AMERICA'S OVERSEAS GARRISONS

America's Overseas Garrisons

The Leasehold Empire

C. T. SANDARS

OXFORD
UNIVERSITY PRESS

Great Clarendon Street, Oxford OX2 6DP

Oxford University Press is a department of the University of Oxford.
It furthers the University's objective of excellence in research, scholarship,
and education by publishing worldwide in

Oxford New York

Athens Auckland Bangkok Bogotá Buenos Aires Calcutta
Cape Town Chennai Dar es Salaam Delhi Florence Hong Kong Istanbul
Karachi Kuala Lumpur Madrid Melbourne Mexico City Mumbai
Nairobi Paris São Paulo Singapore Taipei Tokyo Toronto Warsaw

and associated companies in Berlin Ibadan

Oxford is a registered trade mark of Oxford University Press
in the UK and certain other countries

Published in the United States
by Oxford University Press Inc., New York

© Christopher T. Sandars 2000

British Library Cataloguing in Publication Data

Data available

Library of Congress Cataloging in Publication Data

Sandars, C. T. (Christopher T.)
America's overseas garrisons: the leasehold empire / C.T. Sandars.
Includes bibliographical references and index.
1. Military bases, American—History—20th century 2. United States—Armed
Forces—Foreign countries. I. Title.
UA26.A2 S25 1999   355.7'0973—dc21   99-045917
ISBN 0-19-829687-8

1 3 5 7 9 10 8 6 4 2

Typeset by Best-set Typesetter Ltd., Hong Kong
Printed in Great Britain
on acid-free paper by
Biddles Ltd
Guildford and King's Lynn

PREFACE

The United States, hitherto an isolationist and anti-colonial nation, emerged from the Second World War with an extensive network of military bases around the world and responsibilities for global security on an unprecedented scale. The threat of communism, emanating initially from the Soviet Union but later also from China, coupled with Britain's inability to maintain her pre-war position as a world power, obliged the United States to abandon her wartime plans for Four Power collective security arrangements and develop a global security system of her own. But in undertaking this role, previously discharged by Britain, the United States had relatively few overseas possessions in which to station her forces. For the first time in history, the dominant world power had to maintain the peace largely without the benefit of overseas military bases under its sovereign control. The United States was therefore obliged to build up her global security system through a variety of bilateral and multilateral arrangements concluded, for the most part, with other sovereign nations.

Apart from the few areas where the United States was able to station troops on her own overseas territories, she was compelled to negotiate basing rights with previous wartime partners, former colonial or quasi-colonial possessions, countries which she had occupied, either singly or with her allies, at the end of the war and a number of other nations with whom she had hitherto had no direct security relationship. In each case, the relationship between host nation and the visiting American forces was different and consequently the political constraints on the use of US troops stationed abroad varied from country to country.

In many, but not all, cases the United States leased the military facilities she required overseas from the host nation. To underline the novel aspect of these negotiated relationships with other sovereign powers, the term 'leasehold empire' has been used to characterize the United States post-war global security system. This study aims to chart the development of this system and examine the wide variety of relationships within it. It is not intended to be a comprehensive account of each military base or installation made available to the United States (often referred to, erroneously, as American bases overseas). Nor does the study examine military facilities established by the United States in other countries for specific military operations, in particular the

Vietnam War. The purpose is to illustrate the varying political environments in which the United States sought to build up elements of her global security system after the Second World War and to analyse the problems she encountered as a result of different host nation attitudes and policies.

C.T.S.

London
September, 1999

ACKNOWLEDGEMENTS

Although it grew out of experiences ten years earlier, work on this book commenced in earnest during a sabbatical year at Harvard University in 1995–6 on the Fellows Program at the Center for International Affairs. My first thanks must therefore go to all the faculty and staff at the CFIA, since renamed the Weatherhead Center for International Affairs, who made me so welcome and enabled me to make a start on a long-standing project. In particular I must pay tribute to Steven Bloomfield, Director of the Fellows Program, who shepherds his flock of international Fellows year by year with such sympathy, skill, and enthusiasm.

While at Harvard I benefited from the advice and experience of many colleagues but none more than my academic mentor, Professor Louise Richardson at the Center for European Studies, who applied a rigorous critique to the Fellow's thesis that constituted the first draft of this book. I must also express my gratitude to Colonel Don Higgins USAF, a fellow member of the Fellow's Program, who brought his recent experience as Deputy Director of Operations at Southern Command to bear on the chapter on Panama and to Dr Rudolph Janssens, a participant in the CFIA Japan Program in 1995–6 but now on the staff of the Royal Netherlands Naval College, who kindly commented on the chapter on Japan.

On my return to Britain with a first rough working draft, I was fortunate to receive advice and encouragement from Professor Jack Spence at Chatham House, Dr Gerald Segal at the International Institute of Strategic Studies, who read the chapters on Asia and provided much practical assistance, and finally Professor Michael Clarke at the Centre for Defence Studies at King's College London. It was Michael Clarke who put me in touch with Professor Edwina Campbell at the National Defense University in Washington, who, when tentatively asked whether she would be prepared to look at the chapter on Germany, insisted on seeing the full text and sent back copious comments from the United States. My debt of gratitude to her is immense. She has saved me from many elementary errors and provided me with new insights on a whole range of significant issues. In addition, Professor John Baylis at the University of Wales at Aberystwyth was kind enough to read and comment on the chapters on Britain and her colonies, making a number of very helpful suggestions.

I have also been exceptionally fortunate in the advice and assistance received from former Ambassadors on both sides of the Atlantic. From the United States Monteagle Stearns, formerly American Ambassador to Greece, has applied his wise counsel to the chapters on Greece and Turkey. In Britain I have benefited greatly from the extensive comments made by Lawrence Middleton on South Korea, where he had earlier served as British Ambassador, and finally Sir Alan Munro, recently British Ambassador to Saudi Arabia, was kind enough to review the chapter on the Middle East.

Last but by no means least, I must express my thanks to those who have struggled with the typescript at various stages. In the United States, Suzanne Kendrick typed the whole of the first draft from audio tape and in Britain, Leta Mooney undertook significant additions and amendments. Although I have made most of the more recent revisions myself, there is no doubt that little would have been achieved without their basic groundwork and for this I am deeply indebted to them both. Subsequently, both Cathryn Kemp and Melanie Palmer have provided invaluable help in editing and revising the final text and in particular cross checking footnotes and citations. I am most grateful to them also.

C.T.S.

London
September, 1999

CONTENTS

LIST OF ABBREVIATIONS USED IN THE TEXT

ABM   Anti-Ballistic Missile Treaty
ACE   Allied Command Europe
ANZUS   Australia–New Zealand–United States
ASEAN   Association of South-East Asian Nations
ASW   Anti-submarine warfare
AUTEC   Atlantic Underwater Test and Evaluation Center
AWACS   Airborne Warning and Control System
CENTCOM   Central Command
CENTO   Central Treaty Organization
CIA   Central Intelligence Agency
CFIA   Center for International Affairs
CND   Campaign for Nuclear Disarmament
DEW   Distant Early Warning
DoD   Department of Defense
EDC   European Defence Community
EOKA   Ethniki Organosis Kyprion Aganiston (National
          Organization of Cypriot Combatants)
FMS   Foreign Military Sales
GNP   Gross national product
ICBM   Intercontinental Ballistic Missile
IFOR   Implementation Force
IMF   International Monetary Fund
INF   Intermediate Nuclear Forces
IRBM   Intermediate Range Ballistic Missile
JCS   Joint Chiefs of Staff
MAC   Military Airlift Command
MATS   Military Air Transport Service
MLF   Multilateral Force
NASA   National Aeronautics and Space Administration
NATO   North Atlantic Treaty Organization
NSA   National Security Agency
NSC   National Security Council
PLO   Palestine Liberation Organization
RDF   Rapid Deployment Force

ROK	Republic of Korea
SAC	Strategic Air Command
SACEUR	Supreme Allied Commander Europe
SALT	Strategic Arms Limitation Talks
SEAC	South-East Asia Command
SEATO	South-East Asia Treaty Organization
SFOR	Stabilisation Force
SNF	Short Range Nuclear Forces
SOSUS	Surveillance Sound Under the Sea
SPD	Social Democratic Party (Germany)
USAAF	United States Army Air Force (before July 1947)
USAF	United States Air Force (1947–)
WEU	Western European Union

ABBREVIATIONS USED
IN THE FOOTNOTES

Cmd	Command Papers (1919–56, old series)
Cmnd	Command Papers (1956– , new series)
CNO	Chief of Naval Operations
Col	Column
CRS	Congessional Research Service
DoD	Department of Defense
DO	Defence and Overseas (Committee of the Cabinet)
FCO	Foreign and Commonwealth Office
FO	Foreign Office
FY	Fiscal Year
FRUS	Foreign Relations of the United States
HMSO	Her Majesty's Stationery Office
H of C	House of Commons
JCS	Joint Chiefs of Staff
JSSC	Joint Strategic Survey Committee
OAS	Organization of American States
RSD	Report of Secretary of Defense
SCFR	Senate Committee on Foreign Relations
TIAS	Treaty and International Agreements Series
USAFE	United States Airforce Europe
USGPO	United States Government Printing Office

1

A Tale of Two Empires

Anglo-American Wartime Rivalry

For Britain the Second World War was about her survival as a nation. When Winston Churchill was asked what his war aims were, shortly after becoming Prime Minister, he replied 'I can answer in one word. Victory—victory at all costs'.[1] By contrast, the United States, the last major combatant to enter the war and the only one to experience no direct threat to her mainland territory, enjoyed sufficient time and detachment to formulate wider war aims. These were an amalgamation of Woodrow Wilson's Fourteen Points and Franklin D. Roosevelt's Four Freedoms. Roosevelt, who has been described as 'a rogue Wilsonian',[2] saw the war as an opportunity to create a new world order largely based on the ideals propounded by Wilson in 1918, but with important modifications of his own such as regional policing by the Great Powers.

Common to both Presidents' proposals was an emphasis on self-determination, which Roosevelt considered incompatible with the maintenance after the war of the European colonial empires—particularly the British Empire. In August 1941, four months before Pearl Harbor, he was able to set out his views to Churchill at the Atlantic Conference held on British and American warships off Newfoundland:

I am firmly of the belief that if we are to arrive at a stable peace, it must involve the development of backward countries . . . I can't believe that we can fight a war against fascist slavery and at the same time not work to free people all over the world from a backward colonial policy.[3]

The Atlantic Charter which emerged from this conference contained in clause 3 a firm statement in favour of self-determination. Both countries undertook to:

---

[1] House of Commons (HofC), 13 May 1940. Winston S. Churchill, *Their Finest Hour* (London: Cassell, 1949, 24).
[2] W. R. Louis, American Anti-Colonialism. In *The Special Relationship* W. R. Louis and H. Bull (ed.) (Oxford: OUP, 1986).
[3] W. R. Louis, *Imperialism at Bay* (New York: OUP, 1978).

... respect the right of all peoples to choose the form of government under which they will live; and the wish to see sovereign rights and self-government restored to those who have been forcibly deprived of them.

Churchill claimed that this declaration was intended to apply only to those European countries who had been overrun by Nazi Germany. Moreover, a year later, in November 1942, he made it clear that he had not become the King's First Minister to preside over the liquidation of the British Empire. Nevertheless, the stage had been set, even before the United States entered the war, for an ongoing dispute over the future of Britain's colonial possessions when the war ended.

Hostility to the British Empire was not confined to Roosevelt. In October 1942, the magazine *Life* published an 'Open Letter to the People of England' which put into words a widespread feeling among Americans:

One thing we are not fighting for is to hold the British Empire together... If your strategists are planning a war to hold the British Empire together, they will sooner or later find themselves strategising alone.[4]

Throughout the war senior Americans, both military and civilian, displayed a deep distrust of British motives in planning military operations. Colonel Wedemeyer, one of General Marshall's aides, told him that British plans for Operation TORCH in North Africa 'have been designed to maintain the integrity of the British Empire'.[5] Henry Stimson, the US Secretary of War, agreed. He said 'the British ... are straining every nerve to lay a foundation throughout the Mediterranean area for their own Empire once the war is over'.[6] Later in the war the Americans expressed similar concern over plans prepared by Lord Louis Mountbatten at South-East Asia Command (SEAC) which they dubbed 'Save England's Asiatic Colonies'. Mountbatten had devised plan AXIOM to attack Japan, following the reconquest of Burma, through Malaya and Sumatra. The Americans preferred to attack Japan through China. When addressing the alternative strategies, John Davies, the former American Ambassador to Moscow, now an adviser to Roosevelt, wrote in January 1944 to Harry Hopkins:

SEAC ... is primarily concerned with the re-occupation under British leadership of colonial south-east Asia. The main American concern is to strike the

---

[4] D. Dimbleby and D. Reynolds. *An Ocean Apart* (London: Hodder & Stoughton, 1988).
[5] Ibid.   [6] Ibid.

Japanese where it hurts them most. This is not Sumatra or Malaya. It is in East China, Formosa, Manchuria and Japan itself.[7]

Yet there must be some doubts as to whether these suspicions, grounded in America's own struggle for independence against Britain and rein-forced by the pre-war system of Imperial Preference, were as disinter-ested as they first appeared. The United States already had a colonial empire of her own scattered across the Pacific, mostly in the shape of small island possessions, but including the Philippines, which had been secured with considerable brutality after the defeat of Spain in 1898. Although there was a firm intention to grant independence to the Philippines after the war, there was an equally firm intention, on the part of the American Service Chiefs, not to lose control of the military bases on the islands. Moreover, Roosevelt himself, while preaching self-determination to the British, was pressing the Joint Chiefs of Staff as early as December 1942 to prepare proposals for an extended network of American bases to be established throughout the world at the con-clusion of the war.[8] Dissatisfied with the advice he received, Roosevelt personally despatched a survey expedition one year later to the French possessions in the South Pacific with a view to securing the route from the United States to Australia and New Zealand.

However, Roosevelt was more concerned with the Atlantic than the Pacific. In Henry Kissinger's view, 'to Roosevelt the Atlantic was pos-sessed of the same meaning which the English Channel held for British statesmen'.[9] It was this strategic concept that inspired his proposal to establish American bases on eight British possessions in the Atlantic and Caribbean in return for the fifty over-age destroyers requested by Churchill in 1940. The desire to gain a foothold in these British over-seas territories pre-dated the war. Roosevelt had shown an interest in them as early as 1939 and once the deal was concluded, he declared it to be 'the most important action in the reinforcement of our national defense since the Louisiana purchase'.[10] This was not a short-term wartime expedient. Formal leases were negotiated for ninety-nine years in March 1941. The following month Roosevelt authorized an agree-ment with the Danish representative in Washington to allow American

---

[7] J. Baylis, *Anglo-American Defence Relations 1939–84* (London: Macmillan, 1984). See also Gary Hess *The United States Emergence as a SE Asia Power* (New York: Columbia University Press, 1987).

[8] E. Converse, United States Plans for a Post-War Overseas Basing System, 1942–1948. Unpublished PhD thesis, Princeton University, January 1984.

[9] H. Kissinger, *Diplomacy* (London: Simon & Schuster, 1994, 387).

[10] B. Collier, *The Lion and the Eagle* (New York: Putnam's, 1972, 313).

forces to set up bases in Greenland, and in July 1941 American troops landed in Iceland, with the approval of the local government, to replace British forces who had occupied the island at the outset of the war. Both Greenland and Iceland were Danish possessions at this time, but Denmark was under German occupation and no government in exile had been formed. Once American troops were in place in both territories, Roosevelt declared the whole area between these Danish possessions and North America a part of the Western Hemisphere Defense System.

The measures taken by Roosevelt in the Atlantic, some months before the United States was herself at war, were presented as far-sighted precautions to protect the United States from attack by Nazi Germany. They were also a means, along with the Atlantic Charter itself, of edging isolationist opinion in the United States towards support for Britain. But, consciously or unconsciously, there was a strong element of imperial rivalry underlying Roosevelt's plans, as indicated by his repeated requests to the Joint Chiefs of Staff from 1942 onwards to prepare a plan for a worldwide network of bases after the war. Although these bases were initially to be used by 'The Four Policemen', it is clear that the United States was concerned not just to liberate Britain's colonial subjects, but to equal or replace her influence in the post-war world. In private, American officials were quite open about their ambitions. 'The only possible effect of this war' confided Adolph Berle, Assistant Under-Secretary at the State Department, in his diary, 'would be that the United States would emerge with an imperial power greater than the world had ever seen'. At the same time one of his colleagues, Norman Davis, concluded: 'We shall in effect be the heirs of empire and it is up to us to preserve its vital parts'.[11] By 1944, Admiral King, Chief of Naval Operations, was writing to James Forrestal, Secretary of the Navy, of the need to maintain:

Naval forces in such strength and condition of readiness that they may be moved promptly and in effective force to any part of the world in support of our national policies.[12]

However, in an age when basic airstrips could be used with equal facility by civil and military aircraft, it was the post-war needs of America's civil aviation industry that dictated much of her wartime planning. Imperial rivalry had an eye to commercial advantage as well as strategic

---

[11] Both comments can be found in T. J. McCormick, *America's Half Century* (Baltimore, MD Johns Hopkins University Press, 1989, 33).

[12] Converse. op. cit.

necessity. A paper prepared for the Joint Chiefs of Staff in March 1943 made this clear:

Both for international military purposes and for commercial purposes the Northern, Central and Southern trans-Atlantic routes should be completed and maintained . . . Present air routes to the South-West Pacific should be maintained and developed for military and US commercial purposes.[13]

Post-War Developments

The sheer number of bases established by the United States during the Second World War and the investment made in them, even though many were crude wartime airfields or communications stations, inexorably pushed the Americans into the construction of a post-war global security system building on these facilities. In a statement made in 1945, H. Struve Hensel, Assistant Secretary for the Navy, said, with slightly suspect precision, that the United States had constructed 443 bases during the war, 195 in the Pacific, 11 in the Indian Ocean and Middle East, 228 in the Atlantic area (18 in the North Atlantic), 67 in the Caribbean (including Panama), 25 in the South Atlantic, 55 in North Africa and the Mediterranean, and 63 in Britain, France, and Germany.[14] The first public indication of the United States intention not only to retain some of her wartime bases but to acquire others came in a radio address which President Truman made after the Potsdam Conference on 7 August 1945:

Though the United States wants no profit or selfish advantage out of this war, we are going to maintain the military bases necessary for the complete protection of our interests and of world peace. Bases which our military experts deem to be essential for our protection we will acquire. We will acquire them by arrangements consistent with the United Nations Charter.[15]

Although determined steps to implement these intentions were to be delayed first until the British withdrawal from Greece and Turkey in 1947 and, more significantly, the outbreak of the Korean War in 1950, it was already clear that Roosevelt's 'Four Policemen' would become one global policeman in the post-war years, at any rate in the non-communist world, policing not by territorial conquest but by consent.

---

[13] Joint Strategic Survey Committee (JSSC) 9/1 dated 15 March 1943. Cited in S. Duke and W. Krieger, *US Military Forces in Europe: The Early Years 1945–1970* (Boulder, CO: Westview, 1993).

[14] R. Harkavy, *Great Power Competition for Overseas Bases* (Oxford: Pergamon, 1982).

[15] Public Papers of Harry S. Truman. Cited in Converse, op. cit.

One commentator has suggested that 'the United States expanded its military presence abroad, to the point where it assumed, almost inadvertently and without notice, a role that has been described as Policeman of the World'.[16] This view appears to owe something to Sir John Seeley's famous phrase about the growth of the British Empire—that it was acquired 'in a fit of absence of mind' but was scarcely true of the United States global security system. Although beset by inter-Service rivalries, which were only partially resolved by the creation of the State–War–Navy Co-ordinating Committee in November 1944, planning had proceeded in Washington in fits and starts since the early 1940s on a system of American military bases for the post-war era. The paper for the Joint Chiefs of Staff (JCS) in March 1943 had stated that 'adequate bases, owned or controlled by the United States are essential and their acquisition and development must be considered as amongst our primary war aims'. The paper added somewhat disingenuously 'fortunately such primary war aims in no way conflict with the idea of ultimate collective security'.[17] By November 1943 a subsequent paper, JCS 570/2, was being referred to in Washington as the 'Base Bible'.

These plans did not anticipate the break-up of the wartime alliance and the threat from the Soviet Union. They made no provision for bases in Europe and had to be speedily modified to meet the realities of the Cold War. But in the Atlantic and the Pacific much of the basic infrastructure was in place by 1945. This was supplemented by the growing realization that, contrary to Washington's initial thinking, a continued American military presence would be needed in Europe, Korea, and Japan. Negotiations on the deployment of American forces in these areas were largely complete by the early 1950s. The British Empire took some two hundred years to reach its peak, the global security system of the United States a mere ten years.

By 1947 it was apparent that the Britain could no longer sustain both her pre-war responsibilities and the additional security burdens she had assumed during the war. As a result the United States began to realize that she would be obliged to take on many of Britain's former responsibilities, whether or not she wished to replace Britain as a worldwide power. Britain was suffering the worst winter since 1881, an acute balance of payments crisis, and a disastrous slump in manufacturing output, which fell 25 per cent between January and February. Action by the United States to bring lend–lease to an end and drive a hard bargain over the loans desperately needed by Britain undoubtedly added to her

---

[16] T. Smith, *The Pattern of Imperialism* (Cambridge: CUP, 1981).

[17] JSSC 9/1, op. cit.

difficulties, causing Dean Acheson to remark that 'both enemies and allies were prostrate—enemies by military action, allies by bankruptcy'.[18] Against this background the Attlee government decided to withdraw British support for Greece and Turkey, to proceed with independence for India and to return the Palestine mandate to the United Nations. On 21 February 1947, the Americans were informed of Britain's intention to suspend military and financial aid to Greece and Turkey on 31 March. One State Department official saw the significance of this at once. 'Great Britain' he wrote, 'had within the hour handed the job of world leadership with all its burdens and all its glory to the United States . . .'[19] For British historians the verdict was much the same. Writing in 1991, David Reynolds commented that the decision marked the 'end of Britain's role as one of the major determinants of world events'.[20]

By contrast, the United States ended the war in a dominant position, accounting for some 50 per cent of world economic output. Ernest Bevin, the British Foreign Secretary, commented ruefully 'the United States is in the position today that Britain was at the end of the Napoleonic wars'.[21] This dominance was equally apparent on both sides of the Atlantic. Admiral Nimitz, architect of naval victory in the Pacific, commented in 1947 that the US Navy exercised 'control of the sea more absolute than ever possessed by the British'.[22] To Harold Laski it appeared that 'America bestrides the world like a colossus. Neither Rome at the height of its power, nor Great Britain in the period of its economic supremacy, enjoyed an influence so direct, so profound, so pervasive'.[23] In 1946, even Churchill, while enjoining his audience at Fulton, Missouri, not to discount the resilience of the British Commonwealth and Empire, acknowledged that 'the United States stands at this time at the pinnacle of world power'.[24]

Yet, although the United States ended the war with an extensive network of military bases worldwide and stood poised to replace Britain as a world power, it required the threat of communism to push the Americans into this role. There had been some voices raised at the end of the war, notably that of James Forrestal, the United States first Sec-

---

[18] D. Acheson, *Present at the Creation* (New York: Norton, 1969, 28).

[19] J. Jones, Fifteen Weeks—February–June 1947. In R. Barnet *Allies* (London: Jonathan Cape, 1984).

[20] D. Reynolds, *Britannia Over-ruled* (London: Longman, 1991).

[21] G. Lundestad, *The United States and the World 1945–89*. Washington Paper No. 95. (Baltimore, MD: Woodrow Wilson Center, 1989).

[22] Ibid.   [23] Ibid.

[24] W. S. Churchill, *The Sinews of Peace* (London: Cassell, 1948, 94).

retary for Defense, urging that the basing network should be developed with a view to countering hostility from the Soviet Union. But the military planners were still concerned primarily with staging posts across the Pacific and Atlantic and had given little thought to developing bases in Europe and the Mediterranean. Concern over Soviet intentions gathered pace with George Kennan's 'Long Telegram' of 22 February 1946 and Churchill's 'Iron Curtain' speech at Fulton, Missouri, on 5 March. During the same month, Strategic Air Command was set up with a mission to 'conduct long-range operations in any part of the world at any time'. A year later, on 12 March 1947, the Truman Doctrine was announced and in February 1948 the Prague coup, which brought a communist government to power in Czechoslovakia, underlined the danger to Western Europe. Meanwhile, the Perimeter Defense Strategy for East Asia was under discussion at the State Department. Consistent with General MacArthur's wartime strategy, this envisaged a United States military presence on a chain of islands stretching from the Aleutians through Midway, Okinawa, the former Japanese mandated islands in the Pacific and Guam to the Philippines but not, at this stage, including mainland Japan or Korea.[25] Before the summer was out the Soviet Union had blockaded Berlin and this brought forward a plan, secretly agreed the year before, to deploy B-29 Superfortress bombers to Britain. By the end of the year, it was apparent that China had been lost to the communists and in August 1949 the Soviet Union tested its first atom bomb.

The United States reaction to these developments was to press ahead with signature of the North Atlantic Treaty on 1 April 1949 and to commence work on the policy of containment that became enshrined in NSC-68 completed in April 1950. In apocalyptic terms, this milestone document of 26,000 words assumed that the Soviet Union aimed at 'the complete subversion or forcible destruction of the machinery of government and the structure of society in the countries of the non-Soviet world, and their replacement by an apparatus and structure subservient to and controlled from the Kremlin'. The outbreak of the Korean War two months later appeared to confirm this assessment, reinforcing the need to counter the communist threat by a policy of containment and deterrence. As Kennan's 'Long Telegram' had emphasized, 'the success of the USSR will depend on the degree of cohesion, firmness and vigor which the western world can muster'.[26] This policy required a series of alliances in the Far East to match NATO in the West, together with

---

[25] J. L. Gaddis, *The Long Peace* (Oxford: OUP, 1987, 73).
[26] Extracts from Kennan's Long Telegram. In *The Forrestal Diaries*, W. L. Millis (ed.). (London: Cassell, 1952, 144).

the deployment of bombers from Strategic Air Command to bases from which they could hold the Soviet Union at risk. The range of these bombers was a critical factor in the search for bases in the early post-war years. The United States initially relied on the wartime B-29s and B-36s with a range of 2,000 miles, but in the 1950s these were replaced by America's first jet bomber, the B-47, with a range of 3,000 miles.

In the words of John Lewis Gaddis, containment amounted to 'perimeter defense with all points along the perimeter considered of equal importance'.[27] By the early 1950s, the main elements of this policy were in place. Treaties had been negotiated by John Foster Dulles with Japan, the Philippines, and jointly, Australia and New Zealand in 1951, with South Korea in 1953, and with Taiwan in 1954. In addition, the United States, France, and Britain had been brought into the defence of South-East Asia in 1954 with the creation of the South-East Asia Treaty Organization (SEATO). (An attempt, in which Britain rather than the United States took the lead, to bridge the containment gap in the Middle East with Central Treaty Organization—CENTO—more often known as the Baghdad Pact, foundered with the Iraqi revolution in 1958.) Recording these developments in a report issued in December 1970, a subcommittee of the Senate Committee on Foreign Relations summarized them as follows:

In the post World War Two period, the United States started the construction of a worldwide system of military bases. These bases were to be the foundation of a policy designed to contain the advance of communism in Europe, Africa, the Near East and Asia.[28]

The report rehearsed the treaties entered into by the United States during this period and concluded:

As a result of these policies, by the mid 1960s the United States was firmly committed to more than forty-three nations by treaty and agreement and had some 375 major foreign military bases and 3,000 minor military facilities spread all over the world, virtually surrounding both the Soviet Union and communist China in support of the policy of containment.

The Nature of America's Global Security System

This global security system for the containment of communism has often and inaccurately been termed 'America's post-war empire'. It has

---

[27] J. L. Gaddis, *Strategies of Containment* (Oxford: OUP, 1982).
[28] Senate Committee on Foreign Relations (SCFR). Sub-Committee on US Security Arrangements and Commitments Abroad. 91st Congress, 1970.

further been suggested that the *Pax Britannica* of the nineteenth century was replaced in the second half of the twentieth century by the *Pax Americana*. Typical of this view is the thesis set out by Ronald Steel, a former US foreign service officer, writing in 1967. He characterized the American global security system as:

... an Empire that rests upon the pledge to use American military power to combat communism, not only as a form of imperialism, but even as a social doctrine in the under-developed states.[29]

At the height of the Vietnam War, this was a view perhaps more persuasive than it is at the turn of the century. The 'imperial' interventions of the United States in Guatemala (1954), Cuba (1961), and the Dominican Republic (1965) would also have been fresh in Steel's mind. In a more telling passage he adds:

Although the desire to defend other nations against communism is not an imperial ambition, it has led our country to use imperial methods; establishment of military garrisons around the globe, granting of subsidies to client governments and politicians, application of economic sanctions and even military force against recalcitrant states, and employment of a veritable army of colonial administrators ...[30]

Other American commentators have gone further than this, describing the post-war global security system as 'a hegemonic project', in which American military and economic dominance underpinned and reinforced each other in a consciously planned and co-ordinated campaign to achieve and maintain supremacy for the United States. One proponent of this view is Thomas J. McCormick who has written:

World War II was, for American leaders, a case of 'diplomacy by other means.' They fought the war not simply to vanquish their enemies, but to create the geopolitical basis for a postwar world order that they would both build and lead.[31]

This is not a theory that stands up to serious analysis of the rapid demobilization carried out by the United States at the end of the war and the consequent inability of her leaders to counter Soviet pressure in Europe or the communist takeover in China in the late 1940s. James Forrestal complained in October 1945 that the country was 'going back to bed at a frightening rate'.[32] At this stage, Washington was experiencing

---

[29] R. Steel, *Pax Americana* (New York: Viking, 1967).   [30] Ibid.
[31] McCormick, op. cit., 33.
[32] J. Forrestal to R. Bard 16 October 1945. See W. L. Millis (ed), *The Forrestal Diaries*, 109.

difficulty in finding the 100,000 troops needed for the occupation of Japan, and in February 1948 at the time of the Prague coup, George Marshall commented that 'we are playing with fire while we have nothing with which to put it out'.[33]

In contrast, the Norwegian Geir Lundestad, writing in 1990, has gone to the other extreme suggesting that the United States security system should be termed an 'Empire by Invitation', since many countries both in Europe and South-East Asia worked hard to obtain security guarantees from the United States and welcomed the development of American bases on their territory.[34] This is not an entirely convincing thesis as American bases have proved deeply unpopular in such locations as Okinawa, Panama, and the Philippines, while even those countries benefiting from generous military assistance, for example Greece and Spain, have pressed for reductions in the US military presence.

A more sophisticated view is put forward by Lord Beloff writing in 1986:

In the sense of a direct claim or exercise of sovereignty, the American 'empire' is much smaller than the European empires that have now all but disappeared, but its informal empire, that is the propping up of states and regimes through advice and assistance, and in the last resort military guarantees, is a considerable one.[35]

The term 'informal empire' is one used by Ronald Robinson and John Gallagher to describe the series of arrangements, short of outright conquest, by which Britain advanced her security and economic interests in the nineteenth century, with particular reference to Africa.[36] It could also be extended to cover the special treaty relationships established by the British government in India with the states of the Persian Gulf at the end of the century. Some consider that this concept accurately describes the global security system of the United States. William Roger Louis, writing in 1986, goes so far as to say that 'Robinson and Gallagher's Victorians would have recognised the methods of post World War II Americans'.[37]

[33] *The Forrestal Diaries*, 12 February 1948, 355.   [34] Lundestad, op cit.
[35] Lord Beloff, The End of the British Empire. In *The Special Relationship* (Oxford: OUP, 1986, 257).
[36] The R. Robinson and J. Gallagher thesis was originally set out in The Imperialism of Free Trade, in *Economic History Review*, 1953 and later developed in *Africa and the Victorians* (London: Macmillan, 1961). For a discussion of the thesis see *Imperialism: The Robinson and Gallagher Controversy*, W. R. Louis (ed.) (New York: New Viewpoints, 1976).
[37] W. R. Louis, American Anti-Colonialism. In *The Special Relationship* (Oxford: OUP, 1986, 262).

There is a certain irony in the fact that the United States, which was so intent on dismantling the British Empire in the course of the Second World War, has, through the best of intentions, ended up with a world-wide system of military airfields, garrisons, and naval bases, bearing an uncanny resemblance to the British Empire in its heyday and, in certain cases, established by broadly comparable methods. Paul Kennedy has commented that the maps of major US military deployments worldwide appearing in the *American Defense Annual 1987–88*:

... to historians look extraordinarily similar to the chain of fleet bases and garrisons possessed by that former world power, Great Britain, at the height of its strategic over-stretch.[38]

However, there are important differences between the British Empire and the United States global security system. By any definition, an empire must involve the rule of one nation by another without regard to the wishes of the subject peoples and the transfer of sovereignty to the imperial power. This is the phenomenon referred to by Churchill, when First Lord of the Admiralty before the First World War, as 'our vast and splendid possessions, mainly acquired by violence, largely maintained by force'.[39] Notwithstanding the colonial possessions acquired by the United States from Spain in 1898, and her tendency to ride roughshod over the sovereignty of smaller nations, particularly in Latin America, the American global security system involves no subjugation of other peoples to American rule, nor, apart from the exceptional cases of South Korea, and to some extent Japan, has it involved the United States in reserving for herself the external affairs and defence of client states, which was a cardinal feature of Britain's 'informal empire'.

In setting up her global security system after the war, the United States was obliged to construct an entirely new set of arrangements with the countries where she wished to base her forces. Neither her own anti-colonial traditions, nor the new-found independence of many of the nations concerned, permitted a security relationship in the old imperial tradition. In the immediate post-war years the Americans suffered several rebuffs in their attempt to consolidate the arrangements entered into during the war. Iceland asked for the withdrawal of American troops, Denmark proved reluctant to grant extended basing rights in Greenland, and Portugal took the same line over the Azores. At this time even Ernest Bevin, the British Foreign Secretary, who was later to

---

[38] P. Kennedy, *The Rise and Fall of the Great Powers* (London: Unwin Hyman, 1988).
[39] D. Reynolds, *Britannia Over-ruled* (London: Longman, 1991).

be the foremost advocate of American involvement in Europe, felt that the Americans were pressing too hard for purely military facilities. Instead, he proposed that they should secure access to civil airfields overseas which could be used for military purposes in emergencies.[40] Further afield, the United States ran into similar difficulties in Panama where her request to maintain 131 military installations outside the Canal Zone was turned down.

The growing threat from communism soon reversed these lukewarm attitudes in Europe, but in securing the extensive network of bases needed to implement the policy of containment and deterrence, the United States had to enter into a variety of relationships with different host countries, which in turn set different political parameters to the use of her military forces when deployed from the territories concerned. As early as 1943 a paper for the US Army Air Force had advocated the acquisition of post-war bases by 'purchase, lease or any other inter-government arrangement'.[41] Despite the wartime emphasis on self-determination, there was a substantial colonial element in these arrangements. For a start, the United States retained possessions of her own in the Pacific, notably Hawaii (now a State of the Union), and Guam (an unincorporated territory of the United States). She also took steps to acquire trustee status over other islands which had formerly been subject to a mandate administered by Japan on behalf of the League of Nations. Secondly, the United States was not averse, in the new circumstances of Cold War confrontation, to using other nations' colonial possessions where this suited her, notwithstanding the terms of the Atlantic Charter and subsequent pressure on the European powers to liberate their colonies. The ninety-nine year leases for bases on British territories in the Atlantic and Caribbean had set the pattern here. But the United States was also eager to make use of the strategically placed islands of Ascension and Diego Garcia still held by Britain. In the Mediterranean, an agreement was reached with France for Strategic Air Command to use French bases in Morocco. Finally, the United States maintained what can only be described as a neo-colonial relationship with both the Philippines and Panama until the early and late 1990s, respectively.

Elsewhere, the United States initially enjoyed basing rights by virtue of conquest in the occupied nations of Germany and Italy, Japan and Korea, even though Korea is more properly considered as a liberated

[40] Bevin's Memorandum to Defence Committee, DO(46)58, 13 April 1946. Documents on British Policy Overseas, Series I, Vol IV.

[41] Converse, op. cit.

colony of Japan. Although sovereignty was restored to these nations after the war, their relationship with the United States over the military facilities on their territory continued to be coloured by the memory of defeat and occupation, particularly in South Korea, where the United States retained command of the armed forces after the Korean War, and in Japan where the United States assumed responsibility for external defence. Elsewhere, the United States managed to revive wartime arrangements for the deployment of her forces, after some initial hesitation, in countries such as Greenland, Iceland, the Azores, and Britain, but in each case the arrangements were specific to the country concerned, notwithstanding common membership of the NATO Alliance.

The importance of the Mediterranean in containing Soviet expansion in Europe (and providing a reinforcement route to the Middle East) led to a further set of arrangements with Turkey, Greece, and Spain, even though Spain was not to join NATO until 1982. For a number of reasons these arrangements gave rise to the most difficult political problems encountered by the United States in setting up the global security system. The relative poverty of the countries concerned, the authoritarian and later socialist orientation of some of their governments, and concern over the use of American forces for non-NATO operations all combined to lead to frequent renegotiation of the basing arrangements, coupled with increasing demands for financial assistance. Finally, America's global security system, which had focused in the early postwar years on Europe, the Caribbean, and East Asia, had to be adapted in the 1980s to meet new threats to Western interests in the Persian Gulf and the Indian Ocean. This led to yet another set of arrangements with littoral countries who were in general most reluctant to see American forces permanently stationed on their territory, but content to grant them occasional access and, in some cases, to agree to the pre-positioning of equipment.

There was one exception to this pattern. France was a nation that had been liberated rather than occupied at the end of the war and consequently found herself playing unwitting—and unwilling—host to American and other allied forces in 1945, not only on her mainland territory but also in her North African possessions. The bases built for the United States in Morocco fell victim to the independence movement, but in the early 1950s France was content to play a full part in providing forward bases for American forces on her own territory and establishing infrastructure projects there for NATO as a whole. Following a bilateral agreement with the United States in 1952, bases were made available to the US Air Force in the east and north-east of France while an army base was made available near Paris. A huge supply depot was established at Chateauroux in central France and Bordeaux was used as a transit port for military supplies to American forces in West Germany. In addition, an extensive oil pipeline for NATO use was laid across French territory.

However, with the return of General de Gaulle to power in 1958, differences over the control of American nuclear weapons on French territory came to a head and these were withdrawn together with several US Air Force units in 1959. Seven years later, de Gaulle took the need for self-reliance in defence one stage further. Convinced that the United States would not risk annihilation for the defence of Western Europe, he withdrew France from the military structure of NATO and expelled the remaining American forces from French territory. France consequently became the only host nation in the American global security system, apart from the former colonial territories of Morocco, Libya, and much later the Philippines, to terminate arrangements for stationing American forces on her territory.

It is difficult to find a single generic term to describe the whole spectrum of relationships supporting America's global security system. These relationships range from the total control assured by territorial possession at one end of the spectrum to tentative visiting rights, heavily circumscribed by domestic political concerns, at the other. In the centre of the spectrum we find a wide variety of arrangements with differing political and financial features. It is these arrangements that are described here as the 'leasehold empire', not because the term accurately reflects all the varied arrangements concerned (although many of these were straightforward leases), but because it graphically underlines the novelty of the American global security system. Never before has a single dominant power been obliged to negotiate in this way with the countries in which it wishes to station its forces in order to maintain the peace. General George Marshall accurately foresaw the problem when commenting on a Joint Chiefs of Staff paper in October 1945:

In view of the political complications and difficulties involved in maintaining US personnel and installations on foreign territory in peacetime . . . the State Department should give serious consideration to arrangements by which other nations undertake the load of maintaining required installations in certain areas in return for payment in one form or another.[42]

---

[42] JCS 570/36, 8 October 1945. Cited by Converse, op. cit.

The following chapters will briefly examine each of the different arrangements outlined above and explore the political and financial constraints on the freedom of action enjoyed by the United States in each case.

Strains within the System

One characteristic that the 'leasehold empire' initially shared with the more traditional empires of former years was a reluctance to surrender the military bases it had attained. Commenting on the widespread and durable nature of American commitments overseas in 1970, the Sub-Committee of the Senate Committee on Foreign Relations stated:

Once an American overseas base is established, it takes on a life of its own. Original missions may become outdated but new missions are developed, not only with the intention of keeping the facility going but often to actually enlarge it.

The report went on to say:

Within the government departments most directly concerned—State and Defense—we found little initiative to reduce or eliminate any of these overseas facilities.[43]

This may have been true during the 1950s and 1960s when the concept of strategic denial made the United States reluctant to withdraw from any overseas base which might be acquired by the Soviet Union. But by the 1970s, several factors were emerging which began to erode what had been termed the 'politico-military cement' of the host–guest relationship.[44] In the first place, American supremacy, so dominant in the 1950s, was declining by the 1970s. The withdrawal from Vietnam, the oil shocks of 1973–4, and the suspension of dollar convertibility all undermined the confidence of the poorer host nations in the United States. Seeing America at a disadvantage, some of these nations took the opportunity to drive a harder bargain when basing arrangements came up for renewal. In this sense, the United States experienced many of the nationalist pressures previously directed against the European colonial powers. Secondly, with the beginning of détente and the consequent relaxation of the direct threat to peripheral host nations, the security

[43] SCFR (see note 28).
[44] A. Cottrell and T. Moorer, *US Overseas Bases* Washington Paper No. 47 (Beverly Hills; Saye, 1977).

interests of hosts and guests began to diverge. This was particularly evident in the Mediterranean where bases made available to the United States could be used to serve American national interests as well as the collective security of NATO.

The Yom Kippur War of 1973 brought matters to a head. The United States wished to mount a massive resupply operation for Israel to counter Soviet assistance being given to the Arabs. But of the various European nations approached, only Portugal, still under a dictatorship, agreed to grant the United States staging rights through the Azores. Britain let it be known that a request would not be welcome and the Federal Republic of Germany made it clear that she would not sanction the transfer of military equipment from depots on German territory. The separate nature of American interests in the Middle East was demonstrated on 24 October 1973, when US forces worldwide were placed on heightened alert as a warning signal to the Soviet Union. This action was taken without consulting host nations who were inevitably put at risk by the measure. The American Secretary of State Henry Kissinger later made it clear that the United States could not have accepted any other view and criticized the Europeans for resorting to 'an essentially legalistic argument to the effect that the obligations of NATO did not extend to the Middle East'.[45] These observations only underlined the wide gulf in security perceptions on different sides of the Atlantic.

A further cause for concern among host nations, endemic throughout the Cold War and not confined to a particular period, was the growing disinclination of some countries to accept nuclear weapons on their territory. Even in NATO, not all the member nations were prepared to tolerate nuclear weapons. France, which had initially agreed to the presence of American nuclear weapons, asked for these to be removed in 1959 while pressing ahead with her own nuclear programme. Other members of the Alliance who remained willing to accept nuclear weapons faced intense domestic controversy over the decision taken in 1979 to deploy cruise missiles in Europe in response to the build-up of Russian SS 20 missiles in the Warsaw Pact Countries. Elsewhere, Japan required consultation on the introduction of nuclear weapons from 1960 onwards and this extended to Okinawa after 1972. Restrictions on nuclear weapons were imposed by Spain in 1976 and Panama in 1977. In 1984, Portugal excluded nuclear weapons from the Azores and the Philippines adopted a constitution which banned nuclear weapons in 1986.

---

[45] H. Kissinger, *Years of Upheaval* (London: Weidenfeld & Nicolson, 1982, 711–13).

Other concerns also surfaced in the 1980s. The economic difficulties of the United States mounted and, in 1985, the proponent of the Marshall Plan became the world's greatest debtor nation, with a debt of $3 trillion, largely funded by the purchase of government securities by Japan, for whom the United States continued to exercise responsibility for external defence. In political terms, the use by President Reagan of American forces in Europe for two controversial counter-terrorist actions further underlined the divergence between the security perceptions of host nations and their guests. In October 1985, the *Achille Lauro* affair caused considerable ill-feeling between the American and Italian governments. This was followed in April 1986 by the air strike on Libya which, although supported by Britain's Prime Minister Margaret Thatcher, raised serious questions about the use of American forces stationed in Britain and NATO's purpose on operations conducted in the national interest of the United States. In the late 1980s, events in Panama and the Philippines gave rise to further concern over the mutual dependency which had grown up between the American authorities anxious to safeguard valuable military assets and corrupt and unscrupulous rulers in a position to take advantage of their tenants. The overthrow of President Marcos in February 1986 was marred by the close identification between him and the Americans until shortly before his fall. Similarly, the overthrow and arrest of General Noriega in December 1989, however desirable as an objective, raised considerable concern over the use of American troops stationed in the country, the possible contravention of the Canal Treaty of 1977, and the legal justification for removing Noriega to stand trial in the United States.

In the 1990s, American forces were withdrawn from the Philippines, as a result of natural disaster and nationalist opposition, and are due to be withdrawn from Panama as a conscious act of policy. Elsewhere, the United States has responded positively to the collapse of communism by embarking on a controlled run-down of the global security system. Forces deployed overseas have been reduced to 100,000 in Europe and 100,000 in the Far East, giving the lie both to the earlier observations of the Senate Committee on Foreign Relations and the dire predictions of Paul Kennedy in 1988 that America's worldwide military presence would collapse from imperial overstretch. In the event these predictions proved accurate but for the Soviet Union not the United States. In responding quickly and imaginatively to the changing security environment the United States has done much to ease the tensions that were building up in some host nations at the end of the Cold War, while reassuring her allies that the American global security system will remain in place to meet the threats presented by a more fragmented and volatile world. The Department of Defense annual report to the President and Congress in 1991 summarized the change in American strategy in these terms

The rapidly changing security environment has dictated changes in the overseas deployments of American forces. This will be most noticeable in Europe where a dramatic reduction in US forward-based forces will occur. Even in Asia, where potential regional aggressors have long presented a more likely threat to stability than super power competition, some reductions will occur.[46]

Three years later, the 1994 report spoke of 'reducing overseas base structures to the minimum level necessary to support remaining forward deployed forces',[47] and President Clinton's statement on national security strategy in 1995 indicated that the permanent deployment of forces was only one method of projecting an American military presence overseas, alongside temporary deployments, pre-positioned equipment, continued exercises, port calls and other visits by US forces.[48] Over the period 1989–95 American troops permanently based overseas fell by over 50 per cent from 510,000 to 238,000. The first great power to establish a global security system largely by negotiation with friendly host nations was showing an appreciation of the fact that good guests should not outstay their welcome.

[46] Department of Defense (DoD) Report to the President and Congress, January 1991.
[47] DoD Report to the President and Congress, January 1994.
[48] A National Strategy of Engagement and Enlargement. The White House, February 1995.

2

The Colonial Dimension

Introduction

In building up her global security system after the Second World War, the United States was able to rely in part on a number of overseas possessions of her own where she enjoyed total freedom of action. These were mainly in the Pacific, although Puerto Rico falls into the same category in the Caribbean. By developing the concept of strategic trusteeship under United Nations auspices she was also able to exercise military rights over a number of islands in the Pacific formerly administrated by Japan. Elsewhere, despite the anti-colonial stance adopted during the war, the United States found it convenient to make use of certain overseas possessions held by Britain and, to a lesser extent, France, where agreement could be reached with these colonial powers. The arrangements with France, providing access to bases in Morocco, did not survive the grant of independence in 1956, but Britain continued to hold a number of minor colonial outposts in areas of strategic importance which were of considerable advantage to the United States. Moreover, Britain, being anxious to revive her close wartime partnership with the United States, was more inclined than most other potential host nations to fall in with American plans. As Winston Churchill said in his 'Iron Curtain' speech at Fulton, Missouri, in 1946 'we already use together a large number of islands; more may well be entrusted to our joint care in the near future'.[1] However, if this was a reference to the scheme for strategic trusteeship he was mistaken, for the United States had no intention of sharing access to the Pacific islands with any other power.

The death of Franklin D. Roosevelt removed the leading American opponent of colonialism, whose hostility to the European overseas empires had never wavered. During the war he was recorded as saying to his son Elliot:

---

[1] Churchill's 'Iron Curtain' speech at Fulton, Missouri, 5 March 1946. W.-S. Churchill *Sinews of Peace* (London: Cassell, 1948, 98).

When we have won the war I will work with all my might and main to see to it that the United States is not wheedled into the position of accepting any plan that will further France's imperialist ambitions or that will aid and abet the British Empire in *its* imperial ambitions.[2]

Roosevelt would not live to fulfil this objective and his successor, Harry Truman, took a more pragmatic attitude to European colonialism. Although he refused to supply American transport aircraft to France to enable her to reoccupy Indo-China, he resisted pressure from Chiang Kai-Shek to arrange for the Japanese to surrender Hong Kong to his forces rather than the British. Whereas Roosevelt had throughout the war urged Britain to return Hong Kong to China or transfer the colony to United Nations trusteeship, Truman informed Chiang that: 'No question arises with regard to British sovereignty in the area'.[3]

American ambiguity over colonialism increased as she began to face up to her worldwide security responsibilities after the war and realized that her own territorial assets were limited compared with those still available to the colonial powers. For example in 1946, James Byrnes, the American Secretary of State, asked Britain to 'get or keep under UK control' three airfields in India and one in Burma, which the United States judged to be strategically important, at a time when the socialist government in Britain was fully committed to independence for these two countries. Byrnes also proposed an Exchange of Notes between Britain and the United States establishing 'joint rights in the military installations which had been created in Ascension, Tarawa, Guadalcanal, and the Fiji Islands'.[4] These requests were politely declined by Ernest Bevin but the US Navy was permitted to use the port of Bahrain from 1948 onwards—an example of the United States benefiting from Britain's 'informal' rather than 'formal' empire.

The dilemma for the United States was that in Asia, as in Eastern Europe and the Balkans, the resistance movements which provided the most effective opposition to the Japanese or German occupation were generally communist. Following the fall of China to communism in 1949, the United States was obliged to set aside her antipathy to colonialism as the lesser of two evils and support the colonial powers in the attempt to re-establish their positions in South-East Asia in the face of communist insurgency. Britain managed to defeat communism in Malaya without American assistance but France faced a much more difficult

---

[2] E. Roosevelt, As He Saw It. Cited by H. Kissinger, *Diplomacy* (London: Simon & Schuster, 1995, p 397).

[3] H. S. Truman *Year of Decisions: 1945* (London: Hodder & Stoughton 1955, 380).

[4] Documents on British Foreign Policy Series I, Vol. IV, 1987.

situation in Indo-China. By 1950, the State Department concluded that 'unavoidably the US, together with France, is committed in Indo-China'.[5] This commitment took the form of substantial financial subventions which would have been unthinkable to Roosevelt. On 1 May 1950, Truman publicly announced that American aid would be made available to support the French in Indo-China and by 1952 the United States was paying 60 per cent of France's war expenses. This figure had risen to 80 per cent by 1954, the year in which French forces surrendered at Dien Bien Phu.[6]

It would be a mistake to assume that the United States had embraced colonialism wholeheartedly. She was prepared to make an accommodation with the colonial powers where this suited her own strategic interests. This extended to the direct use of colonial territory where required by the needs of the global security system, together with the use of colonies or former colonies of her own for the same purpose. But where the interests of the United States clashed with those of the colonial powers, particularly in the Middle East where she wished to establish a position for herself, she was quite prepared to pose as the champion of non-communist nationalist movements seeking to free themselves from European influence. On this basis Britain was excluded from the ANZUS Pact in 1951 as the former colonial power but was nevertheless expected to play a full part in SEATO in 1954.

However, it was the Suez crisis in 1956 that marked the most serious breach between the United States and the European colonial powers. The United States rightly refused to support Britain and France in an ill-judged imperialist intervention which threatened to provide the Soviet Union with the entrée she was seeking in the Middle East. John Foster Dulles, who had precipitated the crisis by withdrawing American funding for the Aswan High Dam, was particularly critical of the Anglo-French action. 'What the British and French had done' he said in a memorandum to the National Security Committee (NSC) 'was nothing but the straight old fashioned variety of colonialism of the most obvious sort'.[7] But the steps taken to halt the intervention, involving as they did the humiliation of two of America's closest European allies, were intended to present the United States as an alternative focus of loyalty

---

[5] Foreign Relations of the United States (FRUS) 1950. US 714. Cited by R. Jarvis, The Impact of the Korean War, *Journal of Conflict Resolution*, December 1980.

[6] T. J. McCormick *America's Half Century* (Baltimore, MD: Johns Hopkins University Press 1995, 113).

[7] W. R. Louis, American Anti-Colonialism. In *The Special Relationship* (Oxford: OUP, 1986, Ch. 6, 227).

and leadership to the emerging nations of the Middle East. The memorandum Dulles submitted to the NSC made this clear:

Unless we now assert and maintain this leadership all these newly independent countries will turn from us to the USSR. We will be looked upon as forever tied to British and French colonial policies.

But in undermining the position of Britain and France in the Middle East, which depended on informal empire rather than formal colonialism, the United States found that she had unwittingly created conditions of considerable instability. Nations emerging from the shadow of imperial oversight were more inclined to play the super powers off against each other than to accept uncritically the leadership of the United States. President Eisenhower recognized this in 1957, saying 'the existing vacuum in the Middle East must be filled by the United States before it is filled by Russia'.[8] The Eisenhower Doctrine enunciated in January that year, which pledged economic aid, military assistance, and protection against communist aggression to nations in the Middle East, was designed to plug this gap but it shortly led to co-ordinated military intervention in the area by the United States in Lebanon and by Britain in Jordan. The dilemma posed by the robust United States reaction to Suez has been neatly summarized by Henry Kissinger:

American leaders were striving to combine two incompatible policies: to end Great Britain's imperial role while exploiting the remnants of British influence to build a structure of containment in the Middle East.[9]

Britain and France reacted in different ways to the humiliation of Suez and these reactions were increasingly bound up with each country's nuclear policy. Under General de Gaulle, France turned away from both the United States and Britain, pursuing the chimera of self-sufficiency in security policy which was to lead to the *force de frappe* and, ten years after Suez, withdrawal from the military structure of NATO. In contrast, Harold Macmillan, once he had succeeded Eden as British Prime Minister, determined to restore good relations with the United States through a personal approach to Eisenhower, his wartime colleague from the North African campaign. The co-ordinated action in Lebanon and Jordan provided an early indication of success but Macmillan was greatly assisted in a difficult task by Eisenhower's wish to station in Britain first Thor Intermediate Range Ballistic Missiles and

[8] G. Lundestadt, *The American Empire and Other Studies in US Foreign Policy* (Oxford OUP/Oslo: Norwegian University Press, 1990).
[9] Kissinger, op. cit. 527.

later Polaris submarines. This renewed dependency on Britain as an ally who could offer basing facilities within striking range of the Soviet Union did much to eradicate the memories of Suez, notwithstanding the ongoing problems surrounding the supply of Skybolt and subsequently Polaris missiles to Britain.

Macmillan was equally assiduous in cultivating good relations with the young President Kennedy with whom he established a good rapport despite the difference in their ages. Although Kennedy was not initially well disposed towards an independent nuclear deterrent for Britain, his administration had identified a British colonial territory in the Pacific as a site for further American nuclear tests in the atmosphere. Since the war, the United States had conducted atmospheric nuclear tests at Bikini and Eniwetok atolls in the Marshall Islands, which they had taken over from Japan as UN Strategic Trust Territories. Concerned that further tests might cause difficulties at the United Nations, Kennedy proposed the use of Christmas Island in return for British access to underground testing facilities at Nevada. Christmas Island, located at the centre of the Pacific just north of the Equator, had been annexed by Britain in 1888 and used for atmospheric tests of her own atom bomb during 1957–8. Although the American proposal presented problems for Australia and New Zealand, an agreement was reached which allowed the United States to conduct tests on Christmas Island from May 1962 until the Partial Test Ban Treaty came into force in October 1963.[10]

By the mid 1960s, Britain, under Macmillan's leadership, had embarked on her second wave of de-colonization, granting independence to the majority of her remaining African and Asian possessions. With the British Empire being wound up, neither Kennedy nor Johnson found it necessary to adopt the strident anti-colonial attitudes of their predecessors. Instead, the increasing demands of the war in Vietnam inspired a new-found appreciation for the residual role played by Britain in the Indian Ocean area. Harold Wilson, who became Prime Minister in 1964, initially attempted to capitalize on this appreciation by declaring grandiosely that Britain's frontiers remained on the Himalayas. This declaration was a curious one from the leader of the party which had given independence to India in 1947, and was at odds with Britain's economic plight which made it increasingly difficult to sustain these pretensions. As one economic crisis followed another, progressive withdrawals of British forces from east of Suez and elsewhere were announced in 1967, 1971, and 1974.

[10] R. Lamb, *The Macmillan Years* (London: John Murray, 1995, 303–9).

By now, the United States was thoroughly alarmed. Criticism of Britain's imperial past had largely given way to concern over regional stability in the future. The memoirs of Richard Crossman, a Cabinet Minister in the first Wilson government, spoke of 'thundering telegrams of protest' at Britain's withdrawal plans from President Johnson.[11] The swing in American thinking was later summarized by George Ball, Under-Secretary of State in the Kennedy administration, echoing the comments made in 1957 by Eisenhower:

One cannot dismantle a vast and highly developed power structure such as pre-war colonialism in the brief period of a quarter century without creating power vacuums and power dislocations of major dimensions.[12]

It was this concern at the vacuum left by Britain at the very time that the Soviet Union had managed to leapfrog the containment policy by constructing a blue water navy that prompted the United States to seek ways of replacing Britain in the Indian Ocean area. She was not successful in obtaining permanent basing rights in any of the littoral countries as a substitute for Aden or Singapore, although she was able to continue the arrangements for occasional access in Bahrain and later came to similar agreements with Oman. The only permanent base she was able to establish in the area was at another relic of the British Empire—the remote atoll of Diego Garcia at the very centre of the Indian Ocean.

US Overseas Possessions

The Pacific

Roosevelt may have viewed the Atlantic much as British statesmen regarded the English Channel, but his admirals were more concerned with the Pacific. Britain had agreed early in the Second World War that the Pacific should be treated as an exclusively American theatre of operations, but Admiral Ernest King, US Chief of Naval Operations, took an exceptionally protective view of this theatre. 'What operations are or are not conducted in the Pacific' he stated 'is no affair of the combined Chiefs of Staff since this theater is exclusively American.'[13] Moreover, it was only when he wished to borrow an aircraft carrier from

---

[11] J. Baylis, *Anglo-American Defence Relations 1939–84*. (London: Macmillan, 1984).
[12] Lundestad, op cit.
[13] B. Collier, *The Lion and The Eagle* (New York: Putnam's, 1972, 361).

Britain in 1942 that the Royal Navy learnt anything of King's dispositions in the Pacific.[14]

The US Navy undoubtedly regarded the war in the Pacific as an
opportunity to put into practice the theories that Admiral Mahan had
advanced in the 1890s. In *The Influence of Sea Power on History*, Mahan,
then President of the Naval War College, had regretted America's lack
of colonies which he considered 'the surest way of supporting abroad
the sea power of a country'.[15] Nevertheless, the United States had been
demonstrating discernible colonial tendencies in the Pacific for some
time. In the period 1857–8, three of the Phoenix Islands strung out along
the Equator (Jarvis Island, Baker's Island, and Howland's Island—all
uninhabited today), had been acquired as coaling stations following
Commodore Perry's expedition to Japan in 1852. Midway Island, 1,000
miles beyond Hawaii, had been acquired in 1867 (in the same year
as Alaska) by William Seward, the United States Secretary of State,
who saw no reason why America's manifest destiny should stop at
the west coast. The island gave its name to the decisive battle of the
Pacific war in June 1942 and today forms part of a Naval Defense Sea
Area administered from Hawaii by the Commander-in-Chief Pacific.

Much further south, Captain Meade of the US Navy concluded an agreement in 1872 with local rulers in Samoa, granting 'the
exclusive right of establishing in the said harbour of Pago Pago
on the island of Tutuila a naval station for the use and convenience
of vessels of the United States Government'.[16] Although the Senate
declined to ratify the agreement, the fact that it had been negotiated
by the US Navy launched a protracted three-cornered struggle for
exclusive rights in Samoa between the United States, Britain, and
Germany. This was not concluded until 1899 when a deal brokered by
the United States gave Germany the two largest islands of Samoa
(which they lost to New Zealand in 1914) and the remainder, including
Tutuila, to the United States. Britain turned her attention to the Gilbert
and Ellice islands and the Solomons but American Samoa was annexed
as a US territory and administered by the Secretary of the Navy until
1951 when responsibility was transferred to the Department of the
Interior. Finally, the United States acquired her most valuable possessions in the Pacific in 1898—the Philippines, Guam, and Wake Island as

---

[14] Ibid.

[15] Cited in L. Battistini *The Rise of American Influence in Asia and the Pacific* (Michigan, MI: Michigan State University Press, 1960). I have drawn heavily on this work in my
account of the American annexation of Hawaii.

[16] Ibid.

a result of war with Spain over Cuba, and Hawaii as an indirect consequence of this war. The vexed relationship between the United States and the Philippines is examined in Chapter 4 but the annexation of Hawaii is discussed briefly below.

Hawaii

In 1778, at a time when most of the Royal Navy's available shipping was at full stretch trying to deny independence to Britain's American colonies, an expedition under Captain James Cook landed at the islands of Hawaii in the mid Pacific. Cook named these the Sandwich Islands after his patron Lord Sandwich, First Lord of the Admiralty, and claimed the islands for Britain, tragically meeting his death there the following year. The state flag of Hawaii still features a small Union Jack in the top left-hand corner, but neither the original British name nor British interest in the islands survived American expansion into the Pacific in the nineteenth century. It was New England rather than Britain that showed the earliest sustained interest in Hawaii. Her traders called at the islands en route to China and her churchmen saw them as fertile ground for missionary activity. The first Protestant missionaries arrived from Boston in 1820 but by the middle of the century the American whaling industry was well established in Hawaii, with some 600 whalers calling at the islands in the 1840s. In 1843, a British frigate called at the islands and tried to reassert Britain's claim to them. This claim was resisted with the help of an American protest made by the *USS Constellation* and Hawaii remained independent. But the King of Hawaii remained apprehensive concerning British and French interest in the islands, and in 1851 offered to place them under American protection. President Pierce declined this early opportunity to gain an element of 'empire by invitation' in 1954 and during the Civil War the islands were largely forgotten by the United States.

However, American interest in the islands resumed after the Civil War and at the turn of the century they were acquired by the United States through a mixture of mercantilism, missionary endeavour, and deliberately engineered instability indistinguishable from European colonial practice. Daniel Webster, during his brief spell as Secretary of State, informed Congress as early as 1842 that:

Although the United States has no territorial ambitions in the islands, it could not consent to any other power possessing them or subverting the native government. We might even feel justified consistently with our own principles in interfering by force to prevent them falling into the hands of one of the great powers of Europe.[17]

In 1867, William Seward indicated in a letter to the American agent in Hawaii that he was thinking in terms of annexation:

A lawful and peaceful annexation of the islands to the United States, with the consent of the people of Hawaii, is deemed desirable by this Government.[18]

In a similar letter to the American minister in Honolulu, Seward's successor, Hamilton Fish, outlined the strategic, commercial and religious reasons for acquisition. He saw Hawaii as 'an outpost fronting the whole of our possessions on the Pacific Ocean', and envisaged:

A future that must extend jurisdiction and the limits of this nation and that will require a resting spot in mid-Ocean, between the Pacific coast and the vast domains of Asia, which are now opening to commerce and Christian civilisation.[19]

In 1875, the United States signed a comprehensive commercial treaty with Hawaii, under which the King pledged never to cede the islands to a third power. This treaty was renewed in 1884 with a new clause providing for Pearl Harbor to be placed at the exclusive disposal of the United States as a naval base. The two treaties stimulated the rapid expansion of the American sugar industry so that by the late 1880s the commercial life of the islands was dominated by American sugar plantations, and Americans owned a high proportion of the productive land. In 1887, American residents imposed a settlement on the King which assured white supremacy and came to be known as 'the bayonet constitution'. When the King died in 1891 his sister succeeded him as Queen Liliuokalami and attempted to restore indigenous control over the islands. Disturbances inevitably followed and, in a classic colonial intervention, American marines landed from the *USS Boston* in 1893 'to secure the safety of American life and property'.

The American minister in Honolulu proclaimed Hawaii as a protectorate of the United States but President Cleveland believed it to be morally wrong to annex the islands. He dispatched a personal representative to Hawaii to remove the American flag and re-embark the marines. His successor, William McKinley, was at first undecided over annexation. He submitted an annexation treaty to the Senate knowing that it could not obtain the necessary two-thirds majority to be enacted. However, the war with Spain in 1898 tipped the balance, since Hawaii

---

[17] Cited in L. Battistini, *The Rise of American Influence in Asia and the Pacific*.
[18] Ibid.   [19] Ibid.

was seen as an important staging post for operations in the Philippines. The *New York Independent*, which considered that the islands had been 'taken possession of and annexed religiously . . . two generations ago', reflected the general mood in the United States, proclaiming:

The ripe apple falls into our hands and we should be very foolish to throw it away . . . The possession of Hawaii gives perfect control of the ocean route across the Pacific . . . We need its tropical products and we need its harbors . . . This will give us a dominating influence among all the islands of Oceania.[20]

The hitherto cautious McKinley emerged from the war as an imperialist, believing that 'we need Hawaii just as much . . . as we did California. It is manifest destiny'.[21] He consequently returned to Congress with a Joint Resolution requiring only a simple majority and this passed without difficulty. The islands were formally annexed to the United States in 1898 and became a Territory in 1900. Grover Cleveland was dismayed. 'As I contemplate the means used to complete this outrage' he said, 'I am ashamed of the whole affair.'[22] The *Honolulu Advertiser* more accurately reflected the temper of the American settlers by running a headline 'Hawaii Becomes First Outpost of a Greater America'.

The United States moved quickly to consolidate her position in Hawaii. Pearl Harbor had been established as a coaling station for the US Navy by 1902 and was later developed as a major naval base. The shift from coal burning to oil burning soon allowed the US Navy to cover the Philippines from Hawaii. For the US Army, Fort Shafter, named after an American general who had fought in Cuba, was constructed in 1907 and Schofield Barracks was added in 1909. After the First World War, the strategic importance of Hawaii was greatly enhanced by the Washington Treaties of 1922 which placed restrictions on military construction at Guam and the Philippines. Even so, there were some who felt that Hawaii was being neglected in favour of the long-established Navy yards on the east coast. Writing in the Army and Navy Register in 1922, Rear Admiral Thomas Magruder expressed the opinion:

To-day there are seven Navy yards on the east coast of the United States . . . there is not enough work . . . to justify keeping all these yards in active operation. By disposing of superfluous yards and placing others on an inactive basis

[20] E. May, *The Emergence of America as a Great Power* (London: Harper & Row, 1961, 15).
[21] Ibid. 244.   [22] Battistini, op. cit.

the saving . . . could be used to strengthen the naval base in the Hawaiian Islands. There is where our greatest Navy yard and Navy base should be.[23]

This message was taken to heart with the result that the outbreak of the Second World War saw a formidable concentration of American naval power at Pearl Harbor. Moreover, with the evolution of air power Wheeler Airfield was completed for the US Army Air Force in 1922 and Hickam Airfield, adjacent to Pearl Harbor, in 1938. In addition, a seaplane base was set up for the US Marine Corps at Kaneohe Bay in 1939.

However, the importance of Hawaii for command of the Pacific was just as evident to the Japanese as to the Americans, leading to the attack on Pearl Harbor in December 1941 and the entry of the United States into the Second World War. Not only were the capital ships of the US Pacific Fleet crippled, apart from the three aircraft carriers which were fortuitously absent from Pearl Harbor, but the majority of Army and Navy aircraft were destroyed on the ground at Hickham, Wheeler, and Kaneohe Airfields. Thereafter, Hawaii became the nerve centre for American naval operations in the Pacific. Until he moved to Guam in January 1945, Admiral Chester Nimitz conducted naval operations throughout the Pacific from his headquarters at Pearl Harbor, even when these operations were taking place many thousands of miles distant in the Coral Sea. Subsequently, naval operations in the mid Pacific were planned at Pearl Harbor by Admirals Halsey and Spruance, while those in the South Pacific, leading up to the intended assault on Japan, were conducted from Guam.

Since the end of the war in the Pacific the naval base at Pearl Harbor has played an important part in the Korean War with up to fifty warships under repair there in 1952. In 1959, Hawaii became the fiftieth State of the Union and today houses the Headquarters of the United States Pacific Command, which covers most of the Indian Ocean as well as the Pacific, amounting to some 70 per cent of the world's sea area, together with two subordinate unified commands, US Forces Japan and US Forces Korea. Pearl Harbor now serves as a rear base for the US Seventh Fleet, as well as the main base for the US Third Fleet. Some seventy commands of the US Navy are located at the base, whose main facilities include a naval station, submarine base, naval shipyard, and naval supply industrial centre. In total, there are some twenty-five major military installations on the islands of Hawaii, including Camp H. M.

---

[23] Rear Admiral T. P. Magruder. Army and Navy Register. 25 February 1922. Cited in G. Wheeler, *Prelude to Pearl Harbor* (Columbia, MO: University of Missouri Press, 1963).

Smith, built for the US Marine Corps in 1942. In 1999, there were approximately 46,000 American service personnel stationed at Hawaii, excluding those at sea with the Pacific Fleet, made up of some 15,500 from the US Army, 19,500 from the US Navy, 4,500 from the US Air Force, and over 6,000 from the US Marine Corps. With the end of the Cold War and the United States withdrawal from the Philippines, Hawaii forms one of America's three major basing areas in the Pacific, along with Japan and South Korea.

Wake Island and Guam

Wake Island, midway between Hawaii and Guam, has an area of less than three square miles and a population of only 2,000. The island was named after a British seaman William Wake, who landed there in 1796 but experienced no further contact with the outside world until an American naval expedition visited in 1841. The island was subsequently occupied by American troops on their way to the Philippines in July 1898 and annexed to the United States in January 1899. A commercial seaplane base was established on the island in 1935 but, in common with other American possessions in the Pacific, apart from Hawaii, Wake Island was not fortified prior to the Second World War. The United States felt obliged to abide by an undertaking to this effect given at the Washington Conference of 1921–2 which had limited the capital ships of the American, British, and Japanese navies in the ratio 5:5:3. The agreement by the United States and Britain not to fortify their island possessions in the Pacific was intended to offset the lower ratio of capital ships agreed for Japan. But Japan left the League of Nations in 1933 and declared shortly afterwards that she would no longer be bound by the decisions of the Washington Conference.

Although Japan set about fortifying her mandated islands in the Pacific from 1935 onwards, military construction commenced at Wake Island only in 1941. The island was quickly overrun by Japan following the attack on Pearl Harbor and remained under enemy occupation from 1942 to 1945. Today, the island is administered by the Secretary of the Air Force and the military base, which acts as an emergency landing field and fuel storage depot, is predominantly staffed by civilians who provide air transit and servicing facilities. In 1990, legislation was placed before Congress proposing the incorporation of Wake Island with Guam, but action on these proposals has been deferred because the Marshall islanders have claimed that Wake Island, which they know as Enenkio, was once the site of traditional rituals performed by their Chiefs.

The island of Guam in the Marianas, which lies some 4,300 miles south-west of Hawaii and due east of the Philippines, is of far greater military value to the United States. Guam was discovered by Ferdinand de Magellan in 1521, but claimed in 1565 by Spain, who used it as a staging post on the trade route between Mexico and the Philippines. During the Spanish-American war, Guam was captured by Captain Henry Glass of the *USS Charleston* and was ceded to the United States along with the Philippines at the Treaty of Paris in 1898. In December 1941, Guam, isolated and inadequately defended, was rapidly occupied by Japan and was only recaptured by the United States in August 1944 at a cost of the lives of 7,000 American and 17,000 Japanese troops. In January 1945, the island became the headquarters of the US naval forces in the Pacific. Since the war, the United States has made up for her earlier neglect of Guam. The island has been extensively developed for military use as the one major possession of the United States in the Western Pacific where she enjoys complete freedom of action. The island was administered by the US Navy until 1950 when it became an unincorporated territory of the United States under civil administration. Nevertheless, some 20 per cent of the island's land area of 500 square miles remained under military control until the early 1990s. Congress agreed in 1994 to transfer some 3,000 acres of land from federal to local control and in 1992 the Governor, Joseph Ada, formulated demands, which were conceded in March 1995, for the return of the Naval Air Station at Brewer Field to civil use. Nevertheless, the United States announced a modest expansion in her military facilities at Guam in April 1992 to compensate for the enforced withdrawal from the Philippines. In 1997, the population of the island, at just over 100,000, included nearly 7,000 American servicemen. In 1999, there were still 4,500 US Navy personnel stationed on the island and 2,000 US Air Force personnel.

It is difficult to overestimate the strategic importance of Guam for the United States. For many years, Anderson Air Force Base, constructed in 1944 on the northern tip of the island and rebuilt in the 1970s, was the main Pacific base for Strategic Air Command. In the Vietnam War, Guam became one of the major launching areas for air strikes by B-52 bombers which, because of host nation sensitivities, were unable to use either Japan (apart from Okinawa) or the Philippines. Although the harbour at Apra is relatively small, it provides useful repair and maintenance facilities for the Seventh Fleet and the secure status of the island, as a US territory, led to its selection as one of three bases worldwide for the deployment of Polaris submarines, along with Holy Loch in Scotland and Rota in Spain. Guam has therefore played a vital role in the deterrent posture of the United States, both by sea and by air, and, in conventional terms, the military value of the island has been enhanced by the withdrawal from the Philippines. The convenience of retaining a colonial possession in the Western Pacific is evident. Commonwealth status has been considered for the island from time to time but has secured little support from Congress. In 1982, Commonwealth status was the most favoured option in a referendum which attracted a turnout of only 38 per cent, and in 1987 negotiations commenced on Commonwealth status between the United States and the Guam Commission for Self Determination. The issue was still unresolved in 1995 when President Clinton appointed a team to draft a Guam Commonwealth Act but the future status of the island has not been afforded a high priority by Congress which had failed to give the proposals a full hearing by mid 1999.

The Trust Territories of the Pacific Islands

The Marshall, Mariana, and Caroline Islands lie west of the Philippines and north of New Guinea. Sometimes known collectively as Micronesia, they comprise over 2,000 volcanic islands and coral atolls scattered over a sea area of 7.8 million square miles (an area larger than Australia) but with a total land area of only 700 square miles. With the exception of Guam, which was ceded to the United States, all these islands were sold to Germany for the equivalent of $4.5 million by Spain when her Pacific empire was liquidated in 1898 after defeat in the Spanish-American War. At the outbreak of the First World War, Japan, which was allied to Britain at the time, took the opportunity to occupy these islands. Following the defeat of Germany Japan pressed for full sovereignty over the islands at the Treaty of Versailles. The United States strongly resisted this bid but the outcome was a compromise under which Japan acquired a mandate from the League of Nations over former German possessions north of the Equator, whereas Australia and New Zealand were given a similar mandate south of the Equator (New Zealand acquired control of Western Samoa in this way and Australia acquired the Bismark Archipelago, the Admiralty Islands, parts of New Guinea and the Soloman Islands.) The United States felt she had been out-manoeuvred by Japan and Britain, acting on behalf of Australia and New Zealand, but she was unable to prevent the award of the mandates which became effective in 1920. As a result Japan gained control of extensive strategic assets in the mid Pacific from which she could, in wartime, interrupt communications between Hawaii and the Philippines. Although she was constrained from fortifying these islands under the terms of the mandate in the 1920s, she had no compunction about doing so once she had left the League of Nations in 1933 and renounced the Washington Treaty in 1935. Thereafter, a network of military facilities was established in the islands which included a major Japanese naval base at the island of Truk in the Carolines.

Following the attack on Pearl Harbor, Japan seized Guam, Wake Island, and the Philippines and invaded New Guinea and the Solomon Islands in order to threaten allied communications between Hawaii and Australia. The Japanese advance was checked in mid 1942 at the Battle of the Coral Sea and through allied landings at Guadalcanal in the Solomon Islands. Allied forces under General MacArthur subsequently fought their way through the Solomons and adjacent islands, dislodging the Japanese from some islands and leaving their garrisons isolated on others. As the island-hopping strategy adopted by MacArthur progressed, American bases were established at Kwajalein and Eniwetok in the Marshalls, then Tinian and Saipan in the Marianas, and finally Iwo Jima in the Bonins. Guam was recovered for the United States and the Japanese base at Truk was neutralized. For the final assault on Japan bomber bases were constructed on many of these islands from which B-29 Superfortresses could launch air strikes on the Japanese mainland. Two bases were built on Guam, one on Saipan and two on Tinian, from one of which, North Field, the B-29 *Enola Gay* took off to drop the first atom bomb on Hiroshima on 6 August 1945. At the same time, bases were built for fighter support on Iwo Jima, only 600 miles from Tokyo.

The United States was determined to retain the Japanese-mandated islands after the war, in view of the hostile use to which Japan had put them and the vital importance of possession for future control of the Pacific. The military planners in Washington had made their intentions clear as early as March 1943. However, the acquisition of new overseas possessions was scarcely consistent with the principles of self-determination set out in the Atlantic Charter. Roosevelt decided to square this circle by writing into the United Nations Charter a provision allowing for strategic areas to be designated within UN Trust Territories. James Forrestal, Roosevelt's Secretary of the Navy from 1944, records a Cabinet discussion in March 1945 at which the President advanced the concept:

. . . of what he called multiple sovereignty—that is sovereignty would be vested in all of the United Nations . . . but we would be requested by them to exercise complete trusteeship for the purpose of world security.[24]

Forrestal himself said 'there were a number of places we ought to have for our naval security—Kwajalein, the Marianas, Truk, etc. He [Roosevelt] also included Manus in this category and said he would even be inclined to have military rights on Noumea while leaving the French the economic accruals from new Caledonia'. The President appeared to be unconcerned that New Caledonia was a French possession and that Manus was in the Admiralty Islands mandated to Australia.

After the war, Admiral Nimitz, now Chief of Naval Operations, argued against trusteeship, advocating that the United States should assume sovereignty over the islands. Forrestal recorded him saying in October 1946 that:

The sovereignty of the ex-Japanese mandates should be taken by the United States . . . the ultimate security of the United States depends in major part on our ability to control the Pacific Ocean, that these islands are . . . essential to that control and that the concept of trusteeship is inapplicable here because these islands do not represent any colonial problem nor is there economic advantage accruing to the United States through their ownership.[25]

These comments show the extent to which some elements in Washington were prepared to turn colonialist when the strategic interests of the United States were at stake. However, wiser counsel prevailed and the United States representative to the United Nations pressed for trusteeship, arguing that the course of the conflict had demonstrated the 'paramount strategic importance'[26] of these islands. In 1947, the Security Council agreed that the United States could exercise strategic trusteeship over the Marshalls, the Marianas (excluding Guam), and the Carolines (including Palau). As a result, the Trust Territory of the Pacific Islands came into being, the only one of eleven UN trusteeships to be designated as a strategic trusteeship, a new concept devised solely to meet the military requirements of the United States.

Under Article V of the Trusteeship Agreement the United States was permitted to establish navy, army, and air bases and to erect fortifications on trust territory, to station and employ armed forces in the territory and to declare the whole or part of the area closed for secu-

[24] Cabinet Meeting 9 March 1945. Recorded in *The Forrestal Diaries*, W. L. Millis (ed.) (London: Cassell, 1952, 49–50).

[25] Meeting 22 October 1946 with Truman. See *The Forrestal Diaries*, 213.

[26] J. Woodliffe, *The Peacetime Use of Foreign Military Bases* (Dordrecht: Martinus Nijhoff, 1992).

rity reasons. These were colonial rights in all but name. The islands had simply been taken over from Japan and, in common with other American island possessions in the Pacific, they were administered by the Secretary for the Navy until 1951. From this date, the US Department of the Interior assumed responsibility for the islands but the Marianas remained under military control until 1962. However, the United States took no steps to exercise the extensive rights granted to her to fortify the islands or garrison them with combat troops. Her concern was primarily to ensure that no other power obtained a foothold on the islands, to retain the option to deploy her forces there on a contingency basis (Tinian, Saipan, and Palau were all considered as alternatives to the Philippines at one time or another), and to use the relatively isolated atolls of the Marshall Islands for testing missiles and atomic weapons.

In fact, Bikini atoll was first used for atomic tests in the atmosphere in 1946, before the United Nations had agreed to the proposals for strategic trusteeship. This was followed by an atomic test at Eniwetok in 1947, and the first hydrogen bomb was tested on the same island in 1954. The test programme was not concluded until 1962 by which time a total of 67 tests had taken place. The inhabitants of both islands had been evacuated before the tests began but they were allowed to return to Bikini in 1971 and Eniwetok in 1976. However, evidence of continued contamination was encountered on both islands and the United States was obliged to set up a $150 million trust fund to compensate the islanders for the effects of the test programme. Meanwhile, the inhabitants of Kwajalein atoll had also been resettled to allow the development of a missile test facility in 1961 to track missiles fired from Vandenberg Air Force Base in California. This range, operated by the Army Space and Strategic Defense Command, was one of the two test areas permitted under the Anti-Ballistic Missile Treaty signed by the United States and the Soviet Union in 1972.

It must be doubtful whether the testing of atomic weapons and long range missiles were the strategic uses which the United Nations had in mind when setting up the Trust Territory. However, the Trust Deed obliged the United States to develop political institutions in the islands and to promote economic, social, and educational advancement with the eventual aim of leading the islands towards self-government. The United States started discussions on the future of the islands in 1969 but was to discover, as Britain had earlier, that orderly decolonization can be just as difficult as empire-building. The three archipelagos within the Trust Territory each opted for a different constitutional future and residual difficulties over the island of Palau in the Carolines delayed formal termination of the trusteeship until 1986. By this time, the Marianas had separated from the other islands and elected to become a Commonwealth of the United States (only the second overseas Commonwealth to be set up after Puerto Rico in 1952), the Marshalls had opted for limited independence in 1979, with the United States retaining certain military rights for a further fifteen years, and the Carolines, with the exception of Palau, had become independent as the Federated States of Micronesia.

Palau (sometimes known as Belau) is the name given to the most westerly group of the Caroline Islands closest to the Philippines. In late 1944, these islands had been captured from Japan after bitter resistance, particularly on the island of Peleliu, prior to the American landing at Leyte in the Philippines. Although the United States did not establish post-war bases on the island she wished to keep open the option of doing so, particularly if obliged to withdraw from the Philippines. In moving towards self-government, Palau adopted a constitution in 1979 which banned nuclear weapons from the islands and excluded the use of 'eminent domain' (the American term for compulsory purchase) with regard to the acquisition of land by a foreign power. This was incompatible with the residual military rights that the United States wished to retain and, since a 75 per cent majority was required to amend the constitution, no less than eight referenda were required before a solution was reached in 1986. At that stage, a Military Use and Operational Rights Agreement was concluded which allowed the United States to make contingency use of land on Palau territory for a further fifty years after consultation with the Palau government. At the same time, the United States gave an undertaking to Palau that she would not station nuclear weapons on the islands.

This agreement allowed Palau, as an independent nation, to subscribe to the Compact of Free Association with the United States which had already been adopted by the Marshall Islands and the Federated States of Micronesia. The Compact of Free Association has been described as 'an innovative concept without precedent in United States constitutional history'.[27] Under it, the islands granted to the United States 'a number of rights and prerogatives that limit their own autonomy in exchange for large financial subsidies'. The main limitation on the autonomy of the islands was that the United States remained

---

[27] F. M. Bunge and M. W. Cooke (ed.), *Oceania: A Regional Study* (Washington, DC: The American University, USGPO, 1984, 51, 311).

responsible for their defence and security and retained the right to deny access to the military personnel of any third nation. In this respect, the Compact was not dissimilar to protectorate status which played an important part in Britain's 'informal' empire (although Britain usually reserved for herself control over foreign affairs as well as defence in her protectorates). However, the United States was prepared to pay generously for the rights she retained. The Marshall Islands received $30 million per annum for fifteen years and a substantial rent was paid for continued use of the Kwajalein tracking station for thirty years. A further $400 million of economic assistance was promised to Palau. The Compact came into effect for the Marshalls and the Federated States of Miconesia in 1986 when the UN Trusteeship Council formally brought the Trust Territory to an end but did not apply to Palau until she became independent in October 1994.

Puerto Rico

Although most of America's overseas possessions are to be found in the Pacific, she also holds territory in the Caribbean. The island of Puerto Rico was ceded to the United States in 1898 after the Spanish-American War, and the US Virgin Islands, adjacent to Puerto Rico, were purchased from Denmark in 1917 for $25 million to prevent them falling into German hands. From the outset, the American interest in Puerto Rico and the adjacent islands was strategic. 'The invasion and acquisition of Puerto Rico' it has recently been claimed 'was inextricably tied to the decision to build a canal connecting the Atlantic and Pacific Oceans.'[28] Little was done to develop the island economy which remained largely dependent on sugar plantations. The value of Puerto Rico, in American eyes, lay in its position guarding the approaches to the Panama Canal. The United States was accused by Pedro Albizu Campos, founder of the Puerto Rican independence movement in the 1930s, of being 'interested in the cage not the birds'.[29] Even so, it was not until 1923 that a US Army Base, Fort Buchanan, was built on San Juan Bay and the major naval complex, known as Roosevelt Roads, covering Puerto Rico, its offshore islands of Culebra and Vieques, and the Virgin Islands of St. Thomas and St. Croix was only developed during the Second World War. The purpose of this extensive naval development was allegedly to accommodate ships of the Royal Navy in the event of

---

[28] R. B. Martínez, Puerto Rico's Decolonization. In *Foreign Affairs*, November/December 1997.
[29] Ibid.

a German invasion of Britain. But it must be open to question whether the British Fleet would have retreated to the Caribbean rather than Canada in these circumstances.

The inhabitants of Puerto Rico became American citizens as a result of the Jones Act passed in 1917 but an uneasy relationship persisted between the United States and her Caribbean colony, whose inhabitants spoke Spanish and were steeped in Spanish culture. The independence movement did not attract widespread support but those involved were prepared to adopt extreme measures. In 1936, Campos and other nationalist leaders were imprisoned under the Sedition Act. From 1938 onwards, the Popular Democratic Party under Luis Muñoz Marín began to agitate for independence. But in the post-war period the Nationalist Party under Campos resorted to violence. The party staged an armed uprising in 1950 and later in the year nationalists made an attempt on the life of President Truman. This was followed by an armed assault on an American Congressman in 1954.

The island was granted Commonwealth status in 1952, making it a self-governing incorporated territory forming an integral part of the United States but the Federal Relations Act states that all laws enacted by Congress apply to Puerto Rico, unless deemed locally inapplicable. However, Puerto Rico has never become a State of the Union, despite extensive debate on the future constitutional status of the territory since the war. In 1947, the island first elected its own governor and in 1967, in the first of several referenda, a majority voted to retain Commonwealth status. Notwithstanding this result, the Socialist Party brought the status of Puerto Rico before the United Nations Decolonisation Committee in 1970 and a resolution was passed recognizing the island's right to self-determination.

The onset of the Cold War enhanced the strategic importance of Puerto Rico although this was not to become fully apparent until Castro subscribed to communism in 1959 and the Soviet Navy demonstrated that it could penetrate the Caribbean during the Cuban missile crisis in 1962. Between 1945 and 1957, Roosevelt Roads reverted to maintenance status with different elements being closed and reopened from time to time. However, in 1957 the complex was reactivated as the control centre and testing area for the Atlantic Fleet Weapons Range. Following the missile crisis, Roosevelt Roads also had an important part to play in keeping open the sea lines of communication through the Caribbean to the Panama Canal in the event of war with the Soviet Union.

In 1979, the role of Roosevelt Roads was described as 'a principal naval staging base for conducting training, supporting fleet deployments in the Caribbean and testing weapons systems'.[30] At that time, there were some 3,000 US Navy personnel based at Roosevelt Roads with another 600 personnel from the US Air Force, US Army, and Marine Corps. The base played a significant role in the American intervention in the Dominican Republic in 1965 and in the rehearsal for the invasion of Grenada in 1983. However, even Puerto Rico's status as a Commonwealth of the United States has not shielded military operations at Roosevelt Roads from controversy. Gunnery practice at Culebra evoked considerable protest from the local population in the 1970s, and in 1975 President Nixon ordered the US Navy to leave the island. But this only increased military activity on the neighbouring island of Vieques, where the US Navy occupies some two-thirds of the land area. Accord between the US Navy and the Commonwealth of Puerto Rico on the use of Vieques was finally reached in 1985.[31] However, ill-feeling continued with warships from Belgium and the Netherlands anchored off Vieques being harassed in May 1987 by islanders complaining about target practice and interference with fishing.

A report for the Senate Committee on Foreign Relations in 1979 maintained that the American bases on the island were 'entirely consistent with Puerto Rico's political association with the United States', but acknowledged that there was considerable anti-colonial pressure against the bases in the island and at the United Nations.[32] However, with American troops due to leave Panama in 1999 and activity at Guantánamo in Cuba severely constrained by political factors, Puerto Rico and the US Virgin Islands represent the most secure facilities available to the United States in the Caribbean. As Rear-Admiral O'Connor, Commander of US Forces Caribbean, put it in 1986, 'the one unqualified American military presence in the Caribbean is Puerto Rico, the one certain place'.[33]

Today, the position of Puerto Rico, as an overseas territory of the United States in the Caribbean, remains somewhat anomalous. Most British dependencies in the area, including islands very much smaller than Puerto Rico, have been granted full independence and the two French islands of Martinique and Guadeloupe have become

---

[30] United States Foreign Policy Objectives and Overseas Military Installations. Report for the SCFR. Congressional Research Service (CRS) April 1979.

[31] H. G. Muñiz, US Military Installations in Puerto Rico. In *The Colonial Dilemma*, Edwin and Edgardo Meléndez (ed.) (Boston, MA: South End Press, 1993, Ch. 3).

[32] Congressional Research Service (CRS) 1979.

[33] Muñiz, Ch. 3, *The Colonial Dilemma*.

Departments of France. Puerto Rico, however, remains an appendage of the United States, a pensioner state with an economy largely dependent on transfer payments. Annual per capita income is less than $8,000 and the island has one of the highest crime and drug addiction rates in the world. Over the last 40 years, one-third of the population has emigrated. Against this background, independence has only limited attractions and only the third and smallest political party now advocates this course. The two main parties support continued links with the United States, either as a Commonwealth or a State of the Union but over the last decade there has been continuing debate on the future status of the island without any final resolution.

In 1989, President Bush proposed that a plebiscite be held to determine whether Puerto Rico should proceed to statehood, but this proposal failed to gain the approval of Congress. Instead, a referendum was held in 1991 to determine whether Puerto Rico wished to move to full independence, but this option was rejected by a majority of 53 per cent. In a further referendum in 1993, 48 per cent voted for continued Commonwealth status, 46 per cent for statehood, and only 4 per cent for independence. In 1995, the debate took a perplexing turn. Don Young, Chairman of the House Resources Committee, introduced a bill requiring periodic plebiscites on the island's status. Despite the narrow majority in favour of continued Commonwealth status two years earlier, the bill only allowed a choice between becoming a State of the Union and proceeding to full independence. It was considered that Commonwealth status was a vestige of colonialism which should not be on offer. However, the Resident Commissioner representing Puerto Rico in the House of Representatives opposed the bill and it was withdrawn late in 1996. In its place a further referendum was proposed for 1998 on a full range of constitutional options including Commonwealth status and free association. This passed the House of Representatives by a single vote in March 1998 and in December a further referendum was held on the island but this proved inconclusive—46.5 per cent voted for statehood but 50.2 per cent voted against any of the options on the ballot. And so in the centenary year of Puerto Rico's annexation by the United States, the debate over the future constitution of the island remained unresolved. Furthermore, the islanders themselves, although wedded to Spanish customs and culture, remained uncertain over their status and affiliation, as exemplified by the dispute over language in the early 1990s. In 1991, Spanish was made the official language of Puerto Rico but in 1993 this decision was reversed and English was restored.

Other Colonial Territories

The number of overseas possessions under direct American control was limited, however, as the spurt of imperialism at the turn of the century represented an atypical interlude in the history of a nation dedicated to self-determination and thwarting the ambitions of the European colonial powers. In assuming Britain's role as the primary guarantor of global stability, it was natural for the United States to make use of Britain's more extensive overseas possessions. This process started in 1940, before the United States had even entered the Second World War. Following the war, the United States also established bases in Morocco by agreement with France.

British Bases in the Atlantic and Caribbean

One of Churchill's first actions as Prime Minister was to send Roosevelt a telegram on 15 May 1940 asking for forty to fifty American destroyers to help prosecute the Battle of the Atlantic. Roosevelt replied on 13 August saying that he thought it would be possible to supply at least fifty destroyers, together with some motor torpedo boats and aircraft. In return, he wanted a private assurance that the destroyers would not be turned over to Germany 'if the waters of Great Britain became untenable' but sent to other parts of the British Empire, and secondly, an agreement for the United States to use areas in Newfoundland, Bermuda, the Bahamas, Jamaica, St. Lucia, Trinidad, and British Guyana 'as naval and air bases in the event of an attack on the American hemisphere . . . and the immediate acquisition by the United States and the employment for purposes of training and exercises of bases in these areas—the necessary lands to be acquired by purchase or on a ninety-nine years lease'.[34] The specific nature of the bargain proposed by Roosevelt indicated his concern for the defence of the Atlantic and the Caribbean, the long-term nature of his plans (he had informed King George VI of his interest in the same list of territories in 1939),[35] and his determination to drive a hard bargain. He was prepared to consider either outright purchase or a ninety-nine year lease indicating that the United States wanted a permanent position in these territories, not just short-term arrangements for the duration of the war.

Churchill was at first opposed to giving the United States what he

---

[34] Sir Llewellyn Woodward, *British Foreign Policy in the Second World War* (London: HMSO, 1970, 368).

[35] Baylis, op. cit. 2.

called 'a blank cheque' on the whole of Britain's transatlantic possessions, but the War Cabinet took a broader view: 'The general view of the War Cabinet was that, although, from the point of view of tangible assets the terms of the bargain were not very favourable to us, it was impossible to look at the matter merely as an exchange. It might be the first step in the constitution of an Anglo-Saxon bloc or, indeed, a decisive point in history'.[36]

When he reported to the House of Commons on 20 August 1940, Churchill emphasized the broader strategic significance of the arrangement:

This process means that . . . the British Empire and the United States will have to be somewhat mixed up together. I could not stop it if I wished to. No-one can stop it. Like the Mississippi, it just keeps rolling along.[37]

This arrangement, presaging the widespread development of the 'leasehold empire' after the war, was confirmed in an Exchange of Letters between Lord Lothian and Cordell Hull on 2 September 1940. The exchange provided for the bases to be leased to the United States for ninety-nine years free from all rent or charges, and agreed that the British government would 'grant to the United States for the period of the leases all the rights, power and authority within the bases leased'.[38] A more formal agreement, setting out the terms of each lease and the area to be covered by it, was concluded on 27 March 1941. This agreement conferred sweeping powers on the United States. Article II stated:

When the United States is engaged in war or in time of other emergency . . . the United States may exercise all such rights, power and authority as may be necessary for conducting military operations deemed desirable by the United States.[39]

Furthermore, Article XXIX gave the United States authorities near sovereign powers within the leased areas:

No laws of the territory which would derogate from or prejudice any of the rights conferred on the United States by the lease or by this Agreement shall be applicable within the leased area, save with the concurrence of the United States.[40]

The only reference to consultation appeared in Article I, making it clear that this was to apply only outside the leased areas, and there is no reference anywhere in the agreement to the type of military operations

---

[36] Sir Llewellyn Woodward, op. cit.   [37] Cited in Baylis, op. cit.
[38] Woodward, op. cit.   [39] UK Treaty Series No 2, Cmd 6259, 1941.   [40] Ibid.

the United States would be permitted to conduct from these bases or the extent to which the consent of the British government would be required.

The powers conferred on the United States were such that a case was brought in the US courts after the war to establish whether the bases were 'territories or possessions of the United States'.[41] The US government accepted that sovereignty had not been transferred and later agreed that the United States had no third-party rights over the bases. Nevertheless, the proprietary rights which the Americans felt towards the bases is illustrated by the fact that Senator McFarland of Arizona tried to secure a motion in Congress making permanent ownership of the bases a condition of granting a post-war loan to Great Britain.[42] This motion was rejected by the relatively narrow margin of forty-five to forty votes in the Senate.

Kissinger has commented that the leasing arrangement was primarily of symbolic significance since most of the bases were remote from theatres of war and duplicated other American bases.[43] This was probably true for the bases established in the Caribbean, but in the Atlantic, Bermuda had an important part to play in operations against enemy submarines during the Battle of the Atlantic, and the bases established in Newfoundland, and later Labrador, proved of vital importance both for Atlantic convoy duties and as a staging post in the air bridge to Britain via Greenland and Iceland. The reason that Newfoundland was included in this deal concluded by the British government was that the island remained a British colony until 1949 when it became the tenth Province of Canada. The main naval base established in Newfoundland was at Argentia, Placentia Bay, which was the scene of the Atlantic Conference in August 1941. Work at Argentia was undertaken as a matter of urgency by the US Naval Construction Battalions, known as the 'Seabees', and the base was fully commissioned by the time that the United States entered the war in December 1941. It provided a deep-water harbour free of ice all year-round, from which convoys could be escorted across the Atlantic. The main US Army Air Force base in Newfoundland was Harmon Field, Stephenville, whose primary task was the movement of personnel and equipment to and from the European theatre. Joint facilities were also established with the Royal Canadian Air Force at Gander in Newfoundland and Goose Bay in Labrador, both of which played an important role in the movement of operational

[41] Woodliffe, op. cit.
[42] R. Harkavy *Great Power Competition for Overseas Bases* (Oxford: Pergamon, 1982).
[43] Kissinger, op. cit. 387.

aircraft to Britain by the Atlantic Ferry Organisation. This operation commenced in June 1941 and over 1,300 aircraft had been delivered to Britain by this route before the United States entered the war at the end of the year.

At the end of the war there were over 100,000 American servicemen in Newfoundland and Labrador. The United States left Gander in 1948, which was then developed as one of the main staging points for civil flights across the Atlantic. At Harmon Field an extensive construction programme was carried out between 1947 and 1950 to transform the airfield into a permanent base for the Military Air Transport Service (MATS). The main role of Harmon continued to be the movement of men and equipment to Europe and back until the base closed in 1966. But in 1953, further construction was undertaken to enable a squadron of F102 Interceptor aircraft and supporting tankers to be deployed as a defence against trans-polar attack by the Soviet Union. Goose Bay remained under the control of Strategic Air Command until 1976 when the base closed. But it was reopened as a NATO training base in 1984 providing facilities for the British, Dutch, American, and German Air Forces. The US Navy remained at Argentia, using the base primarily for anti-submarine warfare (ASW) operations until they withdrew in September 1994.[44]

A report for the Senate Committee on Foreign Relations in 1979 recorded the presence of an oceanographic research facility at Argentia with 'acoustic hydrophones planted off-shore . . . designed to provide more detailed information on the . . . ocean environment and transmission of sound in sea water'.[45] This is a rather coy reference to the SOSUS (sound surveillance under the sea) system which the same report openly acknowledges elsewhere. SOSUS, originally code-named CAESAR, was first installed off the east coast of the United States in 1954. Used to detect Soviet submarines worldwide, the system was long treated with the greatest secrecy. However, in recent years it has been reported in open literature that, by the mid 1970s, installations had been established at Newfoundland, Iceland, Bermuda, the Azores, and Brawdy in Britain to cover the Atlantic and that altogether there were thirty-six installations worldwide.[46]

The bases occupied by American forces in Bermuda were not handed

---

[44] For details of the bases in Newfoundland and Labrador I have drawn on John Cardoulis *A Friendly Invasion* (Newfoundland: Breakwater, 1990).

[45] CRS 1979, 18.

[46] R. Harkavy, 'The changing strategic and Technological Basis 1945–52', in U.S. *Military Forces in Europe*, S. Duke and W. Krieger (ed.) (Boulder, CO: Westview, 1993, Ch. 2).

back to the island administration until September 1995. Until that time, the United States occupied three sites, comprising 1,500 acres, or some 10 per cent of the islands' land mass. The largest of these sites was the naval air station at Kindley, covering just over 1,000 acres with extensive landfill on St. David's Island. This air station was constructed in 1941 and occupied successively by the US Army, the US Army Air Force immediately after the war, and the US Navy from 1970 onwards. Bermuda's position, 750 miles from the east coast of the United States, made it an ideal base for ASW operations undertaken by P3-Orion aircraft from Kindley, which also doubled as the island's civil airport. The remaining sites occupied by the United States were the Tudor Hill Laboratory and Naval Annex on the main island of Bermuda, which carried out underwater acoustic research by the US Naval Oceanography Command and served as a SOSUS terminal. The facilities at Bermuda were described as 'strategic, sensitive and classified'—no doubt a reference to the SOSUS installation—in a report by the House Committee on the Armed Services in 1981.[47] Prior to this report a revised agreement was negotiated in 1978, providing the United States with continued leasing rights until 2040, and in the 1980s approximately 1,000 American servicemen and 900 civilians were stationed in Bermuda. Nevertheless, the end of the Cold War has caused the United States to release these facilities earlier than expected.

In the Caribbean, the island bases originally conceived as a picket line protecting the Panama Canal played little part in the war. But during the 1950s the need for offshore testing and tracking facilities for missile systems reawakened American interest in these islands. In 1950, an agreement was signed between the British and American governments which set up a long range proving ground in the Bahamas for the testing of guided missiles and associated training.[48] Related tracking stations were established in Antigua, St. Lucia, Trinidad, and the Turks and Caicos islands. In 1961, a new agreement was negotiated between the United States and the Independent Federation of the West Indies. This allowed the United States to maintain military facilities in Antigua, Barbados, Jamaica, St. Lucia, Trinidad and Tobago, and the Turks and Caicos islands for a period of seventeen years. However, little use was made of this arrangement although oceanographic research facilities were set up at some of the islands. The facilities at Jamaica, St. Lucia, and the Turks and Caicos islands were all closed during the mid 1960s or early 1970s.

[47] Report by House Committee on the Armed Services. 97th Congress, 1st Session, 1981.
[48] UK Treaty Series No 74, Cmd 8189 21 July 1950.

A dispute between the United States and Trinidad developed when Trinidad indicated that she wished to build a new capital for the West Indies Federation on the site of the base made available to the United States at Chaguaramas. The United States refused to close or relocate the base, despite strong pressure from Premier Eric Williams. But the Federation collapsed in 1962 and American interest in the base gradually declined, leading to withdrawal in 1967. The naval facility in Barbados was also closed in 1979 following a breakdown in negotiations over rent to be paid for the base after Barbados had become independent. Elsewhere in the Caribbean the United States agreed to relinquish Atkins Field air base in Guyana when that country became independent in 1966.[49]

Today, the only significant remnants of the 1941 deal in the Caribbean are to be found at Antigua and the Bahamas. In Antigua an oceanographic survey and research site was set up in 1956 and a US Coastguard assistance team was established on the island, providing training for East Caribbean security forces. Neither of these facilities remains in place today but in January 1999 an agreement was signed allowing the USAF to maintain a radar and satellite tracking facility in Antigua. In the Bahamas, the guided missile testing facilities on Grand Bahama were linked to Ascension Island in 1956 and in the 1960s the Atlantic Underwater Test and Evaluation Center (AUTEC) was established on Andros Island.

Post-War Plans in the Pacific

The United States lost the Philippines, Guam, and Wake Island to the Japanese shortly after the attack on Pearl Harbor. Retreating from the Philippines, General MacArthur decided to fall back not on Hawaii but on Australia. United States troops arrived in Australia in 1942 and, with the Japanese trying to launch an attack on Australia from New Guinea, much of the war in the Pacific was fought, in its early stages, in and around British or Australian territory. The battle of Guadalcanal took place in the Solomon Islands and the Battle of the Coral Sea off the north-east coast of Australia. In order to secure the lifeline between Hawaii and Australia, at a time when the Carolines and Marshalls were still in Japanese hands, military facilities had been established throughout the South Pacific, notably at Christmas Island, Fiji, Noumea in New

---

[49] For details of US facilities in the West Indies, I have drawn on H. G. Muñiz, Decolonisation, Demilitarisation, Denuclearisation in the Caribbean. In *Strategy and Security in the Caribbean*, I. L. Griffith (ed.) (London: Praeger, 1991, Ch. 2).

Caledonia (a French colony), and the New Hebrides (an Anglo-French condominium). As the tide turned and the allies moved further north, a large American base was constructed on the island of Manus in the Admiralty Islands (which were administered by Australia under a League of Nations mandate). The planning for post-war bases initiated by Roosevelt originally focused on ways of securing the route to Australia through the French colonies of the Society and Marquesas Islands. Indeed, Roosevelt himself was obsessed with the small French island of Clipperton, 1,000 miles off the Mexican coast. In 1944, he warned Churchill not to take an interest in this island and later suggested transferring sovereignty from France to Mexico to facilitate American strategic interests.

After the war, the United States, in addition to the mandated islands wrested from the Japanese, wished to retain many of the facilities she had established on allied possessions in the Pacific. In April 1946, the American Secretary of State James Byrnes asked for the cession of sovereignty on twenty-five islands in the Pacific, eighteen under British administration and seven under New Zealand administration.[50] Lord Halifax, the British Ambassador in Washington, recommended agreement in principle to joint military installations at Tarawa in the Gilbert Islands, Guadalcanal and Tulagi in the Solomons and Fiji, suggesting that this might assist negotiations on a further loan to Britain, but Ernest Bevin strongly resisted the American approach.[51] In doing so he was backed by Australia and New Zealand who had signed the Canberra Agreement with the United States in 1944, reaffirming their sovereignty over any military facilities established on their territories during the war. Indeed, Australia declined to allow the United States to retain bases anywhere on her territory immediately after the war and arranged for United Nations trusteeships to be set up for New Guinea and the Admiralty Islands, which precluded basing rights for the United States.

Bases in the Middle East and North Africa

The Middle East had not featured in the United States initial post-war plans for military bases since this region was still regarded as a British sphere of influence. A report prepared for the Senate Committee on Foreign Relations in 1979 described the Middle East as 'a secondary area of American foreign policy interest until the post World War II era',

---

[50] Documents on British Foreign Policy Overseas. Series I, Vol. IV, 1987.
[51] Documents on British Foreign Policy Overseas. Halifax to Bevin, Telegram 2540, 20 April 1948.

but one which, following the war 'evolved into a shared interest with the British and French acting as practical overseers'.[52] At the end of the war it became apparent to the Americans that airfields in the region would be required for effective deterrence against the Soviet Union. Britain retained air bases in Iraq until the revolution of 1958 and exerted considerable influence both in Jordan and Egypt prior to the Suez crisis. But her decision to withdraw support from Greece and Turkey in 1947 and her surrender of the Palestine mandate convinced the United States that she would have to play a major role in the Eastern Mediterranean.

However, with the exception of Turkey, the United States was unable to secure permanent bases in the Middle East and, with the build-up of NATO, airfields gradually became available in more advantageous positions. A temporary presence was established in Libya, which had been an Italian colony prior to the war and remained under British occupation for some years afterwards. Towards the end of the war, the United States asked Britain for permission to retain the military air base at Wheelus Field near Tripoli. This was granted and, once Libya had gained independence in 1951, the United States negotiated an agreement with the new government for a twenty-year arrangement from 1951 to 1971. This included the use of an extensive amphibious training area and bombing ranges in the desert, in addition to the use of Wheelus Field which became for a time one of the largest and busiest overseas bases available to the United States. In return, military assistance of $42 million was promised over the period 1954 to 1971. The US Consul-General felt obliged to report to Dean Acheson in October 1951 'we are accused of being the new imperialists who plan to take over the whole of Libya'.[53] Britain had signed a similar agreement in 1953 sanctioning the use of El Adem Field for twenty years, along with other facilities at Benghazi and Tobruk. But both agreements were jeopardized by the overthrow of the Libyan monarchy by Colonel Gadaffi in September 1969. As a result, both the United States and Britain agreed to withdraw from their military facilities in Libya during 1970.

In the course of the North African campaign the United States had established military facilities in the French territories of Morocco, Algeria, and Tunisia and had made extensive use of Dakar in Senegal as a transatlantic supply terminal. Use of these facilities was confirmed in an agreement with the Free French in November 1942 and endorsed

---

[52] CRS April 1979.
[53] W. R. Louis, American Anti-Colonialism. In *The Special Relationship*, W. R. Louis and H. Bull (ed.) (Oxford: OUP, 1986, Ch. 16).

by General de Gaulle in August 1944. But the French soon regretted these arrangements and in June 1945 asked for the return of all the facilities in their African territories. They considered the naval facilities established in Morocco in 1942 at Port Lyautey (later known as Kenitra) to be particularly sensitive. But the United States managed to maintain access to the port which she used as a support base for the early visits to the Eastern Mediterranean by US warships in 1945 and 1946. Moreover, in December 1950 the United States concluded an unpublished agreement with France allowing her to construct five new air bases in Morocco for Strategic Air Command (SAC) on the understanding that these remained under the French flag and French officers were appointed as base commanders.

The French were concerned at the impact which this programme might have on nationalist sentiment and insisted that the bases be built in remote areas. The United States was to bear all the construction costs but the facilities were to be returned to France when no longer needed. The programme was to be implemented as a matter of urgency but inadequate planning and the remote nature of the sites led to delays in completion and increases in costs. Serviceable runways had been laid down at Nouasseur and Sidi Slimane by July 1951 and additional sites had been selected at Benguerir and Boulhaut by June 1952. The fifth base was abandoned and it was not until June 1955 that the four bases, each with 14,000-foot runways, were completed at a cost of $400 million. The strategic value of these bases was questionable, since they were far from the Soviet Union and were developed in parallel with similar facilities in Spain. Indeed, Mohammed V, the King of Morocco, protested that he had not been consulted by France over this arrangement, and when Morocco became fully independent in 1956 the Americans were asked to withdraw. An agreement was finally reached in 1959 whereby the United States agreed to withdraw from the SAC bases by December 1963. An informal arrangement allowed the US Navy to retain a communications facility that it had occupied under separate arrangements at Kenitra but this was phased out by 1978.

United States access to facilities in Morocco was to enjoy a brief revival in the 1980s. In May 1982, a Military Cooperation Agreement was signed by the two governments, initially for six years, which allowed American forces to use Sidi Slimane and Mohammed V international airport at Casablanca in transit, provided host nation approval was obtained in advance. The agreement allowed the United States to construct and maintain facilities at these sites and some $85 million was spent on the airfields. Military aid was resumed and a joint military commission was set up to supervise the provision of aid and equipment. However, this rapprochement was short-lived. In 1984, Morocco signed an 'Agreement of Unity' with Libya and the United States also became concerned that military equipment and supplies provided to Morocco might be used against the Polisario secessionist movement in the western Sahara. As a result, American use of these facilities diminished and the provision of military aid tailed off.

The one British possession in the Middle East which would have been of considerable interest to the United States, both for NATO and national missions, was the island of Cyprus. However, during the late 1950s security on the island remained a constant problem during the EOKA terrorist campaign (whose aim was to unite Cyprus with Greece) and political problems continued to dog the island after independence was granted in 1960. The Treaty of Establishment, concluded between Britain and Cyprus at the time of independence, set up two Sovereign Base Areas at Akrotiri (a Royal Air Force airfield in the south-west of the island) and Dhekelia (a British Army garrison in the south-east of the island). Since Britain retained sovereignty over these areas, comprising some ninety-nine square miles of the island in all, there was, as a Foreign Office Minister informed the House of Commons, 'no requirement for us to obtain the agreement of the Government of Cyprus on the particular use we make of the bases'.[54] Nevertheless, intercommunal hostility between Greeks and Turks on the island, resulting eventually in the Turkish invasion and subsequent partition, together with the divergence of British and American policies over the Arab-Israeli conflict, have made Britain extremely wary of allowing the United States use of these bases. Despite the excellent strategic location of the island for mounting operations in the Middle East, the United States has been authorized to do this on very few occasions. One such was in July 1958 when United States forces landed in Lebanon and British troops were sent in parallel to reinforce Jordan. In describing this operation, John Baylis has written:

The British Navy provided support in the Mediterranean and made facilities in Cyprus available to the United States, while the United States gave logistic support by flying supplies to the British contingent in Jordan.[55]

This was a rare example of Anglo-American action in the Middle East using Cyprus as a staging post. But it is significant that Cyprus was still

[54] Baroness Young in evidence to the House of Commons Foreign Affairs Committee. Minutes of Evidence, 1986–87.
[55] J. Baylis, *Anglo-American Defence Relations 1939–84* (London: Macmillan, 1984).

a British colony at this time and that the joint action taken was in response to the coup in Iraq. There was no Israeli dimension to this operation. The only known example of United States forces being allowed to use Cyprus after independence in relation to the Arab-Israeli conflict occurred after the Yom Kippur War was over in 1974. Minesweeping helicopters were then allowed to stage through Akrotiri to help clear the Suez Canal. However, it has been acknowledged in both countries that the facilities maintained by Britain in Cyprus have occasionally been made available to the United States for intelligence purposes. A report to the Senate Committee on Foreign Relations in 1979 noted that British bases in Cyprus had been used by the United States for 'intelligence collecting flights',[56] and in 1986 it was stated in the House of Commons that a single U-2 aircraft had been based at Akrotiri since 1974 to monitor the peace accords following the Yom Kippur War. The statement in Parliament said that this operation had been 'conducted with the knowledge and agreement of all the govern-ments directly concerned'.[57] This was taken to mean that the Cyprus government had been consulted, although this was not strictly neces-sary. There have also been a number of joint humanitarian missions con-ducted from Cyprus, for example the evacuation of foreign nationals from trouble spots, such as Tehran and Beirut, at various times.

Ascension Island

Another British colony which the Americans found extremely useful because of its strategic location was Ascension Island. This is a barren, volcanic island made up largely of lava and clinker at sea level, but capped by a mountain peak crested with tropical vegetation. Only 34 square miles in area and 9 miles across at its widest point, Ascension lies midway between Africa and South America in the South Atlantic 500 miles south of the Equator. Significantly, the island became a British possession in 1815 and was initially garrisoned by the Royal Navy to prevent Napoleon escaping from St. Helena, some 700 miles to the south-east, where he was exiled after the Battle of Waterloo. The island, which has no indigenous population, has always been administered by the Governor of St. Helena as a British colony. Ascension Island was not included in the leasing arrangement concluded in 1941 which made bases in the Atlantic and Caribbean available to the United States. But American troops arrived on the island in March 1942 and the 38th

---

[56] CRS 1979.   [57] H of C Official Report, 11 February 1986.

Engineer Combat Division quickly constructed Wideawake Field, named after the wideawake terns which frequent the island. By July 1942, a 3,000-foot runway had been constructed and the first American aircraft were using the airfield as a staging post for the movement of men and equipment to the North African theatre. The route used ran down to Recife in Brazil, across to Ascension Island, and from there to Dakar in West Africa and on to support Operation TORCH and other campaigns in the Mediterranean.

By 1943, there were 4,000 US servicemen stationed on the island and the need to retain Ascension Island as a strategic staging post featured in nearly all the plans discussed in Washington during the closing stages of the war. However, the agreement governing use of the island by American forces stipulated that this was to be for the duration of the war and six months thereafter. As a result, most American troops were withdrawn from Ascension in 1945 although some 80 men remained until 1946 and the last US commanding officer did not leave until May 1947. Meanwhile, James Byrnes had written to Ernest Bevin in November 1945, asking for continued rights at a number of British territories including Ascension Island. A memorandum by Bevin to the Defence Committee of the Cabinet on 13 April 1946 concluded with regard to Ascension Island:

The American request is for a 'joint' base on the same lines as those in the Pacific and there should be no difficulty in disposing of this issue on similar lines.[58]

As indicated above, this meant that the request should be resisted and there was no American presence on this island between the end of the war and the mid 1950s.

In 1956, Ascension Island became involved in the missile testing and tracking range set up six years earlier in the Bahamas. An agreement was signed in June 1956 with the wordy and cumbersome title:

Agreement Between the United Kingdom and the United States Concerning the Extension of the Bahamas' Long Range Proving Ground by the Establishment of Additional Sites in Ascension Island.[59]

This agreement gave the United States the right to launch, fly, and land guided missiles in the area of Ascension, establish and use instrumentation and communications systems on the island, and to operate such

---

[58] Paper for Defence Committee of the Cabinet, DO(46)58, dated 13 April 1946. Documents on British Policy Overseas Series I, Vol. IV, 1987.
[59] UK Treaty Series No 25, Cmd 9810.

vessels and aircraft as might be necessary for purposes directly connected with the long range proving ground. The British government was
to provide the sites required free of rent and charges after consultation
with the government of St. Helena. In this way Ascension Island became
the terminal point of a testing ground extending 4,500 miles into the
Atlantic from Cape Canaveral in Florida. A new 10,000-foot runway
was built and paid for by the United States at Wideawake Field, which
was again made available to the Military Air Transport Service under
an agreement concluded in 1962.

The terms of this agreement illustrate the extent to which Britain had
handed over military facilities on the island to the Americans. The first
clause gave the British government the right to land military aircraft at
Wideawake provided the American commanding officer was given 24
hours notice of a single aircraft landing and at least 72 hours notice of
landings by two or more aircraft. The second clause magnanimously
allowed the British government to use any additional facilities it needed
to install at Wideawake. But the third and final clause stipulated that:
'The Government of the United Kingdom shall reimburse the Government of the United States for any readily identifiable additional cost
to the latter arising out of the use of Wideawake airfield by United
Kingdom military aircraft'.[60]

Separate tracking and communications facilities were also set up on
the island in the 1960s by NASA under further agreements between
the two governments. Britain had not maintained a military presence
on the island since the Second World War and as a result she was wholly
dependent on American support in 1982 when Wideawake airfield
became the crucial staging post for operations in the South Atlantic
during the Falklands War. Fortunately, the terms of 1962 agreement
were not rigorously enforced. A Ministry of Defence memorandum to
the House of Commons Defence Committee later stated that the
requirements for advance notice of aircraft landings were effectively
waived during the war and concluded 'at no stage were our operations
adversely affected by any late notification'.[61] This is a classic example of
official British understatement since the United States provided extensive assistance to Britain on Ascension Island in the form of food, fuel,
military supplies, and even the delivery of armaments, much of this at a
time when she was still trying to act as honest broker in the dispute.

---

[60] Exchange of Notes concerning the Use of the Airfield at Wideawake in Ascension
Island by the RAF. Signed 29 August 1962. Treaty Series No 17, Cmnd 1869.

[61] Third Report from the Defence Committee of the House of Commons Session
1982–83. The Future Defence of the Falkland Islands, H of C 154.

The commanding officer of the British Task Force in the South Atlantic later commented that 'Ascension had been transformed from a US communications and satellite tracking station into a forward fleet and air base in a matter of days'. He added that the American colonel at the base had been instructed to give the British every possible assistance but, while the United States was still trying to mediate in the dispute, 'not under any circumstances to get caught doing it'.[62] These instructions emanated from the American Defense Secretary, Caspar Weinberger, a committed Anglophile. His views were not shared by the Secretary of State, Alexander Haig, who, during the early stages of the dispute, was trying to mediate between Britain and Argentina. To placate the Argentinians and underline the neutrality of the United States, Haig proposed to issue a statement saying that Britain's use of American facilities at Ascension Island had been restricted to 'customary patterns of co-operation'. An indignant Margaret Thatcher reminded him that Ascension was a British possession and that the agreements allowing the United States to construct facilities on the island made it clear that sovereignty remained with Britain. Haig agreed to remove any mention of Ascension Island from his statement.[63]

Diego Garcia

Even more convenient in terms of strategic location was the tiny island of Diego Garcia, in the middle of the Indian Ocean. This is a perfect horseshoe-shaped atoll some 14 miles in length from tip to tip, with a lagoon 4 miles across, but with only 10 square miles in total land area. James Horsburgh, a mariner shipwrecked there in 1786, described the atoll as 'one of the wonderful phenomena of the globe'.[64] It has been a British possession since it was seized from France, along with Mauritius, during the Napoleonic wars, but had been little used for military purposes until the 1960s. Writing for the Royal Geographical Society in June 1880, the naturalist Gilbert Bourne asked:

What use would it be to fortify an island ten feet high, which might be completely commanded by a ship sailing outside of it?[65]

However, the United States began to show an interest in the island in 1959. A study for the Joint Chiefs of Staff on 'The Strategic Island

---

[62] Admiral S. Woodward, *One Hundred Days* (London: HarperCollins, 1992, 86).
[63] M. Thatcher, *The Downing Street Years* (London: HarperCollins, 1995, 200).
[64] R. Edis, *The Story of Diego Garcia* (London: Bellew, 1993).   [65] Ibid.

Concept' listed Diego Garcia as one of six islands of strategic significance for the US Navy.[66] This significance increased during the 1960s with the progressive British withdrawal from Aden, Mauritius, and East Africa. The United States saw the need to step into the vacuum created by the second phase of Britain's retreat from empire and once again a British colony appeared to offer a well-placed military base at minimum political and financial cost.

In 1965, Britain set up the British Indian Ocean Territory, which split off Diego Garcia from Mauritius and the islands of Aldabra, Farquhar, and Des Roches from the Seychelles. This was done with the full agreement of the colonial governments of Mauritius and the Seychelles, and in due course the islands of Aldabra, Farquhar, and Des Roches were returned to the Seychelles in 1976. For the moment, however, the Americans were equally interested in all these dependencies. Indeed, Aldabra was originally the first choice for an island base in the Indian Ocean and was only abandoned after a persistent campaign by an individual Member of Parliament, Tam Dalyell, who bombarded the British government daily with parliamentary questions highlighting the ecological damage likely to be caused by a military base on the island.

In December 1966, the initial framework agreement was signed by the British and United States governments in an Exchange of Notes 'Concerning the Availability for Defence Purposes of the British Indian Ocean Territory'.[67] This was a long-term arrangement between the two governments which envisaged that the islands would remain 'available to meet the possible defence needs of the two Governments for an indefinitely long period'. Consequently, the agreement was to run for an initial period of fifty years with an extension of a further twenty years unless either government decided to terminate it. The territories were to remain under British sovereignty but agreed sites were to be made available to the United States without charge, each government to bear the cost of constructing its own facilities once consultation had taken place and agreement reached on the need and location of these facilities. There was no restriction written into the agreement on the type of military operations that could be conducted from the territory, or the extent to which agreement from the British government was required.

---

[66] Cited by K. S. Jawatkar, *Diego Garcia in International Diplomacy* (London: Sangam, 1982).

[67] Exchange of Notes dated 30 December 1976 between David Bruce, US Ambassador in London, and Lord Chalfont, Minister of State at FCO.

In 1968, the United States sought permission to develop an 'austere' communications facility and associated airfield at Diego Garcia. Although Congress did not authorize funding for this project until December 1970, Britain took steps to resettle the 1,200 contract workers employed to gather copra on the island of Mauritius. A payment of £650,000 was made to Mauritius to help with resettlement and this was subsequently increased in the 1980s, when it was revealed that the displaced workers were living in conditions of considerable poverty. Although Britain made no secret of the resettlement programme and the United States had done much the same at Eniwetok and Bikini, the removal of the contract workers later caused considerable controversy when discussed in the United States at hearings of the House Committee on International Relations in 1975. It was also claimed at these hearings by Senator John Culver of Iowa and confirmed by a US Navy witness that Britain had benefited from a waiver of the normal research and development levies on Polaris missile sales to the tune of $14 million in return for the provision of sites at Diego Garcia rent-free.[68]

The last contract workers left the island in 1971 and construction of the airfield by the 'Seabees' started the same year. An interim airstrip was completed by July 1971 and the naval communications station (built under a supplementary agreement signed in 1972)[69] was ready for use by 1973. In the mid 1970s growing concern over the build-up of the Soviet Navy in the Indian Ocean, with bases established at Aden and Berbera, led the United States to seek funding for more extensive facilities on the island. On 5 February 1974, Julian Amery, a Foreign Office Minister, informed the House of Commons that the British government had agreed to an American proposal to convert the naval communications facility to a naval support base by extending the runway to 12,000 feet, deepening the lagoon, and increasing military storage capacity on the island,[70] measures which were considered by Admiral Elmo Zumwalt, a former Chief of Naval Operations, as 'the bare minimum of prudence'.[71]

With this expansion, steps were taken for the first time to exercise a degree of British government control over operations conducted from the island. Amery said that the two governments would consult each other periodically 'on joint objectives, policies and activities in the area'. In normal circumstances, the two governments would 'inform each other

---

[68] House Committee on Foreign Relations. Hearings on Diego Garcia, 5 June 1975. 94th Congress, 2nd Session.
[69] Cmnd 5160.   [70] H of C Official Report, 5 February 1974.
[71] *Baltimore Sun*, 11 July 1975. Cited in CRS, 1979.

of intended movements of ships or aircraft', but in other circumstances use of the facilities would be 'a matter of joint decision of the two governments'. These arrangements were set out in a further agreement between the two governments, signed in 1976.[72] Meanwhile, however, the American proposals had run into difficulty with Congress, where some members were concerned about the escalating arms race in the Indian Ocean. To counter this opposition President Ford was obliged to certify in May 1975 that the plans for Diego Garcia were 'vital to the national interests of the United States',[73] but in September 1975 an amendment to the 1976 Military Appropriations Bill by Senator Culver requested the President to report on the part played by the United States in the resettlement of the island's former inhabitants.

The events of 1979 had a major impact on the United States plans for Diego Garcia and largely removed Congressional opposition to these. In January 1979, the Shah of Iran was overthrown and shortly after the staff of the American Embassy in Tehran were taken hostage by Iranian revolutionary guards. In December that year the Soviet Union invaded Afghanistan. These developments prompted President Carter to prepare plans for a Rapid Deployment Force (RDF) for military operations in the Indian Ocean and Gulf area. Although the United States was in the process of negotiating visiting rights for her forces at Masirah, (an airfield formerly used by the Royal Air Force on an island off Oman) Mombassa in Kenya, and Ras Banas in Egypt, Diego Garcia represented the only permanent base available to support the RDF in the area. The lagoon was capable of accommodating a full carrier task group, and by 1979 sufficient storage capacity had been installed for naval fuel oil and aviation fuel to support a task group of this kind for thirty days. Even so, the island is some 2,500 miles from the Gulf, representing approximately one week's steaming time for warships.

A further expansion of the facilities at Diego Garcia was agreed between the United States and British governments in 1980 and Congressional approval was obtained for the expenditure of $170 million over the following four years. By 1981, the new 12,000-foot runway was able to take B-52 bombers as well as P-3C Orion maritime surveillance aircraft. A new jetty had also been constructed in the lagoon to support a carrier task group and the first maritime pre-positioning support ships had arrived to provide storage of military equipment sufficient for thirty days' operations. By 1991, twelve maritime pre-positioning ships in all were in place at Diego Garcia although these had reduced to five by the

---

[72] Cmnd 6413.	[73] Statement by President Ford, 12 May 1975.

end of the decade with a US Navy presence of 900 service personnel. These measures proved their worth during the Gulf War, when B-52 air-craft based on the island took an active part in operations, supporting by KC-10 and KC-135 tankers. The United States had acquired a second 'unsinkable aircraft carrier' from Britain, this time in the Indian Ocean. Moreover, the resettlement of the contract workers in Mauritius, even though this was challenged in the High Court in Britain in 1999, enabled the American authorities to be reassured by the Congressional Research Service that 'the Diego Garcia is immune to local political developments'.[74]

Conclusion

In developing her global security system after the Second World War, the United States was able to use a number of her own possessions in the Pacific which had been acquired following the Spanish-American War in 1898. As a result of this conflict, the United States not only acquired the Philippines but also Guam in the Pacific and Puerto Rico in the Caribbean. The war also tipped the balance over the annexation of Hawaii where American influence of a commercial and missionary nature had been growing throughout the nineteenth century. The anti-colonial rhetoric deployed by leading Americans so vigorously during the Second World War tended to overlook the fact that Hawaii, as well as the Philippines, had been acquired by traditional colonial expedients, similar to those followed by European empire builders. Hawaii in par-ticular was developed along colonial lines as a major military base from which the United States could exercise control over the Pacific and did not become a State of the Union until 1959.

However, American domination of the Pacific was to be challenged by Japan whose military dispositions in the area were also enhanced indirectly as a result of the Spanish-American War. In 1898, Spain sold all her island possessions in the Pacific, apart from Guam and the Philippines, to Germany. These were occupied by Japan at the start of the First World War and captured by the United States, after excep-tionally bitter fighting in some cases, during the Second World War. The threat posed by Japanese occupation of these islands and the high cost of dislodging Japanese forces from them persuaded the United States to claim quasi-colonial rights over the islands after the war. Like

[74] CRS 1979, 93.

Okinawa and the Bonins, which had been in Japanese hands far longer, the mandated islands in the Pacific were initially treated as the spoils of war. The atomic testing programme at Bikini atoll started in 1946 before the United Nations had agreed to American strategic trusteeship over the islands. This was followed by an extensive testing programme in which the Marshall Islands were used for the same purposes as the European dependencies of Christmas Island and Mururoa.

Over the last hundred years the Marianas, Marshall, and Caroline Islands have been administered in turn by Spain, Germany, Japan, and the United States. Moreover, the United States retained military rights in those islands that opted for independence by means of the Compact of Free Association. Elsewhere, she hung on to her overseas possessions through a variety of constitutional arrangements at a time when Britain and her Commonwealth partners (although not France) were granting their colonies independence. Western Samoa, for example, became independent in 1962 but American Samoa remained an American territory. Fiji became independent in 1970 but Guam was developed as a key military installation in the Western Pacific under direct American control. The smaller island possessions in the Pacific, mostly acquired as coaling stations in the nineteenth century, also remained under American control, administered until the early 1950s by either the Secretary of the Navy or the Secretary of the Air Force, even though they were of limited military value. The same pattern can be seen in the Caribbean where Puerto Rico became a Commonwealth of the United States while Jamaica was granted independence, and the US Virgin Islands remained an American territory while most of the smaller islands under British rule became independent.

In her anxiety to secure her position in the Pacific after the war, the United States pressed her allies to make available to her bases or military facilities on their own colonial territories. Roosevelt expressed a strong interest in the French colonies of New Caledonia and Clipperton Island. James Byrnes followed this up with wholesale demands in the South Pacific. These approaches were rebuffed by Britain, France, Australia, and New Zealand. The wartime pressures which had persuaded Britain, with some reluctance, to lease bases to the United States in the Atlantic and Caribbean no longer applied in the post-war Pacific. However, the position in the Mediterranean was viewed in a different light. The threat there to Greece, Turkey, and to a lesser extent Italy, was all too evident. As a result, Britain allowed the United States to retain Wheelus Field in Libya, and France, not without some misgivings, permitted the construction of four SAC bases in Morocco. These were of only limited tenure since nationalist movements in both countries led to the withdrawal of American forces.

However, the demands of anti-submarine warfare and missile development gave rise to new military uses for those bases secured under ninety-nine year leases from Britain in 1941. In the Atlantic SOSUS terminals were established both at Argentia and Bermuda, and in the Bahamas both an underwater test facility and a missile tracking station were developed. Further afield, the United States was able to make use of two of Britain's island colonies, Ascension Island and Diego Garcia, where nationalist sentiment was not a problem, since there was no indigenous population at Ascension and Diego Garcia was populated only by contract workers. Ascension, in the middle of the South Atlantic, was used to extend the Bahamas tracking facility. Diego Garcia, in the middle of the Indian Ocean, was developed as a traditional military base for purposes of power projection. Of these, Diego Garcia was to be by far the most valuable in strategic terms but also the most controversial in political terms—not just because the contract workers were resettled but also because of the distrust felt by surrounding nations for an American military presence in the Indian Ocean. Political sensitivity, especially in regard to American policy in the Middle East, ruled out the use of Cyprus, where Britain retained two Sovereign Base Areas after independence, despite the key strategic position of this island. Nevertheless, in making wide use for military purposes both of her own and other nations' overseas possessions, the United States showed a significant change of heart from the strident anti-colonial line she had adopted during the war. For her part, Britain, anxious to cement what she regarded as a special security relationship with the United States, was keen to oblige her wherever possible by making her residual colonial dependencies available as elements in America's global security system.

3

The Revival of Wartime Arrangements

Introduction

The United States had invested a considerable amount of money and effort in constructing a worldwide network of military bases during the Second World War and felt that she was owed some return on this investment. There was also the feeling that these bases had been built for the common good of the wartime alliance and should be retained to preserve the collective security of the allies after the war. As James Blaker put it, writing in 1990:

The United States left World War II with the notion that its extensive overseas basing system was a legitimate and necessary instrument of United States power, morally justified and a rightful symbol of the United States role in the world.[1]

Throughout the various planning studies prompted by Roosevelt, the wartime bases established in the Azores, Iceland, and Greenland were consistently given high priority for post-war retention as stepping stones across the Atlantic. Indeed, at a conference between the State Department and the Joint Chiefs of Staff in March 1947, it was agreed that these were the only bases for which the United States should seek permanent long-term rights. It was therefore a considerable blow to the Americans when they were asked to leave each of these territories at the end of the war and James Byrnes, during his short period as Secretary of State, sought the assistance of Ernest Bevin in preserving the American position in these locations.[2] But Bevin, although he was to initiate talks on an Atlantic security pact in December 1947, was not at this stage enthusiastic about a worldwide network of American bases. Only when the full extent of the Soviet threat materialized with the blockade of Berlin in 1948, did he become the main advocate of American involvement in Europe.

[1] J. Blaker, *United States Overseas Basing. An Anatomy of the Dilemma* (London: Praeger, 1990).
[2] Foreign Relations of the United States (FRUS), Vol. VI, 1945. Cited in E. Converse, United States Plans for a Post-War Overseas Military Base System 1942–1948, Unpublished PhD thesis, Princeton University, January 1984.

For their part the Americans made it clear, in the discussions leading up to the North Atlantic Treaty, that the reinforcement of Europe would be critically dependent on use of the mid-Atlantic staging posts. Sir Nicholas Henderson, who participated in these discussions as a young British diplomat, records Charles Bohlen of the State Department saying that 'the United States would in all probability be unwilling to enter into a North Atlantic Treaty unless Norway, Iceland, Denmark (because of Greenland) and Portugal (because of the Azores) had been invited to join as founding members'. He elaborated on this by stating that 'there might be difficulty in sending any substantial assistance unless the United States could at once make use of all naval and air facilities in Iceland, Greenland and perhaps the Azores'.[3]

In the event, the United States forced the pace by issuing a unilateral invitation to Denmark, Iceland, Portugal, and also Italy to join the final negotiations in March 1949 and the signature of the North Atlantic Treaty on 4 April 1949 paved the way for a series of bilateral agreements, allowing American forces to return to Greenland, Iceland, and the Azores in the interests of common defence. It the meantime, the blockade of Berlin had prompted the United States Air Force (until July 1947 the United States Army Air Force) to return to Britain, thereby reactivating the most durable but also the least formal of all America's wartime basing arrangements.

The Atlantic Staging Posts

The Azores

The islands of the Azores, an integral part of Portugal, lie 2,500 miles from the United States and 850 miles from the European mainland. The US Navy had been aware of the strategic importance of the islands as long ago as the 1930s, when an American admiral, with some exaggeration, ascribed to them 'a similar position in the North Atlantic to that of the Hawaiian islands in the Pacific Ocean'.[4] Although the United States only gained a foothold in the Azores towards the end of the Second World War, the role of the islands in the post-war period, both as a staging post for flights across the Atlantic and as a base for anti-submarine operations, has remained central to the American military

---

[3] Sir Nicholas Henderson, *The Birth of NATO* (London: Weidenfeld & Nicolson, 1982, 48).

[4] J. M. O. Sharp (ed.), 'Costs and Benefits of the US Military Presence in Portugal'. In *Europe after an American Withdrawal* (Oxford: OUP, 1990, Ch. 11).

commitment to Europe. A report prepared for the Senate Committee on Foreign Relations in 1979 characterized the Azores as 'a convenient way-station for air traffic en route from the United States to the Mediterranean and other points in Europe'.[5] In a speech to Congress in February 1984, George Shultz, the American Secretary of State, made the same point in far stronger terms. 'The Azores base is pivotal' he said 'if the United States is to react effectively to military challenges in Europe or to threats to Western security outside NATO'.[6]

During the Second World War, the United States initially gave priority to the northern air bridge route to Britain via Canada, Greenland, and Iceland. But the importance of the Azores as a staging post for a mid-Atlantic route to Southern Europe and North Africa quickly became apparent. At an early stage in their post-war planning, even before the United States had obtained landing rights on the islands, the military authorities in Washington had identified their significance for the future. In March 1943, a paper for the Joint Chiefs of Staff commented:

the development of a central Atlantic route via the Azores, if not already in operation, will become a matter of greater interest and importance than any other trans-Atlantic route. Immediate steps should be undertaken and vigorously pressed with a view to obtaining the necessary facilities in the Azores.[7]

Nevertheless, it was Britain who first obtained access to the Azores during the war and the United States who rode in behind her. Portugal had enjoyed an unbroken alliance with England since 1373 and was often referred to as her oldest ally. Despite this, she opted to remain neutral during the war, having concluded a Friendship Treaty with Spain, her fellow fascist neighbour in 1939. Anxious to make use of the Azores during the Battle of the Atlantic, Churchill threatened to seize the islands unless Britain was given access to them.[8] Dr Antonio de Oliviera Salazar succumbed to this pressure and an agreement was signed in August 1943 allowing Britain to set up military facilities on the

[5] United States Foreign Policy Objectives and Overseas Military Installations. Report for the SCFR. CRS April 1979, 50.

[6] A. Vasconcelos, Portugal in Atlantic-Mediterranean Strategy. In *Politics and Security in the Southern Region of the Atlantic Alliance*, D. Stuart (ed.). (London: Macmillan, 1984, Ch. 5).

[7] JSSC 9/1 Enclosure A. Appendix A dated 13 March 1943. Post-War Military Problems with Particular Relation to Air Bases. Cited in S. Duke and W. Krieger (see note 10).

[8] S. Duke, *United States Military Forces and Installations in Europe* (Oxford: OUP, 1989).

island of Terceira. Somewhat disingenuously, Salazar characterized this shift of policy as a change from 'conditional neutrality' to 'active neutrality' representing 'an alliance of the countries on the shores of the Atlantic'.[9]

The Atlantic orientation of Portugal's neutrality was to receive a further push the following year. In November 1944, the United States obtained the agreement of Portugal to construct an airfield on the island of Santa Maria. This agreement gave the United States 'unrestricted utilisation of Santa Maria air base, which would remain . . . under the command of the American Air Force'.[10] Salazar was initially reluctant to extend to the Americans similar rights to those already surrendered to the British but was apparently won over by the argument that the United States could use the Azores as a staging post to the Pacific, where Japan had occupied the Portuguese colony of Timor. The late date of the agreement, as the war in Europe was drawing to a close, gives some credence to this suggestion but a transatlantic flight is not the most obvious way for American forces to reach the Far East.

The agreement signed in November 1944 expired in March 1946 but the United States retained transit rights for eighteen months, and in February 1948 these rights were extended for a further three years. With the development of more powerful transport aircraft, the Azores became a more attractive staging post on the transatlantic ferry route than Iceland and Greenland, although Iceland was to be of greater important for anti-submarine warfare operations against the Soviet Union and Greenland for over-the-Pole deterrent operations and, at a later date, for early warning installations.

In 1946, Lord Halifax, the British Ambassador in Washington, reported that the Americans regarded the Azores as the top priority in the request from James Byrnes, the American Secretary of State, for British help in securing military bases round the world. He added:

We have succeeded in moving the US Chiefs of Staff some way from their original conception of a purely military base in favour of securing civil aviation facilities (readily convertible to military use in an emergency).[11]

However, the growing military threat from the Soviet Union gradually eroded Britain's distaste for overt American military bases and, largely

---

[9] Vasconcelos, op. cit.

[10] Portuguese White Paper. Cited by J. C. de Magalhães, US Forces in Portugal 1943–62. In *US Military Forces in Europe. The Early Years 1945–70*. S. Duke and W. Krieger (ed.) (Boulder, Co: Westview, 1993, Ch. 11).

[11] Documents on British Foreign Policy Overseas Series I, Vol. IV, 1987.

because of the strategic importance of the Azores, Portugal was invited to become a founder member of NATO. Writing of the discussions leading to the signature of the North Atlantic Treaty on 4 April 1949, Dean Acheson said 'the importance of Portugal, possessor of the Azores, to Western European defense was clear enough'. He was less concerned over whether Portugal under Salazar would be an acceptable member of NATO than whether Portugal would be prepared to join without Spain—which he acknowledged would be unacceptable to other European members.[12]

Interestingly, in the light of later events, the Defence Agreement signed between the United States and Portugal in September 1951 was concluded 'pursuant to Article III of the North Atlantic Treaty', and placed a heavy emphasis on NATO responsibilities as the rationale for deploying American forces to the Azores.[13] Article I granted the United States:

In case of war in which they are involved during the life of the North Atlantic Treaty, and within the framework and by virtue of the responsibilities assumed thereunder, the use of facilities in the Azores.

Similarly, Article V spoke of:

Missions charged to the military forces in the Azores, in time of peace as well as in time of war, in harmony with the plans established by the competent organs of the North Atlantic Treaty Organisation.

Under this executive agreement Lajes airfield on Terceira Island was made available to the United States rent-free for an initial period of five years. A supplementary agreement signed in 1957 subsequently extended this arrangement for a further five years. However, by 1961 the United States had become seriously concerned about Portugal's colonial policy in Angola and Mozambique. Military aid was initially reduced from $25 million to $3 million by President Kennedy in 1961 before being increased again to $72 million in 1962 as the 1957 agreement came up for renewal. Moreover, there were reservations in Congress about negotiating a further extension. It was therefore left to the Portuguese government to extend the arrangements unilaterally, with the United States continuing to use Lajes on an *ad hoc* basis until a further agreement was concluded in January 1963.

---

[12] D. Acheson, *Present at the Creation*. (New York: Norton, 1969, 279).
[13] Use of Facilities in the Azores—Defense Agreement between Portugal and the United States of America. Signed 6 September 1951. Treaties and International Agreements Series (TIAS) 3087.

Although the 1951 Defence Agreement envisaged that the facilities made available to the United States in the Azores would be used only for NATO missions, the most spectacular use of Lajes airfield by the USAF was for a national operation in the Middle East. In October 1973, during the Yom Kippur War, the United States needed to mount a massive airlift of military equipment to Israel to counter Soviet assistance to the Arabs. America's other European allies, wary of being associated too closely with the cause of Israel, declined to allow bases on their territory to be used for this purpose. Only Portugal, still under a dictatorship, although Dr Marcello Caetano had now succeeded Salazar, was prepared to accommodate the Americans, and Lajes airfield was used for the airlift. The United States Military Airlift Command (MAC) flew forty-two cargo flights through Lajes in twenty-four hours. The repercussions of the American initiative were profound. Prompt resupply underpinned Israel's victory over the Arabs and thwarted Soviet ambitions to play a decisive role in the Middle East.

Caetano was overthrown in April 1974, thereby ending fifty years of dictatorship for Portugal, but ushering in a period of considerable political instability. There were fourteen governments in Portugal in the period 1974–83 before a stable coalition formed under Mario Soares. The communist party played a dominant role in Portuguese politics in the early years of democracy causing the United States some misgivings and with the advent of democratic government Portugal took a more independent line over the use of military bases in the Azores. In 1980, she made it clear that the use of these facilities by her NATO allies for out-of-area operations would require prior approval and indicated that she would be unlikely to allow the United States to use Lajes for the resupply of Israel in future. Two years later, the socialist Foreign Minister, addressing a meeting of the North Atlantic Council at Funchal, declared 'we must not be regarded as an aircraft carrier on the routes of the Atlantic and the Mediterranean'.[14] In 1986, Portugal spoke out against the American bombing of Libya.

The revival of democracy and the liquidation of her colonial empire allowed Portugal to press the United States for increased military assistance after the restrictive policy previously adopted by Congress because of her record in Africa. Over the period 1975–86, grants of $299 million were provided in connection with the agreement on the Azores bases, out of total US aid to Portugal of just over $1 billion. However, the late 1970s were a period of economic difficulty for the United States

---

[14] Vasconcelos, op. cit. 134.

and she was unable to meet the somewhat exaggerated expectations of the Portuguese. In 1982, Portugal refused an American request for use of the transit facilities in the Azores for the first time, partly to assert her political independence and partly to protest at what she regarded as unsatisfactory levels of American aid. However, this request related not to a significant operational mission, but to the transit of military aircraft purchased from the United States by Egypt which were to be ferried through the Mediterranean. The Portuguese took care not to give too much offence when making their point.

In December 1983, a further agreement was signed to extend American access to facilities in the Azores until February 1991.[15] A Technical Agreement, signed in May 1984, listed the facilities which included Lajes on Terceira, the communications facility at São Miguel, and access to the airports at Santa Maria and Ponta Delgada.[16] Article II affirmed that the agreement was concluded, 'in recognition of Portugal's full sovereignty' and that the defence of the Azores was a Portuguese responsibility. The main agreement, which could be modified at any time provided both governments consented, included words, already used in other bilateral agreements with Mediterranean countries, to the effect that the American administration would 'subject to its constitutional procedures, use its best efforts . . . to assist in mutually agreed programs for the modernisation of the Portuguese defense capabilities'. This assistance was to take a variety of forms, including credits under the Foreign Military Sales (FMS) scheme and outright grants. For the financial year 1983, loans of $52.5 million and grants of $37.5 million were envisaged with loans of $45 million and grants of $60 million for 1984. Similar 'best efforts' were to be made on economic assistance.

But the implementation of these intentions was dependent on Congress and, with the United States facing budgetary difficulties of her own, military assistance to Portugal fell each year between 1985 and 1987. This prompted Cavaco Silva, who had succeeded Mario Soares as Prime Minister in 1985, to call in September 1987 for the renegotiation of the 1983 agreement, claiming that the United States had failed to honour an undertaking to increase military assistance year-on-year. However, the Portuguese stopped short of threats to close or reduce the use of Lajes and the American Secretary of Defense Frank Carlucci,

[15] Exchange of Notes between the United States of America and Portugal regarding the use of Facilities in the Azores. Signed 13 December 1983.

[16] Technical Agreement in Implementation of the Defense Agreement Between the United States of America and Portugal of 6 September 1951. Signed 18 May 1984. TIAS2368.

who had formerly been Ambassador in Lisbon, persuaded Silva to negotiate increased aid without revising the 1983 agreement. Little progress was made and in January 1990, in the course of a visit to Washington, Cavaco Silva again expressed his disappointment and formally asked for a new agreement. Negotiations commenced in January 1991 and in June 1995 a new five-year accord was signed which extended United States access to the bases in the Azores in return for the supply of American military equipment worth $173 million.

The United States retained a small but significant military presence on the islands totalling just under 1,000 USAF personnel in 1999. During the Cold War she had regarded the Azores primarily as an air staging post to Europe, the Mediterranean and the Middle East. In 1970, for example, MAC was making around 550 flights per month through Lajes, using C-5A and C-141 transport aircraft. But the islands should not be seen solely as a mid Atlantic facility for the US Air Force. As the threat from Soviet submarine activity mounted in the Atlantic from the 1960s onwards, the islands came to play a critical role in anti-submarine warfare operations by both the United States and NATO. In 1972, Alexis Johnson, Under-Secretary of State for Political Affairs, stressed the importance of the islands for anti-submarine surveillance in hearings before the Senate Committee on Foreign Relations.[17] A SOSUS terminal was set up at São Miguel on the island of Santa Maria and at the height of the Cold War a detachment of six P3-C Orion anti-submarine warfare aircraft were maintained at Lajes together with the 1605th Military Aircraft Support Wing with a total complement of 2,000 US servicemen. By 1986, a report prepared for the House of Representatives Sub-Committee on Europe and the Middle East commented that 'the ASW support mission . . . is considered to be the more vital of those performed at these facilities'.[18] The report added that it was possible to track Soviet submarines from the facilities in the Azores out to a radius of 1,000 miles and that ASW units located there kept watch over the 4,000 mile sea lane that linked the US Sixth Fleet in the Mediterranean with its major supply depots on the east coast of the United States.

The United States initially regarded the bases in the Azores in much the same light as those in Iceland and Greenland, as essential stepping stones across the Atlantic which had proved invaluable during the war

---

[17] Hearings 1 February 1972. Senate Committee on Foreign Relations Sub-Committee on US Security Agreements and Commitments Abroad. 91st Congress.

[18] US Military Installations in NATO's Southern Region. Report for the House Sub-Committee on Europe and the Middle East. CRS. 99th Congress. 7 October 1986.

and would be needed again for the reinforcement of Europe. The bilateral defence agreements in each case stressed that the facilities were made available to US forces for NATO missions and, for Iceland and Greenland, at the specific request of NATO. For her part, Portugal saw membership of NATO and the bilateral defence relationship with the United States as a means of avoiding the ostracism suffered by Spain and achieving a measure of international acceptance and respectability. This was enhanced by the decision to hold in Lisbon the important meeting of the North Atlantic Council in February 1952 at which NATO force goals were set to meet the Soviet threat following the outbreak of the Korean War.

But both the United States and Portugal developed subsidiary objectives which were at variance with the 1951 Defence Agreement. As the United States acquired other strategic commitments outside the NATO area she wished to use the bases in the Azores to support these. And with Portugal deeply involved in colonial wars in Africa she was tempted to use in this theatre American equipment supplied for NATO purposes even though this was expressly forbidden by the 1951 agreement. The United States became increasingly concerned that aid provided to secure the bases in the Azores would be used, directly or indirectly, to finance conflict in Africa. But the fall of the dictatorship in 1974 raised a new set of problems. The Portuguese expected an increase in aid which the Americans were either unwilling or unable to deliver. As a result, there was a significant change in the bilateral relationship. Portugal had previously been concerned to gain international acceptance as a founder member of NATO. She now came to resemble the other, more recent, allies of the United States in the Mediterranean, Spain, Greece, and Turkey, who were concerned to maximize the financial return on the strategic assets needed by the Americans.

Greenland

In April 1941, eight months before the United States entered the Second World War, Roosevelt authorized negotiations to be opened with the Danish Ambassador in Washington to allow American troops to occupy Greenland, which was constitutionally an island district of Denmark. This course of action was necessary because Denmark was by this time occupied by Germany, no government in exile had been set up, and Roosevelt, ever concerned about the security of the Atlantic, feared that Germany might establish a foothold on Greenland if not preempted by the United States. The Agreement on the Defense of Greenland, concluded in these unusual circumstances on 9 April 1941, recognized the continuing sovereignty of Denmark but granted the United States the right 'to lease for the duration of the Agreement . . . areas of land and water necessary for the construction, operation and protection of the defense facilities specified'.[19] It stipulated that these facilities were to be surrendered to Denmark when there was no longer a danger to peace and the security of North America. Under these provisions, the United States started work in Greenland immediately and by the end of the war had set up seventeen bases, thirteen for the US Army (including the US Army Air Force), and four for the US Navy. The most important bases were those at Søndre Strømfjord, just above the Arctic Circle on the west coast of Greenland, and Nassarssuaq, on the southern tip of the island, both of which played important roles in the northern air bridge to Britain via Newfoundland and Iceland. Nassarssuaq had been completed by the end of 1941 with most of the work finished by the time the United States entered the war.

In June 1946, Robert Patterson, Under-Secretary of War, proposed to James Byrnes, perhaps with the precedent of the Virgin Islands in mind, that the United States should purchase Greenland from Denmark.[20] This proposal was roundly rejected by the Danes in December 1946. Indeed, the Danes were keen to abrogate the agreement signed by their ambassador in 1941, even though they could not adequately defend Greenland themselves, and talks were held with the Americans early in 1948 in an attempt to resolve the problem. No progress had been made by the time that NATO was set up in April 1949 and the new organization was asked to address the issue.

The result was an executive agreement concluded between the United States and Denmark in 1951 which replaced the 1941 agreement and, as with the Portuguese agreement, placed great emphasis on the needs of NATO. The preamble to the 1951 agreement states that both parties:

having been requested by the North Atlantic Treaty Organisation to negotiate arrangements under which Armed Forces of the parties to the North Atlantic Treaty Organisation may make use of facilities in Greenland in defense of Greenland and the rest of the North Atlantic Treaty area . . . have entered into an agreement for the benefit of the North Atlantic Treaty Organisation in the terms set forth below.[21]

[19] Agreement on the Defense of Greenland. Signed in Washington 9 April 1941. TIAS 76.
[20] Converse, op. cit.
[21] TIAS 2292. Cited by J. Woodliffe, *The Peacetime Use of Foreign Military Bases* (Dordrecht: Martinus Nijhoff, 1992).

The agreement was to last for the duration of the North Atlantic Treaty and the two countries agreed to 'establish and operate jointly such defense areas' deemed necessary to the defence of 'Greenland and the North Atlantic Treaty area'. Article I also committed those countries to 'take such measures as are necessary or appropriate to carry out expeditiously their respective and joint responsibilities in Greenland in accordance with NATO plans'.

This emphasis on NATO was slightly disingenuous since the American forces deployed to Greenland were predominantly earmarked for national rather than NATO missions. Article III of the agreement transferred Grönnedal to Danish control, but permitted the United States to retain Søndre Strømfjord and Nassarssuaq. Nassarssuaq was closed in 1957 and Søndre Strømfjord became a joint military–civil airfield, maintained at American expense initially for ferrying short-range aircraft across the Atlantic and later as a supply base for the Greenland radars of the Distant Early Warning Line (DEW line) which stretched across Alaska, northern Canada, and Greenland to detect aircraft flying over the Arctic.

The 1951 agreement also identified Thule as a new defence site for the first time. This station was to become the most important American base in Greenland. Prior to 1951, the main strategic value of the bases in Greenland was as staging posts on the transatlantic ferry route. During the 1950s, this role was overtaken by the need for Strategic Air Command (SAC) to be able to attack the Soviet Union over the Arctic. Thule, in the far north-west of Greenland, is only 900 miles from the North Pole and 2,700 miles from Moscow, enabling B-47 bombers to reach the Soviet Union with only one refuelling. Work began in the summer of 1951 on a base for SAC which was operational in 1952 and finally completed in 1953. Because of the Arctic conditions, construction materials had to be brought in by the US Navy during the short period of six to eight weeks each summer when the sea lanes were free of ice. Thule was also well placed to intercept a Soviet attack over the Arctic on North America and both Nike missiles and Interceptor aircraft were later stationed there.

However, by the 1960s the threat from Inter-Continental Ballistic Missiles had become the dominant strategic concern and a Ballistic Missile Early Warning System was built at Thule as the mid point in a chain of three stations stretching from Clear in Alaska to Fylingdales in Britain. By the mid 1980s, the original early warning radars were out of date and plans were prepared to replace these at all three sites by modern phased array radars giving greater coverage and reliability.

These plans proved controversial, leading to the collapse of the coalition government in March 1987, since some Greenlanders considered that the new phased array radars would violate the Anti-Ballistic Missile (ABM) Treaty signed between the United States and the Soviet Union in 1972. Similar concerns were expressed in Britain over Fylingdales when the British and American governments agreed to modernize the existing early warning system. However, it was made clear that the ABM Treaty did not prohibit the modernization of ballistic missile early warning radars already in existence.

The importance of the military facilities at Thule ensured that the United States retained these beyond the end of the Cold War although the airfield was opened to civil aircraft from July 1996. Elsewhere, reductions in the American military presence were proposed in the mid 1980s. In October 1986, an agreement came into effect under which the land occupied by American forces was reduced from 325,000 hectares to 160,000 hectares with the balance being returned to the indigenous Inuit people. Three years later, in mid 1989, the United States stated that she would no longer require the base at Søndre Strømfjord beyond Spring 1992 since the radars of the DEW line which the airfield served were now obsolete. The Greenland authorities, which had enjoyed a limited measure of home rule since 1979, viewed this development with considerable concern since the airfield was the hub of the territory's internal communications system and also the main access airport for Denmark. It was known that the running costs of the airfield were $25 million a year, which was well beyond the means of the island's population of only 55,000. An appeal was made for NATO funding but this was turned down. After a period of negotiation an agreement was reached in March 1991 which transferred the airfield to Greenland in September 1992 but gave the United States residual rights to use the base in the future if required.[22] Denmark agreed to meet the running costs of the civil airport.

Iceland

At the start of the Second World War, Iceland, like Greenland, was also a Danish possession, although she had reached agreement with Denmark in 1918 that she would gain independence after twenty-five years. However, the strategic position of Iceland, both as a staging post

---

[22] Memorandum of Understanding concerning the use of Sondestrom Aviation Facility, Kulusuk Airfield and other matters relating to US military activities in Greenland. Signed in Copenhagen 13 March 1991. TIAS 12285.

on the North Atlantic ferry route and as a base for the protection of sea-borne convoys, was even more important than that of Greenland. With Denmark under enemy occupation, British troops occupied Iceland in May 1940 in order to secure the island and to deny access to Germany. In July 1941, again some months before the United States entered the war, American troops landed in Iceland at the invitation of the island government to replace the British, who were anxious to redeploy their troops elsewhere. Since she had been promised independence in 1943, Iceland took matters into her own hands and declared independence from occupied Denmark in June 1944. At the same time, with the end of the war in sight, she pressed for American troops, who now numbered some 45,000, to be withdrawn.

On 12 October 1944, an Exchange of Notes was signed between the United States and Iceland, arranging for the reversion of Reykjavik airfield to Iceland with immediate effect. One year later, in October 1945, the United States asked for ninety-nine year leases on other bases on the island, but this request was refused by Iceland. In September the following year Iceland repudiated the 1941 agreement and demanded the withdrawal of American troops, although American Overseas Airlines was allowed to maintain Meeks Field (later renamed Keflavik) as an international airport for five years. This arrangement accorded with the views of Ernest Bevin, the British Foreign Secretary, who had been asked to help maintain an American presence. Earlier in the year he stated in a memorandum to the Defence Committee of the Cabinet that the American Secretary of State James Byrnes had pressed too hard for agreement to a long-term military base. He commented:

We are committed to trying to help the Americans remain in Iceland ... We should urge the possibility of securing civil aviation facilities readily convertible to military use in an emergency (as in the Azores) in lieu of an undisguised military base.[23]

In the event, Iceland joined NATO as a founder member in 1949 at the insistence of the United States, who saw the island as indispensable to the reinforcement of Europe. Mindful of her experiences during the war, she joined the Alliance initially on condition that no foreign forces were stationed on her territory during peacetime. Even so, the decision was not a popular one, provoking intense demonstrations outside the Icelandic parliament (the Althing). The following year, after the outbreak of the Korean War and the sharp rise in international

---

[23] Documents on British Foreign Policy Overseas. Memorandum by Bevin to Defence Committee of the Cabinet DO(46)58, 13 April 1946.

tension which followed, Iceland realized that, with no armed forces of her own, she would have to rely on the United States for her defence. She consequently signed a bilateral Defence Agreement with the United States on 5 May 1951 but, as with Greenland, the text of this agreement indicated that it had been made at the request of NATO and that facilities were to be made available to the United States for the defence of Iceland and NATO as a whole. This was made clear in the preamble:

Since the people of Iceland cannot themselves adequately secure their own defenses . . . the North Atlantic Treaty Organisation has requested . . . that the United States and Iceland . . . make arrangements for the use of facilities in Iceland in defense of Iceland and thus also of the North Atlantic Treaty area.[24]

The agreement also laid down rigorous arrangements for consultation at the outset. Article I stated that 'Iceland will provide such facilities in Iceland as are mutually agreed to be necessary'. Article IV stated that the composition of forces, number of personnel to be stationed in Iceland, and conditions on which they could enter facilities and make use of them would require Iceland's approval. Article III stated that nuclear weapons could not be stationed in Iceland without the prior approval of the Icelandic government. Consultation was to take place through a Joint Defence Council which has met on average twice a month, mainly to discuss US and NATO construction projects.

Provisions for extensive consultation were required because Iceland has in effect entrusted her defence to the United States. The agreement established the all-American Iceland Defence Force, which is a United States Joint Command reporting to Commander-in-Chief Atlantic in Norfolk, Virginia. Although the agreement was concluded 'pursuant to the North Atlantic Treaty of 1949', the United States formally accepted responsibility for the defence of Iceland on behalf of NATO. Nevertheless, total dependency on the United States for defence has not gone wholly unchallenged within Iceland. In 1956, a resolution in the Althing urged Iceland to take over the defence tasks carried out by the United States, even though Iceland still had no armed forces with which to do this. The issue was referred to the North Atlantic Assembly which recommended no change, but the resolution may have prompted a paper prepared for the US Joint Chiefs of Staff in July 1956 on the value of

---

[24] Iceland–United States Defense Agreement. Signed Reykjavik 5 May 1951. TIAS 2266. Cited by Duke, op. cit.

Iceland 'as a US base' (*sic*).[25] This paper listed four vital tasks under-taken from Iceland:

1. Protection of North Atlantic shipping.
2. Air transit to and from north west Europe.
3. Long-range air operations over Europe and the Soviet Union.
4. A fixed submarine detection line from Greenland to the Faroes.

This assessment still placed considerable emphasis on Iceland as a step-ping stone to Europe, either for air transit or for bomber operations. However, the other two tasks foreshadowed the growing importance of Iceland as the central point in what came to be known to NATO navies as the Greenland–Iceland–UK gap.

With the build-up of the Soviet northern fleet during the 1960s and 1970s, based in the Kola Peninsula, it became vital for NATO in time of war to prevent Soviet surface ships and submarines from breaking through the Greenland–Iceland–UK gap into the broader reaches of the Atlantic. Iceland came to be regarded as the 'cork bottling up the Soviet Navy' in the waters of the Arctic. Maritime surveillance therefore became the primary task of the US Air Force based at Keflavik and the SOSUS detection system, with a terminal at Höfn, played an important part in tracking Soviet submarines. The interception of Soviet long-range bomber and reconnaissance aircraft in the Military Air Defense Identification Zone also became a high priority task. F-4C Phantom air-craft, later replaced by F-15 aircraft of the 57th Fighter Interceptor Squadron, were deployed to Keflavik for this mission, supported by tanker and AWACS (Airborne Warning and Control System) aircraft. More Soviet aircraft were intercepted from Iceland than from any other base worldwide. These were mainly Bears and occasionally Badgers, and from mid 1970 the Backfire bomber, which had both greater speed and longer range than the Bear and Badger. By the mid 1980s, there would normally be some thirty NATO aircraft stationed at Keflavik, all on rotation from other bases in the United States or Europe. These com-prised eighteen F-15s, two AWACS E-3s, one KC-135 tanker, and nine P-3C Orions, one of which was normally detached from the Netherlands Air Force from 1985 onwards.[26] In time of war it was planned to deploy four times this number of aircraft to Iceland and also move both a regular and a reserve brigade of the US Army to the island.

[25] JCS 1950/56, 27 July 1956. Cited by Duke, op. cit.
[26] In this brief survey of Iceland defence matters I have drawn heavily on Albert Jonsson *Iceland, NATO and the Keflavik Base* (Reykjavik: Icelandic Commission on Security Affairs, 1989).

In 1974, another proposal was made in the Althing to terminate the 1951 agreement. This was defeated by a petition signed by 50 per cent of the electorate, but led to a further Exchange of Notes between the United States and Iceland on 24 October 1974. Once again, this agreement was proposed by the NATO Council at the request of the Icelandic government. It called for 'the continuation of the facilities and their utilisation by the Iceland Defence Force under the agreement on mutually acceptable terms'.[27] At the same time, the United States agreed to reduce her personnel stationed in Iceland by 12.5 per cent. This amounted to a reduction of only 400 servicemen but numbers are a sensitive issue in an island with a total population of only 250,000. As a further concession it was agreed that the civil air terminal at Keflavik should be separated from the adjacent US military facilities, although the United States undertook to upgrade the joint airfield over a ten-year period. Ten years later in December 1984, a memorandum was signed confirming that any decision to deploy nuclear weapons to Iceland would only be made with the approval of the Iceland government. To underline the country's hostility to nuclear weapons the Althing passed a unanimous resolution the following year declaring Iceland to be a nuclear-free zone. The lingering unease in Iceland over the American military presence is exemplified by the election to the presidency (a largely ceremonial post) in 1980 of Vigdis Finnbogadottir, a non-political candidate opposed to the stationing of American forces at Keflavik. She was returned unopposed in 1984, secured a third term with a 90 per cent vote in 1988 and in 1992 was again returned unopposed for a final fourth term. In response to this undercurrent of domestic criticism, the Iceland government decided in 1984 that it should play a more active part in defence matters and, for the first time, set up a Defence Department with 100 staff within the Ministry of Foreign Affairs.

With the end of the Cold War there were significant reductions in the American military presence. Six F-15s together with the AWACS and tanker aircraft were withdrawn, leaving only four F-15s and six P-3C reconnaissance aircraft with less than 2,500 American service personnel. Nevertheless, the US Secretary of Defense, William Perry, signed an 'Agreed Minute' with Baldvin Hannibalsson, the Icelandic Minister of Foreign Affairs, in January 1994 reaffirming the 1951 Defence Agreement and setting out a number of continuing commitments on the part of the United States until 2001. These included a commitment to

---

[27] Exchange of Notes. Signed Reykjavik 22 October 1974. TIAS 7969.

continue operating the Icelandic Air Defence System, based on Keflavik but with four outlying radar stations, previously funded by NATO, together with an obligation to continue operating the joint civil–military airport at Keflavik (on which the United States had spent $20 million in the 1980s), and to maintain an air–sea rescue service.

Conclusion

After the Second World War, the United States wished to retain the three key staging posts across the Atlantic in the Azores, Iceland, and Greenland. These had been secured by fairly high-handed methods during the war and the host nations were initially reluctant to renew these rights, not least because Iceland had become independent and Denmark felt that the wartime arrangements negotiated on Greenland with her Ambassador in Washington should not be continued. However, the growth of the Soviet threat, the formation of NATO, with all three host nations becoming founder members, and the shock of the Korean War caused a change of heart. Iceland realized that she could not defend herself in the new Cold War environment and Denmark acknowledged that she could not defend Greenland, an area of vital strategic importance with a land mass more than fifty times greater than her own home territory. As a result, Iceland agreed to entrust her defence to the United States, and Denmark was prepared to accept American forces in Greenland, although not in Denmark itself. A report by the Congressional Research Service in 1979 pointed up this inconsistency unsparingly:

By granting the United States basing rights on the island, Denmark has been able to make a substantial contribution to NATO's nuclear shield without violating its own injunction against the stationing of foreign troops on the soil of Denmark proper. In this regard Greenland's remoteness has permitted a United States military presence that otherwise might conflict with Danish perceptions of national sovereignty.[28]

The three host nations took care to draw up precise agreements with the United States emphasizing that American forces were stationed on their territory solely for NATO purposes. This caused no difficulty with Iceland and Denmark, where no non-NATO mission was likely, even though the presence of American troops proved controversial. But the use of the Azores as a staging post for American national operations in the Middle East raised difficult issues for Portugal. These were resolved

[28] CRS April 1979, 25.

in favour of the United States under the isolationist dictatorship of Caetano, but this ready acquiescence was not to survive the advent of democracy.

As a postscript, an interesting insight into the co-ordinated approach adopted by the United States towards the negotiation of basing rights in the early 1950s is provided by Dean Acheson. In his autobiography *Present at the Creation* he describes a stay in Lisbon in February 1952 with the American Ambassador Lincoln MacVeagh, an old friend who had joined the State Department before the war 'to negotiate our base arrangement with Iceland and then towards the war's end moved to Greece, where he gave invaluable help in the rescue of Greece from internal subversion and external attack. Coming to Portugal, he negotiated Portuguese entry into NATO and the Azores base. Arrangements had already been made to move him to Madrid to discuss bases in Spain'.[29]

The Return to Britain

Introduction

The agreements concluded by the United States to secure continued access to military facilities in the Azores, Greenland, and Iceland all referred to the North Atlantic Treaty and made it clear that the facilities were to be used for NATO operations. By contrast, the arrangements made in 1948 for American forces to return to her closest wartime ally, Britain, were initially governed by no formal agreement of any kind and were eventually set out in a single paragraph of only two sentences in a long communiqué summarizing the outcome of talks between Winston Churchill and Harry Truman in January 1952. These two sentences read as follows:

Under arrangements made for the common defence, the United States has the use of certain bases in the United Kingdom. We reaffirm the understanding that the use of these bases in an emergency would be a matter for joint decision by His Majesty's Government and the United States Government in the light of the circumstances prevailing at the time.[30]

Compared to the full agreements negotiated with other host governments and the formal nature of the leases prepared for the Atlantic and Caribbean bases in 1941, this short paragraph is breathtaking in its

[29] Acheson, op. cit. 623.
[30] *Keeling's Contemporary Archives*, *12–19*, January 1952.

brevity. There is no mention of the duration of the arrangements, the nature of military operations contemplated, or the North Atlantic Treaty signed in 1949. Yet in terms of public presentation successive British governments have subsequently relied on the understanding encapsulated in these two short sentences to cover not just the US Air Force missions contemplated in 1948, but the Polaris base set up at Holy Loch, the deployment of cruise missiles in the mid 1980s, and a number of controversial intelligence operations. In doing so, they have attracted considerable criticism in Parliament which rose to a crescendo following the American air strike on Libya in April 1986.

Post-war bases in Britain had not featured at all in the United States planning papers prepared at Roosevelt's request during the war. Wartime planning in Washington was predicated on the assumption that the post-war world would be controlled by Roosevelt's 'Four Policemen', or some variation of this concept, and Britain was understood to be one of the policemen. In general, American officials were slow to discern the decline of Britain—as indeed were the British themselves. American wartime planning also failed to adjust sufficiently early to the Soviet threat and, subsequently, to the part which the atomic bomb would play in deterring this. The one exception was General Carl Spaatz, Commander of the US Army Air Force in Europe, who in the closing stages of the war had devised a Periphery Basing Plan for a series of bases ringing the Soviet Union in continental Europe, although oddly enough not in Britain. He had been warned off this concept by General 'Hap' Arnold, Commander of the US Army Air Force, who described it as 'a subject filled with political dynamite'.[31] Nevertheless, a paper for the Joint Chiefs of Staff in June 1946 saw Britain as the keystone of an initial air offensive against the Soviet Union because of her strategic location and logistic support capacity.[32] The following year, Admiral Forrest Sherman, giving evidence in a closed session to the Senate Armed Forces Committee on 23 January, said:

Our joint concepts envisage that the principal counter offensive efforts against Russia itself would consist of strategic air offensives from bases in the British Isles and in the vicinity of Suez, and perhaps India.[33]

This statement, with its imperial overtones, probably reflected the secret talks which Spaatz, who had succeeded Arnold in February 1946, held in

[31] Letter dated 6 November 1944. Cited by Simon Duke in *United States Military Forces and Installations in Europe* (Oxford: OUP, 1989, 292).
[32] JWPC 496/1, 10 June 1946. Cited by Converse, op. cit.
[33] Evidence of Admiral Forrest Sherman to closed session of Senate Armed Forces Committee, 23 January 1947. Cited in Converse, op. cit.

June that year with Air Chief Marshal Sir Arthur Tedder, Chief of the Air Staff in Britain. It seems likely that these talks were conducted on an Air Force to Air Force basis without political cover by either government. In any event it was agreed that four to five bases in East Anglia would be prepared for the deployment of very heavy bombers by mid 1947. It was evident that these bases were to be used by Strategic Air Command (SAC), which had been set up in March 1946 with the mission, later described by President Eisenhower 'to be constantly ready, on an instantaneous basis, to inflict greater loss upon the enemy than he could reasonably hope to inflict upon us'.[34] Although bombers of SAC made occasional short-term rotational tours to Britain from July 1947, as they also did to West Germany, it was not until the start of the Berlin blockade in June 1948 that a prolonged deployment was envisaged.

The Berlin Blockade

When the United States made a formal request to deploy bombers of Strategic Air Command to Great Britain as a response to the crisis in Berlin, Ernest Bevin accepted with alacrity. He had spent the previous two years trying to dissuade the Americans from pressing too hard for military bases around the world, but he was now concerned at the Soviet threat to Europe and wished to engage the United States in European defence. This partly explains the rapid, informal nature of Britain's response, with no written agreement or conditions. The urgency of the situation was also an important factor. It was necessary to send an unequivocal signal to the Russians and to do so quickly. In this respect, the deployment of B-29 bombers was a successful piece of bluff. It was believed that they were equipped to carry atom bombs because it was known that the bombs dropped on Japan had been delivered by B-29s. But in fact these aircraft had not been modified to carry the atom bomb and those that had, the so- called 'Silverplate' bombers, would not arrive in Britain until 1949. Nor were there any facilities in Britain for handling the atom bomb at this stage. It was not until September 1948 that Colonel Lauris Norstad was authorized to visit Britain to seek agreement on the 'construction of certain necessary buildings and huts for housing components of the bomb at two airfields'.[35]

For their part, the Americans were surprised at the prompt, unconditional agreement they received from Britain. Their Ambassador in

[34] Robert Jackson *Strike Force* (London: Robson 1986, 58).
[35] *The Forrestal Diaries*, (Typescript). Cited by Duke in *US Military Forces in Europe. The Early Years 1945–70*, S. Duke and W. Krieger (ed.) (Boulder, CO: Westview, 1993, 2501).

London, Lewis Douglas, was asked to check that the British government had fully assessed the impact on public opinion.[36] On the other hand, it was clear that the Americans did not just have a temporary deployment in mind. To some extent, the Berlin blockade was the pretext, rather than the reason, for the deployment to Britain. James Forrestal, the American Secretary of Defense, wrote in his diary:

We have the opportunity now of sending these planes and once they are sent they would become something of an accepted fixture.[37]

On 18 July 1948 the first of sixty B-29 Superfortresses flew to Britain to be based at three Royal Air Force (RAF) stations. These were followed by a third bomber group in September 1948, making ninety aircraft in all. In explaining this substantial movement of US aircraft to Britain, the Secretary of State for Air, Arthur Henderson, chose to play down its significance. On 28 July 1948 he told the House of Commons:

Units of the United States Air Force do not visit this country under a formal treaty, but under informal and long-standing arrangements between the USAF and the RAF for visits of goodwill and training purposes. The B-29s at present at RAF stations are here to carry out long distance flying in Western Europe. It has not been decided how long they will stay.[38]

Major General Leon Johnson, Commander of the USAF units in Britain, remained surprised by the lack of formality. In 1949, he wrote 'never before in history has one first class power gone into another first class power's country without an agreement'.[39] But it should be remembered that the two air forces were working closely together on the Berlin airlift. Two of the air corridors to Berlin originated in the British zone of Germany, providing much shorter access routes than the single corridor from the American zone in the south. Between June 1948 and May 1949, the two air forces mounted a total of 200,000 flights into Berlin supplying the beleaguered city with 1.5 million tons of supplies. At the peak period, 8,000 tons of supplies were delivered each day. The RAF contributed approximately 100 transport aircraft to the airlift and the USAF nearly 450. Throughout 1949, Britain was responsible for airlifting all petroleum products into Berlin using chartered tankers. The

---

[36] M. Gowing, *Independence and Deterrence.* (London: Macmillan, 1974). Cited by J. Baylis, The American Bases in Britain. *The World Today*, August/September, 1986.

[37] W. L. Millis (ed.), *The Forrestal Diaries* (London: Cassell, 1952, 430). Cited by Duke and Baylis, op. cit.

[38] H of C Official Report, 28 July 1948. Cited by Duke and Baylis, op. cit.

[39] D. Dimbleby and D. Reynolds, *An Ocean Apart* (London: Hodder & Stoughton, 1988, 177).

large supply depot at Burtonwood in Cheshire was developed as a support and maintenance base for the American transport aircraft engaged in unprecedented levels of flying intensity and was retained by the USAF until 1956.

The airlift was a major military operation which recalled the close partnership established between the British and American armed forces during the war. It was reminiscent of the message which Churchill sent to Roosevelt in August 1940: 'Our view is that we are two friends in danger helping each other as far as we can'[40] and, later, of the passage in his 'Iron Curtain' speech at Fulton, Missouri, in March 1946 when he spoke of a 'fraternal association' between Britain and the United States involving 'joint use of all Naval and Air Force bases in the possession of either country all over the world' and 'the continuance of the intimate relationship between our military advisers'.[41] Moreover, these views were not confined to Britain's wartime leader, now in opposition. Stafford Cripps, Chancellor of the Exchequer in Britain's socialist government, told Forrestal when visiting Washington in October 1948 that 'Britain must be regarded as the main base for the deployment of American power and the chief offensive against Russia must be by air'.[42]

Britain was already accustomed to this intimate relationship in the form of American troops and equipment based in the country during the Second World War. Some 165 military installations had been made available to the US Army Air Force between June 1942 and December 1945. There had been 1.75 million American troops in Britain at the time of D-Day and these too had entered the country without any formal agreements or conditions. Properly prepared agreements and leases were necessary for the bases in the Atlantic and the Caribbean because the United States was still technically a neutral power in 1941. Once she had entered the war these formalities were not considered necessary for the deployment of troops to Britain since international law provides for the stationing of military forces in other countries in time of war. Although a state of war did not exist at the time of the Berlin blockade, the urgency of the joint operations mounted in response no doubt precluded the preparation of legal documents and left Britain, uniquely among the countries playing host to American forces, without any formal agreements covering their deployment or utilization.

[40] Churchill to Roosevelt, 22 August 1940. W. S. Churchill, *Their Finest Hour* (London: Cassell, 1949, 362).

[41] W. S. Churchill, *The Sinews of Peace* (London: Cassell, 1948, 98).

[42] *The Forrestal Diaries*, 460.

Consolidation after Berlin

The blockade was lifted in May 1949 and shortly afterwards the US Joint Chiefs of Staff initiated a study of military basing rights in foreign countries. They were looking for a more permanent basing structure in Britain, not in East Anglia but further inland in the Oxford area. A high priority was placed on obtaining basing rights at Brize Norton, Upper Heyford, Fairford, and one other airfield in the vicinity, still to be identified. (This later turned out to be Greenham Common.) The paper commented that 'the British do not want to make formal, public arrangements to give a foreign power permanent military rights in the UK'.[43] Nevertheless, in January 1950 the US Department of Defense wrote to the British Ministry of Defence asking for 'an indefinite continuation of the right to base and maintain air groups in the United Kingdom'.[44] At official level the Foreign Office, when considering this request, appeared to welcome a permanent military presence by the Americans in Britain. An internal minute argued:

The primary aim of our foreign policy must be to keep the United States firmly committed in Europe ... We must face the fact that this island is strategically well placed as an advanced air base and that we must accept this role.[45]

However, Ernest Bevin was more cautious. He believed that 'a permanent peacetime presence involved quite new principles' and he wanted to put 'the present peacetime arrangements on a more definite basis'.[46] In particular, he wished to ensure that Britain had the right to terminate the arrangement and to clarify the position if the United States intended to conduct operations from airfields in Britain before Britain herself was at war. It was this concern that led to two years of high-level negotiations with the Americans, which came to a head first with Clement Attlee's visit to Washington in December 1950 and secondly with Winston Churchill's visit in January 1952. During these discussions the simple issue of British sovereignty over bases on her own territory became clouded by the different and more complex problem of the extent to which Britain could reasonably expect the United States to consult her on the use of atomic weapons anywhere in the world.

[43] FRUS, Vol. I., 1949, 1976, 302. Cited by Woodliffe, op. cit., 39
[44] DoD Memorandum for the British Government, 11 January 1950. Cited by Duke in Duke and Krieger, op. cit.
[45] Draft Foreign Office (FO) Memorandum, 4 January 1950. Cited by Dimbleby and Reynolds, op. cit. 187.
[46] Bevin's Memorandum to Cabinet, 15 March 1950. Cited by Duke, op. cit.

The first round in these negotiations was the Exchange of Letters between Lewis Douglas, the American Ambassador in London, and Aidan Crawley, Parliamentary Under-Secretary of State for Air, in April 1950 known as the Ambassador's Agreement. This agreement placed no time limit on the deployment of American forces to Britain, but acknowledged the British government's right to terminate this deployment when it so wished. The airfields were to be 'available to the United States Air Force so long as both Governments considered it desirable in the interests of common defence'.[47] What the agreement did not resolve was the much more difficult issue of political control over American operations mounted from bases in Britain during a conflict in which the host nation was not herself involved.

The Sovereignty Issue and the Atom Bomb

During the Korean War, the USAF medium bombardment groups stationed in Britain increased from one to three and one fighter group was added, at Manston in Kent, bringing total USAF personnel in Britain to approximately 10,000 operating 180 aircraft. The increases in American forces in Britain were precautionary measures taken in response to the rise in international tension. But events in Washington gave rise to acute concern in Britain over the use to which these military assets might be put. On 30 November 1950, President Truman, in answering questions at a press conference, gave the impression that the use of the atomic bomb in the context of the Korean War might be left to American commanders in the field. In replying to a direct question about the use of the bomb, he said 'there has always been active consideration of its use', and to other questions not directly connected with the bomb he said that the choice of weapons in Korea was 'a matter that the military people will have to decide'.[48] In the British Parliament, engaged in a two-day debate on foreign affairs, these answers were construed as giving General MacArthur discretion on use of the atomic bomb in Korea. Attlee, under considerable pressure, felt obliged to fly to Washington for discussions.

It was at this point that the two issues of British control over American forces in Britain and their right to be consulted over use of the atomic bomb worldwide became entangled. Britain had, along with Canada, secured the right of consultation on use of the bomb

[47] Memorandum by J. N. Henderson. FO 371|90966, 31 August 1951. Cited by Duke in Duke and Krieger, op. cit. 132.
[48] Acheson, op. cit. 478.

worldwide at the early stages of the Manhattan Project. A meeting of Roosevelt, Churchill, and MacKenzie-King in August 1943 produced the Quebec Agreement which, referring to the atom bomb, said 'we will not use it against third parties without each other's consent'.[49] However, this right of consultation had been surrendered in January 1948. The Americans were now circumscribed by the McMahon Act passed in August 1946 which placed strict limits on cooperation with other countries on atomic weapons technology. There was also a growing feeling in America that, in constitutional terms, the President, as Commander-in-Chief, ought not to restrict his freedom of action to use the atomic bomb if he considered it necessary in defence of the United States. These pressures led Britain to accept, in January 1948, the *modus vivendi*, a secret, unsigned agreement which did not have to be submitted to Congress. Under the terms of this agreement Britain surrendered the right of consultation on the use of the atomic bomb in return for promises on the exchange of technical information which were not fully substantiated. In seeking to pull back an element of consultation, Attlee was attempting to modify the *modus vivendi*.

He very nearly succeeded. Dean Acheson has left a vivid account of how the President and the Prime Minister agreed in a tête-à-tête discussion in December 1950 'that neither of us would use these weapons without prior consultation with the other'. Acheson was aghast. 'I pointed out over and over again', he wrote 'that the President had insisted that no commitment of any sort to anyone limited his duty and power under the law to authorise the use of the atomic weapon if he believed it necessary in the defence of the country'.[50] The result was a compromise communiqué drafted by the British Ambassador, Sir Oliver Franks. It read:

The President stated that it was his hope that world conditions would never call for the use of the atomic bomb. The President told the Prime Minister that it was also his desire to keep the Prime Minister at all times informed of developments which might bring about a change in the situation.[51]

Although Attlee declared himself satisfied with this meeting, it had not given Britain any say on the worldwide use of the bomb. Worse, it did nothing to clear up the unresolved question of military operations conducted from bases in Britain. Sir John Slessor, Chief of the Air Staff, was indignant that the Americans declined to discuss their strategic plan with the British although this was dependent on the use of bases in

---

[49] Duke, op. cit.   [50] Acheson, op. cit. 484.
[51] Communiqué of 7 December 1950. Cited by Duke, op. cit.

Britain. He considered it intolerable that the United States might decide to use the atomic bomb at a time when Britain took a different view. In January 1951, Bevin protested to Acheson 'the British Government has no information as to the strategic plans in support of which these aircraft might be used at short notice nor how far this plan accords with our own.'[52] A further meeting on this issue was held in September 1951 between Herbert Morrison, who had succeeded Bevin as Britain's Foreign Secretary, and General Omar Bradley, Chairman of the Joint Chiefs of Staff, assisted by Paul Nitze of the State Department. At this meeting, the Americans recognized for the first time that:

there must at least be consultation and the British must give their consent, before the United States used atomic weapons from Britain. The American side accepted that the use of British bases involved British sovereignty and that it was therefore natural that the United States would seek acquiescence before launching war from them.[53]

However, the Americans, both for constitutional and domestic political reasons, wished to avoid any suggestion of an outright veto on the use of their forces by another power. Accordingly, work began on the formula that referred to the use of the bases being a matter for joint decision in the light of the circumstances prevailing at the time. A British general election had been called for 25 October and Attlee wished to resolve this before polling day. Truman's agreement was obtained on 17 October to the wording:

The use of these bases in an emergency would be a matter of joint decision by His Majesty's Government and the United States Government in the light of the circumstances prevailing at the time.[54]

This formula, later known as the Truman–Attlee understanding, was not made public at the time, although the British made it clear to the Americans that, if questions on the use of the bases arose during the election campaign, they would be obliged to reply 'there is naturally no question of their use in an emergency without our consent'.[55]

The Churchill–Truman Understanding

As a result of the general election, Churchill became Prime Minister again for the last time. In the early months of his administration he was

---

[52] FRUS, Vol. I., 1951, 822. Cited by Duke in Duke and Krieger, op. cit. 134.
[53] M. Gowing, op. cit. Vol. I., 317. Cited by Duke. See also Baylis, op. cit. for US record of these meetings.
[54] Baylis, op. cit.   [55] Ibid.

asked two parliamentary questions on the American bomber force based in Britain. The first, on 21 November 1951, ran as follows:

Mr Emrys Hughes asked the Prime Minister if he will now take steps to terminate the arrangement by which United States atom bombers are based in the country, in view of the dangers of retaliatory bombing to the people living in the crowded cities of Britain.

The Prime Minister: Certain bases and facilities in the United Kingdom were made available by the late Government to the United States Air Force for the common defence of the United Kingdom and other countries who are parties to the North Atlantic Treaty. This arrangement will continue as long as it is needed in the general interest of world peace and security.[56]

This answer is interesting, both for its reference to the North Atlantic Treaty, which had not featured in any of the previous discussions, and for the acknowledgement that the deployment was an open-ended one. The second question, on 6 December 1951, went to the heart of the concern about separate military operations conducted by the United States. In replying, Churchill made public for the first time the formula in the Truman–Attlee understanding:

Mr Sidney Silverman asked the Prime Minister whether the agreement under which the United States atom bomb forces are permitted to use bases in this country contains the usual provision for their withdrawal in the case that the United States become involved in any war in which the United Kingdom did not wish to be involved.

The Prime Minister: The use of these bases in an emergency would be a matter for joint decision by His Majesty's Government and the United States Government in the light of the circumstances prevailing at the time.[57]

Consequently the communiqué issued in January 1952, at the conclusion of wide-ranging discussions between Truman, Churchill, and their advisers, partly held on the presidential yacht *'Williamsburg'*, did little more than confirm the arrangements already previously agreed by Attlee and made public by Churchill in December. Although Churchill always acknowledged Attlee's role, the formal nature of the January communiqué has over time led to these arrangements becoming known as the Churchill–Truman understanding. In reporting to the House on 26 February in the course of a debate on foreign affairs, Churchill acknowledged that the original understanding had been reached

---

[56] H of C, 21 November 1951, Column (Col) 376.
[57] H of C, 6 December 1951, Col 280.

between Attlee and Truman, but also indicated for the first time that the consent of the British government would be needed:

We reached an agreement about its [the atomic bomb] not being used from the East Anglian bases without British consent. This agreement states in a formal and public manner what had already been reached as a verbal understanding between the late Prime Minister and President Truman.[58]

Expansion and Contraction during the 1950s

In fact, since 1950 the United States Air Force had been pressing ahead with plans for a significant expansion of its presence in Britain. Following the conclusion of the Ambassador's Agreement, General Leon Johnson, now Commander of the Third Air Division, submitted an expansion programme to the RAF in the summer of 1950.[59] This sought to move bomber aircraft from East Anglia to the Oxford area, extend the runway at RAF Mildenhall, provide for hard-standing for B-29 bombers at Mildenhall, Lakenheath, Marham, and Sculthorpe, and obtain additional depot facilities. These plans were embodied in the Special Construction Programme, costed at over $100 million, which was to be funded fifty-fifty by the United States and Britain. In all, some twenty-three additional bases and four depots were envisaged to meet the demands of Strategic Air Command for operating facilities within range of the Soviet Union. The build-up of SAC forces in Britain was such that in 1951 they were split off from the Third Air Division to form the Seventh Air Division of SAC, reporting direct to SAC Headquarters at Omaha, Nebraska. The Third Air Division, retaining responsibility for tactical and logistical activities, became the US Third Air Force with its headquarters initially at South Ruislip. In 1952, there were 45,000 USAF personnel stationed in Britain and by October 1953 the handful of bases occupied by the US Air Force at the time of the Berlin blockade had grown to forty-two in all—twenty-seven bases, depots and other facilities occupied by Third Air Force, and fifteen by Seventh Air Division. Simon Duke, writing in 1987, commented that 'Britain, originally host to two wings of bombers for visits of goodwill and temporary duty, was to become, within the space of three years, America's unsinkable aircraft carrier'. (It was Churchill who gave currency to this phrase during the Second World War but it has been attributed originally to Mussolini.)[60]

[58] H of C, 26 February 1952, Col 964.
[59] S. Duke, *US Defence Bases in the United Kingdom* (London: Macmillan, 1987, 88).
[60] Ibid.

However, the extent of this expansion proved more than Britain could afford under the fifty-fifty funding arrangements, which placed no financial ceiling on her contribution. At a time of considerable financial difficulty, she found herself committed to meeting half the cost of whatever plans the United States proposed. Negotiations were opened on a more equitable financial arrangement and, after some hard bargaining, the Air Base Cost-Sharing Arrangement was signed in September 1953.[61] This Exchange of Letters, which both sides agreed should not constitute a formal agreement, limited Britain's financial contribution to some $70 million, on the understanding that land and facilities required by the USAF were to be provided without charge. In return, the USAF agreed to meet construction costs in excess of $70 million, as well as all future annual maintenance costs.

Throughout the post-war years, the presence of American forces in Britain has been governed by the agreements which Attlee and Churchill reached with Truman on operational matters and by the Cost-Sharing Arrangement of 1953 on financial matters. However, the role of the United States forces in Britain has changed over this period and these changes have resulted in adjustments to the number and location of the bases occupied and the total number of American servicemen stationed in Britain. During the mid 1950s, Third Air Force was building up its tactical fighter bomber capability, organized into three offensive wings at Sculthorpe, Wethersfield, and Bentwaters equipped with a mix of F-84 Thunderstreaks, F-100 Super Sabres, and F-101 Voodoos, and one defensive wing at Manston in Kent equipped with F-86 Sabres. All these aircraft were declared to NATO to be used by Supreme Allied Commander Europe in time of war. Meanwhile, Seventh Air Division's reliance on the short-range B-29 and B-50 bombers in the early 1950s gave way to the longer-range B-47 Stratojet, with an air-to-air refuelling capability, which was deployed to Britain in 1953, initially at Fairford. The advent of the B-52, three years later, coupled with a change in strategic doctrine, much reduced the USAF's dependence on overseas bases, and permanent deployments of SAC units to Britain ceased in 1956.

In the late 1950s, SAC replaced its ninety-day rotational tours at overseas bases with a continuous flying pattern over the Arctic accompanied by shorter three-week deployments at overseas bases where fewer aircraft were kept at 15-minute readiness states known as 'Reflex Alerts'. Furthermore, Britain's own V Bomber Force became operational in the

---

[61] S. Duke, *US Defence Bases in the United Kingdom*, 94–6.

late 1950s. These factors enabled Seventh Air Division to return a significant number of the sites formerly occupied in Britain, retaining only Fairford, Brize Norton, Greenham Common, and Upper Heyford, the core of the bomber bases originally requested in the Oxford area. Over the next few years, SAC was also to withdraw from these bases and by the spring of 1965 all SAC bomber operations in Britain had come to an end. The reason for this was that the bomber itself was being replaced as the prime weapon of deterrence by the Intermediate Range Ballistic Missile (IRBM), deployed by the United States to counter Soviet Intercontinental Ballistic Missiles (ICBMs), whose power was so dramatically demonstrated by the launch of Sputnik in October 1957.

Thor

In March 1957, seven months prior to the launch of Sputnik, Eisenhower and Macmillan had agreed at their conference in Bermuda to deploy sixty American Thor IRBMs to Britain. Since these missiles had a range of only 1,500 miles, forward basing in Europe was essential and Macmillan, anxious to heal the rift with the United States over Suez, was glad to accede to Eisenhower's request to station them in Britain, even though the system was, in the words of a recent commentator, 'despised by the British Defence Chiefs as an inferior first generation system which would soon have to be replaced'.[62] The first of these missiles were stationed at Feltwell in Norfolk with subsequent deployments at a number of other sites in East Anglia, Lincolnshire, and the East Riding of Yorkshire. The brief Exchange of Notes covering this deployment was published as a Government White Paper in February 1958.[63] The agreement made it clear that, although ownership of the missiles would pass to Britain, the nuclear warheads would remain 'in full United States ownership, custody and control' in accordance with United States law. Nevertheless, the agreement repeated the Attlee–Churchill–Truman understanding that:

The decision to launch these missiles will be a matter of joint decision taken by the two Governments. Any such decision will be made in the light of the circumstances at the time.

As predicted by the British Service Chiefs, Thor soon became obsolete

[62] R. Lamb, *The Macmillan Years* (London: John Murray, 1995) 285.
[63] Exchange of Notes Concerning the Supply to the United Kingdom Government of Intermediate Range Ballistic Missiles dated 22 February 1958. Cmnd 406.

with the development of submarine-launched ballistic missiles and, although the first missiles had become fully operational only in mid 1959, they were withdrawn from Britain in 1963. (A comparable system, the Jupiter missile, was withdrawn from Turkey at the same time following the Cuba missile crisis in October 1962.) However, during the five-year deployment of Thor missiles to Britain, the provisions for joint decision on operational use were, exceptionally, reinforced by a dual-key arrangement, requiring action by both British and American servicemen before the missiles could be fired. This arrangement, which appears to cut directly across the Acheson argument that the American President cannot delegate his responsibility for the release of nuclear weapons, has not been applied to any other American systems based in Britain or elsewhere. It was allegedly pressed on Eisenhower by Macmillan in the course of a visit to Washington in June 1958, based on a similar system governing access to the vaults by directors of the Bank of England.

The dual-key arrangements for Thor later gave rise to considerable controversy when ground-launched cruise missiles were deployed to Britain and other European countries in the 1980s. Those hostile to the cruise missile deployment—and more generally to the American military presence in Britain—pressed for dual-key arrangements similar to those applied to the Thor missiles. Mrs Thatcher's government responded that this would involve additional expense and argued that the Attlee–Churchill–Truman understandings required a joint decision before these weapons were fired. The difficulty with this argument was that ground-launched cruise missiles were to be deployed, under a NATO-wide programme, to four other European countries, Belgium, the Netherlands, Germany, and Italy, who had no bilateral understandings of this sort with the United States. At the same time, it is doubtful that the United States would have wished to grant dual-key arrangements to these countries even if she had been prepared to do so for Britain. It is probably more accurate to say that the release of these weapons would have been governed by NATO-wide military planning procedures on the use of nuclear assets which had been evolved since the Attlee–Churchill–Truman understandings.

Holy Loch and Fylingdales

In 1960, Harold Macmillan authorized two significant extensions to the American military presence in Britain. In February, an agreement was signed to permit the construction of a Ballistic Missile Early Warning

Station at Fylingdales on the North Yorkshire moors.[64] This was to be the third of a chain of radar stations designed to detect ballistic missiles launched from the Soviet Union at either Europe or the United States, the other stations in the chain being located at Clear in Alaska and Thule in Greenland. The station at Fylingdales was to be under RAF command and operated by 'the Royal Air Force in accordance with a joint plan which will be developed and agreed by the Royal Air Force and the United States Air Force'. The two governments undertook to pay for different elements of the cost of setting up and operating the station and the agreement was to remain in force for the duration of the North Atlantic Treaty. Although the '4-minute warning' of incoming missiles available to Britain aroused a certain amount of ridicule, no new issues of principle were involved in the construction of this station.

The second agreement, to allow the United States to base Polaris submarines at Holy Loch, announced on 1 November 1960, was a very different matter.[65] This agreement had been reached between Eisenhower and Macmillan at a meeting at Camp David earlier in the year. The Polaris submarine-launched ballistic missile system suffered from the same problems of limited range (about 1,400 miles) as both the early post-war bombers and the Thor missile. Forward basing was therefore required once more and a deal was struck under which, although no explicit links were made, the United States was permitted to use Holy Loch in Scotland as a base for Polaris and Britain purchased one hundred Skybolt missiles for her V bomber force. However, the Skybolt missile was later cancelled by the Kennedy administration and this led to Britain acquiring Polaris for herself in 1963 after difficult negotiations between Macmillan and Kennedy in Bermuda in December 1962.

The first Polaris submarines of the US Navy arrived in March 1961 at Holy Loch, which was the first overseas base for the new weapons system. Others were later developed at Rota in Spain and Guam in the Pacific. The location of the United States main strategic deterrent system in British territorial waters led to renewed debate over the degree of control over its use by the British government, and the extent to which Britain's security was placed at greater risk, rather than enhanced, by playing host to Polaris. The Labour MP Emrys Hughes, a long-time critic of the US military presence in Britain, reminded Parliament that Churchill himself had admitted in 1951 that 'We have made

[64] Exchange of Notes on Ballistic Missile Early Warning System in the United Kingdom dated 15 February 1960, Cmnd 946. TIAS 5313.
[65] H of C, 1 November 1960.

ourselves the target and perhaps the bullseye of a Soviet attack'.[66] This time there was an additional dimension to the debate in that American strategic nuclear weapons were concentrated in one location (unlike the earlier bomber deployments). This location was close to Glasgow, a major population centre, and furthermore in Scotland rather than England, thus feeding the incipient Scottish nationalist movement. John Rankin, a Labour MP from Glasgow, protested 'we are not really an ally of the United States. We are a satellite. We live on an expendable American base'.[67] A further, nationwide, movement which drew strength from the presence of Polaris at Holy Loch was the Campaign for Nuclear Disarmament, which had organized the first of a series of annual marches to the British Atomic Weapons Research Establishment at Aldermaston in March 1958 and gained increased support during the early 1960s.

The problem of British control was complicated by the fact that, although bombers of Strategic Air Command would have flown on operational missions directly from their British bases, the Polaris submarines were designed to spend long periods submerged in distant waters far from their home port. The issue of sovereignty which had finally persuaded the Americans to accept the 'joint decision' formula in 1951 would not apply once the submarines had left British territorial waters. Macmillan, conscious of the political problems this would cause for him, had tried hard to persuade the Americans to extend the consultation provisions to a distance of 100 miles from British territory. This proposal was rejected by the Americans on the grounds, reported by the British Ambassador in Washington, that it would prompt other host nations to ask for similar arrangements 'especially in the Far East and would oblige them to give a series of assurances and undertakings which they would find embarrassing and hampering to operations'.[68]

Faced with this refusal, Macmillan was obliged to acknowledge that Britain had no control over use of the Polaris submarines outside her territorial waters. He first informed the House of Commons on 1 November 1960 that 'it is impossible to make an agreement on all fours with the bomber agreement'. However, he went on in the same statement to say 'wherever the submarines may be, I am perfectly satisfied that no decision to use the missiles will ever be taken without the fullest of possible previous consultations'.[69] A week later, in the course of a

---

[66] Duke, in Duke and Kreiger, op. cit. 145.
[67] H of C, 1 November 1960. Cited by Dimbleby and Reynolds, op. cit.
[68] Lamb, op. cit. 294.   [69] H of C, 1 November 1960. Cited in Duke, op. cit. 1987.

debate on 8 November 1960, Macmillan appeared to concede that the 'joint decision' formula applied only to operations directly launched from British territory or British territorial waters:

As regard facilities in the territory ... we have exactly the same control in an emergency as exists over United States bomber or missile bases in this country. That is to say there will then be joint consultation regarding the use of these facilities.[70]

Nevertheless, in the same debate he admitted that 'consultation might obviously be impossible in circumstances of a sudden surprise attack upon the West. We would, indeed, not wish to insist on prior consultation in such circumstances...'. These contradictory and confusing remarks did little to reassure Macmillan's critics, who were further antagonized by his steadfast refusal to publish the terms of the agreement reached with the United States.

Macmillan's Concerns

Macmillan was clearly never at ease with the Attlee–Churchill–Truman understandings. Various incidents during his premiership caused him to refer to these arrangements in his memoirs as 'constantly being put in jeopardy by the folly of American officers of all ranks'.[71] In making these somewhat harsh comments he undoubtedly had in mind a statement made by Colonel Zinc in February 1958. Zinc, who was to command the first squadron of Thor missiles in Britain, claimed to have full operational control of these missiles, thereby casting doubt on the dual-key arrangements and the 1951 understanding, repeated in the Exchange of Notes on the Thor missiles, which referred to a joint decision by the two governments, not, as Zinc implied, individual military commanders. In June 1958, Macmillan raised his concerns with Eisenhower, according to his memoirs, to obtain a new agreement to replace 'the loose arrangements made by Attlee and confirmed by Truman'.[72] However, no new arrangements were agreed in writing. All that Macmillan achieved was a reaffirmation of the agreements reached in Bermuda in February 1958 that 'the decision to launch the missiles would be a matter for joint decision by the two governments'.

In a second incident in July 1960, an RB-47 reconnaissance aircraft on a mission from Brize Norton in Oxfordshire was shot down by the

[70] H of C, 8 November 1960. Cited in Woodliffe, op. cit.
[71] H. Macmillan *Riding The Storm* (London: Macmillan, 1971, 475). Cited by Baylis, *Anglo-American Defence Relations, 1939–84* (London: Macmillan, 1984).
[72] Ibid. 494.

Russians over the Arctic Ocean. The Russians claimed that the aircraft had been located within their territorial waters. The Americans denied this, but the incident caused grave embarrassment, coming soon after the U-2 incident in May 1960, which led to the collapse of the Paris Summit, and at a time when the U-2 pilot, Gary Powers, was still on trial in the Soviet Union. Eden had forbidden U-2 aircraft to operate from Britain but Macmillan, clearly ill at ease in the House of Commons, was obliged to admit that other intelligence-gathering flights had taken place for a number of years from British bases under the Attlee–Churchill–Truman understandings. He claimed that 'everything that takes place from the bases will be known to the respective political heads of both countries'.[73] However, he was clearly less confident in private than he made out in public. According to his memoirs, in July 1960 he determined 'to look carefully again at the precise terms of the agreements for the American bases in order to ensure that they were water-tight'.[74]

By 1962, it was apparent that Macmillan's concern had resulted in periodic reaffirmation of the original Attlee–Churchill–Truman understandings. Answering a question in the House of Commons not long after the Cuba missile crisis, he stated:

The pledges given to Lord Attlee in October 1951, to Sir Winston Churchill in January 1952 and by President Eisenhower's Administration in 1958, and now reaffirmed by President Kennedy last year, of course hold and they cover any use of bases in this country by the American Administration.[75]

The references to Eisenhower clearly relate to the agreement on Thor missiles in 1958, but mention of reaffirmation by President Kennedy in 1961 appears to introduce a new element into the debate. This was not picked up at the time, but some twenty years later the British Defence Secretary Michael Heseltine disclosed in May 1983:

That agreement is ratified and reaffirmed every time a British Prime Minister or President of the United States changes and each of them personally examines the agreement and reaffirms their satisfaction with it.[76]

From this it seems that the practice had been adopted at some stage, possibly between Kennedy and Macmillan, of reaffirming the original agreements at each change of President or Prime Minister. Dr David Owen, a former British Foreign Secretary, made the same point on 17

---

[73] H of C, 25 July 1960. Cited in Woodliffe, op. cit.
[74] H. Macmillan, Pointing The Way. Cited by Baylis, op. cit. 1984, 238.
[75] H of C, 6 November 1962.
[76] *The Listener*, 2 June 1983. Cited by D. Campbell, *The Unsinkable Aircraft Carrier* (London: Paladin, 1986, 308).

April 1986 when he spoke of agreements made by 'Attlee with Truman, Churchill with Truman and those of successive Prime Ministers'.[77]

Changing Roles

By 1964, the full complement of ten Polaris submarines was stationed at Holy Loch and two years later the withdrawal of American forces from France saw the relocation of some 8,000 US servicemen to Britain. Among the major units to redeploy to Britain were a tactical reconnaissance wing to Upper Heyford and a troop carrier wing and airborne command post to Mildenhall. These joined the 48th Tactical Fighter Wing—the Statue of Liberty Wing—which had moved from Chaumont to Lakenheath in 1959 equipped with F-100 Super Sabres. Overall numbers nevertheless declined from the peak of some 43,000 personnel in the late 1950s. With the withdrawal of SAC units from Britain, bases at Brize Norton, Fairford, and Greenham Common had been returned to RAF control in the mid 1960s, but these and other bases were retained as standby or recovery bases. Moreover, as the USAF's strategic nuclear assets were withdrawn from Britain, they were replaced by tactical nuclear weapons. Dual-capable aircraft, such as the Phantom, were stationed from 1965 onwards at Alconbury and the twin base of Woodbridge–Bentwaters.

Subsequently, the new F-111 fighter bombers were deployed to Upper Heyford in 1970 and Lakenheath in 1977. As a consequence, the number of American servicemen in Britain levelled off at some 30,000 during the 1970s and early 1980s, but there was no reduction in the number of bases and other facilities occupied by the US armed forces. The switch in strategic concepts from a policy of massive retaliation to one of flexible response had a significant impact on the deployment of American forces in Britain. The original post-war role of the 'unsinkable aircraft carrier' had been that of a strike carrier from which to hold the Soviet Union at risk of nuclear attack. With NATO now planning for more extended war in Europe, involving considerable reinforcement from the United States, Britain became more of a support carrier. It was estimated that in wartime some 40 per cent of NATO aircraft would be assigned to Britain,[78] which would become a huge marshalling yard and storage depot for the air war over Europe.

This role required the retention of over one hundred bases and other facilities in Britain. In addition to Holy Loch, where Poseidon submarines

---

[77] H of C, 16 April 1986, Col 943. Cited by Duke, op. cit. 1990, 301.
[78] Duke, op. cit. 1990.

replaced Polaris in 1971, there were eight main operating bases occupied by the US Air Force. In addition to the F-111 fighter bombers stationed at Lakenheath and Upper Heyford, A-10 Thunderbolts or 'tank-busters' were deployed to Woodbridge–Bentwaters from 1979 onwards for rapid deployment to the Continent in the event of war. Two standby bases were identified at Sculthorpe and Wethersfield and an additional ten airfields in RAF hands were designated co-located operating bases. Reconnaissance aircraft were located both at Mildenhall, where the SR-71 Blackbird arrived in August 1970, and Alconbury, where the TR-1 was deployed in 1982. Both stations had additional roles. An 'aggressor' squadron of F-5 aircraft was stationed at Alconbury to provide training in Soviet Air Force tactics, and Mildenhall, which became the headquarters of Third Air Force in 1972, housed an airborne command and control unit, together with aircraft of Military Airlift Command. In the early 1980s, Fairford was reopened as a base for KC-135 tanker aircraft and, following the NATO decision of December 1979, Greenham Common and Molesworth (a disused wartime bomber base) were designated as bases for the deployment of ground-launched cruise missiles. Ninety-six cruise missiles were stationed at Greenham Common in 1984 and provision was made for a further sixty-four at Molesworth from 1986 onwards. However, the build-up at Molesworth had not been completed by the time the INF Treaty was signed in December 1987 and all the missiles were subsequently withdrawn from both bases, as required by the treaty, with provision for inspection of the storage bunkers.

These main bases were supported by a host of secondary facilities across the country, many with an intelligence gathering or communications role. The intelligence facilities, some operated jointly, some nationally, derived from the secret agreement concluded in 1947, known simply as 'US/UK', to which the old Commonwealth was later admitted, and the Burns–Templer agreements of 1948–50.[79] These agreements consolidated the exceptionally close relationship on intelligence matters which had grown up during the war in which Britain was for some time the senior partner. In 1952, an interception facility was established at Kirknewton near Edinburgh. This was followed by a communications centre at Chicksands in Bedfordshire which in 1964 acquired a huge circular antenna known colloquially as the 'elephant cage'. A naval monitoring station was set up at Edzell in Scotland in 1960 in connection with the Polaris programme and a SOSUS terminal was established at Brawdy in South Wales. Finally, the working partnership between the British Government Communications Headquarters and the United

---

[79] Baylis, op. cit. 1984.

States National Security Agency (NSA) led to the NSA assuming administrative control of Menwith Hill station in Yorkshire in 1966. For many years this facility was referred to as a defence communications site and it was not until the mid 1990s that it was officially acknowledged as a field element of the NSA.[80]

Opposing Views on the American Presence

The extent and variety of American military assets stationed in Britain, the strategic importance of some of these assets (SAC bombers, Polaris and Poseidon submarines, and the Fylingdales Early Warning System), together with the informal nature of the arrangements governing these deployments, all made Britain a unique overseas basing area for the United States. The ready acceptance of the return of American forces to Britain after the Second World War caused some surprise at the time but in both social and political terms Britain probably provided a more favourable environment for the deployment of American troops than any other foreign nation. In social terms, a network of Community Relations Committees, linked to the major bases and chaired by well-known local figures, exists to foster good relations between the bases and the surrounding communities. In political terms, the approvals required from the British government to change the disposition of American forces or equipment or embark on new construction work at the bases are regarded as an administrative rather than a legal matter and, although spelt out in Parliamentary answers from time to time, are exercised with a light touch. Henry Kissinger has remarked on the close and informal nature of the relationship between Britain and the United States on security issues during the post-war period:

The ease and informality of the Anglo-American partnership has been a source of wonder—and no little resentment—to third countries. Our post-war diplomatic history is littered with Anglo-American 'arrangements' and 'understandings', sometimes on crucial issues, never put into formal documents.[81]

However, Kissinger did not always get the cooperation he expected from Britain. During the Yom Kippur War of 1973 there was some concern expressed by the host government when American forces in Britain, along with those in other countries, were placed on heightened alert, without prior consultation, as a warning to the Soviet Union.

[80] H of C, 12 July 1995.
[81] H. Kissinger, *The White House Years* (London: Weidenfeld & Nicolson 1979). Cited by Baylis (1984).

Prime Minister Edward Heath made a point of declining to endorse the alert and, when it came to the use of bases in Britain for American operations in support of Israel, Kissinger commented somewhat ruefully that 'We were given to understand . . . that it would be appreciated in London if we did not use British bases either for the airlift or for intelligence collection in the Middle East. There was never a formal refusal because it was made plain we should not ask'.[82]

At the same time, the concerns over the use of American forces in Britain demonstrated by both Attlee and Macmillan illustrate that Britain's eagerness to tie the United States firmly into the defence of Europe was often modified by an underlying worry over sovereignty and the feeling that the Americans were inclined to take their British hosts too much for granted. Although broadly supported by majority opinion in Britain, the American presence has attracted considerable criticism both on environmental and political grounds. Environmental criticism tended to be confined to the immediate neighbourhood of bases where operations caused a severe noise problem. In the early 1950s, the main offender was Greenham Common where the town of Newbury had expanded close to the base since the war. In the early 1980s, the decision to reopen Fairford for tanker operations by the KC-135, a particularly noisy aircraft, was strongly opposed by the local community, and in the late 1980s the need to re-route the flight pattern for the ageing F-111s when taking off from Upper Heyford caused considerable distress in nearby villages.

Political protest was more widespread. The Campaign for Nuclear Disarmament (CND), which has exercised a varying degree of influence on the Labour Party over the years, attracted considerable support during the 1960s and 1970s with its annual marches to Aldermaston, although these were directed as much against British as American nuclear weapons. The deployment of cruise missiles to Greenham Common in the mid 1980s added a new dimension to the protest movement. At this point, CND found itself largely eclipsed by a variety of other protest groups, especially all-women groups, who mounted a vigil outside the base and occasionally succeeded in breaking through the perimeter fence. A number of violent demonstrations were staged at the base and off-base exercises involving convoys with training missiles were regularly harassed by protesters. Fears of a similar level of protest activity at Molesworth were never fully realized because of signature of the INF Treaty which led to early withdrawal of the missiles.

---

[82] H. Kissinger, *Years of Upheaval* (London: Weidenfeld & Nicolson, 1982, 709).

The Air Strike on Libya

In a generally hostile book entitled *The Unsinkable Aircraft Carrier*, first published in 1984, a left-wing journalist, Duncan Campbell, described Britain as 'an emergency parking lot for Strategic Air Command', and suggested that there had been a 'de facto policy of open house' since the US Air Force returned to Britain in 1948.[83] He was also strongly critical of the arrangements for 'joint decision', believing that the United States saw this as an informal understanding, not a binding agreement, which would not oblige her to accept a British veto over military operations which she intended to launch from Britain. These views were put to the test in April 1986 when President Reagan sought and obtained from Thatcher agreement to use F-111 aircraft and supporting tankers based in Britain for an air strike on Libya.

The informal nature of the arrangements for basing American forces in Britain and the widespread ignorance of these arrangements by the general public were severely shaken by the news that F-111 aircraft based at Lakenheath and Upper Heyford, refuelled by tankers specially deployed to Mildenhall, had been used on the night of 14 April 1986 to bomb military targets in Libya in retaliation for terrorist attacks against American servicemen in Germany. Margaret Thatcher came under immediate attack in the House of Commons from a wide spectrum of political opinion wanting to know whether she had given her consent to the operation and, if so, on what grounds. Public disquiet was fuelled by the fact that Britain was the only country in Europe that had cooperated with the United States. Both France and Spain had refused overflying rights for the F-111s from Britain, thus necessitating a round trip of 5,600 miles with four refuelling operations by 28 tankers. Indeed, some of the tankers were redeployed to Britain from Spain, who protested that this was in breach of her own agreements with the United States. There was also considerable suspicion voiced that the F-111 aircraft based in Britain were not strictly necessary for the operation, in which carrier-based aircraft in the Mediterranean also took part. It was suggested that aircraft from Britain had been used largely to gain political support for the raid, although subsequent experience in the Gulf War with precision guided munitions later gave credence to the American view that the Pave Tack system, with which only F-111s were equipped, did much to minimize civilian casualties.

Margaret Thatcher maintained that the United States had sought Britain's consent to the operation under the Attlee–Churchill–Truman

[83] Campbell, op. cit. 14, 91.

understandings, and that she had given her consent on condition that only specific military targets clearly related to terrorism were attacked. She justified the action taken by reference to the right of self-defence under Article 51 of the United Nations Charter, the threat of state terrorism and the need to support the United States, on whom the defence of Europe relied. In replying to a barrage of criticism in the House of Commons, she said that it was 'inconceivable' that Margaret Thatcher would refuse this request from the United States.[84] In this she may have been influenced by President Reagan's support for Britain during the Falklands War in 1982 and the murder of a young policewoman by officials from the Libyan Embassy in London exactly two years before in April 1984. She confirmed, on a more authoritative basis, that the Attlee–Churchill–Truman understandings were renewed at each change of administration in Britain or the United States and maintained that they had worked well on this occasion. Nevertheless, neither Members of Parliament nor the public at large were *au fait* with these understandings and it had been generally believed that American forces were stationed in Britain for NATO purposes only. It had certainly never been envisaged in the early 1950s that these forces might be deployed on national operations unconnected with NATO, and the realization that Britain's arrangements with the United States were less rigorous than those of other countries caused some concern. Many took the view that Britain had acquiesced too readily in a private quarrel between the United States and Libya, which had been building up for some time in the Gulf of Sidra, and regretted that Thatcher had not taken a more independent line.

The Recent Rundown

With the end of the Cold War the American military presence in Britain, whose primary role had been the reinforcement of continental Europe, was scaled down significantly. In 1992, it was announced that the A-10 tank-buster aircraft were to be withdrawn and that the two Tactical Fighter Wings of F-111 fighter bombers were to be replaced by two squadrons of F-15E fighters (one of which transferred from Bitburg in Germany). At this stage it was envisaged that the total number of combat aircraft in Britain might decline from 250 to 48. This proved to be an overestimate as there were still some 66 USAF combat aircraft in Britain in 1998. Nevertheless, with the departure of the A-10s the

[84] H of C, 15 April 1986, Col 726.

USAF withdrew from Woodbridge–Bentwaters in January 1993. In February 1993, the British government announced that Greenham Common was to be sold, although the missile storage bunkers remained open to inspection under the INF Treaty. The F-111s left Upper Heyford in October 1993, to be followed by the remaining fighter aircraft in December. The USAF withdrew from the base in September of the following year.

By 1998, with the rundown virtually complete only some 13,500 American service and civilian personnel remained in Britain.[85] Of this number, 1,200 mainly civilian personnel were located at Menwith Hill and many of the service personnel were liaison staff scattered in small numbers over a large number of sites. The operational elements of the American military presence were concentrated in just three major bases, Alconbury–Molesworth with 1,400 personnel, Lakenheath–Feltwell with 5,300, and Mildenhall with 4,200. The 66 combat aircraft remaining consisted entirely of F-15s stationed at Lakenheath, although there were also refuelling tankers, transport aircraft, and helicopters stationed elsewhere. This represented a substantial reduction from the forces deployed in Britain at the height of the Cold War. But in proportional terms the reduction was far less than that experienced in Germany where there had been a huge rundown of ground forces. The American military presence in Britain remained the second largest in Europe, but only just, for by 1999 the total of American service personnel permanently stationed in Britain, at 10,700, was almost the same as that in Italy prior to the increases required to support operations in the Balkans. However, Third Air Force remained in being with its headquarters at Mildenhall and acquired additional responsibilities. Under HQ United States Air Force Europe at Ramstein, Third Air Force covered all USAF activity north of the Alps, while Sixteenth Air Force based at Aviano in Italy covered activity south of the Alps with particular responsibility for operations first in Bosnia and subsequently in Serbia and Kosovo. However, Britain too provided direct support for USAF operations in Serbia and Kosovo in 1999 by permitting B-52 bombers to fly missions from RAF Fairford as she had done during the Gulf War.

---

[85] H of C, 2 March 1998, Col 490.

4

Neo-colonial Bases

Introduction

In searching for suitable overseas bases after the Second World War, the United States always assumed that, in addition to the territories she possessed overseas, she would be able to retain military facilities in other countries where she had hitherto enjoyed colonial or quasi-colonial rights. In this respect, American practice differed markedly from that of Britain, which had been so roundly criticized as an imperial power by Franklin D. Roosevelt and others during the war. American planners drawing up lists of facilities required by the United States after the war placed the Philippines and the Panama Canal Zone high on their list of priorities. They also assumed that the United States would retain the naval base at Guantánamo in Cuba. By contrast, Britain retained no military facilities in India or Pakistan when these countries were granted independence in 1947 (a year after the Philippines) and, although she retained her African and East Asian colonies for some time longer, she generally liquidated her military presence in these on independence. The sole exception to this practice was the retention of the Sovereign Base Areas in Cyprus after 1961.[1]

The United States, however, retained extensive military facilities in both the Philippines and Panama throughout the Cold War period, casting some doubt on the degree of sovereignty enjoyed by these countries, which remained heavily dependent on the United States in both economic and security terms. The dominant position of the United States in Panama and the Philippines initially gave her considerable freedom of manoeuvre in developing military bases there. But in both countries this advantage came to be eroded by association with local rulers, Ferdinand Marcos in the Philippines and Manuel Noriega in

[1] The Five Power Arrangements providing military assistance to Malaysia and Singapore cannot be construed as a colonial hangover as they involved Australia and New Zealand as well as Britain.

Panama, who were corrupt, undemocratic, and unscrupulous. Moreover, the local populations resented the military bases as a vestige of colonialism, even though many local workers depended on them for their livelihood. In both countries, a dangerous and unhealthy dependency had grown up between the Americans and their hosts by the 1980s. The United States considered the strategic assets located in Panama and the Philippines to be so important that they were obliged to condone the excesses of the local rulers who enriched themselves while impoverishing their countries. For their part, the local rulers became increasingly dependent on the access and other payments made by the Americans to secure their tenure, knowing that they were well placed to drive a hard bargain in negotiations. During the 1980s, a pattern of fraudulent elections, political assassinations, and blatant disregard for democratic principles developed in both countries, leading to a popular revolution in the Philippines and an embarrassing military intervention by the United States in Panama. For very different reasons the United States undertook to withdraw her forces from both countries during the 1990s.

Throughout this period, the US naval base at Guantánamo in Cuba remained an extraordinary enclave in increasingly hostile territory. Although the United States was bitterly opposed to Fidel Castro's regime she was unable, for wider strategic reasons, to make use of the military facilities available to her in Cuba to secure her political objectives. For broadly similar reasons, Castro was unable to take decisive action against the base at Guantánamo, although he engaged in minor harassment from time to time. An uneasy stalemate therefore developed which persists to this day, leaving Cuba the only undivided sovereign territory to have accommodated both Soviet and American military bases within her borders at the same time.

The Philippines

The Acquisition of the Philippines

Americans have inevitably found it difficult to reconcile their own anticolonial history with the acquisition of overseas territories at the turn of the century. The Philippines, acquired from Spain at the Treaty of Paris in 1898, were the largest of these possessions and some sought to defend their acquisition by suggesting that the United States exercised a uniquely beneficial form of imperialism. Cordell Hull, Roosevelt's Secretary of State, who pressed in 1944 for 'early, dramatic and concerted announcements' by the colonial powers on self-government for their overseas possessions,[2] nevertheless considered the United States colonial policy in the Philippines to be 'a perfect example of how a nation should treat a colony or dependency'.[3] However, most imperial powers have justified their policy by varying degrees of paternalism and there is little evidence that American imperialism in the Philippines was significantly different from that pursued by other colonial powers. There was no obvious connection between the dispute over Cuba which led to war with Spain in 1898 and the acquisition of Spanish possessions in the Pacific, half a world away and 5,000 miles from the west coast of the United States. However, the advocates of expansion, chiefly Theodore Roosevelt, together with Senators Lodge and Beveridge, were quite clear in their aims. In a direct reference to British use of sea power, Senator Beveridge set out their objectives:

The trade of the world must and will be ours. And we will get it as our mother has told us how. We will establish trading posts throughout the world as distributing points for American products. We will build a Navy to the measure of our greatness . . . The Philippines are logically our first target.[4]

As Assistant Secretary of the Navy, Roosevelt had pressed President McKinley to attack the Philippines as soon as war broke out with Spain, having appointed Commodore Dewey to the Far East and ensured that he was waiting with a fleet at Hong Kong. The Spanish fleet was defeated on 1 May 1898 at Manila Bay and the Treaty of Paris, ceding the Philippines to the United States, was concluded on 10 December.

McKinley had been a reluctant imperialist, taking five months and many nights of prayer to decide whether to annex the Philippines. His first thought was to obtain only a naval base in the islands and later to annex only the island of Luzon, but he eventually agreed to acquire the whole territory for payment of $20 million compensation to Spain. Somewhat disingenuously he commented:

Without any original thought of complete or even partial acquisition, the presence and success of our arms at Manila imposes on us obligations we cannot disregard.[5]

---

[2] Memo to Roosevelt, 8 September 1944. Cited in T. Smith, *The Pattern of Imperialism* (Cambridge: CUP, 1981); and G. Hess, *The US Emergence as a South East Asia Power* (New York: Columbia University Press, 1987).

[3] Letter to W. Phillips, 18 November 1942. Cited by David Reynolds, Wartime Alliance. In *The Special Relationship*, W. R. Louis and H. Bull (ed.), (Oxford: OUP, 1987).

[4] L. Battistini, *The Rise of American Influence in the Pacific* (Michigan, MI: Michigan State University Press, 1960).

[5] Ibid.

These sentiments would have been wholly familiar to a British or French imperialist. Indeed, Rudyard Kipling, the apostle of British imperialism, was urging on the Americans while McKinley hesitated. It is not generally appreciated that Kipling's exhortation to 'take up the white man's burden' was addressed not to his fellow countrymen but to the United States while she was debating whether or not to make the Philippines an American colony.

The decision was not universally popular in the United States. Thomas B. Read, Speaker of the House, commented that his country had bought ten million Filipinos at $2 per head. Mark Twain thought that the Stars and Stripes should be replaced by the Skull and Crossbones. 'We cannot' he wrote, 'maintain an Empire in the Orient and a Republic in America'.[6] However, the decision was even less popular in the Philippines, where the local inhabitants had, perhaps naively, assumed that the defeat of Spain by the United States would ensure their independence. It took some two years and 70,000 American troops, two-thirds of the US Army, to suppress the popular revolt led by Emilio Aguinaldo and pacify the islands. The war cost $170 million and the lives of 200,000 Filipinos.

The acquisition of the Philippines led inevitably to rivalry between the United States and Japan over control of the Pacific. For the time being this rivalry was suppressed by the secret agreement concluded in 1905 by William Howard Taft, known as the 'Agreed Memorandum', which preserved the American position in the Philippines and the Japanese position in Korea. Recognizing that the Philippines were too far away to be adequately protected, the United States made similar agreements with Japan in 1908 and 1917. Even Theodore Roosevelt, once President, foresaw the difficulty of defending the islands against Japanese attack. 'The Philippines', he commented, 'form our Achilles' heel'.[7]

In the years following the First World War the United States put her trust in the Washington Treaties concluded in 1921–2 by the Secretary of State Charles E. Hughes. These allowed no new military construction in Guam, the Philippines, and the islands west of Hawaii. For their part, the Japanese were prevented from fortifying the former German colonies which they had acquired at the end of the war under the terms of the League of Nations mandate and this restriction was confirmed by the treaties. Consequently, the naval base at Subic Bay, although

---

[6] S. Karnow, *In Our Image. America's Empire in the Philippines* (London: Century, 1990, 92). See also G. Vidal, *The Nation*, January 1986.

[7] Battistini, op. cit.

established in 1904, remained largely unfortified during the inter-war years, much to the chagrin of the US Navy, which, with the advent of oil burning, was now far better placed to protect the Philippines from Hawaii. In 1930, Rear-Admiral Yarnell, appearing before the Senate Committee on Foreign Relations, made his views plain:

This nation never provided the essentials necessary to a naval defense of the Philippines even when no treaties existed and most probably never would have provided them even if no treaties were signed.[8]

Independence Proposals

By the 1930s, the United States was giving active consideration to independence for the Philippines, long before the European powers were prepared to contemplate independence for their colonies. But there was considerable ambiguity about the future of American military installations on the islands. As early as 1924, the General Board of the Navy Department declared 'In case independence is granted, the United States must retain a naval station in the Philippines'.[9] The Hare–Hawes–Cutting Act of 1933 reflected this view by authorizing the United States to retain whatever military bases it wished. President Manuel Quezon objected to this provision as incompatible with independence for the Philippines. Franklin D. Roosevelt, as vigorous in opposing imperialism as Theodore Roosevelt had been in advocating it, was prepared to meet Quezon's demands and close the bases. The Tydings–McDuffie Act of 1934 set the date for independence in ten years' time and allowed for the United States to surrender all military facilities except her naval bases, on which negotiations were to take place within two years of independence. However, by 1944, when the ten years had elapsed, the United States had been ejected from the Philippines, which were under Japanese occupation.

In these circumstances the United States Congress passed a Joint Resolution reversing the 1934 Act with Quezon's agreement. The passage on bases read:

After negotiation with the President of the Commonwealth of the Philippines ... the President of the United States is hereby authorised ... to withhold or acquire and to retain such bases ... as he may deem necessary for the mutual protection of the Philippines and of the United States.[10]

[8]   G. E. Wheeler, *Prelude to Pearl Harbor* (Columbia, MO: University of Missouri Press, 1963).
[9]   Ibid.
[10]   Joint Resolution No 93. Cited in G. E. Taylor, *The Philippines and the United States: Problems of Partnership* (London: Praeger, 1964).

The war with Japan and the occupation of the Philippines had radically altered American strategic thinking. The islands were initially seen as bases for prosecuting the war against Japan but, with the Japanese surrender, it was apparent that they could be used as the means of projecting American power more generally in the Far East. In 1945, plans prepared for the Joint Chiefs of Staff requested twenty-four army facilities and thirteen navy facilities in the Philippines in addition to the retention of Subic Bay and Clark airfield.[11] In May that year Truman signed a preliminary statement with Quezon's successor, Sergio Osmeña, calling for 'the fullest and closest military cooperation'.[12] This was intended to pave the way for an agreement on the future of the American bases to be ready at the time of independence. However, negotiations ran into difficulties on questions of jurisdiction. The United States wanted unlimited criminal jurisdiction over American troops whether on or off the bases while the Philippine authorities sought full jurisdiction outside the bases. These arguments were to continue over a considerable period despite secondary agreements reached from time to time.

The Bases after Independence

The Philippines became independent on 4 July 1946, but the Treaty of General Relations, which transferred sovereignty from the United States, excluded 'the use of such bases . . . as the United States of America, by agreement with the Republic of the Philippines, may deem necessary to retain for the mutual protection of the United States of America and of the Philippine Republic . . .'.[13] It was not until 14 March 1947 that the Military Bases Agreement was signed.[14] This gave the United States rent-free leases of ninety-nine years at Subic Bay, Clark airfield and fourteen other sites, with access to a further seven sites, if required 'by military necessity', in return for the provision of military aid and agreement by the Americans not to retain a base in Manila. Neither government could abrogate the agreement unilaterally. President Manuel Roxas, a keen supporter of the bases, who had succeeded Osmeña a year earlier, expressed his satisfaction, saying 'the

[11] W. J. Berry, *US Bases in the Philippines: The Evolution of the Special Relationship* (Boulder, CO: Westview, 1989).
[12] Karnow, op. cit. 331.
[13] Treaty of General Relations between the United States of America and the Republic of the Philippines. Signed 4 July 1946. TIAS 1568.
[14] Agreement between the United States of America and the Republic of the Philippines Concerning Military Bases. Signed 14 March 1947. TIAS 1775.

establishment of these bases, not for aggression but for defence, will guarantee our own safety and advance the cause of peace worldwide'.[15] This statement acknowledged, obliquely, that the bases were to be retained not primarily for the defence of the Philippines—the facilities involved were far in excess of what was required for this—but for the projection of United States power in the Pacific. Indeed, the Philippine government, although playing host to these installations, obtained no formal security guarantee in return from the United States at this stage. This would not be granted until August 1951, in parallel with the Peace Treaty with Japan, in the form of the Mutual Defense Treaty, one of a series of defence treaties which John Foster Dulles negotiated with America's allies in the Pacific, first as Special Consultant to Dean Acheson and later as Secretary of State. These treaties were designed to secure acceptance in the region for the Japanese Peace Treaty and each contained broadly similar wording on security. Article IV of the treaty with the Philippines read:

Each party recognises that an armed attack in the Pacific Area on either of the parties would be dangerous to its own peace and safety and declares that it would act to meet the common danger in accordance with its constitutional processes.[16]

In 1954, Dulles confirmed to the Philippines Foreign Secretary that 'an armed attack on the Philippines could not but be also an attack on the military forces of the United States', and as such would be instantly repelled. This declaration was not entirely welcome to the Senate who felt that it extended the terms of the 1951 treaty without their approval.[17]

Meanwhile, the issues of jurisdiction had been resolved in favour of the United States. The American authorities were to administer the bases as if they were sovereign territory, exercising jurisdiction both over their own forces and over the Filipinos working on the bases. They also gained jurisdiction over offences perpetrated outside the bases if committed by an American serviceman on duty or if the injured party was an American serviceman. In addition, the US Navy continued to administer the town of Olangapo, with a population of some 60,000, adjacent to Subic Bay, as it had done since 1920. In these circumstances it was not surprising that many Filipinos saw the bases as symbols of

[15] H. W. Brands, *Bound to Empire* (Oxford: OUP, 1992).

[16] Mutual Defense Treaty between the United States of America and the Republic of the Philippines. Signed 30 August 1951. TIAS 2529.

[17] SCFR Sub-Committee on US Security Agreements and Commitments Abroad. 91st Congress, 1970.

continued American dominance and felt that their independence was more nominal than real. This impression was reinforced by the economic provisions of the Philippine Trade Act of 1946 which, although stipulating that there should be free trade between the two countries for eight years, pegged the peso to the dollar and established quotas on exports from the Philippines to the United States but not vice versa. Another aspect of neo-colonialism was the assistance provided by the Central Intelligence Agency in putting down the Hukbalahap rebellion during the 1950s. But above all, the Filipinos felt that the American bases had not protected them from the Japanese in 1941, that their sacrifices during the war were not fully appreciated, and that the United States was retaining the bases to serve their own wider interests rather than to protect the Philippines themselves. One million Filipinos had died in the struggle to expel the Japanese and Manila had been devastated in house-to-house fighting. In the words of one commentator 'what was not destroyed during the Japanese occupation was likely destroyed during the liberation'.[18]

Revisions to the 1947 Agreement

Filipino resentment of the bases grew in the 1950s with the increase in American military activity after the outbreak of the Korean War and the realization that the 1947 agreement contained less favourable terms on jurisdiction than the NATO Status of Forces Agreement signed in 1951 and the parallel agreement signed with Japan in 1953. It was considered intolerable that Japan, the defeated enemy, should obtain more favourable treatment than the Philippines, an ally and former colony. As the United States wished to expand the bases, President Magsaysay attempted to negotiate a revision to the Military Bases Agreement. Inconclusive discussions were held in 1954 and further talks commenced in 1956 following a meeting between Magsaysay and Vice-President Nixon. President Eisenhower, who had served in the Philippines before the war, agreed that sovereignty rested with the Philippine government, but refused to accept any restrictions on use of the bases during an emergency. 'It would destroy the utility and one of the major purposes of having bases there', he said, 'We should stand very firm'.[19]

Negotiations were broken off by the Americans in December 1956

---

[18] Berry, op. cit.
[19] Eisenhower Papers, 21 August 1956. Cited by Brands, 271.

but resumed in 1958 between the US Ambassador Charles Bohlen and the Philippine Foreign Minister Felixberto Serrano. This time an agreement was reached in October 1959 which stated, *inter alia*:

Use of the bases for United States military missions not falling within the 1951 Mutual Defense Treaty or the 1954 South East Asia Collective Defence Treaty requires prior consultations.[20]

The two treaties mentioned refer only to hostile attacks on the Philippines (which would necessarily involve an attack on American forces stationed there) and thereby preclude use of the bases for offensive operations by United States forces when there is no threat to the Philippines unless the consent of the host government has been obtained. This interpretation was subsequently confirmed at a hearing of the US Senate Sub-Committee on Agreements and Commitments Abroad in 1969. The Sub-Committee was told that offensive air operations against Vietnam from the Philippines had not been authorized, since these would have required consultation under the Bohlen–Serrano Agreement.[21]

The 1959 agreement also removed neo-colonial grievances by returning jurisdiction over the port of Manila and the town of Olangapo to the Philippine authorities. A Philippine Liaison Officer was established at each base and a Mutual Defense Board was set up to consider grievances and disputes. But no progress was made on the outstanding issues of criminal jurisdiction. Congress was not prepared to see any concessions made and the American Secretary of State Christian Herter instructed Bohlen not to discuss the matter since 'no mutually satisfactory agreement is possible on this item'.[22] However, the most significant feature of the 1959 agreement for the future was the decision to reduce the leases on the bases from the original ninety-nine years set out in the Military Bases Agreement to a new period of twenty-five years. After some delay this provision came into effect in an Exchange of Notes signed in September 1966 so that the original leases were now due to expire in 1991. Both governments could agree to terminate the leases earlier, but after 1991 either government could unilaterally give one year's notice of termination.

---

[20] Memorandum of Agreement signed 12 October 1959. Cited in J. Woodliffe, *The Peacetime Use of Foreign Military Bases* (Dordrecht: Martinus Nijhoff, 1992).

[21] Symington Hearings. US Senate Committee on Agreements and Commitments Abroad 1969. 91st Congress. Cited in Robert Pringle *American Interests in the Islands of South East Asia* (New York: Columbia University Press, 1980).

[22] Berry, op. cit. 101.

The Marcos Years

With the election of Ferdinand Marcos to the presidency in 1965, the Philippine government began to adopt a much tougher negotiating stance. Over a period of twenty years this increasingly came to resemble blackmail with the periods between negotiations reducing to the point where they became virtually continuous with ever higher compensation costs being demanded. The process started with the formal agreement in 1966 that the period of lease on the bases would be reduced from ninety-nine to twenty-five years. A relatively modest aid package of $45 million was also agreed, although the United States, throughout this and subsequent negotiations, held firm to the principle that the provision of military and economic aid was a separate issue which should not be construed as rent for the bases. But in the late 1960s, hostility to the American bases was fuelled by opposition to the war in Vietnam. Marcos had agreed to send a contingent of Army engineers, 2,000 strong, to Vietnam—a move that he had opposed when first suggested by his predecessor, President Macapagal. Many Filipinos saw this as further evidence of subservience to US foreign policy interests and demonstrations against the war and Philippine involvement in it intensified.

To re-establish his nationalist credentials before the 1969 elections, Marcos decided on a further round of negotiations on the bases. In January 1969, his Minister for Foreign Affairs, Carlos Romulo, publicly questioned whether the bases were necessary for the defence of the Philippines. In July, Raul Manglapus, a former Minister of Foreign Affairs, who was to return to this post under President Aquino, issued a statement saying that the bases had become 'deadly irritants' adversely affecting US–Philippine relations and contributing to the weakening of the social fabric in the Philippines.[23] The growing distrust was not helped by hearings before the Senate Sub-Committee on US Security Agreements and Commitments Abroad (the Symington Hearings) in the autumn of 1969 at which Senators Symington and Fulbright indicated that they did not believe the United States should respond to an attack on the Philippines unless American forces were attacked. Fulbright also criticized retention of the bases on the grounds that they supported the existing political regime in the Philippines.[24] Against this unpromising backdrop discussions on the bases began again in October 1969 but, not surprisingly, failed to make progress.

[23] Ibid. 100.
[24] The Symington Hearings. Cited by Berry, 143–4.

Marcos made a formal request for further negotiations in June 1972 but once again difficulties over criminal jurisdiction, compounded on this occasion by the onset of Watergate, caused discussions to be suspended in July 1974. With the resignation of President Nixon and the advent of President Ford, Marcos raised the issue once again, hinting that the Philippines would abrogate the 1947 agreement unless better terms were obtained. On a visit to Manila in December 1975, Ford agreed to further negotiations 'in clear recognition of Philippine sovereignty'. A new round of negotiations started in 1976, with the Americans seeking to show their resolve to remain in Asia following the withdrawal from Vietnam, and Marcos intent on increasing US military and economic assistance. At the end of the year, in the lame duck period between the Ford and Carter administrations, Henry Kissinger made an offer of aid worth $1 billion over five years for retention of the bases. Marcos refused this and in February 1977, negotiations were resumed with a Democrat administration under President Carter, who had made concern for human rights one of the main features of his election campaign. On the American side, the negotiations were initially handled by the young Richard Holbrooke, later to make his name at the peace talks on Bosnia held at Dayton, Ohio, in 1995, but then only thirty-five and Assistant Secretary of State for Asia.

After three years of negotiations, involving interventions by Vice-President Mondale and Senator Daniel Inouye of Hawaii, who warned Marcos that Congress would not approve the aid figure proposed by Kissinger, an agreement was reached early in 1979. This agreement, officially titled 'Arrangements Regarding Delineation of US Facilities at Clark Air Base and Subic Naval Base' [25] was regarded as an amendment to the Military Bases Agreement of 1947 rather than a new agreement. It was signed by the Foreign Minister, Carlos Romulo, and Richard Murphy, the American Ambassador, on 7 January 1979 and met many of the host nation's demands. Reductions were agreed in the size of the bases at Subic Bay and, more extensively, Clark Airfield where 100,000 acres, or 90 per cent of the overall base area, was returned to the Philippine authorities. All bases occupied by American forces were recognized for the first time as military establishments belonging to the Philippine government. Consistent with practice in NATO and elsewhere, the Philippine flag was to be flown at the bases and Filipino base comman-

---

[25] Full title: Arrangements Regarding Delineation of United States Facilities at Clark Air Base and Subic Naval Base; Powers and Responsibilities of the Philippine Base Commanders and Related Powers of the United States Facility Commanders and the Tabones Complex. Signed 7 January 1979. TIAS 9224.

ders were to be appointed with responsibility for perimeter security at the bases. However, Article II was to cause some difficulties in the future by enjoining the Philippine and American commanders at the bases to be guided by the seemingly incompatible objectives of 'full respect for Philippine sovereignty on the one hand and the assurance of unhampered US military operations on the other'.

On aid, the United States undertook, in parallel letter from President Carter, to make 'best efforts' to secure a sum of $0.5 billion from Congress over the next five years. This was a good result for the Americans, representing only 50 per cent of the figure previously offered by Kissinger and rejected by Marcos. Nevertheless, it was still a huge increase over the $45 million agreed in 1966, and such a sum made it increasingly difficult to preserve the fiction that this was not a rental payment. Furthermore, the United States was obliged to accept that the agreement would be reviewed every five years until 1991, when the revised twenty-five year lease expired. There were no changes on criminal jurisdiction since this was not a major concern of President Marcos.

With a further review due in 1984, Marcos began to prepare the ground in characteristic manner. In 1982, he secured President Reagan's agreement to further negotiations and the following year he informed visiting Congressmen that the United States would be asked to remove the bases unless a satisfactory price was obtained, indicating that he was looking for a $900 million aid package. A little later, Carlos Romulo, deploying pressure tactics once more, released a letter from the Soviet Union seeking closer military relations with the Philippines. These tactics appeared to be successful. In a surprisingly short time an agreement was reached—in June 1983—between the American and Philippine Ambassadors which restated Philippine sovereignty over the bases and endorsed the need for prior consultation over 'the operational use of the bases for military combat operations'. The United States agreed to notify the Philippine government of any major changes in force levels, equipment, or weapon systems and undertook to try to improve conditions in areas surrounding the bases, especially the towns of Olongapo and Angeles adjacent to Subic Bay and Clark Field, respectively.[26] Moreover, the Reagan administration was more accommodating than its predecessor on aid. A side letter from the President, accompanying the agreement undertook to make 'best efforts' to provide the $900 million over five years which Marcos had requested. In summary:

[26] Defense Memorandum of Agreement. Signed 1 June 1983. TIAS 10699.

To a significant extent the 1983 Amendment permitted the United States to continue to use the bases in pursuit of its own national security interests in return for increased compensation for the Marcos regime.[27]

However, the assassination of Benigno Aquino in August 1983 plunged the country into crisis and Congress declined to approve the proposed aid programme, passing a Concurrent Resolution tying future aid to free, fair, and honest elections. The 'snap elections' called in November 1985, in which Marcos declared himself the winner, clearly failed to meet this test and led directly to his downfall in February 1986. Under President Corazon (Cory) Aquino, a further review of the bases commenced in 1987 but this provided little respite for the United States. With the return of democracy to the Philippines a new Constitution had been approved by popular referendum which stipulated that foreign military bases would 'not be allowed in the Philippines, except under a treaty duly concurred in by the Senate and . . . ratified by a majority of the votes in a national referendum'. Moreover, President Aquino had been swept into power by a popular revolution hostile to the Marcos regime and consequently to the Americans, who were seen as having supported Marcos for too long. Both Aquino and Raul Manglapus, her Foreign Minister, who had long been opposed to the American presence, saw the bases as an infringement of Philippine sovereignty and determined to drive as hard a bargain as possible. They pressed for still higher aid payments and included in their demands reduction of the Philippine national debt, then standing at $30 billion.

An interim agreement was reached between Manglapus and the American Secretary of State George Shultz, in October 1988. Under this, the United States was granted access to the bases for the three years until 1991 but the cost was a package of economic and military aid worth some $480 million per annum. This was a rise of 140 per cent on the annual figure of $180 million suggested by Marcos. The United States was buying time but at very considerable cost. She may have considered this a reasonable price to pay to support the fledgling democracy established under President Aquino and subsequent negotiations showed that they were prepared to continue with a substantial level of financial support beyond 1991. But 1991 saw a combination of natural disaster, reassessment of the threat, and Philippine intransigence, as described below, that finally persuaded the United States to withdraw completely from the Philippines. Before discussing the decision on final withdrawal it is necessary to assess the value of the bases to the United States and

---

[27] Berry, op. cit. 282.

the damage done to America's standing in the world by her association with Ferdinand Marcos.

The Value of the Bases

In their heyday, the two American bases at Clark Field and Subic Bay were considered by American defence specialists as 'probably the most important basing complex in the world'.[28] In the 1970s, some 40,000 Filipinos were employed at these and other military installations throughout the Philippines. By the end of the 1980s, this figure had risen to nearly 70,000, making the American services the second largest employer in the country after the Philippine government. Clark Field, which had a complement of 8,000 servicemen in the mid 1970s and covered 130,000 acres, was the second largest US Air Force base after Vandenberg in California, with a storage capacity for aviation fuel of 25 million gallons, equivalent to that at Kennedy Airport in New York. It served as 'the US air logistics hub for the South-West Pacific.[29] The main role of the US Third Tactical Fighter Wing, stationed at Clark, was the training of US Air Force units in Korea and Japan. Associated with Clark was a large bombing and gunnery range at Crow Valley but no operational missions were flown from the base.

Subic Bay was the largest naval base west of Hawaii, with 4,500 servicemen on site in the mid 1970s, and capable of accommodating two forward based aircraft carriers. The home of eight separate US Commands, its mission was to act as a forward base and repair facility for the US Seventh Fleet. Naval repair work could be undertaken there more economically than in either the United States or Japan and as result, 60 per cent of all repair work for the Seventh Fleet was carried out in the Philippines. The four floating dry docks at the base could handle any size of warship except an aircraft carrier. On average, ten to fifteen ships per day could be docked at Subic Bay, which also embraced the largest naval supply depot in the world. The associated naval air station at Cubi Point, commissioned in 1956 after five years construction, had an 8,000-foot runway and could, if required, accommodate 400 naval aircraft on detachment from their carriers. Some distance to the north, the important communications base at San Miguel

[28] A. Cottrell and R. J. Hanks, *The Military Utility of US Bases in the Philippines* (Washington, DC: Center for Strategic and International Studies, Georgetown University, 1980).
[29] US Foreign Policy Objectives and Military Installations. Paper for the SCFR. CRS. April 1979.

provided links throughout the Pacific. In 1974, the *New York Times* described Subic Bay as 'a base that has everything a fleet could want: repair shops, an air station . . . its own mountains for ship to shore gunnery practice, enough beaches for the Marines to practise amphibious landings'.[30]

The United States military authorities regarded their bases in the Philippines as essential long before the communist threat emerged, first in the Soviet Union at the end of the Second World War and later in China. Planning during the war assumed that the bases would be used initially for the expected assault on Japan and later to underpin the role that the United States saw for herself in the Pacific. After the war, the Philippines came to represent a key element in the perimeter containment strategy developed to counter the communist threat. General MacArthur, with long-standing family links to the islands, needed no persuading of their importance. But the loss of China in 1949, the outbreak of the Korean War in 1950, and the defeat of the French in Indo-China in 1954 all greatly enhanced the strategic position of the Philippines. A paper prepared for the Joint Chiefs of Staff in 1958 said of the bases in the Philippines:

These bases are therefore an essential part of a worldwide base system designed to deter communism. Any reduction in this base system creates a point of weakness which invites communist aggression.[31]

During the Vietnam War, the bases at Subic Bay and Clark Field became staging posts for movements to and from Vietnam. Although no offensive operations were directly launched from the Philippines, Subic Bay acted as a rear base for the Seventh Fleet, accommodating 215 ship visits a month at the height of the war in 1967 with a record forty-seven ships in port in October 1968. Once the war was over there were some in the State Department who were prepared to reconsider the need for the bases. Francis Underhill, a State Department official, wrote:

Our relations with the Philippines can never be normal while our bases remain. For the Filipinos they create contradictions and strains which twist and warp every aspect of their attitudes towards us.[32]

But the Department of Defense argued that the loss of Vietnam made it more, not less, important to retain the bases in the Philippines. This

---

[30] A. Cottrell and T. Moorer, *US Overseas Bases*, Washington Paper No 47. (Beverly Hills, CA: Sage. 1977).

[31] Paper for Joint Chiefs of Staff (JCS) by Chief of Naval Operations (CNO). Cited in Brands, 270.

[32] Cited in Brands, op. cit. 305.

attitude was echoed in a study published in 1977 which concluded 'without Subic Bay the US Seventh Fleet could not possibly be maintained at its present force level and operational effectiveness'.[33] When giving evidence to the House Committee on Foreign Affairs on the 1979 agreement, Richard Holbrooke said of the bases 'They are no longer rear bases supporting forward positions on the littoral of the Asian continent. They are forward positions in the Western Pacific'.[34] This view reflected the value of the Philippine bases, not just for power projection in the Pacific and the South China Sea, but, from the mid 1970s, embracing an additional role as the main logistics base for deployments into the Indian Ocean following Britain's withdrawal from East of Suez. A report for the Senate Committee on Foreign Relations in 1979 endorsed this appreciation. 'The bases', it said, 'fulfil, or are intended to fulfil, military missions far beyond the South-West Asia or South-West Pacific area'. The authors stressed that the naval facilities in the Philippines 'are essential, or at the very least very important, to the total fulfilment of key extra-regional missions' but felt that 'Clark's contribution to major political and military objectives appears to be much less than that of Subic' and that 'a strong rationale exists for reducing the size and functions of Clark Air Base'.[35]

It was the relative scarcity of secure bases in the Indian Ocean, apart from Diego Garcia, that persuaded the Carter administration to play down the human rights record of the Marcos government and conclude the revised bases agreement in 1979. The fall of the Shah at the start of the year and the Soviet invasion of Afghanistan at the end of 1979 re-focused the strategic thinking of the United States on the Indian Ocean and the Gulf. But the lack of bases in the area underlined the importance of the Philippines. In 1980, US naval units were obliged to deploy right across the Indian Ocean from the Philippines during the abortive attempt to rescue the American hostages in Iran. This point was well recognized at the start of the Reagan administration. The initial briefing prepared for George Shultz by the State Department pulled no punches on the value of the bases:

Our relationship with the Philippines is dominated by our interests in the maintenance of unhampered use of our military facilities at Subic and Clark. The

---

[33] Cottrell and Moorer, op. cit. 56.
[34] Hearings of the House Committee on Foreign Assistance Legislation for Fiscal Year (FY) 1980–81, 65–66.
[35] CRS April 1979, 9, 64.

facilities are essential for our strategic posture in the Far East, as well as the Indian Ocean areas.[36]

The Marcos Record

But as developments during the 1970s increased the military importance of the bases for the United States, the record of the Marcos government was deteriorating rapidly, causing increasing difficulties for the Americans in political terms. This placed the United States in an acute dilemma well summarized by Ambassador David Newsom in 1977:

In seeking to achieve our current goals and objectives in the Philippines, we face a serious but not unique dilemma. We have certain national security objectives, namely the retention of our military bases, which we can only achieve by reaching agreement with a leadership considered by many in the United States—and the Philippines—to be in violation of the accepted norms of human rights.[37]

The first step in the downward spiral had occurred in 1971 when Marcos suspended Habeas Corpus. The following year, he declared martial law and thereafter ruled by decree. Benigno Aquino, the main opposition leader, was jailed, newspapers and radio and television stations were shut down, and demonstrations were banned. In response, Congress amended the Foreign Assistance Act in 1974 to reduce or terminate security assistance to foreign governments violating human rights and in 1976 an amendment to the International Security Assistance Act not only banned security assistance to governments consistently violating human rights, but required the President to make an annual report to Congress on each country receiving security assistance. The following year, the State Department listed the Philippines as one of six countries violating human rights. However, Marcos responded to this criticism with a none too subtle threat to the bases. A committee was appointed 'to determine whether the military pact with the United States effectively provided protection for the nation or increased the danger to our country because of the provocation of others'.

The elections for the National Assembly held in April 1978 were blatantly fraudulent but President Carter, who had come to office determined to take a firm stand on human rights, was obliged to swallow his scruples in order to secure a new basing agreement. The advice he

---

[36] Briefing for Schultz by Paul Wolfowitz, State Department. Cited by Brands, 312.
[37] Newsom to State Department, 15 November 1977. Cited by Brands, 312.

received from the new Ambassador, Richard Murphy, in November 1978 was uncompromising:

If the human rights report on the Philippines receives the same sort of media interpretation in 1979 as it did in 1978, which put the Philippines at the bottom of the human rights barrel in East Asia, I fear there would be a very serious impact on base agreement prospects in both the United States and the Philippines.[38]

In 1980, Benigno Aquino was released from jail and left for the United States for heart surgery. Martial law was lifted in January 1981 but the presidential elections that followed were even more suspect than the elections for the legislature in 1978. When the opposition parties boycotted the elections, Marcos persuaded a former Defence Minister, Alejo Santos, now in his seventies, to stand as his 'opponent'.

The result—as expected—was a further victory for Marcos which encouraged him to embark on wholesale plunder of his country during the 1980s. American military aid under the 1979 agreement amounted to some 25 per cent of the Philippine defence budget. This allowed the Philippine armed forces, described by Ambassador Newsom as 'the most corrupt organisation in the Philippines', to enrich themselves considerably.[39] Members of the government did the same under a system which came to be known as 'crony capitalism'. By the early 1980s, the Marcos government owned or directed one hundred corporations, including three large government holding companies—the Philippine National Bank, the Re-development Bank of the Philippines, and the National Development Company—whose assets grew by nearly 700 per cent in this period. Meanwhile, the real economy was in a tailspin. Foreign debt totalled $25 billion in October 1983, an increase of $6 billion on the previous month, and the gross national product fell by 6 per cent in 1984 and 4 per cent in 1985.

The assassination of Benigno Aquino on his return from the United States in August 1983 marked the beginning of the end. Further elections for the legislature were held in 1984, at which Marcos is alleged to have spent 5 billion pesos—or some 10 per cent of the national budget—to get his candidates returned. Facing increasing erosion of his authority, not least from criticism by the Catholic leader Cardinal Jaime Sin, Marcos brought forward the next presidential elections from 1987 to 1986. Cory Aquino decided to oppose Marcos, prompted by the acquittal of General Ver on charges of assassinating her husband. Although Marcos declared himself the winner of the election, Cory

[38] Brands, op. cit.   [39] Ibid.

Aquino refused to accept the result. A campaign of civil disobedience followed, supported by the Catholic Church, and in February 1986 the defection of both the Defence Minister and Chief of Police, together with a revolt by junior officers of the armed forces, precipitated the collapse of twenty years of corrupt misrule by the Marcos family.

The Attitude of the United States

What was the attitude of the United States to the increasingly tyrannical and corrupt behaviour of the Marcos government? Some, such as Admiral William Crowe, Commander-in-Chief Pacific Command, saw the dangers sufficiently early. In September 1984, he said 'there is no hope for my naval base with that guy as President of that country'.[40] The same point had already been made by the more responsible elements of the American press. In October 1983, George Kahin of the *New York Times* argued that the dependence of the United States on the bases in the Philippines was entangling the country in internal Philippine politics. This brought no credit to the United States and he urged that the military facilities should be transferred to Guam or Australia.[41] Some thought was being given to this fall-back solution in official circles. In September 1984, Richard Armitage, Assistant Secretary of Defense, disclosed at a Senate hearing that the United States had leased land on Guam and Tinian against the possibility of withdrawal from the Philippines.[42]

But overall successive administrations were unable to either influence Marcos or make a break with him and so supported him long after he had become a political liability. President Johnson, obsessed with the war in Vietnam, needed both the bases in the Philippines and a token engineer battalion from the Philippine army to participate in the war. Carter reluctantly shelved his concern over human rights because of strategic developments in the Indian Ocean and the Middle East. But it was Reagan who was most uncritical in his support for Marcos and only just managed to jump from the sinking ship as it went down. In September 1982, he described Marcos as 'a respected voice for reason and moderation',[43] and at a news conference on 11 February 1986, just days before the fall of Marcos, Reagan was supporting him by saying 'I don't know anything more important than those bases'.[44]

---

[40] Brands, 329. See also Karnow, 407.
[41] G. Kahin, *New York Times* 12 October 1983. Cited by Richard Betts, Global Deterrence. In *Security Interdependence in the Asia Pacific Region*. James Morley (ed.) (Lexington, MA: Lexington Books, 1986).
[42] Karnow, 407.   [43] Ibid. 388.   [44] Ibid. 414.

Even so, the freedom of manoeuvre enjoyed by the United States at these neo-colonial bases was severely constrained. Despite the dominant position of the United States in the Philippines, both militarily and economically, and the scant regard for Philippine sovereignty immediately after the Second World War, American use of the bases was subject to increasing restrictions during the post-war period. The Bohlen–Serrano Agreement of 1959 required prior consultation on any military operations not deriving directly from an attack on the Philippines. However, the Exchange of Notes accompanying the 1979 agreement stated:

Consistent with its rights and obligations under the 1947 agreement as amended, the United States shall be assured of unhampered military operations involving its forces in the Philippines.[45]

Both the United States and the Philippines may have intended to draw a distinction between day-to-day operations at the bases for training and exercise purposes and combat operations launched from the bases against other countries. But this distinction was not spelt out in the agreements and the apparent inconsistency between the obligation to consult the host nation and the right to unhampered military operations was never satisfactorily resolved.

At the same time, the Philippine government, under pressure from its Asian neighbours, was trying to demonstrate its independence from American influence. As early as 1964, Nehru had questioned whether the Philippines were fully independent and consequently eligible for the Non-Aligned Movement. Moreover as a founder member of ASEAN (Association of South East Asian Nations) in 1967, the Philippines felt uncomfortable with the Bangkok Declaration which stated that 'All foreign bases are temporary and remain only with the concurrence of the countries concerned'. In 1975, Vietnam pressed the point by arguing that the Philippines should not attend a conference of the Non-Aligned Movement because of the US military presence on her territory. Possibly in response to this criticism, the Philippines opened diplomatic relations with Vietnam in 1976 and, in a communiqué dated 12 July, both countries pledged 'not to allow any foreign country to use one's territory as a base for direct or indirect aggression and intervention against the other country or other countries in the region'.[46] This also appears to be inconsistent with the concession on 'unhampered military operations' granted to the United States in 1979. It seems that Marcos may

---

[45] Woodliffe, op. cit.
[46] Communiqué of 12 July 1976. Cited by Pringle, op. cit.

have been trying to be all things to all men but the perception in the American press was that the United States could not rely on unfettered freedom of action from the Philippine bases. An assessment by a political commentator based on an article in the *Washington Post* of 15 September 1982 concluded:

Manila's shift to a more independent policy towards the Third World and its greater stake in the Arab world for overseas jobs and oil, raised doubts about whether Washington would be assured the free use of Subic and Clark in the event of a Middle East crisis.[47]

Final Withdrawal

Following the fall of Marcos in February 1986, the Philippines prepared a new Constitution which was approved by referendum in February 1987. Under its terms the future of the bases required the approval of the Senate and subsequently a popular referendum. Another feature of the Constitution was a ban on the deployment of nuclear weapons on Philippine territory. Article II, section 8 stated that 'the Philippines, consistent with its national interest, adopts and pursues a policy of freedom from nuclear weapons in its territory'.[48] This wording went considerably further than the Senate Resolutions in 1958 forbidding the deployment of ballistic missiles and the construction of launch sites without the consent of Congress, which had been incorporated in the Bohlen–Serrano Agreement. Moreover, it could not be reconciled with the US Navy's traditional stance of neither confirming, or denying the presence of nuclear weapons on board its warships. In June 1988, the Philippine Senate passed a bill by nineteen votes to three which would, had it become law, have banned the 'development, manufacture, acquisition, testing, use, introduction or storage' of nuclear weapons in the Philippines. Although the Senate's bill was defeated in the House, these developments caused grave concern in the United States. George Shultz warned against the spread of the 'New Zealand virus' and told the Senate Appropriations Committee that the United States and the Philippines would 'have to part company' if the bill became law.[49]

Negotiations on the future of the bases commenced again in May

[47] Richard Betts, op. cit. Based on an article in the *Washington Post*, 15 September 1982.
[48] J. Gerson and B. Birchard (ed.), *The Sun Never Sets*, (Boston, MA: South End Press, 1991).
[49] *New York Times*, 17 June 1988. Cited by Berry, op. cit.

1990, since the interim agreement reached by Shultz and Manglapus was due to expire in 1991. Discussions took place against a background of violent confrontations between police and demonstrators opposed to the bases. They were not helped by the decision of the US Congress to reduce aid to the Philippines by $96 million, which Aquino regarded as a violation of the 1988 agreement. However, negotiations were interrupted on 15 June 1991 by the eruption—for the first time in 600 years—of Mount Pinatubo volcano situated some ten miles from Clark Field and twenty miles from Subic Bay. This was one of the major volcanic events of the century with a force eight times greater than that of Mount St. Helens in the United States. Clark Field was declared a total loss immediately. The naval base at Subic Bay was covered with one foot of volcanic ash but had reopened by mid July. Subsequent negotiations on the bases therefore focused on the future of Subic Bay.

After negotiations that had, on and off, stretched over fourteen months, an agreement was reached in August 1991 which would have allowed the United States to remain at Subic Bay for a further ten years subject to a 'base related compensation' package of $200 million per annum. However, in September 1991 the Philippine Senate, led by Senator Agipato Aquino, the President's brother-in-law, exercised its rights under the 1986 Constitution and rejected this agreement by twelve votes to eleven. The United States was offered a three-year phased withdrawal but declined to accept this and negotiations broke down altogether in December 1991 when President Aquino ordered American forces to leave the Philippines by the end of 1992. The mood of the country, always ambivalent about the bases, had hardened since the interim agreement of 1988 and so had President Aquino's attitude. 'The time has come', she said, 'to close the books on a colonial vestige'.[50]

With the end of the Cold War and the collapse of the Soviet Union, the United States found that she could after all manage without the bases which had earlier been regarded as indispensable. The military aircraft based at Clark Field had already been redeployed to Alaska and Clark's training functions had been reallocated elsewhere in the United States. The naval forces stationed at Subic Bay and the tasks undertaken there were redeployed mainly to Japan and Hawaii. But the United States was also able to make a virtue out of necessity by relying more on occasional access arrangements with friendly countries and less on permanent bases. The Secretary of Defense's Report

---

[50] *Financial Times*, 18 September 1991. Cited in Woodliffe, op. cit.

to the President and Congress in January 1994 summarized the position as follows:

With the loss of American bases at Clark and Subic Bay in the Philippines, the US focus has turned away from permanent basing structures towards establishing access arrangements with many nations in the area. These new arrangements range from the formal access agreement negotiated with Singapore to arrangements under consideration with such countries as Malaysia, Australia and Thailand.[51]

Panama

The US Stake in Panama

The decision to colonize the Philippines in 1898 gave added impetus to a scheme which had been under consideration by the United States for many years, to construct a canal across the Isthmus at Panama. This too was an imperial enterprise conceived on a grand scale by Theodore Roosevelt. It involved the United States in helping to separate Panama from Colombia (in contravention of earlier treaty commitments), the construction of a canal by the Army Corps of Engineers, the creation of the Canal Zone bisecting the new state, in which the United States was virtually sovereign, and the domination of Panama by the United States on a quasi-colonial basis throughout the twentieth century. As in the Philippines, the strategic importance of the Panama Canal to the United States led to an unhealthy mutual dependency between the two countries.

For much of the century control of the canal was a strategic imperative for the United States. The Panamanians, for their part, hoped for economic benefits from the canal but, as in the Philippines, keenly resented the dominant American presence in their country. The issue in Panama was not so much the military bases established there by the United States (although there were prolonged disputes over these) as the existence of the canal itself within the semi-sovereign Canal Zone. Finally, the Americans in Panama, no less than in the Philippines, found themselves increasingly locked into an acutely embarrassing relationship with the *de facto* ruler of the country who was a petty despot and racketeer. In both countries this embarrassment came to a head in the 1980s, although the host nation governments had been growing ever

---

[51] Secretary of Defense Report to the President and Congress, January 1994. Part II, 21.

more autocratic since the 1970s. Manuel Noriega in Panama shared many faults with Ferdinand Marcos in the Philippines. But he was also an acknowledged drug dealer who, after the failure of various indigenous revolts against him, had to be removed by a forceful military intervention which did little for the worldwide reputation of the United States.

The United States interest in Panama commenced in the 1840s. The Ridlack–Mallinaro Treaty, concluded in 1846, allowed American passengers unrestricted transit rights across the Isthmus, provided the United States guaranteed their security and upheld the sovereignty of Colombia over Panama. (Panama had declared independence from Spain in 1821 but had opted for incorporation in the Federation of Gran Colombia in 1822.) Under the treaty, the United States was granted the right of military intervention in Panama to protect transit facilities and this right was exercised thirteen times between 1846 and 1902 in a series of military landings lasting from one day to sixty-three days. However, it was the California gold rush, beginning in 1848, which greatly increased the number of American travellers across the Isthmus and gave rise to a sizeable American community in the country. The Panama Railroad Company, having received an exclusive concession from the government of Colombia, started work on a railway across the Isthmus in 1850 and, by agreement with the Provincial Governor, this work took place in a 'Yankee Strip' where American justice prevailed, making it the forerunner of the Canal Zone. In the period 1848–69, over 350,000 passengers travelled to California via Panama, with nearly 225,000 making the return trip. The frontier town atmosphere which prevailed at the time has been described by Michael Coniff in terms which continued to characterize the American association with Panama through to the twentieth century:

The huge American community contained many enterprising and productive people, but they tended to be arrogant, greedy, demanding, insensitive and contemptuous towards Panamanians.[52]

In effect, Panama was already a United States protectorate in all but name, as the government of Colombia increasingly left maintenance of law and order in the region to the Americans. As with the British Empire, informal imperialism preceded the bid for territory but, as the Suez Canal neared completion in 1869, William Seward, America's

---

[52] M. L. Coniff, *Panama and the United States: The Forced Alliance* (Washington, DC: University of Georgia Press, 1992). I have drawn heavily on Coniff in the account of events leading up to the 1903 Treaty and much of what follows.

expansionist Secretary of State, sent an agent to Bogotá to sign a Canal Treaty with Colombia. Treaties signed in 1869 and 1870 established a twenty-mile zone for a canal with free port facilities at each end, but the Colombian Senate rejected the first treaty and the United States Senate the second. As a result, it was a French company, headed by Ferdinand de Lesseps, fresh from his triumph at Suez, which first started work on a sea-level canal, much to the chagrin of the Americans. President Rutherford Hayes expressed the United States determination to secure control of the canal in a message to Congress in 1880:

The policy of this country is a canal under American control. The United States cannot consent to surrender this control to any European power.[53]

In pursuance of this policy, the United States mounted her largest military intervention in Panama to date in 1885, at a time when work on the French canal was in progress, to restore order following a revolt by Panama against Colombia. However, the first French canal company went bankrupt in 1888 and it was not until 1894 that a second French company was formed, which in 1898 abandoned the concept of a sea-level canal in favour of one that used locks and reservoirs.

By the end of the century, the United States was making little secret of her imperial pretensions in the area. It was in 1895 that Richard Olney, the American Secretary of State, made his renowned declaration:

The United States is practically sovereign on this continent and its fiat is law upon subjects to which it confines its interposition.[54]

The pretext for this sweeping restatement of the Monroe Doctrine was a dispute between Britain and Venezuela over the precise borders of British Guiana, on which the United States wished to arbitrate. The details of the dispute have long been forgotten but Olney's provocative phrase was taken as a clear indication that the United States intended to play an imperial role in the affairs of Central and South America.

Matters came to a head as a result of the Spanish-American War of 1898. The Treaty of Paris established the United States as a Pacific power by transferring to her Spain's colonies in the Philippines, Guam, and Wake Island. The acquisition of these Pacific territories also persuaded the United States to annex Hawaii. With colonial possessions spanning the Pacific, the need for an American-controlled canal at Panama became compelling. It had, for example, taken the *USS Oregon* sixty-

---

[53] Coniff, op. cit.
[54] G. Smith, *The Last Years of the Monroe Doctrine* (New York: Hill & Wang, 1994, 24).

eight days to sail from San Francisco to Cuba via Cape Horn to join the battle of Santiago de Cuba.

The 1903 Treaty and Construction of the Canal

Events now unfolded swiftly in favour of the United States. In 1899, Colombia was again wracked by an insurrection, known as the War of a Thousand Days, which rekindled Panama's hopes of independence and gave the United States a further justification for renewed military intervention. Meanwhile, the second French company had no greater success with its canal than the first. Theodore Roosevelt became President of the United States in 1901 and the following year the Spooner Act gave him authority to negotiate with Colombia for the construction of a canal in Panama. Early in 1903, a treaty was agreed between the two Foreign Ministers (the Hay–Herran Treaty) which, for a consideration of $10 million, gave the United States the right to construct a canal and take a 100-year lease on territory either side of the route. But this treaty was rejected by the government of Colombia, leading those Panamanians with an interest in the canal and their own independence to become concerned that the United States would turn to an alternative route through Nicaragua. They therefore began plotting secession from Colombia and at the same time engaged Philippe Burnau-Varilla, a Frenchman formerly employed on the abortive canal planned by de Lesseps, as their agent to maintain contact with the United States. Burnau-Varilla visited Roosevelt and Hay in Washington, who convinced him that the United States would support an independent Panama, notwithstanding the provisions of the Ridlack–Mallinaro Treaty.

In November 1903, a further revolt broke out in Panama against Colombia. The *USS Nashville* was on hand to provide protection for the new nation which was immediately recognized by the United States. Colombia failed to recover the secessionist province, but the threat of recovery allowed Burnau-Varilla to conclude a treaty for the construction of a canal on behalf of the Panamanians which was exceptionally favourable to the Americans. This treaty was signed by Burnau-Varilla while the official Panamanian delegation was still sailing to the United States to commence negotiations. The Panamanians threatened to disown the treaty but Burnau-Varilla persuaded them that, if they did so, the United States would withdraw her protection for the new nation, leaving it to be reabsorbed by Colombia. Faced with a *fait accompli*, Panama reluctantly approved the treaty on 2 December 1903.

The Hay–Burnau-Varilla Treaty was based on the Hay–Herran Treaty which Colombia had earlier rejected. It gave the United States the right to build and operate a ship canal across the Isthmus of Panama and created a Canal Zone ten miles wide. The United States was to be the sole protector of the canal and was empowered to acquire any other land 'where necessary and convenient' for this purpose. The concession was to last 'in perpetuity' and the United States was granted the right to intervene in the internal affairs of Panama 'to re-establish public peace and constitutional order'. The United States agreed to guarantee the independence of Panama, but had to a large extent compromised that independence by acquiring an area of some 500 square miles in the centre of the country over which she was virtually sovereign. The key passages on the status of the Canal Zone ran as follows:

Panama grants to the United States all the rights, power and authority . . . which the United States would possess and exercise if it were the sovereign of the territory . . . to the entire exclusion of the exercise by the Republic of Panama of any such sovereign rights, power or authority.[55]

This was an unequal treaty, even by the standards of the time. Philippe Burnau-Varilla, although employed by the Panamanians as their agent, had sold out to the United States. The infant republic had to make the best of a bad job. In May 1904, Panama formally transferred the Canal Zone to United States jurisdiction. Moreover, Article 136 of the Constitution of Panama gave the United States the right to use troops to keep the peace throughout the country. It is little wonder that a British diplomat commented in 1910, 'It is really farcical to talk of Panama as an independent state. It is simply an annex to the Canal Zone'.[56]

The US Army Corps of Engineers succeeded where the two French canal projects had failed. Construction of the American canal commenced in 1904 and was completed ten years later on the day that Germany invaded Belgium in 1914. The entry of the United States into the First World War in 1917 put the Canal Zone onto a war footing. Work on Fort Clayton, the first of a series of military fortifications, had started in 1911 and the senior American Army officer now assumed the powers of governor in the Canal Zone. The extent of American dominance over the country as a whole was demonstrated by the fact that American troops were used to supervise elections in 1908, 1912, and 1918. The United States also occupied Chiriqui province, on the border with Costa Rica, until 1920, but dropped a plan to build bases on the island of Taboga in the face of public protest.

---

[55] Cited in Coniff, op. cit.   [56] Coniff, op. cit. 80.

The American Military Presence

In the inter-war period, further military bases were constructed both within the Canal Zone and outside. The largest base outside the zone was the Rio Hato Air Base built on land leased from private citizens in 1939 on the Gulf of Panama and the United States War Department demanded 999-year leases on several other sites. But military expansion was offset by a treaty signed in 1936 under Franklin D. Roosevelt's 'Good Neighbor' policy which removed some of the most onerous provisions of the 1903 treaty. The protectorate status for Panama was dropped and the right to acquire additional land at will to protect the canal was ended. The annuity payment for use of the canal was increased from $250,000 to $430,000 and equal treatment was assured for American and Panamanian employees. Not surprisingly, the United States Senate was reluctant to approve this treaty and did so only in 1939.

The Second World War saw the strategic importance of the canal emphasized as never before. With the United States Navy engaged simultaneously in the Pacific and Atlantic, rapid transit between the two theatres was essential. Although attack by either Germany or Japan was unlikely, the security of the canal was given a high priority. When President Arnulfo Arias, naively encouraged by the Atlantic Charter, pressed for improved terms on the military leases and more economic aid, Roosevelt threatened to occupy the bases. The United States, even if not directly implicated, was certainly relieved when Arias was replaced by President De la Guardia in a coup in 1941. De la Guardia proved more amenable to American influence, making a declaration of war on the enemy powers in December 1941 and agreeing to requests for additional military bases. A total of 134 additional military installations were built by the Americans during the war (although many of these were simply searchlight stations or observation posts) and 69,000 American troops were deployed in Panama by 1943.

The first signs of popular resentment at the American presence emerged shortly after the war. The United States wished to retain thirteen of the 134 wartime installations outside the Canal Zone and a Defence Sites Agreement was drawn up in 1947. But there were riots in Panama City over these proposals and the Panama Assembly rejected the agreement by fifty votes to nil, forcing the United States to abandon these installations. In 1953, President José Remón called for further changes to the 1903 treaty but the agreement reached in 1955 did not alter the fundamentals. The annuity payment for the canal was increased to $1.93 million and certain railroad properties in Panama City and

Colón were returned to Panama. However, the United States secured a continued lease for the use of Rio Hato Air Base and refused to accept any changes to those provisions of the 1903 treaty which granted virtual sovereignty to the United States within the Canal Zone. John Foster Dulles, the American Secretary of State, insisted that bases constructed within the Canal Zone were authorized under the 1903 treaty.

Nationalist Pressure for Change

As was to be expected, the Suez crisis in 1956 had a considerable impact on Panama. The United States maintained that the situations in Panama and Suez were quite different. President Eisenhower, who had been instrumental in the humiliation of Britain and France over Suez, was most anxious with regard to Panama 'to head off any developments ... comparable to what had occurred in Egypt'.[57] A package of wage increases and social improvements was introduced in the Canal Zone. But the seeds of political protest had been sown. In 1958, the first 'flag riots' occurred as a result of students trying to display the Panamanian flag in the Canal Zone. The following year fighting resumed, with 120 people wounded, several by American soldiers. Although Eisenhower agreed in 1960 to the Panamanian flag being flown alongside the Stars and Stripes in the zone, further flag demonstrations broke out in 1964, leading to renewed violence, which left twenty-four Panamanians and four Americans dead. On this occasion, Panama broke off diplomatic relations with the United States in protest. In response, President Johnson agreed to make concessions and in September 1965 it was announced that the United States was prepared to abrogate the 1903 treaty, acknowledge Panama's sovereignty over the canal, and share the responsibility for operating it. By 1967, these principles had been incorporated in three draft treaties. One provided for joint administration of the canal until 1999, another gave the United States the right to dig a new sea-level canal, and the third gave the United States the right to defend the canal for one hundred years.

Despite the radical shift in the American position represented by these draft treaties, they did not satisfy public opinion in Panama. The commission proposed to run the Canal Zone was still dominated by the Americans and the continuation of the American bases, which were to remain until 2004, was deeply unpopular. President Robles was impeached on grounds of corruption but also for his part in negotiating

---

[57] Coniff, op. cit.

the treaties. Nevertheless, the United States had for the first time been prepared to concede sovereignty over the Canal Zone to Panama and the way had been cleared for final revision of the 1903 Treaty. Further discussions took place in 1974 between Henry Kissinger and veteran Special Envoy Ellsworth Bunker for the United States and Foreign Minister Juan Tack for Panama. An agreement was initialled in February 1975 which, among other provisions, reduced the fourteen main American bases to four. However, this was blocked in Congress by Senators Strom Thurmond and Jesse Helms, strongly supported by Governor Reagan of California. When progress stalled, President Omar Torrijos, who had seized power from Arnulfo Arias in October 1968, tried to apply pressure to the United States by re-establishing diplomatic relations with Cuba (rather as Marcos would play the Vietnam card in the Philippines). But serious negotiations had to wait for the advent of the Carter administration in 1977.

The 1977 Canal Treaty

President Carter saw the Panama Canal as an obstacle to better relations with South America as a whole and he had made renegotiation of the 1903 treaty a campaign issue. For good measure he had added:

I will certainly look with favor on the possible reduction in the number of bases . . . possibly a reduction in the number of military forces we have there.[58]

In resuming negotiations in 1977, the new administration was able to build both on President Johnson's proposed treaties and on the further drafts agreed between Kissinger and Tack. The treaty agreed in 1977, twenty years after the Suez crisis, set an end date of the turn of the century for a quasi-colonial arrangement which had become increasingly difficult to justify. But, in making concessions, the United States was no doubt influenced in part by the fact that the strategic rationale for the canal was now much diminished. The US Navy now maintained separate fleets in the Atlantic and Pacific. Large American warships, particularly aircraft carriers, could not use the canal and the proportion of American seaborne trade passing through the canal was dropping year by year.

The terms of the 1977 treaty closely resembled those agreed ten years earlier under Johnson. The United States agreed to cede legal jurisdiction over the canal over a period of three years, but administrative

---

[58] Carter, 2 June 1976. Cited by W. LaFeber, *The Panama Canal* (Oxford: OUP, 1989).

responsibility for the canal was to be shared until 1999, with an American majority on the nine-member Panama Canal Commission until 1989. The United States also agreed to withdraw her forces from Panama by 31 December 1999. After that date 'only the Republic of Panama shall operate the canal and maintain military forces, defence sites and military installations within its national sovereignty'. In the interim period, the bases were divided into defence sites, to remain under American control until 1999, and other 'areas of military co-ordination' where security responsibility would be shared. The United States also undertook 'to endeavor to maintain its armed forces in normal times at a level not in excess of' the levels prior to the treaty. A separate Implementation Agreement empowered the United States to 'station, train and move military forces within Panama', but this agreement enjoined the United States to ensure that her armed forces abstained from any interference in the internal affairs of Panama.[59] Even so significant residual rights were retained by the United States. The Canal Treaty gave her the right 'to protect and defend the canal' and the parallel Neutrality Treaty, guaranteeing the permanent neutrality of the waterway, included an amendment by Senator Byrd of West Virginia to the effect that the two nations 'shall have the right to act against any aggression or threat directed against the canal or against the peaceful transit of vessels through the canal'.[60]

The Panama Canal Treaty was approved by referendum in Panama and ratified by the US Senate in April 1978 by sixty-eight votes to thirty-two, one more than the two-thirds majority required. But the terms had provoked bitter controversy in Congress. Senator De Concini of Arizona said he could only support the treaty if it contained a condition allowing the United States to intervene to safeguard the canal after 1999 'including the use of military force in Panama to reopen the canal'.[61] The final text therefore included a perpetual right for the United States to intervene if the neutrality, security, or functioning of the canal was threatened and Panama reluctantly accepted this. Moreover, Senator Nunn of Georgia had introduced a further last-minute condition in March 1978 stating that nothing in the treaty should preclude the two nations from conducting negotiations towards the maintenance of United States military facilities in Panama after 1999.[62] The

[59] J. Woodliffe, *The Peacetime Use of Foreign Military Bases* (Dordrecht: Martinus Nijhoff, 1992).
[60] United States Foreign Policy Objectives and Overseas Military Installations. Report for the SCFR. CRS April 1979.
[61] LaFeber, op. cit.   [62] CRS April 1979.

way was therefore open for a continued American military presence into the next century if agreed by both parties.

It could be argued that the various amendments written into both the Panama Canal Treaty and the Neutrality Treaty in the US Senate, after negotiations had been concluded between the two governments, tilted the agreements further in favour of the United States. But the fact that the two treaties were approved by the Senate owed much to enlightened self-interest. A report prepared for the Senate Sub-Committee on Foreign Relations shortly after the debates on the treaties concluded:

It was the sense of the Senate that the security of the Panama Canal would be best served by responding to the national aspirations of the Panamanian people.[63]

The point was made that the canal, operated by a series of locks, was highly vulnerable to sabotage 'that would have been likely had Pana-manian nationalism been fostered by a Senate rejection of the treaties', and that no reasonable number of American troops could have pro-tected the canal in the face of nationalist subversion.

Role of the Bases

At the time of the 1977 treaty the United States had eleven significant military bases in Panama, all in the Canal Zone, together with the Head-quarters of Southern Command at Quarry Heights. The Rio Hato Air Base had been returned to Panama some years earlier when Tor-rijos had refused a request to extend the lease. This left Howard and Albrook Air Force Bases, built in 1948, one on each side of Panama City, three relatively small naval bases, and six major army bases. Of the army bases, those at Forts Clayton, Davis, Kobbe, and Armador, at which American infantry units were stationed, were designed to defend the canal. But at Fort Sherman, the US Army had set up a jungle warfare training school during the Second World War and at Fort Gulick, the School of the Americas had been established in 1946. This facility had trained over 30,000 military officers from all over Latin America by the 1970s. Torrijos himself was a graduate of the school but he later demanded its removal, characterizing it as 'this great colonial encampment'.[64] Neither of these bases could be justified as defending the canal. Moreover, those bases whose primary role was to defend

---

[63] Ibid. 204.   [64] LaFeber, op. cit.

the canal also had secondary objectives, such as intelligence gathering, and command and control of United States forces deployed elsewhere in Latin America. The Panamanians understandably felt that the American troops in their country, numbering some 10,000 at this time, were stationed there not for the common defence of the two countries but to serve the national interests of the United States. This bred considerable resentment, particularly when, during the 1980s, American national interests were pursued in alliance with Colonel Manuel Noriega.

The Noriega Problem

President Torrijos died in a plane crash in July 1981, leaving a vacuum to be filled by Colonel Noriega. Noriega had played a key part in helping Torrijos survive a counter coup in December 1969 and since 1970 had been head of the Panamanian intelligence service. As such, he had developed close links with the Central Intelligence Agency (CIA) and these were to be revived in the 1980s when the CIA was actively involved in Panama on programmes supporting the Contras in Nicaragua and the junta in El Salvador. In 1984, the supply of arms to the Contras by the United States became unlawful for a short period as a result of legislation passed by Congress. In pursuing this policy clandestinely, Colonel Oliver North and his associates made Noriega a co-conspirator in an illegal scheme, a role which Noriega eagerly embraced believing that it gave him a further hold over the US authorities.

Noriega was not to head the Panamanian government until December 1989, shortly before the American invasion to remove him. Instead, he preferred to remain the power behind the throne, rigging elections to ensure that his preferred candidate became President and deposing him later when he became too independent. From 1982 to 1986 Panama had five puppet Presidents of this kind. One such was Nicolás Barletta, made president by Noriega in 1984, although the veteran Arnulfo Arias, now 83, appeared to have won his third ill-fated election for president. The American Secretary of State George Shultz attended Barletta's inauguration and this was seen as a further sign that the United States was prepared to turn a blind eye to Noriega's malpractices. However, Barletta did not last long. In July 1985, he was removed from office by Noriega who felt that he was applying the economic strictures of the International Monetary Fund too rigorously.

From 1983 onwards, Noriega was *de facto* Commander of the Panama

Defence Forces, described by Representative Steven Solarz of New York as 'the closest thing to a government version of the Mafia anywhere in the world'.[65] (One is reminded of Gladstone's notorious description of conditions in the Kingdom of the Two Sicilies in 1851 as 'the negation of God erected into system of Government'.) The rackets run by Noriega and his military colleagues included the control of duty-free shops, and the sale of visas, passports, and residence permits. But above all, Noriega was involved in the drug trade, having forged close links with the Medellín cartel in Colombia. Colombian cocaine was shipped through Panama and Panamanian banks were used to launder the proceeds. This was known to certain United States authorities who nevertheless condoned his activities in return for help in the campaign against the Contras.

The parallels with American tolerance of President Marcos are uncanny. In September 1985, Noriega arranged for the assassination of Hugo Spadafora, a political opponent who had begun to publicize his drug-dealing activity. As with the assassination of Benigno Aquino in the Philippines, this marked the beginning of the end for Noriega. In 1986, his drug trafficking and other criminal activities were exposed by Seymour Hersch in the *New York Times*. The following year, the Iran–Contra scandal broke in the United States and Noriega's role in this emerged. In February 1988, the Department of Justice filed indictments against him in Florida on thirteen counts of drug trafficking and racketeering. The Department had at one point thought of naming the whole of the Panama Defence Forces as a racketeering enterprise, but decided against it. Following the indictment, President Delvalle tried to dismiss Noriega but found himself ousted and replaced by a puppet President, Manuel Solís Palma. These events provoked a period of increasing opposition in Panama, met by ruthless repression, further fraudulent elections, more than one attempted coup, and intense pressure by the United States behind the scenes to persuade Noriega to step down.

But the policies pursued by certain United States authorities in Central America had created a monster which they could no longer control. In May 1989, Noriega invalidated an election which independent observers considered had been won by Dr Guillermo Endara. The United States stepped up sanctions. The Organisation of American States attempted to mediate. But the Panama Defence Forces, thoroughly corrupted by Noriega, stood by him despite the economic

[65] Ibid.

collapse of the country and the breakdown of law and order. Noriega resisted all attempts to depose him, both by the Panamanians and the Americans. On 15 December, the Panamanian National Assembly was induced to declare that the country was 'in a state of war with the United States'. Attacks on American servicemen intensified. One Marine officer was shot dead and another American serviceman was wounded. A third was beaten up while his wife was threatened. In the end, President Bush had little option but to order military intervention and Operation Just Cause was launched on 20 December 1989.

Although the cause was undoubtedly just, the circumstances were a severe setback for the image of the United States in Latin America. Just twelve years after the Canal Treaty and ten years before the final American withdrawal from Panama, the United States found herself obliged to revert to a colonial style intervention of the kind specifically ruled out in the treaties of 1977. A force of 24,000 troops was used, half of whom were already stationed in Panama, giving other host nations around the world some cause for concern over American respect for their sovereignty. This was the largest American force deployed in Latin America since the Spanish-American War in 1898 and the largest operation conducted by the United States anywhere in the world between Vietnam and the Gulf War. The invasion was roundly condemned by the Organisation of American States, by twenty votes to one, and deplored by the international community at large. Although exact numbers are far from certain, it is estimated that over 500 were killed including 27 American servicemen. After a farcical stand-off at the Papal Nuncio's residence, Noriega, despite his record still the *de facto* head of a friendly government, was flown to Florida for trial, even though the United States had no jurisdiction over his activities in Panama. He was subsequently sentenced to 40 years imprisonment in the United States for drug trafficking and related offences in April 1992.

Dr Endara, who was not consulted over the arrest and removal of Noriega, was sworn in as the new President by the American authorities at Albrook Air Force Base. Not surprisingly, he was widely seen as an American puppet and this impression was confirmed by his subsequent actions. In July 1990, it became known that his government had accepted American funds to set up a Council for Public Security which was to maintain links with the CIA and in December, Endara sought the assistance of American forces in suppressing an uprising in contravention of the 1977 Canal Treaty. For this, moves were made to impeach him in March 1991 but the case was dismissed by the Legislative Assembly.

The Future

Although the Panama Canal Treaty of 1977 clearly provided for the withdrawal of American forces from Panama by 31 December 1999, both parties began to have second thoughts as the deadline approached. In January 1992, the United States was proposing to accelerate the rundown and 3,000 troops were withdrawn the following year. Southern Command, which had assumed responsibility for American forces in the Caribbean from Atlantic Command in June 1997, moved from Panama to Miami in October and US Army units were redeployed to Puerto Rico. However, the Clinton administration had meanwhile developed plans to retain a residual military presence in Panama to combat the drug trade and the US Senate unanimously adopted a resolution proposed by Senator Jesse Helms urging the government to renegotiate the withdrawal provisions of the Canal Treaty. For their part, the Panamanians began to face up to the economic consequences of withdrawal. It was realized that the bases contributed some $500 million a year to the local economy and that little progress had been made with plans to convert the American military infrastructure—some 43,000 acres of land and 5,000 buildings—to economic use. In May 1993, a poll in the newspaper *La Prensa* indicated that 70 per cent of Panamanians wanted the Americans to stay.

In these circumstances, a delicate game of cat and mouse developed. Neither side wished to make the first move. The government of Panama, hoping to secure compensation for the extension of American basing rights, feigned indifference and waited to be wooed. The United States, thinking of a limited residual presence without significant payment, did not wish to appear too eager. However, Clinton agreed to explore the options with President Pérez Balladares, who in September 1995 confirmed for the first time that an American military presence might remain in Panama beyond 1999. By now, the United States was thinking in terms of a multinational centre to counter drug trafficking (the Centro Multilátero Antinarcótico) which she felt might be more acceptable to the government of Panama. It was envisaged that this might be located at Howard Air Force Base with some 2,500 troops and a number of surveillance aircraft whose mission would be to identify and track drug traffickers rather than conduct operations against them. In February 1997, William Cohen, the American Defense Secretary, stated that 'It will be important that we have some sort of residual contact and presence in Panama'.[66] John Negroponte was appointed to head the

---

[66] *Janes Defence Weekly*, 12 February 1997.

American negotiating team on the project in November but, with both countries reluctant to take the initiative, substantive negotiations were slow to commence. In his annual report to the President and Congress in April 1997, William Cohen would go no further than to say:

The two Governments agreed to hold exploratory talks to discuss possible stationing of some forces in Panama beyond December 31 1999 in order to promote stability and improve the co-ordination, co-operation and synchronisation of counter drug activities in the region.[67]

It therefore seemed likely, as the century drew to a close, that the United States would be bidding to retain a residual presence in Panama and that the local government would be striving to drive a hard bargain for the privilege. However, the government of Panama, conscious of growing domestic opposition to the retention of anything resembling an American base after 1999, declined to sign a bilateral accord with the United States on the Centro Multilátero Antinarcótico. In January 1998 discussions began with Brazil, Colombia, and Mexico in an attempt to give a more convincing multinational character to the project, but these broke down in June and the United States was obliged to look elsewhere for a base in Latin America to counter drug trafficking.

Conclusion

The State of Panama was largely a creation of the United States by virtue of the assistance given to the new nation in her bid to free herself from Colombia. In playing the role of midwife to the new nation, the United States was able to secure a highly advantageous treaty for the construction of the Panama Canal and with it the acquisition of an extraterritorial military base in a prime strategic location. It is scarcely surprising that Panama, bisected by the Canal Zone in which the United States was virtually sovereign, became an American colony in all but name. There could be no pretence, as there was in other host nations, that American forces were stationed in the country for any other purpose than the furtherance of the United States own strategic interests, both in Panama and elsewhere in Central America.

What is surprising is that, faced with endemic protest against the American military presence and political dominance, the United States should have agreed in the late 1970s to withdraw from Panama by the end of the century. Although this decision was taken far later than the

---

[67] Annual Report by the Secretary of Defense to the President and Congress for FY 1998. Published April 1997. (USGPO, 15).

comparable processes of de-colonization undertaken by the European powers, the Panama Canal Treaty nevertheless represented the first deliberate decision to withdraw from an element of the United States global security system. The decision pre-dated the end of the Cold War by a decade and, although undoubtedly influenced by the declining strategic significance of the Canal, owed more to the belated recognition that the quasi-colonial position of the United States in Panama was no longer compatible with the forces of nationalism and self-determination which America was pledged to support. In a speech to the General Assembly of the Organisation of American States in June 1978, President Carter expressed the hope that the Canal Treaty would mark 'the beginning of a new era of inter-American understanding reflecting a new spirit of commitment and cooperation'.[68] At the time, this was a widely held view in Washington. Although the treaty was concluded by Carter, who staked the reputation of his administration on securing ratification from the Senate, much of the preparatory work had been undertaken in earlier years by Johnson and Kissinger.

However, the United States was to find, in common with the European powers before her, that disengagement from a quasi-colonial position could sometimes be just as difficult as acquiring or maintaining such a position. In Panama, these difficulties were compounded for the United States by the fact that withdrawal was announced twenty years before it was due to be completed and that in the interim period she chose, in pursuit of President Reagan's policies in Nicaragua and El Salvador, to use her position in Panama as a base for controversial and, at times, unlawful activities in Central America. These activities involved an association with Manuel Noriega on the part of various US agencies which could neither be justified nor adequately controlled. And, in turn, this association led inexorably to a further act of colonial intervention by the United States in the internal affairs of Panama in 1989. Although discussions were held in 1998 with a view to retaining a residual United States military presence in Panama beyond 1999, based on a multinational centre to counter drug trafficking, these proved abortive and, as the end of the century approached, it looked as though the withdrawal of American forces would be completed as planned, bringing to an end almost 100 years of quasi-colonial status for the country.

---

[68] Speech to the General Assembly of the OAS, 21 June 1978. Cited in CRS April 1979.

Guantánamo

History of the Base

The great naval base at Guantánamo fits less easily into a chapter on
neo-colonial bases than those in the Philippines and Panama. Events in
Cuba had been the pretext for the Spanish-American war of 1898 but,
ironically, Cuba was allowed to gain her independence in 1902, after a
short period of United States occupation, whereas Puerto Rico and all
Spain's former colonies in the Pacific were annexed. In the period
leading up to the war, Congress had passed a Resolution demanding
that Spain relinquish sovereignty over the island but pledging that the
United States would not 'assume sovereignty, jurisdiction or control' in
her place. The mood was very different after the war and these scruples
were not applied to the Philippines, Guam, Puerto Rico, or even Hawaii.
Even so, the United States imposed considerable restrictions on Cuba's
independence. The Platt Amendment of 1901 gave the United States the
right to intervene in Cuba and maintain military bases there. This piece
of American legislation was incorporated in the Constitution of the
newly independent Cuba in 1902 as a quid pro quo for American withdrawal, and the right that it conferred was exercised with little com-
punction in the early years of the century. Both in 1912 and 1917, United
States Marines were landed in Cuba to keep the peace and protect
American property following insurrections against the government.
Cuba was also used as a base from which to deploy American troops to
Haiti in 1915 and to the Dominican Republic in 1916. In this sense a
quasi-colonial relationship existed between the United States and Cuba
until the overthrow of Fulgencio Batista by Fidel Castro in 1959. Certainly the terms and conditions on which the United States retained the
base at Guantánamo could not be described as those freely negotiated
between independent sovereign powers.

Guantánamo is the oldest United States base on foreign territory and
the first example of what is here termed the 'leasehold empire'. The
Treaty of Relations signed by the United States and Cuba in May 1903
leased the land required for the base indefinitely. The duration of the
lease was to be 'for the time required for the purposes of coaling and
naval stations', which in effect meant for as long as the United States
wished to retain the base. The annual rent was fixed at $2,000 in gold,
which was reassessed as $3,386 in 1934 when the United States went off
the gold standard, and recalculated again in 1959 at only $3,403. Article
III of the treaty contained language on sovereignty very similar to that

found in the Hay–Burnau–Varilla Treaty with Panama concluded at the same time. The relevant clauses read:

While on the one hand the United States recognises the continuance of the ultimate sovereignty of . . . Cuba over the . . . areas of land and water on the other
. . . Cuba consents that . . . the United States shall exercise complete jurisdiction and control over and within the said areas.[69]

In 1934, a new Treaty of Relations was signed between the United States and Cuba. Under this, the United States right of intervention set out in the Platt Amendment and incorporated in the 1903 treaty was dropped. But the United States retained the lease on Guantánamo which, together with other provisions of the 1903 treaty, was to remain in force 'until the two contracting parties agreed to the modification or abroga-tion of the stipulations'.[70] In effect there was no change to the right enjoyed by the United States to remain at the base as long as she wished since the treaty could only be amended by consent.

Value of the Base

Guantánamo has been described as the best deep water port in the Caribbean. It is a natural harbour some 14 miles across with a rapidly sloping ocean floor to 150 fathoms which can accommodate fifty war-ships at a time. The overall area of the base comprises 45 square miles on the south-eastern tip of Cuba opposite Haiti. One-third of this area is water. There are some 1,400 buildings at the base, which is protected by a 24-mile perimeter fence and overlooked by hills with gun emplace-ments capable of threatening the whole base area if artillery were installed in them. The base area was also dependent until 1964 on sup-plies of fresh water from mainland Cuba (in this respect resembling the dependency of Hong Kong on mainland China). When Castro cut off the water supply in February 1964, water was brought in by tanker and has subsequently been provided by desalination plants. There are two airstrips in the base area, one with a runway of 8,000 feet, but no combat units are permanently stationed at Guantánamo. For most of the Cold War period the main units at the base were the Fleet Training Group and Fleet Marine Ground Defense Force. In 1978, there were 1,800 US Navy personnel stationed at the first of these units and 400 US Marines

---

[69] J. Woodliffe, *The Peacetime Use of Foreign Military Bases* (Dordrecht: Martinus Nijhoff, 1992).
[70] Ibid.

at the second. A report for the Senate Committee on Foreign Relations in 1979 concluded:

The military value of Guantánamo rests more on its availability in the event of a contingency . . . than in its day-to-day peacetime training function which presumably could, if necessary, be performed at other bases with training responsibilities.[71]

As with other Caribbean bases, including some of those leased from Britain, Guantánamo had a significant role to play in the Second World War. It guarded the approach routes to the Panama Canal and the Windward Passage between Cuba and Haiti. The base also served as an assembly point for convoys proceeding across the Atlantic. Since the war, the base has served mainly as a training facility for the US Atlantic Fleet, complementing Roosevelt Roads at Puerto Rico. While Batista remained in power there was little friction between the US Navy and the Cuban authorities. US Ambassador Philip Bonsal wrote of his expectations when taking up his appointment in 1959:

I assumed that the treaty under which the United States held the Guantánamo naval base would remain in force. It was nevertheless my hope (which I kept to myself) that it might be possible eventually . . . to achieve a modification of the status of Guantánamo that would give Cuba a participation in its operation similar to that enjoyed by our NATO allies in the American bases on their soil. But unfortunately the Cuban-American alliance was to be destroyed, not modified.[72]

The Base in Baulk

The seizure of power by Fidel Castro in 1959 and his subsequent adoption of communism has left Guantánamo in a unique position as the only American base in a communist country. Throughout the subsequent thirty years of acute hostility between the United States and Cuba, the base remained on the island as the victim of an uneasy stalemate on the chessboard of the Cold War. Despite the abortive Bay of Pigs invasion in 1961, the missile crisis and the accompanying naval blockade in 1962, a continuing trade embargo and the absence of diplomatic relations, neither the United States nor Cuba has made any decisive move to modify the status quo. Castro could, if he wished, abrogate

---

[71] United States Foreign Policy Objectives an Overseas Military Installations. Report for the SCFR. CRS April 1979.

[72] P. Bonsal, *Cuba, Castro and the United States* (Pittsburgh, PA: University of Pittsburgh Press, 1972).

the 1903 lease, despite the need for bilateral agreement in the 1934 treaty, but has clearly feared an outright American invasion if he did so. He has therefore declined to accept the peppercorn rent and contented himself with harassing the base from time to time, for example by cutting off the water supply in 1964 in retaliation for the seizure of four Cuban fishing vessels off Florida by the United States. During the missile crisis Castro tried to make the withdrawal of American forces from Guantánamo one of the Russian conditions for ending the crisis, but Khruschev ignored him.[73] For their part, the Americans have been equally reluctant to take any provocative action which might lead to further pressure on the base. It is noticeable that no land-based operations against Cuba from Guantánamo were contemplated during the missile crisis, although reinforcements were sent to the base. Reinforcements were again despatched to Cuba in 1979 by President Carter in response to a scare, which proved to be unfounded, that a new Soviet combat brigade had been established on the island. In an uncharacteristic piece of sabre-rattling, Carter authorized a mock amphibious landing. 1,800 Marines were involved and they stayed at the base for a month.

Earlier in 1979, the report prepared by the Congressional Research Service had concluded that Guantánamo 'has military value but is not indispensable'.[74] Both the training and surveillance functions could be carried out at Roosevelt Roads in Puerto Rico. That judgement is probably still valid today, although the value has become more symbolic than real. Although the huge base is now something of an anachronism, the United States cannot, for political reasons, make significant reductions in her military presence at Guantánamo, far less withdraw from the base. In 1999, 1,000 US Navy personnel and 400 US marines remained at the base. The military value of the base has already diminished with the collapse of the Soviet Union and will diminish further with the American withdrawal from Panama in 1999. But the war of nerves with Castro continues, fuelled by conservative elements in Congress, and no American President can sanction changes at Guantánamo until relations with Cuba have returned to normal. Meanwhile, the facilities at the base give rise to periodic embarrassment since they act as a magnet for refugees, both from Cuba itself and from Haiti.

[73] C. A. Robbins, *The Cuban Threat* (New York: McGraw Hill, 1983).
[74] CRS April 1979.

5

From Conquest to Containment:
The Legacy of Occupation

At the end of the Second World War, the United States found herself with occupation forces deployed not only in Germany and Japan, the two principal enemy powers which she had defeated, but also in two associate nations whose position was less easy to determine. In Europe, Italy had made a separate peace with the allies in 1943 and had thereafter hoped to be treated as a co-belligerent. In Asia, Korea, which had been colonized by Japan in 1910, was expecting to be liberated rather than occupied. (Occupation forces were also maintained for ten years in Austria but were withdrawn following signature of the Austrian State Treaty in 1955 which guaranteed the neutrality of the country.)

The United States had not originally envisaged retaining long-term garrisons in any of these four countries, least of all in Korea, and in most of them a rapid rundown was put into effect. But the onset of the Cold War, heralded by the Prague coup and the Berlin blockade in 1948 and intensified by the Korean War in 1950, prompted the early return of American forces in substantial numbers, particularly in the divided nations of West Germany and South Korea. Although the former enemy powers and their associates all became partners in the United States global security system, playing a key role in the policy of containment, the aura of guilt, defeat, and occupation lived on, particularly in West Germany and Japan. There was tacit recognition, acknowledged during the discussions on German reunification in 1990, that the heavy concentrations of American forces in these two countries served not only to deter aggression from hostile neighbours, but also to reassure friends and allies that a resurgence by the former enemy powers would not be permitted. The phrase 'double containment', coined to describe this concept, was applied originally to Germany but it could equally well be applied, with its connotation of residual occupation, to Japan. Even in the mid 1990s, several years after the end of the Cold War, the United States pledge to maintain 100,000 troops both in Europe and Asia was built around a substantial military presence in Germany and Japan. The declared aim of these continuing deployments was to ensure stability in Central Europe and East Asia, respectively, but an undercurrent of conquest and control remained.

The residual psychology of occupation has exercised a continuing influence on the perceptions of the United States and host nations alike, with the result that the terms and conditions under which American forces remained in the four nations occupied after the war differ quite markedly from those applying elsewhere. For example, the broad acceptance of the American military presence by the authorities in Japan (if not always the people) can be contrasted with the confrontational postcolonial relationship in the Philippines which came to an end amidst mutual recrimination in 1992. And in the Mediterranean, the stationing of substantial American forces in Italy, including ground forces, has given rise to none of the political posturing and frequent renegotiation occasioned by the lesser deployments of mainly air and naval forces in Spain, Greece, and Turkey.

The legacy of American occupation needs to be considered separately in Asia and Europe because of the different strategic environments in the two continents and the different role played by the United States in these distinct theatres. In Europe, occupation was a collective undertaking. Germany was initially occupied by the four victorious powers (who remained in Berlin in this capacity until 1990) and for a short time Britain shared occupation duties in Italy with the United States. With the division of Germany and the creation of NATO, first Italy and later Germany were permitted to rearm and become fully integrated members of the Alliance. West Germany, as the nation most threatened by the Warsaw Pact, became a huge encampment for allied forces not only from the United States but also Britain and France (both former occupying powers, although no French troops were assigned to NATO after 1960), and Canada, Belgium, and the Netherlands. Although the United States was the only NATO ally to maintain forces in Italy on a permanent basis, the deployment of American troops in both West Germany and Italy, while forming part of the United States global security system, clearly served the collective aims of the North Atlantic Alliance.

In Asia, by contrast, the United States played a lone hand. Her primary concern was with Japan, which she saw as providing a key component in the great sweep of offshore islands, sometimes known as the Great Crescent, stretching from the Aleutians in the north to the Philippines in the south, from which American power could be projected over the Asian mainland. The Strategic Concept Plan adopted by the United States in October 1945 recommended:

An outer perimeter of bases from which to reconnoiter and survey possible enemy actions, to intercept his attacking forces and missiles, to deny him use of such bases and to launch counteractions.[1]

Developments in Korea were to modify this initial conception by compelling the United States to maintain substantial forces on the peninsula and the war in Vietnam embroiled American troops on the mainland of Asia for a decade. But the value of Japan lay in the long-term availability of strategic bases close to the mainland over which, as a result of conquest and occupation, the United States had a relatively free hand. This was particularly true of Okinawa, an island far from mainland Japan but close to China, on which the United States started a massive military construction programme as early as 1947, and over which she retained occupation rights until 1972, twenty years after they had been relinquished for the rest of Japan.

The United States took great care to ensure that she alone occupied Japan. Although the Peace Treaty with Japan was signed by a number of nations in 1951, the parallel Security Treaty was a bilateral agreement between Japan and the United States. This treaty made it clear that the United States had the right to station forces in Japan, not just for the defence of the country itself but to maintain stability in the Far East as a whole. The United States position in Korea was initially very different. For the purposes of post-war occupation, the country was divided at the 38th Parallel with the Soviet Union and the invasion of South Korea in 1950 brought fifteen other countries to her defence in addition to the United States. But at the conclusion of the war the United States emerged in a dominant position in South Korea. She retained operational control of the South Korean armed forces and the fragile republic was wholly dependent on the United States for her security. The war had also consolidated the United States position in Japan which had served as a rear base for United Nations operations on the Korean peninsula.

There were thus significant differences between those elements of the United States global security system in Asia, where she remained largely autonomous, and those in Europe where, although the pre-eminent

---

[1] Strategic Concept and Plan for the Employment of US Armed Forces. Signed October 1945 by Robert Patterson Secretary of State for War. Cited by F. Shiels, *America, Okinawa and Japan* (Washington, DC: University Press of America, 1980).

partner in the Alliance, she shared her security responsibilities with a number of allies. Even so, there were important common features to the deployment of American forces in the occupied nations which spanned the geographical divide. One such feature was a certain similarity of approach to the principal enemy powers of Germany and Japan. Another was the fact that both Germany and Korea became divided nations faced with an imminent communist threat which required the deployment of substantial American ground forces within their borders.

American thinking on post-war policy towards the defeated enemy powers inevitably focused on Germany and Japan. Little detailed planning was undertaken for Italy and none at all for Korea. The earliest proposals for the defeated enemy powers had concentrated on punitive measures to dismantle their war economies and restructure their societies. For Germany, the Morgenthau Plan, put forward by the US Secretary to the Treasury, had advocated reducing the country to a largely agrarian economy, but this was not supported by his Cabinet colleagues who remembered the lessons of Versailles. In addressing the Asian theatre it was agreed at the Cairo conference in 1943 to 'restrain and punish the aggression of Japan' and this prompted General MacArthur to concentrate initially on breaking up the 'zaibatsu'—the powerful industrial enterprises that had supported the war effort and were seen as part of the military establishment.

However, the defeat and subsequent impoverishment of the two dominant economic and military powers flanking the Soviet Union left a vacuum which Stalin was quick to exploit. The increasing hostility of the Soviet Union persuaded the United States that she had to revive rather than suppress her former enemies. On 7 November 1947, James Forrestal, the American Secretary of Defense, told the Cabinet that restoring the balance of power in Europe and Asia depended on rebuilding 'the two nations we have just destroyed'.[2] At the State Department, George Kennan, the main architect of containment and now Head of the Policy Planning Staff, argued that the first priority of the United States should be to counter the dominance of the Soviet Union on the Eurasian land mass. 'That balance', he wrote, 'is unthinkable as long as Germany and Japan remain power vacuums'. American policy, he continued, should seek to restore the strength of Germany and Japan:

[2] W. L. Millis (ed.), *The Forrestal Diaries.* 7 November 1947 (London: Cassell 1952, 327).

to a point where they could play their part in the Eurasian balance of power and yet to a point not so far advanced as to permit them again to threaten the interests of the maritime world of the West.[3]

The switch from a punitive to a supportive policy was known as the 'Reverse Course' in Japan but the term could have been applied equally to West Germany, for whom the benefits of the Marshall Plan were far greater. In Germany, the United States took steps to integrate the Western Occupation Zones into a single economic unit with a common currency which was to gain maximum advantage from the Marshall Plan and play a major part in the reconstruction of Europe. In Japan, the Dodge Plan aimed to revive industrial productivity and increase export competitiveness largely through domestic austerity measures. But with most of her traditional markets lost during the civil war in China, Japan was not to recover until the Korean War revived demand for her heavy industries.

Despite the steps taken to revive the former enemy powers, the financial arrangements governing the deployment of American and other allied forces owed much to the legacy of occupation. Whereas the United States was often obliged to secure access to bases elsewhere, including some NATO countries, through the generous provision of economic and military aid, defence facilities were made available to her free of charge in West Germany and Japan. Moreover, as the economies of the former enemy powers recovered to the extent that they, and to a lesser extent South Korea, became major trading competitors of the United States, the demand for offset or infrastructure payments to defray the stationing costs of American forces became increasingly strident. West Germany, Japan, and South Korea were all obliged at different times to make a substantial contribution to the cost of the troops billeted on them even though they had no say in the deployment decisions and no control over the costs incurred. The success of the host nation economies, which undoubtedly owed something to American military protection, was the main factor behind the offset demands, especially as the economic pre-eminence which the United States had enjoyed in the early post-war years began to decline in relative terms. Nevertheless, these demands were popularly regarded as occupation costs in West Germany and Japan and it is noticeable that, although they were never applied to Italy, offset payments were sought only from countries occupied after the war. Negotiations on offset were particularly difficult in West Germany (where Britain also sought a contribu-

---

[3] M. Schaller, *The American Occupation of Japan* (Oxford: OUP, 1985).

tion to her stationing costs) and, except for Berlin where true occupation costs continued to be paid until 1990, offset payments were discontinued in the mid 1970s. However, offset and infrastructure payments have continued on an increasing basis for both Japan and South Korea.

Further evidence of the subordinate status of the two principal enemy powers is to be found in the constraints imposed by their post-war constitutions on any military action outside their own borders. For Japan, the Constitution adopted in 1947 renounced the use or threat of force to settle disputes and, although, following the Korean War, Self Defence Forces were permitted from the mid 1950s, a ceiling of 1 per cent of GNP (gross national product) was applied to the Japanese defence budget until 1987. In contrast, West Germany was required to raise substantial armed forces once she had joined NATO in 1955 and these were deployed to guard three sectors of the inner German border alongside her NATO allies. However, the Basic Law of 1949 was widely believed to prohibit the use of these forces outside the NATO area. As a result, neither country felt able to participate in the Gulf War and attempts to deploy forces on secondary activities in support of the coalition aroused bitter political controversy. A difficult period of reappraisal followed in both countries. But in 1992, legislation was passed in Japan permitting the Self Defence Forces to be deployed for logistics or humanitarian purposes with UN peacekeeping missions and in 1994 the Constitutional Court in Germany ruled that under the Basic Law the country's armed forces could in fact participate in international military operations outside the NATO area within the framework of multilateral collective security systems (such as the United Nations, NATO, and the Western European Union), provided each operation was approved by the Bundestag. Thus, the two principal powers defeated in the Second World War, which had subsequently hosted heavy concentrations of American troops for reasons of internal as well as external containment, finally felt themselves sufficiently trusted to play a part in international security operations.

Although there were a number of features common to the deployment of United States forces in West Germany and Japan, as the two principal enemy powers, there were also important parallels between the stationing of American troops in West Germany and South Korea as the two front-line nations of the Cold War. The imminent threat to both countries required the deployment of substantial American ground forces which, as the relative economic power of the United States declined, she found it increasingly hard to sustain. Furthermore, the war in Vietnam first diverted forces from West Germany, the principal front-line state of the Cold War, and in the disillusion that followed, bred a growing distaste for the deployment of ground forces overseas in substantial numbers. This distaste, coupled with the economic difficulties which the Vietnam War had done much to engender, led the United States to propose a series of troop withdrawals from both West Germany and South Korea, and to place a growing emphasis on reinforcement to meet her obligations to West Germany. The withdrawal proposals were put forward by Presidents Nixon and Carter for South Korea and Senator Mansfield for West Germany. The motives for these proposals were understandable, not least in the context of burden-sharing by the European members of NATO, but they conveyed the impression that the United States was eager to reduce her forces in those countries where the threat was greatest while striving to retain them, not always successfully, in host nations at some distance from the front line.

6

From Conquest to Containment: Asia

Japan

Initial Post-war Planning

The United States was determined to take sole control of Japan after the Second World War but did not initially envisage permanent military bases on the main islands. As the war drew to a close, Admiral Leahy, President Truman's Chief of Staff, was adamant that not a single island should be surrendered to 'even partial control of another nation'.[1] In a similar vein, Truman himself wrote to James Byrnes, his Secretary of State, in January 1946 stating that the United States should 'maintain complete control of Japan and the Pacific'.[2] The determination to keep the other allies out of Japan was evident at the Foreign Ministers' Conference in London in September 1947, at which both Britain and the Soviet Union were rebuffed by Byrnes. But sole control did not encompass plans for a permanent military presence on the 'mainland' or home islands. At this stage, the Joint Chiefs of Staff were concerned to deny Japan to the Soviet Union, not to develop offensive bases on the home islands. Their thoughts had long been focused on the Ryukyus, a string of islands stretching south-west from Japan proper towards Formosa, as Taiwan was then known.

The largest of these islands is Okinawa, scene of a particularly bloody battle during the closing stages of the war, when, prior to the dropping of the atomic bombs, it was seen as an essential springboard for the invasion of Japan. Although not needed for this purpose, American military planners had for some time envisaged a major United States base on the island in the post-war period. Both Marshall and MacArthur saw the Ryukyus as a key strategic location for American forces after the war. MacArthur had long advocated a base on Okinawa but did not consider bases on the home islands to be necessary until the outbreak of the Korean War. General Marshall had written to President Truman in July 1945 saying:

[1] M. Schaller, *The American Occupation of Japan* (Oxford: OUP, 1985, 54).
[2] Schaller, op. cit. 62.

The mere possession by the United States of positions within range of troubled areas should be a useful influence for peace and stability. Among the areas of potential trouble after the war is that bordering the Yellow Sea. A base in the Ryukyus therefore is particularly desirable, with the remainder of those islands de-militarised and in friendly hands.[3]

It is difficult to understand this early emphasis on the Ryukyus. They face China rather than the Soviet Union, which was the immediate post-war threat. The Yellow Sea is bordered by China on one side and Korea on the other and would be better controlled from Kyushu, the most southern of the four home islands. Vladivostok, home of the Soviet Eastern Fleet, is over 1,000 miles to the north of Okinawa but only half that distance from northern Honshu (the main island of Japan) and Hokkaido, the most northern of the four home islands, abuts the Kurile Islands which had been occupied by Russia at the end of the war. Yet, all the wartime and post-war plans for United States military bases placed the Ryukyus in the highest priority category and made no mention of permanent bases on the home islands of Japan.[4]

The State Department did not share the Pentagon's interest in the Ryukyus. The first drafts of a possible peace treaty which they prepared in March 1947 made no provision for bases either in Japan or Okinawa. As with Germany, the initial American emphasis on post-war planning for Japan envisaged a short, punitive, period of occupation to eradicate the culture of militarism and break up the powerful economic enterprises that had supported the war effort. Following agreement at the Cairo Conference to 'restrain and punish the aggression of Japan', the newly formed State–War–Navy Co-ordinating Committee had given instructions in December 1945 that the dominant industrial combines known as 'zaibatsu' should be broken up. MacArthur was a keen supporter of this policy, declaring that Japan should become 'the Switzerland of the Pacific'. In keeping with the American determination to prevent further aggression by Japan, the new Constitution put in place in May 1947 contained sweeping clauses that went far beyond those applied to Germany. Article 9 stated categorically that:

The Japanese people forever renounce war as a sovereign right of the nation and the threat or use of force as a means of settling disputes . . . land, sea and air forces will never be maintained. The right of the belligerency of the State will not be recognised.

[3] F. Shiels, *America, Okinawa and Japan* (Washington, DC: University Press of America, 1980, 85).
[4] E. Converse, United States Plans for a Post-War Overseas Military Base System 1942–48. Unpublished PhD thesis, Princeton University, January 1984.

However, growing concern over Soviet post-war policies and the evident economic impoverishment of Japan led to a reappraisal of policy in Washington which was given further impetus by the Truman Doctrine announced in March 1947 and the Marshall Plan unveiled in June. One result of this reassessment was the Reverse Course policy designed to rebuild the economy of Japan instead of running it down. George Kennan, Head of the Policy Planning Staff at the State Department, was just as concerned with the political and economic aspects of containment as with the security structures required. He became gravely concerned at the economic plight of Japan and commented in October 1947 that 'the socialisation of Japan had proceeded to such a point that . . . it would not be possible, under the present economic machinery, for the country to support itself'.[5] In April 1948, the United States launched the Economic Recovery in Occupied Areas Program under which aid could be provided to Japan and in December Truman signed the stabilization decree which gave official blessing to the Reverse Course. The main feature of this was the Dodge Plan, devised by a prominent American banker, which aimed to revive the industrial productivity of Japan and improve her export position through reductions in domestic purchasing power.

In parallel, there was a significant shift in the thinking of the Joint Chiefs of Staff who began to see mainland Japan as a launching pad for deterrent action against the Soviet Union and even toyed with the idea of rebuilding the Japanese armed forces as a counterweight to the USSR. A Joint Chiefs of Staff (JCS) study completed in April 1947 concluded:

Of all the countries in the Pacific area, Japan deserves primary consideration for current US assistance designed to restore her to economic and military potential.[6]

However, MacArthur, wielding virtually plenipotentiary powers in Tokyo, remained strongly opposed to permanent military bases in Japan, or the creation of a Japanese army. A visit to him by George Kennan in March 1948 failed to modify his views. These remained wedded to an offshore defence concept for the Far East, taking in the Aleutians, Midway, the former Japanese mandated islands, the Philippines, and Okinawa, but not mainland Japan. Back in Washington, the Joint Chiefs of Staff continued to press for forward bases in Japan but

---

[5] W. L. Millis (ed.), *The Forrestal Diaries*. 31 October 1947, (London: Cassell, 1952, 316).
[6] Schaller, op. cit. 90.

recognized that any peace treaty making provision for these would require agreement by the wartime allies, with these provisions almost certainly being rejected by China and the Soviet Union. A paper prepared in June 1949 argued that continued occupation of Japan would provide 'the United States with staging areas from which to project our military power to the Asiatic mainland and the USSR'.[7]

The deadlock resulting from the divergent views of the State Department, the Pentagon, and MacArthur continued until the fall of China to the communists in October 1949 provided further impetus to the debate. Truman indicated in December that he was prepared to contemplate a peace treaty without Soviet participation[8] and MacArthur was persuaded to consider the retention of American forces on the Japanese mainland as part of a defensive shield after the occupation of Japan had ended. The State Department initially hoped that communist China would break with the Soviet Union as Tito had done in Yugoslavia, but the conclusion of a thirty-year Treaty of Friendship in February 1950 between China and the Soviet Union showed this to be wishful thinking in the short term. In contrast, relations between China and the United States continued to deteriorate and the situation in Indo-China, where France came into conflict with the Viet Minh nationalist movement opposed to the restoration of colonial rule, gave increasing cause for concern. In April 1950, John Foster Dulles, a Republican, joined the State Department as a measure designed to cement Truman's bipartisan foreign policy and was given the task of negotiating a peace treaty with Japan. However, little progress was made before the outbreak of the Korean War on 25 June 1950.

The Impact of the Korean War

The invasion of South Korea by the North had a cataclysmic effect on American foreign policy worldwide, but the impact on Japan was particularly marked. As United Nations forces were initially forced back into a narrow enclave around Pusan, Japan, only 150 miles away across the Korean Straits, became the main supply depot and rear operating base for the allied war effort. This role continued and expanded following the allied landings at Inchon and the advance of United Nations forces up the Korean Peninsula. Moreover, the purchasing programmes set up by the Americans in Japan in support of the war prompted the

---

[7] JCS paper. Strategic Evaluation of US Security Needs in Japan, 9 June 1949. Cited in Schaller, op. cit. 167.
[8] Schaller, op. cit. 246.

first steps towards economic recovery. Procurement by the allied military authorities amounted to $800 million in 1951–2, and had reached $3 billion by 1954. This inflow of capital bridged the dollar gap from which Japan was suffering and the military needs of the United Nations provided an outlet for Japan's heavy industry, whose traditional markets in China had been closed since the end of the war. The Toyota vehicle plant, for example, was saved from bankruptcy by the demands of Korea.

The war also saw the birth of Japan's Self Defence Forces. In July 1950, MacArthur directed the Japanese government to form a National Police Reserve of 75,000 men initially to guard American bases while US troops were in Korea. This led in time to legislation passed in 1954 allowing the Ground Self Defence Force to be established. But most significantly, the war in Korea prompted the United States to press ahead with a peace treaty and persuaded the State Department to accept a continued American military presence in Japan. Ironically, Prime Minister Shigeru Yoshida, when indicating that he too was content with these conditions, made a whimsical reference to American progress after independence from Britain: 'If Japan becomes a colony of the United States', he said, 'it will eventually become stronger'.[9] Throughout the 1970s and 1980s it looked as though he would be proved right.

The 1951 Security Treaty

The peace treaty between the Allied Powers and Japan was signed by 48 nations in San Francisco in September 1951. The Soviet Union attended the ceremony but did not sign the treaty. It was made clear in the treaty that Japan and the Allied Powers were to be treated as 'sovereign equals' with full sovereignty being restored in April 1952. In parallel, a bilateral Security Treaty was signed between the United States and Japan which acknowledged that Japan could not defend herself, gave the United States sweeping rights to maintain her own armed forces in Japan, but stopped short of placing on the United States a binding obligation to use these forces for the defence of Japan. Indeed, the Security Treaty emphasized that the United States was entitled to use her military forces in Japan for wider security purposes. The treaty also included a clause allowing American forces stationed in Japan to be used for internal security purposes at the request of the Japanese government.

[9] Schaller, op. cit. 257.

The 1951 Security Treaty runs to only two printed pages. The preamble stated that 'Japan will not have the effective means to exercise its inherent right of self defense because it has been disarmed', and went on to say:

Japan desires, as a provisional arrangement for its defense, that the United States of America should maintain armed forces of its own in and about Japan so as to deter armed attack on Japan.

This led on to a further clause in the preamble stating:

The United States of America, in the interests of peace and security, is presently willing to maintain certain of its armed forces in and about Japan, in the expectation, however, that Japan will itself increasingly assume responsibility for its own defense ... always avoiding any armament which could be an offensive threat or serve other than to promote peace and security ...

The key provisions on basing rights were set out in Article I as follows:

Japan grants, and the United States of America accepts, the right ... to dispose of United States land, air and sea forces in and about Japan. Such forces may be utilised to contribute to the maintenance of international peace and security in the Far East and to the security of Japan against armed attack from without, including assistance given at the express request of the Japanese Government to put down large-scale internal riots and disturbances in Japan, caused through instigation or intervention by an outside power or powers.

Article II stated that Japan would not grant bases or other rights to any third power without the United States consent and Article IV stated that the treaty would expire when United Nations arrangements or other collective security arrangements were deemed satisfactory by both governments. In effect, duration was to be open-ended.

The Japanese came to see this as an unequal treaty dictated by the United States alongside the Peace Treaty from a position of strength as the occupying power. The terms were certainly advantageous to the United States. There was no restriction on the use which could be made of her military forces in Japan. Instead, they could be used fairly freely throughout the Far East. The treaty confirmed Japan's dependence on the United States for defence, but did not contain the provision to 'act to meet the common danger' in the event of an armed attack which had featured in the treaties concluded at the same time with the Philippines and jointly with Australia and New Zealand (the ANZUS Treaty). The Japanese also found the references to United States intervention on internal security matters deeply distasteful, despite the caveats surrounding these.

The 1960 Treaty of Mutual Co-operation and Security

Japan first attempted to revise the terms of the Security Treaty in 1955 but this request was rejected by Dulles, who, notwithstanding the terms of the Constitution imposed by the United States, was only prepared to consider a more balanced treaty if Japan was to rearm as Germany had done. In 1958, the Japanese Prime Minister Nobosuke Kishi visited Washington and obtained the administration's reluctant agreement to revising the treaty. Two years of hard bargaining followed before a new Treaty of Mutual Co-operation and Security was signed in 1960. This treaty has remained in force until today but was exceptionally unpopular at the time of signature. Mass demonstrations in Tokyo obliged President Eisenhower to cancel a visit in June 1960 and Kishi was compelled to resign shortly afterwards.

At first sight, it is difficult to understand the strength of popular protest against the 1960 treaty. Many of the more objectionable provisions of the 1951 treaty were removed. Article II allowed Japan to maintain and develop her capacity to resist armed attack (but it has to be acknowledged that rearmament was never popular with the bulk of the population). Article IV stated that the parties would consult together 'whenever the security of Japan or international peace in the Far East is threatened'. Moreover, Article V brought the United States defence commitment to Japan into line with those afforded to the Philippines, Australia, and New Zealand in 1951, and South Korea and Taiwan in 1953 and 1954, respectively. The standard formula used in all these treaties and now extended to Japan was:

Each party recognises that an armed attack against either party in the territories under the administration of Japan would be dangerous to its own peace and safety and declares that it would act to meet the common danger in accordance with its constitutional provisions and processes.

Furthermore, the right of the United States to intervene in internal security matters was dropped and it was separately agreed that the United States would no longer maintain ground combat troops in mainland Japan.

The treaty was negotiated between two sovereign powers and this was acknowledged in the parallel Exchange of Notes between Kishi and Christian Herter, the American Secretary of State, which for the first time set out important provisions for consultation between the two governments. One such provision stated that 'major changes' in the deployment of US armed forces, equipment, and facilities in Japan would be subject to prior consultation, and Herter, at a later Senate hearing, stated that consultation meant approval by Japan.[10] This provision was taken to cover nuclear as well as conventional equipment. A further provision ensured that consultation would take place before the United States embarked on military operations from Japan. This provision was quite unambiguous:

The use of facilities and areas in Japan as bases for military combat operations to be undertaken from Japan shall be the subject of prior consultation with the Government of Japan.[11]

Moreover, the United States government followed this up with a communiqué saying 'The United States Government has no intention of acting in a manner contrary to the wishes of the Japanese Government'.[12]

These concessions were not sufficient to win over popular opposition to the 1960 treaty which stemmed partly from its terms and partly from the way in which it was handled by the Japanese government. Many Japanese felt that the 1960 treaty reinforced Japan's dependency on the United States for defence and confirmed her subservience to United States regional interests, which could involve them in American conflicts in Asia. The provision in Article VI which came to be known as the 'Far East Clause' caused particular concern:

For the purpose of contributing to the security of Japan and the maintenance of international peace and security in the Far East, the United States is granted the use by its land, air and naval forces of facilities and areas in Japan.

The fact that the Japanese Foreign Minister was unable to define the Far East when pressed on this issue only added to the sense of unease. In addition, there was no fundamental change to the rights of the United States to maintain bases in Japan and the treaty could not be abrogated by either party for ten years, after which it could be abrogated by either party giving a full year's notice. These very real concerns were compounded by Kishi's tactics on ratification. Anxious to secure ratification before Eisenhower's visit in June 1960, he extended the session of the Diet and, using strong-arm tactics, rushed the ratification through the Lower House in late May. This led to students occupying the Diet building, Eisenhower's Press Secretary James Hagerty being mobbed when he arrived for a preliminary visit and Eisenhower's visit being cancelled,

---

[10] C. J. Lee and H. Sato, *US Policy Towards Japan and Korea* (London: Praeger, 1982).

[11] J. Woodliffe, *The Peacetime Use of Foreign Military Bases* (Dordrecht: Martinus Nijhoff, 1992).

[12] F. Greene, *Stresses in US–Japan Security Relations* (Washington, DC: Brookings Institution, 1975).

with Kishi resigning the following day. Nevertheless, the treaty became effective on 20 June 1960 since the Lower House had ratified it and no further action was needed by the Upper House.

It has been suggested that much of the protest occasioned by the 1960 treaty represented dissatisfaction with Kishi, who had been Minister of Industry and Commerce in General Tojo's wartime Cabinet and was only released from prison in 1948. Hayato Ikeda succeeded Kishi as Prime Minister but Japanese politics in the late 1960s were dominated by Eisaku Sato. Although a much more skilful politician than Kishi, he too provoked criticism of the Far East Clause in the treaty by stating in 1965 that the United States could use the bases in Japan—short of flying direct combat missions—for support missions during the Vietnam War, since the war posed a threat to peace and security in the Far East. This may seem somewhat disingenuous in view of the United States role in the war, but by giving verbal support to the United States on Vietnam, Sato was able to obtain from President Johnson a reaffirmation of the American commitment to the defence of Japan. In a communiqué issued on 31 January 1965 Johnson stated:

The President re-affirms the United States determination to abide by its commitment under the Treaty to defend Japan against any armed attack from outside.[13]

However, Sato's main achievements were to persuade Johnson to return the Bonin Islands to Japan in 1968 and to secure a promise from President Nixon in November 1969 that Okinawa would be returned to Japanese jurisdiction in 1972. On the strength of these achievements Sato secured re-election in December 1969 and in 1970, the Security Treaty was extended without controversy after its first ten-year period. It now continues from year to year unless either country gives notice of an intention to abrogate.

Okinawa

Okinawa is the largest island in the Ryukyu chain, which extends for 800 miles between the southern Japanese island of Kyushu and Taiwan. It was the site of a bitter three-month battle between April and June 1945 when 12,000 American troops, 75,000 Japanese troops, and 150,000 islanders were killed. The island had been a Japanese Protectorate since 1872 and the islanders felt that they had been sacrificed to gain time for the defence of mainland Japan. The number of islanders killed amounted

[13] Ibid.

to one-fifth of the total population and equalled the number that died in
Nagasaki and Hiroshima combined. The brutality of the fighting and the
islanders' sense of betrayal by the mainland Japanese do much to explain
their continuing resentment towards both the United States and the government in Tokyo. By the same token, the intensity of the battle for
Okinawa may have been a factor in America's determination to retain
the island after the war as a major military base. This determination was
already clear in the Potsdam Declaration of July 1945, which placed strict
limits on the sovereignty of Japan after the war, stating:

Its sovereignty shall be limited to Honshu, Hokkaido, Kyushu, Shikoku and
such minor islands as we determine.

The future of the Ryukyu islands was left open but the United States
was already in occupation and in October 1945 a paper for the Joint
Chiefs of Staff made it clear that:

All Japanese mandated islands and Central Pacific islands detached from Japan,
including the Bonins and Ryukyus, will be brought under exclusive United
States strategic control.[14]

The following year, a further JCS paper dealt specifically with
Okinawa which it saw as 'a springboard from which to exercise some
stabilising influence over the area around the Yellow Sea'.[15] The State
Department took a very different view, arguing that the Ryukyus should
be demilitarized and returned to Japan. A paper prepared by the State
Department in June 1946 showed some residual signs of anti-colonial
sentiment:

For the United States to take over any part of the Ryukyu islands would be
contrary to its policy of opposing territorial expansion, whether for itself or for
other countries . . . The establishment by the United States of a permanent base
at Okinawa or elsewhere in the Ryukyu islands would be likely to provoke
serious international repercussions and would be politically objectionable.[16]

However, these arguments failed to gain the day and by March 1948
George Kennan could be counted in the military camp. His memorandum to George Marshall following his visit to MacArthur in Tokyo
placed particular emphasis on Okinawa:

Okinawa would be made the center of our offensive striking power in the West
Pacific area. It would constitute the central and most advanced point of a U-
shaped US security zone embracing the Aleutians, the Ryukyus, the former

---

[14] JCS 570, 21 October 1953. Cited in Shiels, op. cit.
[15] JCS 1619, 10 September 1946. Cited in Shiels, op. cit.
[16] State Department paper, 27 June 1946, mentioned in JCS 1619/5, 5 September 1946.
Cited in Shiels, op. cit.

Japanese mandated islands, and of course Guam. We would rely on Okinawa-based air power, plus our advanced naval power . . .'[17]

With the containment policy gaining ground, it is scarcely surprising that Okinawa remained under a military government from 1945 to 1950, and that a massive programme of military construction was commenced in 1947. This construction programme eventually absorbed some 75,000 acres, or 25 per cent of the total land area of the island. The triumph of communism in China in 1949 enhanced the importance of Okinawa, which is only 500 miles from Shanghai and the same distance from Taiwan. The huge construction programme therefore continued in the early 1950s until some 120 military facilities, including 19 major bases, were established on the island. These included the largest complex of bases for the US Marine Corps outside the United States, housing 19,000 Marines, major air bases for the Marines at Zukeran and Futenma, and for the US Air Force at Kadena, accommodating twenty squadrons of aircraft, further bases for the US Army, and a small port and naval base. At the height of the Vietnam War in the 1960s, some 45,000 American servicemen were stationed at Okinawa, compared with only 40,000 on the home islands of Japan. Since Okinawa remained occupied enemy territory, separate from mainland Japan, it was not initially covered by the 1960 Treaty on Mutual Co-operation and Security. This allowed nuclear weapons to be stored on the island, both for the B-52s stationed at Kadena Air Force Base and with the Mace B missiles manned by the US Army.

The 1951 Peace Treaty gave the United States 'powers of administration, legislation and jurisdiction' over the Ryukyus, and a parallel Exchange of Notes between Acheson and Yoshida provided for United States control over the islands 'as long as conditions of threat and tension exist in the Far East'.[18] These arrangements reflected the concept of residual sovereignty—not dissimilar to that applied in Panama and Cuba—under which Japan recognized that the United States had the right to apply for United Nations Strategic Trusteeship if she wished, but that sovereignty would ultimately return to Japan. In fact, Acheson had considered applying for Strategic Trusteeship some years before but the outbreak of the Korean War reinforced the status quo. It was also recognized that the Soviet Union would have been able to veto an application for Strategic Trusteeship in the Security Council.

---

[17] G. Kennan to G. Marshall, 14 March 1948. Cited in J. L. Gaddis *The Long Peace* (Oxford: OUP, 1987, 73).
[18] Lee and Sato, op. cit.

Under the Eisenhower administration, the United States showed no sign of relinquishing Okinawa. In 1953, Richard Nixon, as Vice-President, visited the island to declare that 'the United States will continue to control Okinawa so long as the communist threat exists'.[19] The following year Eisenhower himself went further in his State of the Union message, saying 'we shall maintain indefinitely our bases in Okinawa'.[20] But elsewhere disquiet was expressed. An article by Ralph Braibanti in the *American Political Science Review* of December 1954 said 'the present statelessness of the Ryukyus is bewildering and degrading'. The inhabitants, the article added, were 'citizens of neither Japan nor the United States'.[21] Reflecting this disquiet, the Senate Committee on Foreign Relations set up a study on the future of Okinawa in 1959 and a further study was put in hand by President Kennedy in 1961. However, the Vietnam War greatly enhanced the importance of Okinawa for the United States. From 1968 onwards, B-52 bombing raids on Vietnam were undertaken from Kadena Air Force Base. As a result, President Johnson declined to return Okinawa to Japan in 1967 when the return of the Bonin Islands was agreed. Although prepared to consider the return of the Ryukyus within 'a few years', Johnson decided to play for time by setting up yet another advisory committee on the issue.

It was not until the Nixon administration that a breakthrough was made. Although the war in Vietnam was still in progress in 1969, with by now more than 50,000 troops stationed on Okinawa, Nixon agreed on reversion to Japan in principle when he met Sato in November that year. Nixon may have been swayed partly by intense political pressure in Japan, with large demonstrations against American jurisdiction over the island and the use of the bases for operations over Vietnam. But retention of Okinawa under direct American control was also inconsistent with the Guam Doctrine spelt out by Nixon in July 1969, in which he had urged regional powers to take on greater responsibility for their own defence.

The bargain announced in the Nixon–Sato communiqué of 21 November 1969 gave Japan the primary responsibility for defending Okinawa but allowed the United States to retain the bases on the island. Reversion to Japan was promised for 1972 'provided there was no detriment to peace and security in the Far East'. Moreover, Japan was obliged to acknowledge for the first time that the security of Japan and

---

[19] Shiels, op. cit.   [20] Ibid.
[21] *American Political Science Review*, December 1954. Cited in Shiels.

the wider security of the Far East were directly related. In his speech to the National Press Club in Washington, Sato agreed that it was 'impossible adequately to maintain the security of Japan without international peace and security in the Far East and, therefore, the security of countries in the Far East was a matter of serious concern to Japan'. He went on to acknowledge that South Korea was essential to Japan's security and promised that Tokyo would respond 'promptly and positively' to requests from the United States to use the bases in Japan to repel an attack on South Korea. However, Sato was more cautious on Taiwan. Although the United States had urged him to include in his speech identical wording to that used on South Korea, he merely acknowledged that Taiwan was 'also an important factor for the security of Japan'.[22]

There are several interesting features to this bargain. First, the reversion of Okinawa to Japan brought the island squarely within the terms of the 1960 treaty. Among other points this meant that nuclear weapons could no longer be stored on the island without the consent of the Japanese government. Secondly, any combat operations launched from Okinawa would also require the consent of the Japanese government and the fact that the Americans pressed Sato for specific references to operations in defence of South Korea and Taiwan indicates that they intended to honour the commitment to consultation. Finally, Sato was obliged to reaffirm, as he had already done in 1965 over Vietnam, that the security of Japan was inextricably bound up with the wider security of East Asia, which American troops were in Japan to maintain. However, the term 'Far East', which had caused such trouble in 1960, was no better defined in 1969 and the United States retained a relatively free hand over peacetime deployments throughout the area.

Notwithstanding reversion in 1972, the American military presence continued to breed resentment among the people of Okinawa, who felt that they were bearing a disproportionate share of the overall burden—75 per cent of American military installations in Japan were concentrated on Okinawa which represented only 1 per cent of Japan's land area. The US Marines occupied a complex of bases covering some 10 per cent of the island known collectively as Camp S.D. Butler and also had an air base of their own at Futenma. In 1978, two-thirds of the Third Marine Division were still stationed in Okinawa. The role of these units was described as 'a combat reserve force maintained for amphibious or

---

[22] Greene, op. cit.

other operations throughout the US Pacific Command areas'.[23] At the end of the Cold War, the United States still had 28,000 troops in Okinawa compared to 20,000 in the rest of Japan, and in May 1993, the Governor of the Prefecture, Mashide Ota, stated that 'the people of Okinawa feel that Japan as a whole—not only Okinawa—must share in the burden of providing land for American military bases'.[24]

Difficulties over jurisdiction, land rights, and environmental damage continued to cause ill-feeling between the United States authorities and the local population. But it was not until the mid 1990s that matters came to a head with the rape of a 12-year-old schoolgirl in September 1995 by three American servicemen. This caused an outcry in Okinawa, fuelled by the initial reluctance of the American authorities to surrender the suspects to the local police until formally charged. The fact that all three American servicemen were black no doubt inflamed feeling on the island although this was not widely reported abroad. A renewed anti-American campaign resulted, led by Masahide Ota, who, exercising his powers as Governor of the Prefecture, declined to renew many of the leases for land within the military bases, thus pitting the island authorities against the national government in Tokyo. Significant concessions were needed to resolve this issue. First a joint meeting of the Defence Secretaries and Foreign Ministers of both countries in September 1995 agreed on a set of minor measures. The American naval port at Naha and Yomitan airfield were to be returned to the island authorities while restrictions were placed on live artillery firing and parachute drops. But the furore over Okinawa provided an unwelcome backdrop to the summit between between President Clinton and Prime Minister Ryutaro Hashimoto in April 1996, obliging the United States to make further concessions which are described below.

Mainland Bases

The military installations retained by the United States on the four home islands of Japan were also extensive. No US Army combat units were stationed on the home islands once the occupation was over but the headquarters of US Army Japan, consisting mainly of administrative and support staff, was located at Camp Zama, some 40 miles from Tokyo. The headquarters of both the Seventh Fleet and the Fifth Air

---

[23] United States Foreign Policy Objectives and Overseas Military Installations. Report for the SCFR. CRS April 1979.

[24] Article in *Navy Times*, 31 May 1993.

Force were also located near Tokyo. By 1970, there were a total of 125 military facilities in American hands, of which 30 were major bases. The most numerous of these were Air Force bases, of which there were six at Yokota, Misawa, Itazuke, Tachikawa, Iwakumi, and Atsugi. Of these, only Misawa at the northern end of Honshu and Iwakumi in the south were remote from centres of population. Misawa housed the 432nd Fighter Wing equipped with F-16s and was also used for anti-submarine warfare surveillance of the Seas of Japan and Okhotsk by P-3C Orions. At Iwakumi, nearly 200 aircraft were stationed in the 1970s, including helicopters of the 1st Marine Aircraft Wing, providing support for the US Marines based in Okinawa, should they be required to deploy to the Asian mainland. Yokota, only 24 miles from Tokyo, served as the head-quarters of US Forces Japan and Fifth Air Force. The aircraft stationed there were mainly tasked for air reconnaissance, air defence training, and transport duties.

Many of these air bases attracted considerable local opposition. Atsugi, a naval air station, was particularly unpopular because of night landing practice. In May 1968, a USAF aircraft from Itazuke crashed at Kyushu University with the result that the base was placed on standby status. Tachikawa also attracted violent opposition from students who had camped at the end of the runway in December 1969, temporarily closing the base. In addition, there were two large naval bases at Yokosuka and Sasebo. Yokosuka, nearly 20 miles from Tokyo and covering some 500 acres, was the home of the Seventh Fleet. It had the only dry dock in the Western Pacific capable of taking an aircraft carrier, and in the 1970s it was the home port for the aircraft carrier *USS Midway* and ten other US warships. Sasebo was mainly a storage depot for fuel and munitions but ship repair could also be undertaken both at the base and at nearby industrial facilities since the US Navy enjoyed free docking facilities at Sasebo Heavy Industries from 1968 onwards.

Apart from main bases, there were also two bombing ranges, six ammunition depots, and a training area of 45,000 acres for the use of the Marine Corps at the foot of Mount Fuji. As one commentator declared, 'by 1970 it had become increasingly obvious that the United States had far too many active bases in Japan'.[25] In December that year, the two governments announced plans to reduce American forces in Japan by 12,000 men, with two F-4 Phantom squadrons moving from Misawa to South Korea, the air base at Itazuke reverting to Japan and

[25] R. Paul, *American Military Commitments Abroad* (New York: Rutgers University Press, 1973).

the naval base at Sasebo being run down. However, it was still calculated that 70 per cent of American bases and 77 per cent of American
troops on the home islands were located within 60 miles of Tokyo (the
equivalent of 30,000 foreign troops in the New York Metropolitan
area).[26] In 1971, the Senate Sub-Committee on US Security Agreements
and Commitments Abroad commented that US forces 'hold an excessive number of facilities within and around Tokyo', including four
military golf courses, a 450-acre ammunition dump, and the Mito
bombing range. The Sub-Committee went on to make the following
recommendation:

American facilities which are considered essential should be promptly con-
verted to joint use, as has been done in other countries, and we should move to
give up entirely those facilities which today are in the main justified on the basis
of convenience.[27]

The presence of so many military facilities used by an outside power in
a country where land is at a premium inevitably caused continuing friction with the local population. A study for the Brookings Institution in
1975 by Fred Greene listed the main environmental problems as overcrowding at Naha, the capital of Okinawa, which was hemmed in by military installations, the spread of Tokyo towards the Air Force Base at
Yokota, and Japan's pressing need for land and water adjacent to the
naval base at Yokosuka. The author commented 'even those Japanese
who are anxious to maintain the base system call for a greater sensitivity to Japan's needs'.[28]

But resentment was not confined to environmental issues. Many
Japanese remained hostile to the bases on political grounds, seeing
them as a reminder of the occupation period and the continuing
dependency of Japan on the United States for defence. There was also
a strong feeling that the bases served American rather than Japanese
interests which could drag Japan into an American war in Asia.
Moreover, the Japanese Self Defence Forces with, for example, more
P-3C Orion aircraft than any other allied nation, appeared to be
structured and equipped largely to support those of the United States.
Japanese perceptions of the American presence were confirmed by
evidence given by Alexis Johnson, Under-Secretary of State, to the
Senate in 1970:

[26] R. Paul, *American Military Commitments Abroad*.
[27] SCFR. Sub-Committee on US Security Agreements and Commitments Abroad, 91st
Congress 1970.
[28] Greene, op. cit. 53.

Our facilities and bases in Japan, as well as Okinawa, are not so much related to the defence of Japan and Okinawa as they are to our ability to support our commitments elsewhere.[29]

The Brookings Institution study concluded that 'antagonism to the US force and base presence has grown, especially as Japan has recovered its economic strength'. Another commentator, writing in 1973, pointed to the different political factors in Japan, Germany, and South Korea:

Unlike the closeness in purpose which Americans have with the Germans and Koreans as far as US troops on their soil are concerned, the Americans appear to many Japanese to have seized bases in their country through conquest and to hold them stubbornly for purposes not entirely consistent with their own aspirations and policy.[30]

Consultation and Nuclear Weapons

This feeling of resentment was fostered by continuing concern over consultation and anxiety over nuclear weapons. Arrangements for consultation pre-dated the 1960 Security Treaty, for Kishi and Eisenhower had set up a US–Japan Security Consultative Committee in 1957. Following signature of the Security Treaty and the parallel Exchange of Notes providing for consultation, the Japanese government went to some trouble to set out the changes in force levels and equipment which would require their agreement. These parameters were set fairly high—an army division, a naval task force or a USAF unit of 75 aircraft in terms of force levels, and nuclear weapons, intermediate or long-range missiles in terms of equipment—giving the American a reasonably free hand at lower levels.[31] But many felt that consultation over US operations from the bases in Japan was inadequate and this seemed to be confirmed by the opening statement made to a Senate hearing in 1970 by Alexis Johnson, who had been US Ambassador in Japan before returning to the State Department. Referring to the consultation provisions of the 1960 Security Treaty he said:

There has been no occasion since the Treaty went into effect under which the United States has asked for consultations in accordance with this understanding.[32]

It was apparent that the Japanese government had not, for their part, asked for consultations either and this suggested that both governments

---

[29] Lee and Sato, op. cit. 41.   [30] Paul, op. cit. 48.   [31] Greene, op. cit. 65.
[32] Ibid.

were content to play down the need for consultation. However, there had been a series of incidents during the 1960s which had prompted popular protest at American actions. First, it was discovered shortly before signature of the 1960 Security Treaty that three U-2 aircraft had been stationed in Japan, allegedly for 'high level weather observation'. This revelation, coming shortly after the detection of the U-2 piloted by Gary Powers over the USSR and the subsequent collapse of the Paris Summit, was one of the factors behind the outcry in Japan over the 1960 treaty. Secondly, the United States informed the Japanese government in 1965 that B-52 aircraft returning from a combat mission over Vietnam might need to divert to Itazuke air base because of adverse weather conditions over Guam. Although the aircraft eventually landed at Okinawa, this too prompted considerable protest by the socialist opposition. Finally, the *USS Enterprise* was ordered to the Sea of Japan following the seizure by North Korea in January 1968 of the unarmed reconnaissance ship *Pueblo* and called briefly at Sasebo, where she was greeted by hostile demonstrations claiming that she was on a military mission.[33]

These concerns were echoed by a nagging anxiety over the deployment of nuclear weapons, a particularly sensitive subject for the Japanese. The Japanese government had refused an American request in the 1950s to deploy Honest John missiles armed with nuclear warheads and, although slow to ratify the Nuclear Non-Proliferation Treaty, had made it clear that they would not permit nuclear weapons to be deployed on the Japanese home islands. This was one of the sticking points in the negotiations over the reversion of Okinawa. The three non-nuclear principles—not to possess, produce, or permit the introduction of nuclear weapons into Japan—were first formulated in 1966 and incorporated in a non-binding resolution of the Diet in 1971. Speaking in 1966, Prime Minister Sato declared:

We ardently desire to stamp out nuclear weapons. We do not venture to possess them ourselves and are determined not to permit them to be brought into this country.[34]

Yet, as elsewhere, this firm expression of policy was difficult to reconcile with the traditional line of the US Navy that they would neither confirm nor deny the carriage of nuclear weapons on American warships. It was long suspected that ships of the Seventh Fleet had nuclear weapons on board and in 1974 the opposition made specific allegations

---

[33] F. C. Langdon, *Japan's Foreign Policy* (Vancouver: University of British Columbia Press, 1973).

[34] Ibid. 138.

that the *USS Midway* was carrying nuclear weapons while in a Japanese port. The United States stood by the 'neither confirm nor deny' formula. The Japanese government stated that consultation would be needed before nuclear weapons were brought into Japan and no consultation had been sought. This issue continued to cause problems for both governments until the Nuclear Posture Review, completed by the Pentagon in October 1994, removed tactical nuclear weapons from the aircraft carriers and other surface ships of the US Navy. Overall, the impression left, both on consultation over conventional combat operations and nuclear weapons in American warships, was that the two governments remained equally anxious to maintain a low profile. The United States took care not to launch combat missions directly from Japanese territory, but Japan was content to be guided by the United States on foreign policy matters for much of the Cold War period and was reluctant to make an issue of consultation, regardless of popular feeling on this subject.

A More Symmetrical Security Relationship?

An attempt was made in 1978 to reduce the asymmetries in the security relationship between the United States and Japan. Joint US–Japan Guidelines on Defense Co-operation were drawn up to encourage more bilateral exercises, intelligence-sharing, and military planning studies. However, Japan's continuing economic growth and her mounting surplus on trade with the United States underlined the most fundamental asymmetry of all—the world's second largest economic power was still precluded, for constitutional and historical reasons, from playing a full part in her own defence. Instead, she looked to the United States to guarantee her security. While the reasons for this unique relationship made sense in 1945, when United States military and economic power was predominant, they no longer did so in 1985, when the United States had become the world's largest debtor nation and had a $50 billion trade deficit with Japan. Concern at the 'free ride' enjoyed by Japan on defence, which had undoubtedly contributed to her impressive economic progress, mounted steadily in the United States. This took the form of pressure on Japan by the Carter administration to increase her own defence budget, which had, by unwritten convention, been capped at 1 per cent of gross national product since the mid 1970s.

This pressure met with little success and in 1981, President Reagan tried an alternative approach, saying that the United States expected her allies to take on more military missions. In response to this, Prime

Minister Zenko Suzuki promised that the Japanese Navy would in future extend coverage of the trade routes approaching Japan out to a distance of 1,000 miles. The following year, Suzuki over-ruled his Finance Minister to secure a growth of 4.6 per cent in the Japanese defence budget without breaching the limit of 1 per cent of GNP. In 1985, Prime Minister Yasuhiro Nakasone, who had been Director General of the Defence Agency under Sato, made a further attempt to raise this ceiling. He was unable to secure immediate agreement to his proposal. Instead, the Cabinet approved a Force Improvement Programme which was implemented over the years 1986–90. This allowed for the purchase of more F-15s, modernization of Japan's F-4 Phantoms, the replacement of Nike missiles by Patriot, and an increase in the destroyer force from fifty to sixty. As a result, Japan now has a significant air defence, anti-submarine warfare, and coastal defence capability, which complements the offensive capability of the United States. She can boast of armed forces totalling 240,000, a 140-ship navy, and some 330 combat aircraft. Moreover, Japan's economy continued to grow steadily through the 1980s with the result that her defence budget increased at a faster rate than most NATO nations and was one of the largest in the world at the end of the decade.

The 1 per cent ceiling was eventually breached in 1987 and the level of Japanese defence spending was no longer an issue with the United States by the end of the Cold War. However, a parallel campaign had been under way throughout the 1980s to offset the cost of stationing American troops in Japan through increased host nation support. In 1977, Japan made offset payments of $580 million and these were increased to $1 billion in 1979, representing 30 per cent of the local costs incurred by the United States (excluding military salaries). In 1980, it was agreed that Japan would meet the salaries and social security benefits of 22,000 local employees at the bases and in 1981 she began to pay for military construction projects planned by the Americans. Under these arrangements, Japan was contributing $2.5 billion per annum in host nation support in 1988. By the early 1990s, this contribution had risen to $6 billion per annum, which was equivalent to 70 per cent of the United States local costs, excluding military salaries. This was a far higher portion of these costs than West Germany had been prepared to pay under the offset arrangements which had been terminated in 1976. The Japanese claimed that they were paying $20,000 for each American serviceman on their territory, whereas Germany had never paid more than $5,000. None the less, Congress, confronted by

Japan's huge trade surplus with the United States, continued to press for an even higher contribution from the host nation. The Japanese have been reluctant to agree to this, arguing that they have no control over the costs incurred by the United States. They also point out that host nation support is only one element in the overall equation on burden-sharing, arguing that the other elements which need to be taken into account are the increases in Japan's own defence budget, the contribution to overseas aid programmes, and contributions either in cash or in kind to allied operations such as the Gulf War and United Nations peacekeeping.

However, with respect to peacekeeping Japan, in common with Germany, has been slow in coming to terms with the wider international role expected of her, constrained as she was by Article 9 of the post-war Constitution. At the time of the Gulf War she first made a financial contribution of $4 billion to the allied war effort in September 1990 but was obliged to raise this by a further $9 billion in January 1991. Despite total expenditure of $13 billion Japan had attracted more criticism than gratitude for her belated and grudging response to the crisis. Furthermore, a proposal to send six minesweepers to the Gulf in a non-combatant role after the war provoked considerable controversy at home. This led to legislation passed in June 1992 which allowed the Self Defence Forces to participate in United Nations peacekeeping operations in a logistics or humanitarian role, although the approval of the Diet was required if more than 2,000 men were allocated to any one operation. On this basis, a contingent of 1,800 was sent to Cambodia in September 1992 and further contributions were made to United Nations missions in Mozambique in 1993 and on the Rwanda–Zaire border in 1994. These tentative steps on the wider world stage, some 45 years after the end of the Second World War, helped to move the security relationship with the United States away from total dependency towards an incipient but still very one-sided sense of partnership.

But these were very modest steps. As the Cold War came to an end and the United States reassessed the needs of her global security system, it was remarkable how little the security relationship with Japan had altered despite the immense change in the relative economic weight of the two countries. In 1950 the American economy had been 26 times larger than that of Japan. In 1994 it was only 1.4 times larger. Yet neither country appeared willing to consider a radical change in the asymmetrical security relationship which had persisted since 1945. It suited the United States to station the majority of her forces in Asia in Japan, particularly after the withdrawal from the Philippines in 1992 since, notwithstanding the environmental and political pressures, especially in Okinawa, at government level Japan remained one of the more accommodating and compliant host nations in the global security system. The 1960 Treaty on Mutual Co-operation and Security gave the United States considerable flexibility in using Japan as a base for power projection in the Far East. This was acknowledged, along with the American role in the defence of Japan, in the Military Posture Statement prepared by the Department of Defense Joint Staff for 1989:

United States bases in Japan play a vital role in Japan's defense and provide operational and logistics bases for US operations throughout North-East Asia.[35]

For her part, Japan gained substantial economic benefits from running a relatively small defence budget in proportion to her national wealth. For political and historical reasons she was in no hurry to adopt a more assertive defence policy. Instead, she was content to meet an increasing share of the in-country security costs incurred by the United States. It suited her to remain a subordinate partner to the United States in security terms while increasingly challenging her guardian on the economic front.

After the Cold War

With the end of the Cold War, the United States made a series of attempts to give a semblance of greater equality to the security relationship. In January 1992, President Bush issued jointly with the Japanese Prime Minister, Kiichi Miyazawa, the Tokyo Declaration on United States–Japan Global Partnership in which the two countries agreed to cooperate in promoting international security. Moreover, political support in Japan for the American military presence increased rather than diminished following the end of the Cold War. Hitherto, the socialist opposition had been hostile to the American alliance but the short-lived coalition government led by the socialist Prime Minister Tomiichi Muruyama from April 1994 to January 1996 saw the erosion of this hostility and the growth of all-party support for the American security connection. The Clinton administration reaffirmed the security relationship between the United States and Japan in February 1993, but the start of the administration was dominated by increasingly acrimonious commercial disputes between the two countries, with the trade deficit reaching a record $65 billion in Japan's favour in 1994. To counter this Joseph

[35] *US Military Posture FY 1989*. Prepared by the Joint Planning Staff. (USGPO, 26).

Nye, Assistant Secretary of Defense, launched an initiative in January 1995 designed to revive the security relationship, which was in danger of faltering as the commercial climate deteriorated, and in April 1996, a security summit meeting took place between President Clinton and the new Prime Minister Ryutaro Hashimoto. This meeting had been carefully prepared but it was inevitably influenced by both the aftermath of the Okinawa rape case in September 1995 and the more recent confrontation between the United States and China over Taiwan in March 1996.

The Okinawa incident was by no means unique. There had been similar cases over the years but the rape of a 12-year-old schoolgirl attracted widespread media attention, acted as a catalyst for the pent-up grievances of the islanders and focused discussion on the heavy concentration of American forces remaining on Okinawa after the end of the Cold War. In these circumstances, the United States was obliged to make a number of concessions to local opinion. It had already been agreed that the naval port of Naha and the airfield at Yomitan should be returned to the island authorities. At the summit it was confirmed that Futenma air base and ten other sites, comprising 20 per cent of the land used by the Americans, would be returned over a period of five to seven years and that some American troops would be transferred from Okinawa to the home islands. The details were settled in a Special Action Committee on Okinawa which reported in December 1996 but plans for an offshore helicopter base to replace Futenma were later costed at $2 billion, and in December 1997 local residents voted against proceeding with the project. Moreover, the reduction in American troops turned out to be only 5 per cent and Mashide Ota campaigned vigorously for further withdrawals. In June 1996, local elections on the island returned a majority of candidates opposed to the American military presence and in September that year Ota arranged a plebiscite at which 90 per cent of the islanders voted for further reductions in the bases. Meanwhile, he declined to renew some 3,000 leases for land required at the bases until compelled to do so by a ruling of the Supreme Court which was consolidated by legislation in the Diet in April 1997. By now, Ota's dispute was as much with the government in Tokyo as with the United States, and Hashimoto was obliged to visit Okinawa with promises of financial assistance. Tension continued on the island until a governor more sympathetic to the American military presence was elected in November 1998.

For the United States, concessions on Okinawa were an exercise in damage limitation but China's attempt to intimidate Taiwan in March

1996, prior to the Taiwanese presidential elections, provided a timely reminder of the risks of conflict in Asia just before the security summit in Tokyo. In response to a series of Chinese missile tests in the Straits of Taiwan the United States was able to demonstrate her continuing commitment to Taiwan and her other allies in the region by dispatching two carrier battle groups to the Straits. The incident underlined the relevance of the United States military presence in Asia following the end of the Cold War and the importance of access to secure bases from which American forces could be deployed. Against this background it was appropriate for Clinton and Hashimoto meeting in April to reinforce the US–Japan Security Treaty of 1960 and proclaim an 'Alliance for the Twenty-First Century'. The United States agreed that her force levels in Japan would remain unchanged, despite minor redeployments between Okinawa and the home islands, while Japan agreed to play a more active role in regional defence, to participate in joint naval exercises outside territorial waters, and to take a more prominent part in international peacekeeping operations. It was agreed that 'instability and uncertainty persist in the region' where 'there were still heavy concentrations of nuclear force', and it was acknowledged that the United States–Japan security relationship 'remains the cornerstone for maintaining a stable and prosperous environment in the Asia-Pacific region'. Specifically the two countries agreed to

Bilateral policy co-ordination, including studies in bilateral co-operation in dealing with situations that may emerge in the areas surrounding Japan, that will have an important influence on the security of Japan.[36]

These undertakings, which were developed in new Guidelines on Joint Defense Operations in September 1997, were presented as evidence that Japan had come of age in security terms and was at last accepted as a partner by the United States rather than a dependent. But in reality very little has changed. The United States continues to maintain substantial forces in Japan, including the military bastion she has built up on Okinawa, primarily to underwrite the security of East Asia as a whole, with the defence of Japan herself being a secondary and somewhat unlikely eventuality. In pursuit of this objective, which she sees as a long-term commitment, the United States stations 39,000 troops in Japan, made up of 16,600 Marines, 14,000 USAF personnel, 7,000 US Navy personnel, and a small US Army contingent of under 2,000. The main force elements are the Marine Expeditionary Force in Okinawa, a carrier battle group of the Seventh Fleet based at Yokosuka,

---

[36] Joint Declaration on Security. 17 April 1996.

and one and a half Tactical Fighter Wings with some 90 combat aircraft, mainly F-15s and F-16s. The role of these forces is to support South Korea if required, to project American power in the region, and to ensure stability in Asia by deterring a struggle for power between Japan and China. In effect 'double containment' is at work in Japan no less than in Germany, but Japan is still expected to provide extensive logistic support for the American forces on her territory and her own Self Defence Forces still have a relatively limited role which largely complements the forces of the United States.

What has changed is that the role of Japan in providing a convenient offshore base for American power projection in Asia is now openly acknowledged and is broadly accepted within Japan. The references in the text of the April 1996 communiqué to regional instability and uncertainty and 'situations which may emerge in the areas surrounding Japan' have aroused none of the hostility or suspicion which the Far East Clause of the 1960 treaty originally prompted. A number of developments over the intervening years may account for this. The memories of the wars in Korea and Vietnam have faded. Despite the difficulties of the late 1990s, Japan has grown significantly in self-confidence as a result of her economic success since 1945. Moreover, the sense of partnership evoked by references to bilateral policy co-ordination and studies in bilateral cooperation has no doubt done much to placate Japanese *amour-propre*.

But it may be that Japan has become reconciled to her role. In 1983, Nakasone described Japan in an interview with the *Washington Post* as a large aircraft carrier for the United States, echoing the phrase that Winston Churchill had used to describe Britain during the war.[37] Both offshore islands provided a friendly and accommodating environment for the deployment of American troops but while Britain prided herself on her close military partnership with the United States (which may have contributed to her relative economic decline), Japan seemed content to remain a military dependency of the United States while building up a huge trade surplus with her protector. Yet, at the end of the twentieth century, with the Soviet Union no longer a military threat, there remains something disturbing about the sight of the world's second largest economy (still responsible for 13 per cent of global production despite her economic difficulties) playing host to the forces of the world's sole surviving superpower. The two nations appear to be

---

[37] J. Auer, Defense Burden Sharing and the US–Japanese Alliance. In M. Mochizuki, *Japan and the United States* (London: Brassey's, 1991, Ch. 2).

locked in an embrace which they are unable or unwilling to break. Kissinger has predicted that 'The New World order, with its multiplicity of challenges, will almost certainly oblige a country with so proud a past to re-examine its reliance on a single ally'.[38] But there is little sign of any radical re-examination so far and it appears that neither nation wishes to make significant changes to the status quo.

South Korea

Post-war Planning and Military Government

Situated on the mainland of Asia, South Korea was never intended to be part of the United States global security system. No fighting had taken place in Korea during the Second World War and at the end of the war the United States had not originally proposed to occupy the country, even though it had been under Japanese domination since the turn of the century. The Treaty of Portsmouth, brokered by Theodore Roosevelt in 1905, which ended the Russo-Japanese War, had recognized Japan's 'paramount political, military and economic interest in Korea'. At the same time, William Howard Taft, then the United States Secretary of War, had concluded a secret agreement with Japan giving her a free hand in Korea on condition that she did not interfere with the United States in the Philippines. Five years later, Japan, with the acquiescence of the Western powers, formally annexed Korea and thereafter Americans gave little thought to the 'Hermit Kingdom' until obliged to do so by the exigencies of the Second World War. The Cairo Declaration of 1943, signed by the United States, Britain, and China, had promised 'that in due course Korea shall become free and independent'. The cautious note in the declaration reflected Franklin D. Roosevelt's uncharacteristically colonialist view that 'the Koreans are not yet capable of exercising and maintaining an independent government'.[39]

Drawing on American experience in the Philippines, Roosevelt envisaged a 40-year period of trusteeship for Korea before she achieved full independence. But the military authorities in Washington, believing that they faced a long battle to conquer Japan itself, followed by further campaigns against Japanese forces in Asia, were wholly unprepared to

---

[38] H. Kissinger, *Diplomacy* (London: Simon & Schuster, 1994, 26).
[39] Minutes of a meeting of the Pacific War Council, 12 January 1944. Cited by G.-K. Kinderman. In H. C. Hinton *The US–Korean Security Relationship: Prospects and Challenges for the 1990s* (London: Pergamon/Brassey's, 1988).

assume responsibility for Korea in 1945. No detailed planning had been undertaken since the Cairo Declaration and the sudden surrender of all Japanese forces after the dropping of the atom bombs consequently found the United States without a settled policy on Korea. Although Stalin had endorsed the provisions of the Cairo Declaration at the Tehran Conference in 1943, it soon became apparent that, unless an American presence could be quickly established in the country, the Soviet Union would gain sole occupation. It was therefore arranged for Soviet troops to accept the surrender of Japanese forces north of the 38th Parallel and for American troops to do the same to the south. This proposal, which was to have far-reaching consequences for the peninsula, was prepared in Washington, in some haste, at midnight on 10/11 August 1945 by two American officers to meet a request for urgent advice from the State–War–Navy Co-ordinating Committee. One of the officers was a Major Dean Rusk, who was later to became President Kennedy's Secretary of State.

The United States was agreeably surprised that Stalin readily accepted what was intended to be a temporary demarcation line along the 38th Parallel, which placed the capital Seoul in the American sector. But in the absence of any firm American plans for the country, it was not until 3 September 1945, some three weeks after the Japanese surrender, that the US Seventh Infantry Division under General John Hodge landed at Inchon to commence the occupation of South Korea. General Hodge had been chosen by General MacArthur, who was preoccupied with Japan, mainly on the grounds that he was readily available in Okinawa. Hodge, a tough combat general who had risen from the ranks, had no political experience and little guidance from Washington on how to administer a former Japanese colony. His limited instructions prevented him from extending formal recognition to any indigenous political organizations but he found himself in a country expecting to be liberated rather than occupied. The surrender of Japan had given rise to an intense burst of spontaneous political activity in the hope of early self-government. Seeing this activity as a threat to his authority, Hodge declined to deal with the emerging political groups awaiting him and turned first to the Japanese colonial administration to run the country and, when this approach caused a public outcry, to direct military rule, based on the colonial system and employing many Koreans who had served the Japanese.

Under the United States military government little was done to develop a moderate coalition of political forces which might run the country once the occupation came to an end. Concerned at the consolidation of a communist regime in the North and the considerable sympathy for communism in the South, the American authorities allowed political power in the South to be built up by Syngman Rhee, a 70-year-old political exile known for his strong anti-communist stance, whom they had brought back from the United States. Instead of laying a firm foundation for a moderate democratic system of government for the future, the military government alienated those who might have developed such a system and unwittingly paved the way for forty years of authoritarian government reinforced by the threat from the North and the fragile security situation in the South.

The official American handbook on South Korea has acknowledged that:

The three-year occupation period following the liberation of Korea was characterised by uncertainty and confusion, stemming largely from the absence of a clearly formulated policy for Korea and intensification of the conflict between the United States and the Soviet Union.[40]

The fundamental problem was that the political aspirations of the Koreans proved incompatible with the deliberations of the Allied Powers. Roosevelt's trusteeship scheme had been endorsed in modified form after his death at a meeting of Foreign Ministers in Moscow in December 1945. It was agreed that the United States, Britain, the Soviet Union, and China would set up a Joint Commission to work out arrangements for a Four Power Trusteeship to run for five years 'to guide the Korean people towards full independence'. But discussions between the United States and the Soviet Union broke down over which political groups to consult. Only the communists (under instruction) were prepared to agree to trusteeship and the Soviet Union maintained that only those agreeing to trusteeship should be consulted. Faced with this impasse the United States submitted the future of Korea to the United Nations General Assembly in September 1947 and secured acceptance of an American resolution setting up a Temporary Commission (in place of the Joint Commission) to observe elections to a Korean National Assembly by the end of March 1948. The Americans hoped that the country would be reunited and would gain its independence following free elections held under United Nations supervision. However, the Soviet Union declined to cooperate with the United Nations Temporary Commission and in May 1948 the United States, exasperated by Soviet obstruction, proceeded with separate elections in the South which were won by Syngman Rhee.

[40] A. M. Savada and W. Shaw (ed.), *South Korea. A Country Study*, Washington, DC: Federal Research Division. Library of Congress (USGPO).

The independent Republic of Korea was established in the South in August 1948 and the Democratic People's Republic was set up in the North in September. Neither government recognized the other and each claimed sovereignty over the whole peninsula. Despite this unsettled situation the United States, faced with growing military commitments in Europe and reluctant to maintain troops on the Asian mainland, proceeded with plans for an early withdrawal of her occupation forces. In April 1948, President Truman had endorsed an assessment made by the Joint Chiefs of Staff in September 1947 that the United States had 'little strategic interest in maintaining its present troops and bases in Korea' and that the occupation forces 'could well be used elsewhere'.[41] This was entirely consistent with the American desire to disengage from the Asian mainland and rely on the Pacific island chain as the outer defensive perimeter of the United States. George Kennan, in a lecture to the National War College on 11 October 1948, asserted that 'you do not need to hold positions on the Eurasian land-mass to protect our national security',[42] and the following year General MacArthur spelt out the policy in a newspaper interview:

. . . Our line of defence runs through the chain of islands fringing the coast of Asia. It starts from the Philippines and continues through the Ryukyu archipelago, which includes its main bastion, Okinawa. Then it bends back through Japan and the Aleutian Island chain to Alaska.[43]

The Effect of the War

The new South Korean government protested at the proposed withdrawal, but in December 1948 the United Nations passed a resolution calling for the withdrawal of all foreign troops from Korea. The Soviet Union complied by the end of the year, and by June 1949 47,000 American troops were withdrawn from South Korea, leaving only 500 men in a Military Advisory Team, whose task was to build up the fledgling South Korean army. This consisted of some 65,000 men previously employed as paramilitary police using military equipment donated by the United States. An initial tranche of equipment valued at $1.5 million was delivered by the end of 1949 with further allocations

[41] JCS Memorandum to Secretary of Defense, 25 September 1947. JCS 483/44. Cited by L. S. Bok, *The Impact of US Forces in Korea* (Washington, DC: National Defense University Press, 1987). For Truman's endorsement see Lee and Sato, op. cit. 9.

[42] J. L. Gaddis, *The Long Peace* (Oxford: OUP, 1987).

[43] 1 March 1949. Cited in *The Sun Never Sets*, J. Gerson and B. Birchard (ed.), (Boston, MA: South End Press, 1991).

worth $10.2 million promised under the Mutual Defense Assistance Act which Truman had signed in October. Twelve months after the American withdrawal, on 25 June 1950, North Korea invaded the South. Some felt that Dean Acheson had inadvertently encouraged the invasion by his speech on 12 January 1950, in which he had made it clear, in accordance with Washington policy at the time, that Korea lay outside the American defence perimeter and as such could not be guaranteed against military attack. However, Acheson now saw the invasion as 'an open, undisguised challenge to our internationally accepted position as the protector of Korea'.[44] The United States was convinced that the invasion had been masterminded by the Soviet Union and foreshadowed a similar offensive in Europe. In a speech characteristic of this view Truman declared:

The attack on Korea makes it plain beyond all doubt that communism has passed beyond the use of subversion to conquer independent nations and will now use armed force and war.[45]

Although the United States had no treaty commitment to South Korea, she immediately dispatched three divisions from Japan and, with the Soviet Union boycotting the Security Council, she was able to mobilize a coalition under United Nations auspices to counter the invasion. Sixteen nations joined the coalition, including Turkey, (who sent a large contingent because she was anxious to gain admission to NATO), but the United States played the dominant role, suffering 140,000 casualties with 33,000 dead during the three-year war. By the time of the armistice signed at Panmunjon in July 1953, the United States had become fully committed to the defence of South Korea and saw no alternative to maintaining substantial forces in the country to deter the continuing threat from the North. South Korea, occupied by the United States against her will in 1945, had unwittingly become an integral part of the United States global security system eight years later.

In part, the continuing military presence by the United States was required to persuade Syngman Rhee to accept the armistice, even though he declined to sign it, not wishing to perpetuate the division of his country. The conclusion of the Mutual Defense Treaty between the United States and the Republic of Korea in October 1953 also helped to overcome Rhee's objections but South Korea is still technically at war with the North. Despite the continuing threat from the North,

---

[44] Lee and Sato, op. cit.

[45] Richard Detrio, *Strategic Partners: South Korea and the United States* (Washington, DC: National Defense University Press, 1989).

and the marked difference in the security environment, the terms of the Mutual Defense Treaty with South Korea closely resemble those previously agreed with the Philippines and jointly with Australia and New Zealand. The United States made no commitment to maintain troops in South Korea, but Article IV stated that:

The Republic of Korea grants, and the United States of America accepts, the right to dispose United States land, air and sea forces in and about the territory of the Republic of Korea, as determined by mutual agreement.

The key provisions on assistance in the event of attack, which were identical in all three treaties, appeared in Articles II and III. Article II provided that:

The parties will consult together whenever the political independence or security of either of the parties is threatened by external armed attack.

Article III developed the provisions on consultation in a manner identical to those offered to the Philippines, and Australia and New Zealand:

Each party recognises that an armed attack in the Pacific area on either of the parties in territories now under their respective administrative control ... would be dangerous to its own peace and safety and declares that it would act to meet the common danger in accordance with its constitutional processes.[46]

For a country that had just emerged from a three-year war that threatened its very survival, these provisions fell some way short of a cast-iron security guarantee. They were a good deal less robust than the commitment to common defence in the North Atlantic Treaty (although a considerable improvement over the terms of the 1951 treaty with Japan, which contained no such commitment until revised in 1960). Many South Koreans felt that the emphasis on consultation and the lack of any automatic response to repel an armed attack represented an inadequate recognition of their security needs.

Whatever the terms of the treaty, the outcome of the Korean War and the continuing threat from the North made South Korea a front-line member of the United States global security system and one, by force of circumstance as well as the legacy of occupation, in which the American military authorities occupied a dominant position. In the Taejon Agreement of 1950, Syngman Rhee had placed all South Korean forces under the command of General MacArthur as United Nations

---

[46] Mutual Defense Treaty between the United States of America and the Republic of Korea. Signed 1 October 1953. TIAS 3097.

Commander and this arrangement continued after the armistice, with the senior American officer in South Korea retaining operational control of South Korea's armed forces. In 1968, following the seizure of the *Pueblo* by North Korea, a Security Consultative Committee was set up which was to meet annually. In 1976, a series of annual joint military exercises known as TEAM SPIRIT was inaugurated which brought together 100,000 American and South Korean troops. Military integration was taken one stage further in November 1978 with the creation of the United States–Republic of Korea Combined Forces Command under an American General. This arrangement, which replaced the Taejon Agreement of 1950, created a Combined Field Army made up of the US Second Infantry Division and the ROK Third Army with staff positions shared evenly between the two nations. The small residual contingent of United Nations troops was henceforward restricted to supervision of the armistice.

Meanwhile, all South Korea's military equipment was purchased from the United States on the advice of the American Military Mission, although no tanks or heavy equipment were supplied in the early years for fear that South Korea would implement Syngman Rhee's threat to 'March North'. There was a widespread perception that South Korea had become a military dependency of the United States who dictated her foreign and defence policy. For example, South Korea had no direct contacts with Japan on security issues until the 1980s. These were all channelled through the Americans. South Koreans tended to take a gloomy view of their country's dependency status. Writing in 1982, Lee and Sato concluded:

The three year Korean War established South Korea as a United States client state par excellence in the areas of military, economic and diplomatic relations.[47]

Some American commentators have been almost as severe:

Out of four decades as a Japanese colony, South Korea emerged in 1945 into two decades of existence, if not exactly an American client state, at any rate a state dependent on the United States for survival.[48]

The Political System in South Korea

While there were military advantages for the United States in this degree of dependency and integration, there were also political pitfalls

[47] Lee and Sato, op. cit.
[48] H. C. Hinton, The US–Korean Relationship: An American Perspective. In *The US–Korean Security Relationship: Prospects and Challenges for the 1990s* (London: Pergamon/Brassey's, 1988).

arising from responsibility for the defence of a country governed by a succession of repressive and authoritarian regimes. To some extent, the Americans themselves were to blame for the dilemma in which they found themselves by relying on the hardline anti-communists who surrounded Syngman Rhee. They had also been obliged to resort to force themselves, in order to keep the peace during the occupation period, thereby setting a precedent for dealing with public order problems which South Korean governments were only to happy to emulate. In the autumn of 1946, disturbances broke out in Taegu, provoked mainly by economic distress, which the South Korean police could not contain. American troops were compelled to step in to restore order and impose martial law. Subsequently the overriding needs of security, brought home first by communist subversion and reinforced by the traumatic experiences of the Korean War, were deployed as justification for a series of restrictive measures by autocratic governments with little regard for human rights. But the United States felt obliged to support these governments. When General Park Chung Hee seized power in 1961, the State Department welcomed the 'hopeful and constructive signs' shown by the new regime and President Kennedy promised full economic and military support.[49] Park's successor, General Chun Doo Hwan, was one of the first foreign leaders to be invited to visit President Reagan in 1981, and American backing enabled him to survive a major financial scandal in 1982.

The governments of Rhee, Park, and Chun over the period 1952–87 were all autocratic. The pattern was established by Syngman Rhee who had ruthlessly suppressed a military revolt at Yosu in October 1948 with the loss of 2,000 lives, and had followed this up with a purge of the army, widespread arrests, and imprisonment of members of the National Assembly. Authoritarian government provided the framework for strong economic growth from the 1960s onwards but the processes of government were characterized by corruption, manipulation of the Constitution, student revolt, resort to martial law, suppression of human and political rights, and even political abduction and assassination. By 1987, when a more democratic government took office, the Constitution adopted in 1948 had been amended on nine separate occasions. During the Korean War, Syngman Rhee was re-elected under martial law in 1952, and two years later he forced measures through the National Assembly granting himself exemption from the constitutional limit of two four-year terms. But in 1960, he was

[49] D. S. Lewis (ed.) *Korea: Enduring Division? Keesing Special Reports.* (London: Longman, 1988, 52).

compelled to resign as a result of student agitation and widespread rioting following a blatantly rigged election. He was succeeded after a short interval by Park who staged a military coup in May 1961. The National Assembly was dissolved, martial law was declared, and political activity was banned.

Park retired from the army in August 1963 and was elected President as a civilian in December. But his government was dominated by former military officers and Park himself perpetuated his rule by tinkering with the Constitution in 1969 and again in 1972, first to give himself a third term and then unlimited tenure. Martial law was declared in 1964, following extensive student demonstrations against the proposal to restore normal relations with Japan and also in 1972 when the 1962 Constitution was suspended and the National Assembly once more dissolved. In 1973, the opposition leader Kim Dae Jung was abducted from Tokyo by the Korean CIA. The following year, Park's wife was killed in an assassination attempt and in 1979, in the midst of further student riots and an uprising in Pusan, Park himself was assassinated in a restaurant by the Director of the Korean CIA, who disagreed with his handling of the disturbances. So ended a regime which has been described as a 'dictatorship punctuated by electoral manoeuvres of limited scope and dubious morality'.[50]

Park was replaced by Chun who instigated a coup in December 1979. Chun was a disciplinarian who believed that South Korea 'obviously requires the leadership and control of the military'.[51] Opposition to his regime crystallized the following year in a prolonged uprising in Kwangju. Students and other dissidents battled with the army and police for nine days in May 1980 before the rising was brutally suppressed with the loss of over 200 lives. A further period of repression followed which was intensified after the assassination plot perpetrated by North Korean agents in Rangoon in October 1983. Although Chun himself survived, seventeen members of his entourage, including several Cabinet Ministers, were killed. But the external threat failed to quell protest at home. The mid 1980s were a turbulent period with mass rallies and demonstrations in 1986 and 1987, and the main opposition leaders, Kim Dae Jung and Kim Young Sam, in and out of house arrest and exile abroad. The unrest was driven in part by the fear that Chun, like Park, would not step down when his presidency ended in 1988. At times, the country appeared to be out of control, with pitched battles between protesters

[50] D. S. Lewis. 64.   [51] Ibid. 70.

and police an almost daily occurrence. Since the protesters believed that the United States supported Chun, attacks on American institutions were a common occurrence, with several offices of the US Information Service being occupied and even set on fire. In the same vein, pressure built up at a later stage to move the US military headquarters from its prime site in Itaewon in central Seoul and this pressure was eventually successful.

In June 1987, General Roh Tae Woo, who had played a key role in bringing Chun to power, realized that opposition demands would have to be met. His proposals for reform were accepted by Chun who kept his promise to retire in 1988. Roh subsequently won the first direct presidential election in South Korea for sixteen years (largely because the Kims failed to agree on a single candidate), and the first peaceful transfer of power took place in the history of the Republic. But popular agitation continued with student demonstrations threatening to disrupt the Seoul Olympics in 1988 and rallies of over 200,000 in the capital in the early 1990s. It was only with the election of Kim Young Sam in 1992 that South Korea had a President with no military background for the first time since 1960. Kim came to power as a radical reformer on a strong anti-corruption ticket. Chun and Roh were tried and imprisoned both for corruption and for treason in connection with the 1980 coup. But Kim was unable to eradicate the prevailing culture. His own family was implicated in further financial scandals and in the mid 1990s his former Ministers of Health and Defence were jailed for corruption while another minister and a presidential aide were arrested. It was not until the presidential election in December 1997, won by Kim Dae Jung, that South Korea experienced its first peaceful transfer of power to an opposition party. Meanwhile, demonstrations continued in the more liberal political environment, prompted partly by labour disputes and partly by political disaffection. Some of these demonstrations were overt protests against the American military presence. In May 1996 students demanded that American forces should withdraw from South Korea and that the United States should accept some responsibility for the Kwangju massacre. The demand for withdrawal was repeated at demonstrations in Seoul in August 1996.

The US Dilemma

In these circumstances it is easy to sympathize with the American commentator who declared in 1988 that:

Americans, both official and unofficial, have tended to be unhappy with the South Korean political system since 1948.[52]

The problem for the United States was that, although the opposition groups in South Korea held her in part responsible for the character and policies of these autocratic regimes, in reality her ability to influence events within the Republic was limited, particularly under Park. The South Korean armed forces, nominally under American command, had a hand in all the major transfers of power between 1953 and 1987. In 1960, a South Korean army division was detached from its United Nations duties in an attempt to restore order in Seoul following the fraudulent election in April. This pattern was repeated in 1961, when South Korean troops were again removed from the joint United Nations Command to help Park seize power. And in 1979, the coup launched by Chun was secured by the timely intervention of army units moved from the border by General Roh Tae Woo without the knowledge of the American commander, General John Wakeman. Although the United States was not directly involved in these interventions, she inevitably became identified with local leaders who had gained power by force.

The United States did what she could to express disapproval of the more extreme measures implemented by these authoritarian regimes but her representations were not always successful. In 1971, Congress voiced its concern about human rights under President Park by amending the Foreign Assistance Act to require the State Department to report on the human rights record of countries receiving aid. But in 1972, following a leadership crisis over relations with the North, Park took emergency powers, suspending the Constitution and curbing the freedom of the press. Three years later, in May 1975, Park made it a crime to criticize the Constitution. Again in 1976, President Ford, in response to pressure from Congress, protested at a series of political trials mounted by Park's government but without any noticeable effect. American pressure had a greater impact on President Chun. It is believed that this prevented a full-scale military response to the Kwangju uprising in 1980 and the following year strong representations were made against the death sentence imposed on the opposition leader Kim Dae Jung as a result of the uprising. As a mark of displeasure, the United States declined to attend the annual meeting of the Security Consultative Committee and on this occasion American action suc-

[52] Hinton, op. cit.

ceeded in getting the death sentence commuted. The United States also played an important part in persuading Chun to accept reform and step down in 1987.

American Force Reductions

Despite the integration of American and South Korean forces in the republic, the continuing threat from the North and the American commitment to resisting this, the extent of South Korea's dependency on the United States left the country feeling vulnerable and insecure. South Korea was severely shaken by Nixon's rapprochement with China in 1972, and the subsequent admission of the People's Republic of China to the United Nations at the expense of Taiwan. But the main cause of disquiet were the proposals under Presidents Nixon and Carter to reduce American troops in South Korea. As in West Germany, the other divided country directly faced with a communist threat, the United States came to resent the high level of ground forces she was obliged to station in South Korea and made various attempts to reduce these, first to meet the demands of the war in Vietnam and later for wider strategic and economic reasons. In addition, South Korea, in common with other allies of the United States in South-East Asia, came under increasing pressure to send forces of her own to Vietnam, notwithstanding the ever-present danger on her northern border.

Following the Korean War, American troops in the Republic were progressively reduced from 360,000 men to approximately 60,000. Two US Army divisions were retained, one guarding the western section of the Demilitarised Zone north of Seoul, and the other held in reserve south of Seoul. These were backed by tactical nuclear weapons and approximately 100 combat aircraft at six major air bases. In 1957, the United Nations Command declared that it would no longer be bound by the force limits set out in the Armistice because of repeated violations by North Korea but made no immediate move to increase its forces. The following year, China proposed that all outside troops be removed from Korea. The United States declined to withdraw her troops and China, seeing her bluff called, withdrew her forces unilaterally. Thereafter, the United States garrison was maintained at much the same levels throughout the 1960s, although additional Air Force units were despatched to South Korea following the seizure of the *Pueblo* by North Korea in January 1968 and the detention of her crew for eleven months. Similar reinforcement action was taken in response to the North Korean attack on an American reconnaissance aircraft over the Sea of Japan in April 1969, and the killing of two American officers with an axe at Panmunjon in August 1976.

During the Vietnam War, South Korea, in common with Thailand and the Philippines, came under considerable pressure from President Johnson to make a contribution to the American war effort. Initially, South Korea was prepared to supply only a small number of non-combat troops, including an army field hospital, since she was naturally concerned not to weaken her defences against North Korea. However, she was more concerned that American forces should not be withdrawn to fight in Vietnam and an assurance was obtained in a letter signed in July 1965 by General Beach, Commander of US Forces in Korea, and Ambassador Winthrop Brown stating that 'the US decision that there would be no reduction in force levels remained unchanged' and that 'no US troops would be withdrawn without prior consultation with the Republic of Korea'.[53] This assurance was reaffirmed by Vice-President Hubert Humphrey in February 1966 and President Johnson in November 1966. South Korea drew some comfort from these assurances and had by 1969 increased her troops in Vietnam to 50,000, organized, directed, and financed entirely by the United States, which also made available a military modernization package of $140 million to South Korea in 1970.

However, the 1965 agreement on force reductions was to provide little reassurance under President Nixon. The Guam Doctrine of 1969, stating that America's Asian allies must do more in their own defence, was a severe shock to South Korea. Worse was yet to come. In March 1970, Nixon unilaterally announced the withdrawal of one of the two American infantry divisions stationed in South Korea. There had been no prior consultation with the South Korean government, which argued that unilateral withdrawal would be destabilizing, would cause concern to Japan, and remove any chance of negotiating reciprocal reductions in the North. As these arguments made little headway in Washington, the South Korean authorities felt obliged to adopt unorthodox countermeasures. Advertisements opposing the withdrawal were taken out in the *Washington Post*. Threats were made about leaving one section of the Demilitarised Zone unguarded, and hints were dropped about the withdrawal of South Korean troops from Vietnam. However, none of these more drastic measures

[53] Lee Suk Bok, op. cit.

was implemented, and in March 1971 the 20,000 men of the US Seventh Infantry Division left South Korea, leaving South Korean troops to guard the whole of the 155 miles of the Demilitarised Zone for the first time. American forces in Korea now comprised the Second Infantry Division, the 38th Air Defense Brigade equipped with Nike Hercules and the 4th Missile Command equipped with Honest John and Sergeant Missiles. The embittered government of South Korea had demanded a further military modernization package of $4 billion in compensation. Only $1.5 billion was conceded and this took many years to deliver.

Following these reductions, the American withdrawal from Vietnam and the rapprochement with China touched a raw nerve in South Korea. President Ford did his best to reassure the South Koreans, underlining in 1974 'the determination of the United States to render prompt and effective assistance to repel armed attack against the Republic of Korea in accordance with the Mutual Defense Treaty of 1954'.[54] However, in the 1976 presidential campaign the Democratic candidate, Governor Carter, made a campaign pledge to withdraw all United States ground forces from Korea over a period of four to five years. Once elected, President Carter was determined to honour this pledge, even though the proposed withdrawal was strongly opposed by Congress, the Joint Chiefs of Staff, and the CIA in the United States, and by both Korea and Japan overseas. A plan was drawn up to withdraw 6,000 troops by 1978 and the remainder by 1981/82.

The proposed withdrawal was badly handled from start to finish, causing grave offence to an important ally. In 1977, Vice-President Mondale informed the Japanese in Tokyo of the new administration's intentions, but failed to visit Seoul for consultations. In country, General John Singlaub, Chief of Staff of the US Eighth Army in Korea, expressed his concern in an interview with the *Washington Post*. He was reprimanded by President Carter and relieved of his command. At home, the President's proposals caused Congress to pass the Foreign Relations Authorisation Act in 1978 requiring that the withdrawal should be jointly decided by the President and Congress. Many in Congress were opposed to any withdrawal at all. Others wished to obtain parallel reductions from North Korea. With the South Koreans again lobbying intensively in Washington against withdrawal and inviting eminent Americans to Seoul, the waters were considerably muddied by scandal.

---

[54] Lee and Sato, op. cit.

A South Korean businessman was alleged to have distributed $750,000 to Congressmen in order to gain their support.[55]

Eventually, President Carter was obliged to climb down when new intelligence data, released in January 1979, indicated that North Korea had forty divisions rather than the twenty-nine earlier assumed, and 2,600 tanks, not 2,000. Carter visited Seoul in June 1979 but no announcements were made at that time. It was left to his National Security Advisor, Zbigniew Brzezinski, to announce the following month that the withdrawals had been suspended. As a face-saver, South Korea agreed to increase its defence budget from 5.5 per cent of GNP to 6 per cent from 1980 onwards. The whole episode did considerable damage to American credibility, not only in Korea but also in Japan which was strongly opposed to the withdrawal. There had been minimum consultation, both over the original proposal and the change of policy two and a half years later. Commenting on the debacle in 1982, Lee and Sato stated that 'South Koreans were ill disposed to tolerate procedural discourtesy or diplomatic insult on so fundamental a question as their own national security'.[56]

Realignment and Recovery

President Reagan took office determined to improve relations with South Korea. Concern over the domestic policies of the South Korean government took second place to the worldwide struggle against communism. President Chun received an early invitation to visit the new president, notwithstanding his record at home. A joint communiqué issued in Washington after the meeting in February 1981 stated that the United States 'has no plans for withdrawing US ground forces from the Korean peninsula'.[57] The United States also promised to 'make available for sale to Korea appropriate weapons systems and the defense industry technology necessary for enhancing Korea's capability for deterring aggression'. The following month, at the annual meeting of the US–Korea Security Consultative Committee in San Francisco, Casper Weinberger, Secretary of Defense, followed up this pledge by promising to sell thirty-eight F-16 aircraft to Korea and provide credit concessions on the military sales package of $327 million. At the 1982 meeting, Weinberger reaffirmed the formula earlier used by President Ford, promising

[55] Byung-joon Ahn, South Korea and Taiwan. In *Security Interdependence in the Asia Pacific Region*, J. Morley (ed.), (Lexington, MA: Lexington Books, 1986, Ch. 4).
[56] Lee and Sato, op. cit.
[57] *State Department Bulletin*, March 1981, Vol. 81, No 2048. Cited by R. Detrio.

'prompt and effective assistance to repel invasion'.[58] President Reagan made a return visit to Seoul in November 1983.

The Korean Peninsula is the one area of East–West conflict that has remained virtually unaffected by the end of the Cold War. In the late 1980s, the catalogue of atrocities committed by North Korea continued with the destruction of a South Korean airliner over Burma by a bomb and, with a high level of tension persisting, substantial American forces have remained in the South. In July 1989, the United States and the Republic of Korea reiterated their commitment to retaining US troops in South Korea as long as the governments and peoples of both countries wanted them.[59] With the end of the Cold War, President Bush announced plans to reduce American forces in Asia from 135,000 to 120,000, with some of these reductions being made in South Korea. However, President Clinton reassured South Korea of the American commitment to her defence when he visited Seoul in July 1993 and reaffirmed this commitment in April 1996. Under Clinton, the United States has pledged to maintain 100,000 American troops in Asia with 36,000 of these in South Korea. Ground forces of 27,000 men comprise the major element of this deployment. An enhanced infantry division is based at Camp Casey, 25 miles north of Seoul and 12 miles south of the border, with a further smaller detachment at Camp Humphreys, 50 miles south of Seoul. The US Air Force contributes a further 9,000 personnel and approximately 90 combat aircraft, mainly F-16s based at Kunsan and Osan, the headquarters of Seventh Air Force. These forces are supported by a significant infrastructure system with military ports at Pusan and Inchon and an extensive military pipeline linking the major bases. In 1996 plans were implemented to preposition a heavy brigade set of equipment in South Korea to facilitate reinforcement. Overall, the support system is not dissimilar to that established within NATO, albeit on a smaller scale. But while the threat faced by NATO has receded with the end of the Cold War, that facing South Korea remains.

From the mid 1960s onwards South Korea achieved a remarkable rate of sustained economic growth, averaging over 9.5 per cent for the years 1963–83 and generating a trade surplus with the United States from 1982, which rose to $4,000 million in 1985 and $9,500 million in 1987. This exceptional economic performance inevitably gave rise to demands in the United States for offset or burden-sharing on the costs of

---

[58] Byung-joon Ahn, op. cit.
[59] DoD Annual Report to the President and Congress for FY 1991. January 1990.

stationing American forces in the country. Similar demands had arisen in relation to both Germany and Japan but the pressures on South Korea were less severe and arose very much later. The vehicle devised for meeting these demands was the Combined Defense Improvement Program under which South Korea made further purchases of American defence equipment, predominantly F-16 aircraft. It was not until 1989 that the US Department of Defense reported that the Republic of Korea had promised to increase direct financial support for American forces stationed on her territory. In 1990, the Department's annual report stated, somewhat optimistically, that South Korea was contributing $300 million a year in support costs and in 1991 an increase of 115 per cent in this contribution was promised.[60] But these undertakings remained largely unfulfilled. Only $150 million was paid in 1990/91 and in November 1995, the United States found it necessary to conclude a new burden-sharing agreement with South Korea under which she undertook to meet support costs of $330 million a year rising by 10 per cent a year thereafter. However, in the autumn of 1997 South Korea, in common with other nations of the Pacific Rim, ran into severe economic difficulties which required the International Monetary Fund to put in place its largest ever rescue package of $57 billion. Gross national product declined by 5 per cent in the first six months of 1998, and it must be doubtful whether any burden-sharing targets agreed with the United States will survive the economic restructuring that has followed.

Continuing Stalemate

In the late 1990s, the Korean Peninsula remains caught in a time warp, representing the last unfinished business of the Cold War. For a time it looked as though relations between North and South would improve. The first discussions between the two countries at Premier level took place in late 1990 and the following year an Agreement on Reconciliation Non-aggression and Exchanges of Co-operation was signed. But this limited progress was blighted by the suspected development of a nuclear weapons programme by North Korea in the last years of Kim Il Sung's rule. Although an agreement had been reached to ban nuclear weapons throughout the peninsula in December 1991, North Korea

---

[60] DoD Annual Reports for 1991 and 1992, published January 1990 and 1991, respectively.

decide to boycott further discussions on nuclear matters in January 1993 and in March threatened to withdraw from the Nuclear Non-Proliferation Treaty, suggesting that she had a weapons programme of her own under development.

The United States took steps to remove this threat by negotiation, supported by both carrots and sticks. To allay North Korea's fears, President Bush had removed American tactical nuclear weapons from Kunsan in 1991, allowing President Roh to declare that there were no nuclear weapons based in South Korea. In addition, the annual TEAM SPIRIT exercises, which North Korea had chosen to stigmatize as rehearsals for an invasion, were cancelled in 1992 and from 1994 onwards. To reassure South Korea, the United States agreed to equip her forces there with a six-battery battalion of Patriot missiles which were deployed in April 1994. At the same time, the United States entered into negotiations with North Korea and these bore fruit in October 1994 with the signature of an 'Agreed Framework'. Under this agreement, North Korea agreed to halt her nuclear programme in return for the supply of light-water reactors by an international consortium (70 per cent funded by South Korea) and the provision of alternative energy in the form of 500,000 tons of heavy fuel oil a year. Although the agreement alleviated the nuclear threat to South Korea, both North and South Korea used the negotiations to secure related objectives—the North to open a direct dialogue with the United States for the first time, while keeping the South at arm's length, and the South to reinforce the American security commitment to their country.

South Korea succeeded in this objective, obtaining a series of commitments from President Clinton to keep American forces in country as long as the local people needed them. These represented a marginal improvement on the terms of the Bush commitment of 1989 which had spoken of the governments and peoples of both countries requiring an American military presence. The death of Kim Il Sung in July 1994, followed by a period of political uncertainty, economic collapse, and famine in the North, may have reduced the threat of a major conventional attack on South Korea but suspicions remained that North Korea was continuing work on a nuclear weapons programme. In August 1998 she launched a multi-stage missile which crossed Northern Japan and she subsequently denied access to an underground facility believed to house a nuclear weapons capability. On a visit to Seoul in November 1998 President Clinton was obliged to warn North Korea that Congress would be reluctant to fund the 1994 agreement while these suspicions remained. Meanwhile, the North has continued with its long-standing policy of military probes and incursions. In April 1996, she declared that she was withdrawing from the Armistice Agreement of 1953 and mounted a number of minor incursions into the Demilitarised Zone. This was followed in September 1996 by the discovery of a North Korean submarine stranded on South Korea's east coast. A further North Korean submarine was discovered in similar circumstances in June 1998, and in December 1998 a third submarine was sunk by the South Korean Navy after approaching the port of Yosu. These incidents were followed by a naval confrontation in the Yellow Sea in June 1999 during which a North Korean gunboat was sunk during a dispute over fishing rights.

Conclusion

With South Korea under direct threat from the North for much of the post-war period, the American military presence in the Republic has been, in some respects, closer to that in West Germany, the other divided nation of the Cold War, than that in Japan, where post-war occupation was exploited to serve the United States wider strategic interests. In South Korea, as in Germany, American troops were deployed to meet an immediate and specific threat across an internal frontier. But in both countries, the United States has at times remained reluctant to maintain ground forces at the level considered necessary by a nervous and insecure host nation. In East Asia, this reluctance is hard to reconcile with the heavy concentration of American forces, predominantly US Marines, on the island of Okinawa. Indeed, South Korea was so concerned to retain American forces on her territory that at one stage she offered the United States the island of Cheju, off the south coast of the peninsula, as a replacement for Okinawa should this become necessary.

In West Germany, the American ambivalence on forward defence was prompted largely by the feeling, more prevalent in Congress than in successive administrations, that the Europeans should do more to safeguard their own security. In South Korea, the uneasy security relationship with the United States under Nixon and Carter can be attributed partly to the aftermath of Vietnam and partly to the need for economy. But underlying these factors, as set out in the Nixon Doctrine enunciated in Guam in 1969, was the periodic concern felt by the United States about the permanent deployment of ground forces on the Asian mainland. Even when South Korea was the only non-communist regime in East Asia north of Thailand, following the fall of Vietnam, Laos, and Cambodia, the United States pressed ahead with reductions in her forces there. The South Koreans were reassured by President Reagan's more aggressive posture towards communism and the agreement in 1989 to maintain American troops in South Korea as long as both countries wanted them. But they were concerned by President Bush's plans to reduce American forces in Asia and it was not until President Clinton made a firm commitment to maintain 100,000 American troops in Asia, with 36,000 of these in Korea, that this recurring anxiety was allayed. Even so, the South Koreans were concerned that the United States would not be able to meet the requirement formulated in the 'Bottom-Up' review of October 1993 to fight and win two nearly simultaneous major regional conflicts—especially as there was talk in Washington, later denied, that this really amounted to a 'Win . . . Hold . . . Win' scenario.[61]

The twists and turns of American policy on South Korea since 1945 have been described as 'cycles of abandonment followed by re-engagement'.[62] It is ironic that these shifts of policy occurred in the host nation where, of all those in the post-war security system, the United States held the most dominant position through command first of the United Nations forces and thereafter of the Combined Field Army. It was only in December 1994 that the Chairman of the Korean Joint Chiefs of Staff assumed operational command of the combined forces in time of peace (with operational control reverting to the United States in time of war). But dominance in the military sphere carried limited influence on the domestic policies of successive South Korean governments, which, because of the siege mentality pervading the country and the absence of any prior democratic tradition, became progressively out of line with the values which the United States claimed to uphold. This was a pattern repeated elsewhere, particularly in the Philippines and Panama. While it was the loss of support in his own party, coupled with pressure from the United States, that persuaded Chun to accept reform in 1987, he cannot have been blind to the withdrawal of American support from Marcos the year before. But neither in Panama nor in the Philippines were the indigenous armed forces under American command. It was this factor in South Korea which caused difficulties for the United States under a series of authoritarian governments headed

---

[61] L. Middleton. In *The Korean Peninsula in Transition*, T. Y. Kong and D. H. Kim (ed.), (London: Macmillan, 1997).

[62] Hinton, op. cit.

by figures with a military background. Although South Korea could be described as a client state in security terms, the United States found herself in the unenviable position, until recently, of commanding the armed forces of a country whose domestic policies, prior to 1987, were frequently distasteful and sometimes unacceptable. In reality, her influence over these policies was limited but dissident opinion in the country, with its own ideological agenda, was not prepared to acknowledge this.

7

From Conquest to Containment: Europe

West Germany

The Post-war Occupation

The United States had not originally intended to station forces in West Germany permanently, as part of her post-war global security system, any more than she had in the other occupied territories of Japan, Korea, or Italy. The division of Germany and the blockade of Berlin persuaded Harry Truman that a continuing military commitment to Europe by the United States would be needed. But, notwithstanding signature of the North Atlantic Treaty in 1949, it was the outbreak of the Korean War in June 1950 that provided the pretext needed for both the return of American troops to Germany in substantial numbers and the eventual rearmament of the Federal Republic. Thereafter, West Germany became the cornerstone of the United States global security system during the Cold War, with a far greater concentration of American forces than any other host nation. In common with Japan, and to a lesser extent Italy and South Korea, the terms and conditions on which American forces were deployed in West Germany owed much to the residual legacy of occupation. The initial arrangements for the return of American forces in strength were made before sovereignty was restored to the Federal Republic of Germany in 1955 and the City of Berlin remained formally under occupation by the United States, Britain, France, and the Soviet Union until 1990, with the last elements of their garrisons departing only in 1994. However, in one respect West Germany was unique. No other country in the global security system also played host to the forces of five other nations in addition to those of the United States. The forces originally deployed in the American, British, and French occupation zones were joined, as NATO's integrated military structure was established, by those of Canada, Belgium, and the Netherlands.

In June 1945, the four victorious powers announced that they would 'station forces and civil agencies in any or all parts of Germany as they may desire'.[1] However the Western allies envisaged that their occupation forces would remain for a short period to supervise the eradication of militarism and National Socialism and would then be withdrawn. 'Nothing in the previous record of American diplomacy suggested in the late 1940s a long-standing American troop presence in Germany. Once the short term needs of the occupation had been met, it was assumed ... that US soldiers would eventually be withdrawn'.[2] The Potsdam Declaration of August 1945 made provision for demilitarizing Germany by stating that 'the production of arms, ammunition and implements of war, as well as all types of aircraft and sea-going ships, shall be prohibited and prevented'.[3] This was broadly in line with the surrender terms imposed on Japan. A more extreme plan prepared by Henry Morgenthau, the United States Secretary of the Treasury, advocated that Germany be reduced to a pastoral society. Although this plan was not adopted as United States government policy, the intentions behind it were for a time reflected in the instructions given to the American Military Governor, General Lucius Clay, by the Joint Chiefs of Staff.

Thus, the initial emphasis of the American occupation was on retribution rather than restitution—a policy which was to be rigorously pursued in the Soviet occupation zone but was modified in the three Western zones as the full extent of Germany's economic difficulties became apparent. Britain, for example, found herself obliged to divert scarce supplies of food and fuel from her own people to sustain economic life in her occupation zone. Fortunately, General Clay was able to interpret his instructions flexibly and within two years a 'Reverse Course' had been charted for Germany, as for Japan, but on a far grander and more generous scale. The increasingly belligerent behaviour of the Soviet Union and the desperate economic plight of Western Europe prompted the United States to announce in 1947, first the Truman Doctrine and then the Marshall Plan. As General George C. Marshall noted:

The restoration of Europe involves the restoration of Germany. Without a revival of Germany's production there can be no revival of Europe's economy.[4]

---

[1] Declaration Regarding the Defeat of Germany. Signed Berlin 5 June 1945. Cited by H. Haftendorn, A Structural View. In *Homeward Bound? Allied Forces in the New Germany*, D. G. Haglund and O. Mager (ed.) (Boulder, CO: Westview, 1992, 22).

[2] D. G. Haglund, American Troops in Germany. In Haglund and Mager, op. cit. Ch. 6.

[3] S. Duke, *United States Military Forces and Installations in Europe* (Oxford: OUP, 1989).

[4] T. J. McCormick, *America's Half Century* (Baltimore, MD: Johns Hopkins University Press, 1995, 80).

Although economic reconstruction became the new policy for Germany in the Western occupation zones, the withdrawal of American troops continued to gather pace. In May 1945, the United States ended the war with sixty-nine divisions in Germany, totalling 2 million men. By mid 1946, this number had decreased to 340,000 and by 1947 to 135,000. With some 1.5 million men needed in the Pacific and 600,000 to be returned home for demobilization in the United States, the American withdrawal has been termed 'an organised rout'.[5] Individual servicemen were moved according to length and location of service resulting in the fragmentation and dispersal of military units. Although James Byrnes had announced in Stuttgart in September 1946 that American troops would remain in Germany, there was no immediate thought of reversing the rundown, despite the blockade of Berlin in June 1948 and the signature of the North Atlantic Treaty in April 1949. Truman, commenting on the signature of the Brussels Treaty, had declared 'It is of vital importance . . . that we keep occupation forces in Germany until peace is secured in Europe', but this was not seen as a long-term commitment.[6] It is worth recalling that NATO was originally conceived not as an integrated military alliance with American ground forces deployed in Europe but as a political alignment safeguarding the values of the West with provision for mutual military assistance in time of trouble. In consequence, the United States initially saw her military role in the Alliance as limited to the provision of naval and strategic air force units while focusing on those planning groups concerned with the Atlantic and North America. Ground forces were to be provided by the Europeans, predominantly the French. This broad division of labour was endorsed by the North Atlantic Council meeting in Washington in January 1950.

Following the merger of the Western occupation zones in 1948, first for economic and then for political purposes, the Federal Republic of Germany came into being in September 1949 with the enactment of a new constitution known as the Basic Law. The Occupation Statute, signed by the Allied Powers on 21 October 1949, brought military government to an end but allied forces remained in West Germany and the Statute gave the allies reserved powers in relation to 'the protection, prestige and security of allied forces, dependants, employees and representatives'. An Allied High Commission remained in place with

---

[5] W. Mako, *US Ground Forces and the Defense of Central Europe* (Washington, DC: Brookings Institution, 1983, 6).
[6] E. May, *The Federal Republic of Germany and the United States* (Boulder, CO: Westview, 1984).

extensive residual powers, which allowed for the resumption of full authority in an emergency, but the number of American troops continued to decline until a level of only 75,000 was reached in 1950. These troops had been concerned in the early post-war years primarily with social programmes designed to eradicate National Socialism and restore democratic government at local level. They were only lightly equipped, as if for police duties, and their morale was low.

The exception, consistent with the American concept of her future role in the defence of Europe, was the United States Army Air Force, which had become the United States Air Force in July 1947. Although the Periphery Basing Plan proposed for Europe by General Carl Spaatz had been abandoned, Strategic Air Command (SAC) was anxious to demonstrate a global capability. Six B-29 bombers were sent to Rhein-Main airfield for 12 days in November 1946 and nine were sent to Giebelstadt, near Würzburg, for 10 days in July 1947. In October 1947, General Curtis LeMay, Commander of United States Air Force Europe, began to build up Fürstenfeldbruck airfield to accommodate three squadrons of B-29s for periodic visits. (West Germany was considered too vulnerable for the permanent deployment of SAC assets, hence the deployments to Britain, Spain, and Morocco.) However, the Berlin airlift in 1948/49, with operations from the American zone mainly conducted from Rhein-Main and Wiesbaden, consolidated the position of the USAF in Germany and in January 1951, Twelfth Air Force was created as the tactical arm of US air assets in the country with its headquarters at Ramstein.

It was the outbreak of the Korean War in June 1950, widely believed at the time to have been instigated from Moscow, that persuaded the United States to reinforce Europe with ground troops, and NATO as a whole to consider what might be necessary to resist a Soviet attack. In the words of John McCloy, US High Commissioner in West Germany, 'Korea brought Europe to its feet'.[7] The whole thrust of the security debate in Europe switched from the need to restrain Germany to the importance of defending Europe as far to the east as possible. On 9 September 1950, President Truman announced that he had 'approved substantial increases in the strength of United States forces to be stationed in Western Europe'. Four divisions were added to the two already in place and these began to arrive in May 1951. But Truman added that he expected this commitment to be matched by the European members of NATO:

[7] McCormick, op. cit. 107.

A basic element in the implementation of this decision is the degree to which our friends match our actions in this regard. Our plans are based on the sincere expectation that our efforts will be met with similar action on their part.[8]

The European members of the Alliance did their best to meet this challenge. The communiqué of the North Atlantic Council issued from New York in September 1950 declared that the state of war with Germany was terminated, that the three occupying powers would increase their forces in Germany, including Berlin, and would treat any attack on the Federal Republic or on Berlin as an attack on all three powers. The communiqué also announced:

The establishment, at the earliest possible date, of an integrated force under centralised command, which shall be adequate to deter aggression and to ensure the defence of Western Europe.[9]

In December 1950, General Eisenhower assumed the post of Supreme Allied Commander Europe (SACEUR) which met the need for centralized command. But as the Soviet Union had some thirty combat divisions in East Germany and 175 divisions overall, the requirement for forces adequate to deter aggression and ensure the defence of Western Europe pointed inevitably towards German rearmament. In September 1950, the North Atlantic Council had been able to agree only that the Federal Republic should be authorized to form 'mobile police formations' and should be 'enabled to contribute' to the common defence in some yet unspecified way.[10] But by the end of the year the Council had acknowledged that German participation in the common defence 'would strengthen the defence of Europe without altering the purely defensive character of NATO'.[11]

Redeployment and Rearmament

The Joint Chiefs of Staff in the United States had been considering the rearmament of West Germany prior to the Korean War, but Truman had commented 'as wrong as can be' on a Department of Defense report he saw canvassing these proposals.[12] However, 'the Korean War made it politically possible to bring the German rearmament policy out of the

---

[8] D. Nelson, *A History of US Military Forces in Germany* (Boulder, CO: Westview, 1987*a*).
[9] Ibid.
[10] Communiqué of North Atlantic Council. December 1950. NATO 1949–89. Facts and Figures. Brussels, 1989.
[11] Nelson, op. cit.   [12] May, op. cit.

closet'.[13] Dean Acheson began to argue for rearmament as part of a package involving the return of American troops to Germany, and Konrad Adenauer, who had become Chancellor of the Federal Republic in August 1949, saw the debate on rearmament as a means of regaining full sovereignty for West Germany. For understandable reasons, France remained strongly opposed to rearmament, with Robert Schuman, the French Foreign Minister, regarding the proposal as 'unthinkable'. The policy was equally unpopular with the opposition in West Germany. In November 1949, Kurt Schumacher, the leader of the Social Democratic Party who believed that Germany could only be reunited by remaining neutral, had castigated Adenauer as 'Chancellor of the Allies'.

The outcome of the debate on West German rearmament, which ran from 1950 to 1955, was crucial to the long-term commitment of American troops to Europe. The concept of rearmament, strongly advocated by Acheson at the United Nations General Assembly in 1950, was initially anathema to France who, as an alternative, put forward the Pleven Plan, under which units of a new German army, no larger than 6,000 men each, would serve in a wider European army under the authority of the European Defence Community (EDC). A draft treaty setting up the EDC was agreed in February 1952 but the scheme faltered because of failure to agree on parallel proposals for political integration, and in August 1954 the French National Assembly rejected it. With the demise of the EDC, France was reluctantly persuaded to accept that the German armed forces would be rebuilt on a national basis and the United States, who saw this as the only solution to the European security problem, acknowledged in return that she would be obliged to maintain a long-term military presence in West Germany, both to deter the Soviet Union and reassure France. But John Foster Dulles, who had become President Eisenhower's Secretary of State in 1953, spoke of 'an agonising reappraisal' by the United States following the collapse of the EDC. To forestall this Anthony Eden, the British Foreign Secretary, embarked on an intensive round of diplomacy in London and Paris aimed at bringing West Germany both into the Brussels Treaty of 1948 and the North Atlantic Treaty of 1949.

Eden's diplomacy was successful in concluding the Paris Agreements in October 1954 which were ratified early in 1955. These agreements ended the allied occupation of West Germany, acknowledged the Federal Republic of Germany as a sovereign nation, allowed the new

---

[13] McCormick, op. cit. 106.

nation to raise its own armed forces, looked forward to the Federal Republic joining NATO, and permitted other NATO forces to remain on West German territory in the interests of common defence. Sovereignty, however, was not absolute. Because of the division of Germany and the anomalous position of Berlin, which remained formally under Four Power occupation, the former occupying powers retained certain reserved rights, which they were eventually to exercise in 1990, relating to Berlin, reunification and the conclusion of a final peace settlement. These reserved powers included the right to continue stationing forces on West German territory. Another reserved power, not removed until 1967, was the right of the allies to resume authority if any emergency threatened the security of West Germany before the federal government had worked out suitable crisis plans of its own.

With these reserved powers in place, known colloquially as 'victory rights', the deployment of American forces in West Germany was viewed by both parties in a different light from deployments freely negotiated elsewhere. West Germany continued to pay occupation costs in the Federal Republic until 1957 and to meet the costs of the occupying powers in Berlin thereafter. These amounted to DM1.9 billion a year when they were finally discontinued with signature of the Final Settlement in 1990. Moreover, it was not until 1961, six years after she had joined the alliance, that West Germany became a party to the NATO Status of Forces Agreement, a multilateral agreement signed in 1952 setting out the terms and conditions on which members of the alliance deployed troops on each other's territory. Despite the transfer of sovereignty the shadow of occupation lingered on, with West Germany contributing considerably more to the infrastructure required by the allied forces stationed on her territory than was common elsewhere in the Alliance. In addition to the free provision of barracks, airfields, and training areas, for which no charges were made between NATO allies, West Germany made housing, schools, and hospitals available without charge to the forces of the United States and other allies stationed on her territory.

The document covering the deployment of allied forces on West German territory was the Convention on Relations Between the Three Powers and the Federal Republic of Germany, originally signed in May 1952 as a lead-in to the proposed European Defence Treaty, but amended to form part of the Paris Agreements which came into force in May 1955.[14] Article IV described the deployment of allied

---

[14] Convention on Relations between the Three Powers and the Federal Republic of Germany. Signed 23 October 1954. TIAS 3425.

forces as a right rather than an arrangement agreed between sovereign nations:

Pending the entry into force of the arrangements for the German Defence contribution, the three powers retain the rights ... relating to the stationing of armed forces in the Federal Republic. The mission of these forces will be the defence of the Free World, of which Berlin and the Federal Republic form part.

Despite the nature of the rights conferred, Article IV emphasized that the allied powers wished to exercise these with the consent of the host nation:

The Federal Republic agrees that, from the entry into force of the arrangements for the German Defence contribution, forces of the same nationality and effective strength as at that time may be stationed in the Federal Republic ... The three powers do not desire to exercise their rights regarding the stationing of armed forces in the Federal Republic ... except in full accord with the Federal Republic.

Likewise, Article V obliged the three powers to consult the Federal Republic 'with regard to all questions concerning the stationing of these forces ...'. In parallel, the Three Power Declaration on Berlin, signed on 3 October 1954, stated that the three powers 'will maintain armed forces within the territory of Berlin as long as their responsibilities require it'. The separate status of Berlin was later confirmed in the Quadripartite Agreement signed by all four occupying powers in September 1971.

Following the Paris Agreements, the Federal Republic of Germany became a sovereign nation on 5 May 1955 and was formally admitted to NATO the following day. She had committed herself to creating a West German army of twelve divisions comprising half a million men. To achieve this, conscription was introduced in 1956 but even so the target had to be reduced to 350,000 and this was not attained until 1961. In parallel, American force levels in West Germany increased again to some 250,000 by the early 1950s. By 1952, there were five US combat divisions assigned to NATO's Central Command and American forces remained broadly at this level until the demands of the Vietnam War began to cause withdrawals in the mid 1960s. The concentration of American forces in Germany was formidable. One-quarter of a million men represented 70 per cent of American troops in Europe and 25 per cent of American forces worldwide. (In Europe, Britain played host to the next largest concentration of American forces but came a long way second to West Germany with only 30,000 at the peak period in the

1970s.) Some 60 per cent of American military installations overseas were located in Germany. The US Army contingent comprised two corps of the US Seventh Army located in the centre section of NATO's Central Army Group, where, in the layer-cake formation adopted by the Alliance, they were flanked by two West German corps. The headquarters of the V Corps was located at Frankfurt and that of VII Corps at Stuttgart. This deployment of American ground forces was determined not by an objective assessment of the most likely line of a Soviet attack but by the location of the United States occupation zone agreed at the end of the war. Hence, the most powerful forces of the alliance were located in the southern Länder of Bavaria, Hesse, and Baden-Württemberg, a predominantly mountainous area, while the traditional invasion route across the North German plain was defended by a mixture of Dutch, German, British, and Belgian forces. This misalignment was to cause considerable difficulty when the United States belatedly decided to reposition some of her forces in the 1980s.

As to air assets, in the 1950s the US Twelfth Air Force in Germany consisted of fighter-bomber groups equipped with F-84 aircraft initially based at Fürstenfeldbruck and Landstuhl, backed by tactical reconnaissance groups at Fürstenfeldbruck and Neubiberg. In 1957, Twelfth Air Force was reallocated to the United States and replaced in West Germany by Seventeenth Air Force, which had been obliged to withdraw from Morocco. By the 1970s, the assets of Seventeenth Air Force comprised three tactical fighter wings based at Hahn, Spangdahlem, and Ramstein, equipped with F-4 Phantoms for close support, and a fourth tactical fighter wing at Bitburg equipped with F-15s for air superiority. These bases were supported by a tactical control wing at Sembach, an airlift capability at Rhein-Main, and a tactical reconnaissance wing at Zweibrücken. Sembach originally served as the headquarters for Seventeenth Air Force but was replaced by Ramstein in the 1980s. In peacetime Seventeenth Air Force comprised 300 aircraft and 40,000 men, only 15 per cent of the total NATO aircraft in Europe. However, wartime plans allowed for an additional thirty squadrons of 600 aircraft to reinforce Europe within 10 days, mostly to be based at co-located operating bases, of which there were seventeen in the Federal Republic of Germany.

Because of the continuing Soviet threat to West Germany, there was initially little risk of American troops stationed there being used for purposes unacceptable to the host nation. But there were significant diversions of men and equipment to other theatres during the Cold War period. Substantial numbers of troops were withdrawn from West

Germany to meet American commitments in Vietnam and in 1973, equipment was shipped to Israel during and after the Yom Kippur War, occasioning, unusually, a strong public protest from the Federal Government in the following terms:

Weapons deliveries using West German territories or installations from American depots in West Germany to one of the warring parties cannot be allowed. The West German Government is relying on America to finally halt deliveries from and over West Germany.[15]

US Force Reductions and Social Consequences

The pressure from the United States to reduce her forces in West Germany in the 1960s and 1970s stemmed partly from the belief that the European allies were not doing enough, and partly from the demands of the war in Vietnam which, at its height, absorbed half a million American troops, including ten Army divisions and other independent units. The feeling that the Europeans were not pulling their weight had been expressed as early as the mid 1950s by President Eisenhower. 'Unhappily' he said, 'the European nations have been slow in building up their military forces and have now come to expect our forces to remain in Europe indefinitely'.[16] However, until the mid 1960s the United States maintained her forces in Germany at a constant level and even increased these in response to international tension. Following the construction of the Berlin Wall in August 1961 an additional 42,000 American troops were deployed to Europe and three infantry divisions in Germany were mechanized. But the demands of the war in Vietnam built up from the mid 1960s onwards and, when the American economy ran into difficulties in the late 1960s and early 1970s, Congress began to press for the withdrawal of American ground forces from Europe and a greater contribution to burden-sharing from the European members of the Alliance. This gave rise to the new concept of dual-basing which aimed to make use of improvements in military transport aircraft to reduce the numbers of troops permanently stationed in Germany and rely on rapid reinforcement in an emergency. The first major airlift occurred in 1963, when 15,000 men and over 100 tonnes of equipment were moved from the United States to West Germany in 63 hours. This initial exercise was later to develop into the annual REFORGER

[15] H. Kissinger, *Years of Upheaval* (London: Weidenfeld & Nicolson, 1982).
[16] G. Lundestad, *The American Empire and Other Studies* (Oxford: OUP Oslo: Norwegian University Press, 1990).

airlifts, commencing in 1968, which, by the end of the Cold War period, were transporting an entire corps of 100,000 reservists from Texas to West Germany.

However, the troops withdrawn for service in Vietnam could not be returned rapidly in a crisis. One commentator concluded that 'the way in which these forces were gathered is widely judged to have had a deleterious impact on the overall US ground posture'.[17] Over the period 1966–73, approximately 100,000 American troops were withdrawn from Europe to meet the demands of Vietnam, of whom 60,000 came from Germany. In 1968 alone, 28,000 American troops left Germany for the United States leaving their heavy equipment behind. The level of American armed force levels in the Federal Republic dropped from 262,000 in 1965 to 215,000 in 1967, and fell below 200,000 in subsequent years. This caused concern to West Germany, not only because of the erosion of her security but also because the feedback from Vietnam gave rise to severe disciplinary problems among American troops in Germany. Until the end of the 1950s, many West Germans still thought of American troops in their country as occupation forces but from the mid 1950s to the mid 1960s, according to opinion polls, approval of the American military presence steadily grew, reaching nearly 60 per cent in 1966. The repercussions of Vietnam and associated disciplinary problems were to erode this favourable reaction. Relations with the host nation population were strained throughout the late 1960s and 1970s and only recovered in the early 1980s when *Der Spiegel* found that no more than 12 per cent of the population wanted American forces to withdraw from Germany.[18] However, this favourable trend was again weakened in the mid 1980s when the deployment of cruise and Pershing II missiles revived the underlying hostility to the stationing of nuclear weapons on West German territory.

The impact of the Vietnam War on American forces in Germany ran deep. Many of the best officers and NCOs were creamed off to serve in Vietnam. In 1968 it was estimated that US Army units in Germany were 50 per cent short on their complement of Majors and 60 per cent on Captains and Lieutenants. This was also a period of growing racial tension in the United States, fostered by the civil rights movement and exacerbated by the assassination of Martin Luther King in 1968. Afro-American troops accounted for 14 per cent of the US Army in Germany during the 1970s, but accounted for two-thirds of the serious crime

[17] Mako, op. cit. 20.
[18] D. Nelson, *Defenders or Intruders? The Dilemmas of US Forces in Germany* (Boulder, CO: Westview, 1987b).

recorded. Poor accommodation contributed to a ghetto-like existence in which Afro-American servicemen felt increasingly isolated in a predominantly white community. This sense of isolation was exacerbated for American troops, white as well as black, by the decline of the dollar against the Deutschmark in the 1970s which reinforced the tendency to remain on base when off duty. In 1967, the dollar bought DM3.90. After the collapse of the Bretton Woods system in 1971, the rate fell to DM2.50 in 1975, and in October 1978 it reached a new low of DM1.72. American servicemen increasingly found themselves the poor relations of their more prosperous German hosts.

1971 was a particularly bad year for the US Army in Germany. In February, part of a barracks at Camp Pieri near Wiesbaden was destroyed by arson. In July, a racial brawl led to a trial known as 'the Darmstadt 29' which was attended by well-known civil rights lawyers from the United States and attracted much unfavourable publicity. In August, American troops refused to take part in a three-day exercise and 100 soldiers were charged with insurrection. Two years later, the US authorities were compelled to take penal powers to combat drug abuse among American servicemen, suspending certain constitutional rights. It was a revealing sign of the times that the *International Herald Tribune* welcomed the fact that there were only two underground US Army newspapers in Germany in April 1975 whereas there had been ten a few years previously.[19]

A comprehensive study of American forces in Germany by Daniel Nelson in 1987 concluded that morale, discipline, and readiness of American troops in Germany declined markedly during the period of the Vietnam War, with a significant increase in drug abuse and racial disturbances, giving rise to strained relations with the local authorities in the surrounding areas.[20] The same author concluded in a separate study that 'The Germans are fully aware that the crime rates are substantially higher among US forces than among the forces of any other NATO ally'.[21] Another commentator writing in 1989 concluded:

In the Federal Republic of Germany constant reports of drug abuse and racial tension among US servicemen conspired to create an atmosphere of tension and led effectively to the segregation of US forces from German society.[22]

However, it must be stressed that these adverse social developments were most apparent in those units of the US Army that tended to be

---

[19] *International Herald Tribune*, 23 April 1975. Cited in Nelson, (1987*b*).
[20] Nelson (1987*a*).   [21] Nelson (1987*b*, 68).   [22] Duke, op. cit. 68.

concentrated in predominantly urban areas. In the occupation period, American and other allied troops had generally moved into former Wehrmacht barracks which were often located in town centres. In the Frankfurt area, for example, the four towns of Hanau, Wiesbaden, Darmstadt, and Giessen, with a total population of 600,000, played host to 77,000 American servicemen, civilian employees, and family members. One in every eight people in the area was an American citizen. By contrast, the six bases occupied by the USAF in West Germany were all in rural areas where the American presence, although even more dominant, was beneficial to the local economy. At Bitburg, for example, 11,000 American citizens almost equalled the 12,000 local inhabitants but one in seven of these obtained work on the base which employed 80 nearby firms.[23] Overall, some 66,000 Germans worked for the US military authorities in 1990, ensuring that the economic benefits of the American presence did much to offset the adverse social impact.

Offset and Burden-sharing

The burden-sharing debate in Congress, which overlapped with the final stages of the Vietnam War, was largely instigated by the Senate minority leader Mike Mansfield. From 1966 to 1971 he introduced a series of resolutions, calling for reductions in American troops in Germany, as a means of putting pressure on the Federal Republic to make higher offset payments. Mansfield then switched tactics abandoning resolutions from 1971 to 1974 in favour of amendments to Appropriations Bills, calling for reductions of 50 per cent in American military forces in West Germany. One such amendment briefly passed into law in September 1973, causing panic in the Federal Republic, until this provision was struck out in conference of the two Houses of Congress one month later. These pressure tactics, sustained over a period of eight years, were strongly resented by the Federal Republic, which rightly maintained that American troops were stationed in West Germany for the benefit of the Alliance as a whole and ultimately to safeguard the security of the United States. The Germans felt that they had already made a significant contribution to the local costs incurred by United States forces through the various offset agreements which ran from 1961 to 1976 and that, in being pressed to do more, they were being penalized for the accidents of geography and history. Insofar as higher payments

---

[23] H. Bebermeyer and C. Thimian, The Economic Impact of Stationing US Forces in the FRG. In *Europe After an American Withdrawal*, J. Sharp (ed.), (Oxford: OUP Stockholm International Peace Research Institute, 1990, Ch. 6).

were demanded as the American economy deteriorated in the early 1970s, West Germany felt that she was being asked to pay indirectly for the costs of the Vietnam War and American economic mismanagement.

The various offset negotiations had proved a running sore in US–West German relations since the initial negotiations in 1961. The costs of maintaining American troops in West Germany during the late 1950s caused no particular difficulty. The American economy still occupied a dominant position in the world and the inflow of dollars to West Germany helped to overcome the severe dollar shortage which was holding back economic development throughout Europe. But during the 1950s, the German economic miracle was gathering pace. Following Ludwig Erhard's currency reform in 1948, industrial production in West Germany had risen by 50 per cent and by 1954 her gross national product had soared by a 200 per cent. By the mid 1960s West Germany had become the world's third largest industrial power and its second leading exporter. At the same time, the locally incurred costs of American troops in Europe had, by 1960, reached $600 million a year and the American economy was finding it progressively harder to meet these. Negotiations on offset were opened but Adenauer was strongly opposed to any payments in cash which, he thought, could be construed as occupation costs. An agreement was therefore reached under which the Federal Republic would buy $1.2 billion of American military equipment over a two-year period and increase its contribution to the NATO infrastructure fund from 14 per cent to 20 per cent of the total.

This agreement was repeated by further two-year agreements of similar value until the mid 1960s, but over the next ten years offset negotiations became progressively more difficult. In 1965, the economic miracle faltered, with West Germany recording a current account deficit. The following year, the economy failed to show any growth for the first time since 1955 and because of extensive earlier purchases there was no scope left for further procurement of American military equipment. Moreover, the Starfighter aircraft, one of the main items purchased, was particularly unpopular having suffered a series of crashes with a high number of fatalities. West Germany grudgingly agreed to the purchase of US Treasury bonds to ease the American balance of payments difficulties, starting with purchases of $500 million in 1967 and rising to combined purchases of bonds and equipment of $2 billion for the period 1969–71. In 1971, a new element was introduced whereby West Germany agreed to contribute $186 million to the cost of modernizing barracks occupied by American troops. The overall package covered 80 per cent of the foreign exchange costs incurred by the United States but the final offset agreement for the period 1973–5 showed a reduction on this figure. The end of the Bretton Woods system in 1971 and the subsequent floating of the dollar eased the United States balance of payments problems for the time being, even though American servicemen in Germany were to suffer the consequences. Moreover, the oil crisis of 1973/74 caused major foreign exchange difficulties for the Federal Republic of Germany. As a result, President Ford and Chancellor Schmidt agreed to terminate the offset arrangements in 1976, replacing them by the multilateral Defence Improvement Programme for NATO as a whole.

The Nunn Amendments

At the same time as agreement was being reached not to continue with offset negotiations, the annual pressure by Senator Mansfield for troop reductions was finally laid to rest by an alternative initiative from Senator Sam Nunn. In 1974, a report on the structure of United States forces in NATO by the Brookings Institution[24] addressed the skewed deployment of American forces in Germany for the first time since the occupation. The report recommended that two American divisions in West Germany should be moved from the south of the country to the north, that the ratio of combat troops to support troops should be increased, and that the essential supply routes for reprovisioning American forces in Germany should be realigned from west to east instead of north to south. The north/south supply route using the port of Bremerhaven had been forced on NATO when France withdrew from the integrated command structure in 1967. There was consequently little that could be done about this, but Senator Nunn picked up the other two points in the Brookings Institution report and incorporated them in an amendment which passed into the 1974 Defence Procurement Bill. This amendment required the United States to reduce support troops in West Germany by 18,000 and increase combat troops by a similar number. Accordingly, two new combat brigades were created and, while one of these was housed at Weisbaden in southern Germany, the other, an armoured brigade of 3,800 men, was stationed at Garlstedt near Bremerhaven in northern Germany. The costs of these changes were shared equally between the United States and the Federal Republic.

[24] *US Force Structure in NATO: An Alternative*, (Washington, DC: Brookings Institution, 1974).

However, this was not the end of the proposals to reposition American forces. In the early 1980s a new tactical doctrine for the air–land battle in Germany was adopted by the US Army. This aimed to replace the static defensive strategy hitherto followed with a more aggressive mobile defence designed to disrupt an enemy invasion by counter-offensives deep into his own territory. The doctrine required United States forces to be located closer to the inner German border in order to launch an early counter-attack instead of being deployed for defence in depth. In 1981, Senator Nunn proposed amendments designed to achieve this relocation but problems of cost and land acquisition appeared insuperable to the Federal Republic, which was beginning to experience a period of considerable economic strain. Total costs were put at DM11–13 billion, which neither the German nor the American authorities could afford. Instead, a new host nation support agreement was signed in 1982, in which the United States agreed to double the size of her forces in West Germany in a crisis and the Federal Republic agreed to provide 93,000 reservists to furnish logistic support for these reinforcements. The Federal Republic also agreed to pay DM150 million in new storage costs to underpin these reinforcement plans and to use a further 2,000 reservists to guard the stocks left in country.

Nuclear Issues

The most contentious issue arising from the American military presence in West Germany, however, was not burden-sharing or troop withdrawals but the deployment of nuclear weapons. The Federal Republic of Germany was bound by the Paris Agreements of 1955 not to build or manufacture nuclear weapons, but faced with an overwhelming preponderance of hostile conventional forces on the other side of the inner German border, she realized that nuclear weapons deployed by her NATO allies were essential to her security and that she would need access to tactical nuclear weapons herself to fulfil her NATO responsibilities. In the early stages of the Cold War, decisions on nuclear defence for Germany were taken almost exclusively by the United States regardless of the impact on the host nation. By 1951, the Pentagon was developing a new doctrine, named Project VISTA, which involved the development of low-yield atomic bombs for tactical use, the build-up of a tactical nuclear capability on the part of the US Air Force, and a tactical nuclear role for the US Army. This inevitably led to plans to deploy tactical nuclear forces in West Germany to supplement the strategic forces maintained in Britain, Spain, and Morocco.

In October 1953, the United States announced that tactical nuclear weapons would be used in any major nuclear conflict in Europe and by the end of the year the first such weapons, dual capable 8-inch howitzers, were assigned to American forces in Germany. By the end of 1954 there were six battalions of 8-inch howitzers, six battalions of Honest John, and one battalion of Corporal surface-to-surface missiles on West German territory, all in American hands. However, the build-up of nuclear weapons was accompanied by some strikingly insensitive exercise planning. In June 1955, exercise CARTE BLANCHE postulated an attack on West Germany leading to the use of 300–400 nuclear weapons for defensive purposes, leaving 1.7 million Germans dead and 3.5 million wounded. The result was uproar in the Bundestag and the West German press which prompted the first stirrings of the German anti-nuclear movement.

German concern over the possible use of nuclear weapons on her territory was intensified by the 'New Look' introduced by Eisenhower when he became President in 1953 and adopted by NATO in December 1954. The National Security Council (NSC) document 162/2 prepared in October 1953 summarized the 'New Look' by stating that the United States would in future 'consider nuclear weapons to be as available for use as other munitions'. This policy was prompted partly by the collective failure of NATO to meet the ambitious—and quite unrealistic—targets for conventional forces set at the Lisbon summit in 1952 and partly by Eisenhower's wish to hold the American defence budget at a figure no higher than $35–40 billion. (The Radford Plan, developed in 1956 to follow up the 'New Look' but never implemented, envisaged the reduction of the US Army by half a million men as a cost-saving measure.) The 'New Look' placed greater reliance on nuclear weapons, under what came to be known as the 'tripwire strategy', to defeat a conventional attack from the East. But within a few years, the threat of a Soviet first strike on the West with nuclear weapons was dramatically demonstrated by the launch of Sputnik in October 1957. In December 1957, a meeting of the North Atlantic Council at Heads of Government level agreed that NATO should hold stocks of nuclear weapons ready for use and that Intermediate Range Ballistic Missiles (IRBMs) should be made available to SACEUR. (This decision paved the way for the deployment of Thor missiles to Britain, and Jupiter to Italy and Turkey the following year.)

The NATO planning document MC-70, also agreed in December

1957, followed the thrust of the 'New Look' by indicating that conventional forces should be used largely as a means of buying time to prepare for a nuclear exchange. The notion of even a short phase of conventional war on their territory was not a welcome one to the Germans. But the alternative was equally unwelcome. In the course of the American dispute with China over the offshore islands of Quemoy and Matsu, John Foster Dulles advanced the concept of 'Massive Retaliation' on 12 January 1954, implying resort to nuclear weapons whatever the degree of provocation. The United States, he said, would 'depend primarily upon a great capacity to retaliate, instantly, by means and at places of our choosing'.[25] Although first raised in the East Asian theatre, it was evident that this concept characterized American thinking on the struggle with communism worldwide. In September 1958, Dulles was to write to Harold Macmillan 'our entire military establishment assumes more and more that the use of nuclear weapons will become normal in the event of hostilities'.[26]

These developments in American thinking did little to reassure the West Germans. But the controversy over the use of nuclear weapons was fanned by the actions of their own government. In October 1956, Franz Joseph Strauss, the Federal Defence Minister, called for nuclear armament for the Bundeswehr, by now guarding several important sectors of the inner German border. This led directly to the Göttingen Appeal by 18 West German nuclear scientists, advocating total rejection of nuclear weapons by the Federal Republic and a bitter five-month 'Campaign Against Atomic Death' launched by the Social Democratic Party. However, Adenauer won the federal elections in September 1957 (the only absolute majority in the history of the Federal Republic), and in March 1958 the Bundestag agreed to the acquisition of delivery systems for tactical nuclear weapons by the German armed forces. By November that year, the Bundeswehr had taken delivery of the short range free-flight missile Honest John. Two medium-range subsonic nuclear armed missiles, Mace and Matador, were also made available to West Germany, to be replaced later by Redstone and, from 1969, by Pershing I. All these weapons remained under the control of SACEUR with the warheads in American custody and the authority for release vested in the American President.

However, by the 1960s it was feared that the strategy of 'Massive Retaliation' might no longer prove credible to the Soviet Union who, having acquired a second strike capability, would find it hard to believe

[25] Dept of State Bulletin 30. 25 January 1954, 108.
[26] R. Renwick, *Fighting With Allies* (London: Macmillan, 1996, 168).

that the United States would expose her own cities to a Soviet nuclear strike in order to prevent minor territorial aggrandizement in Western Europe. In its place, the doctrine of Flexible Response, worked up by the American Defense Secretary Robert McNamara, was adopted by NATO in December 1967, allowing, as its name implies, a more flexible response to aggression which could involve the initial use of conventional forces and tactical nuclear weapons instead of an immediate resort to a strategic nuclear strike. This approach relied on a significant increase in tactical nuclear weapons already deployed to West Germany, both as land-based missiles and as bombs to be delivered by the British and United States Air Forces. By 1975, the United States had 7,000 nuclear warheads in Europe, the majority of which were deployed in Germany. The following year the F-16, a nuclear capable combat aircraft, replaced the ageing F-4 in Seventeenth Air Force, with three squadrons being deployed to Hahn.

Although the West Germans were relieved at the demise of 'Massive Retaliation', the new doctrine was scarcely more palatable, raising as it did the prospect of a period of intense conventional conflict on German soil, possibly followed by nuclear exchanges first at tactical and secondly at strategic level. In the words of one recent commentator, the new doctrine 'ensured that any limited war in Europe would be total war for the Germans'.[27] This seemed to be borne out by the description of the projected land battle in the US Army Operations Manual issued some years later. 'Combat in Germany will automatically involve repeated, almost continuous battle for cities, towns, villages and adjacent built-up areas'.[28] Moreover, there was an inherent tension in the concept of flexible response. For the Europeans it meant a short conventional phase followed by early escalation, but for the Americans it meant postponing the resort to strategic nuclear weapons for as long as possible. The commentator cited above added somewhat cynically that 'the purpose of American forces in Europe was not simply the declared one of deterring a Soviet attack on West Europe but also the undeclared one of containing a hot war in Europe to Europe'.

Continuing concern on nuclear policy was accentuated for West Germany by two disputes in which sudden switches of policy by the United States severely undermined the confidence of the Federal Republic. The first was President Kennedy's proposal for a Multi-Lateral

---

[27] E. Kirchner and J. Sperling, From Instability to Stability. In *The Federal Republic of Germany and NATO* E. Kirchner and J. Sperling (eds.) (London: Macmillan 1992, 11).

[28] Mako, op. cit. 35.

Nuclear Force (MLF) put forward in 1962 to give the European members of NATO a greater role in the deterrence strategy of the Alliance while discouraging them from acquiring nuclear weapons of their own. But the concept of multinational mixed-manned naval units equipped with nuclear missiles, which could be launched only on the authority of the American President, held few attractions for the Europeans. Chancellor Erhard was reluctantly persuaded to accept the scheme on behalf of West Germany only to see it abandoned by Lyndon Johnson in 1965.

The one benefit to emerge from the collapse of MLF was greater provision for consultation on nuclear matters between members of the Alliance. In 1962, the spring meeting of the North Atlantic Council had developed the Athens Guidelines under which Britain and the United States had undertaken to consult their allies prior to the use of nuclear weapons 'time and circumstances permitting' and an exchange of information was agreed on the role of nuclear weapons in the defence of NATO. Four years later, in 1966, a substantive discussion of nuclear planning issues took place at the May/June meeting of the North Atlantic Council and at the December meeting the Nuclear Planning Group was set up to discuss strategic defence and the possible use of tactical nuclear weapons. At the outset only seven members of the Alliance participated but West Germany was one of these and membership allowed her to play a full part in the evolution of nuclear policy for the Alliance, while underlining her unique territorial concerns as the most likely battlefield for a major East–West conflict.

Notwithstanding West Germany's involvement in nuclear planning, a further incident occurred in 1977 in which she was severely embarrassed by a late change in American policy. On this occasion there was, potentially, a more direct impact on West German territorial concerns than that which might have arisen from the MLF proposals. The cause of the dispute was the so-called 'neutron bomb', more properly known as the 'Enhanced Radiation Weapon', which was intended to kill people while leaving buildings intact. This device was a gift to the anti-nuclear demonstrators who criticized it as a capitalist weapon designed to safeguard property. President Carter initially said that he would deploy the system in Europe only if European members of NATO requested it. With considerable reluctance, Chancellor Schmidt of West Germany made a formal request, only to be embarrassed five months later when Carter reversed his decision and decided not to proceed with the weapon. 'No convincing rationale was presented for Washington's sudden reversal of course.'[29]

[29] J. A. Reed, *Germany and NATO* (Washington, DC: National Defense University Press, 1987).

However, two years later, in December 1979, it was Schmidt who was the leading proponent of what came to be known as NATO's Twin Track (or Double Track) decision to counter the deployment of Soviet SS-20 intermediate nuclear missiles in East Germany by the stationing in Europe of Pershing II and ground-launched cruise missiles (known as Intermediate Nuclear Forces or INF). In parallel, negotiations were to be opened with the Soviet Union on overall reductions in the number of Intermediate Nuclear Forces deployed on both sides of the East–West divide. A total of 572 NATO missiles were to be deployed in five countries, including West Germany, commencing in 1983. But as part of the Twin Track decision, steps were also taken to reduce the overall number of nuclear warheads deployed in Europe—1,000 older nuclear warheads were to be withdrawn from Europe with the new missiles being accommodated within the reduced levels. Moreover, in October 1983 NATO took the decision at Montebello to withdraw a further 1,400 obsolete nuclear weapons from the European theatre by 1988 and modernize those that were left. The obsolete weapons withdrawn, most of which were deployed on West German territory, included Honest John, Nike Hercules, and Pershing IA.

The INF deployment policy was to prove as controversial in Germany as elsewhere. In November 1980, the Krefeld Appeal was launched in opposition to the INF deployments and soon collected one million signatures. Over the period 1981–3, immediately prior to deployment, demonstrators took to the streets in numbers not seen since the 1930s and in the 1983 Bundestag elections the Peace Movement and the Green Party, capitalizing on hostility to INF, secured a total of 27 seats. The revival of the anti-nuclear movement was not confined to Germany. As the official NATO handbook remarked:

The debate on nuclear issues between 1980 and 1983 was on a scale which had not been heard for many years. The period saw the growth of the campaign for nuclear disarmament and a proliferation of protest groupings and demonstrations in several countries, attracting massive media coverage and commanding international public attention.[30]

Nevertheless, deployment went ahead and the Twin Track policy eventually proved successful. President Reagan proposed talks with the Soviet Union on INF in 1981 and, although she withdrew from the negotiations in November 1983, following delivery of the first missiles, the Soviet Union, faced with a determined stand by NATO, finally agreed to the 'zero option' put forward by the United States. The INF Treaty was signed in December 1987 providing for the elimination

---

[30] NATO Facts and Figures, 126.

of all American and Soviet land-based missiles with a range between 500 and 5,500 kilometres. This allowed NATO to halt the deployment of missiles planned but not yet completed and required the United States to eliminate all those missiles already deployed under the Twin Track policy.

However, the INF Treaty did not cover short range nuclear forces (known as SNF) and West Germany quickly realized that, with no intermediate missiles left in the European theatre, she was the only country at risk from those missiles of 500 kilometres range or less retained by the Warsaw Pact. A further debate ensued on whether to replace NATO's short range nuclear missile Lance. The United States, backed by Britain, believed it essential to protect her own troops stationed in West Germany with short range missiles. But West Germany, having acquiesced in the removal of those missiles which played an important part in committing the United States and her other NATO allies to her defence, was reluctant to agree to the modernization of a lesser category of weapon which could only be used on German territory. At times, the debate grew acrimonious. At the Wehrkunde conference in January 1989 the US Defense Secretary Frank Carlucci threatened a withdrawal of American troops if Lance was not replaced, but at the NATO summit in May it was agreed to postpone a decision until after the German federal elections in December 1990. Chancellor Kohl immediately informed the Bundestag that no successor to Lance was needed but by the close of the year the Berlin Wall had come down and the end of the Cold War was in prospect. By the spring of 1990, the United States was prepared to cancel the project to replace Lance and in September 1991, with Germany reunited and the Warsaw Pact formally dissolved, President Bush announced that all land- and sea-based tactical nuclear weapons would be withdrawn from Europe.

After the Cold War

It was in Germany that the Cold War had commenced and it was in Germany that it came to an end swiftly and unexpectedly. 'Almost overnight the military situation was transformed and no other country experienced the change as intensely as Germany.'[31] Following the breach of the Berlin Wall in November 1989, events moved at a bewil-

[31] J. J. Anderson and J. B. Goodman, Mars or Minerva? A United Germany. In *After the Cold War*, R. Keohane, J. Nye, and S. Hoffman (ed.) (Cambridge, MA: Harvard University Press, 1993, 35).

dering pace. 'The sober path to reunification soon became a speedway.'[32] In February 1990, it was agreed that the four former occupying powers should meet the authorities of West and East German to discuss reunification and frame a final peace settlement. These talks were concluded in September 1990 and Germany was reunited on 3 October. Mikhail Gorbachev had originally held out for a neutral united Germany outside NATO, but the London Declaration issued by NATO in July 1990, offering a new era of partnership with the countries of the Warsaw Pact, a statement that members of the two Alliances were no longer adversaries and a new military strategy for NATO (later known as the New Strategic Concept), allowed him to reach agreement with Chancellor Kohl that the new Germany could remain a member of NATO. This enabled the former German Democratic Republic to leave the Warsaw Pact in September 1990. On 1 April 1991, the military activities of the Warsaw Pact ceased and on 1 July that year the organization was formally dissolved. By the end of the year, following the abortive coup in August, the Soviet Union itself had been dissolved and the Cold War was effectively over. The hostile forces ranged against each other for nearly forty-five years could be scaled down or dispersed.

The Treaty of Final Settlement which emerged from the 'Two Plus Four' talks required the occupying powers to vacate Berlin and Soviet troops to leave East Germany by the end of 1994. The treaty also required the combined armed forces of the reunited Germany to be reduced to 370,000 by 1995 but it made no provision for the withdrawal of NATO forces from West Germany. Of the six Western allies stationing troops in the Federal Republic during the Cold War, Canada, Belgium, and the Netherlands decided to withdraw their forces completely. Britain and France retained forces in Germany at much reduced levels, the one to show solidarity with the United States, the other to demonstrate her preference for a European defence identity. However, it was the future role of the United States, which had first withdrawn from Europe and then returned in strength, that caused most debate. President Bush had declared in 1990 that 'militarily significant US forces must remain on the other side of the Atlantic as long as our allies want and need them'. Among German citizens there were mixed views about this need. In September 1990, with reunification clearly in prospect, an opinion poll recorded that 60 per cent of the population felt their relationship with American forces in Germany to be 'good to very good'.[33]

---

[32] Ibid. 27.
[33] EMNID Institute Poll. Cited by H. Pohlman, The Domestic Impact of Allied Troops in Germany. In Haglund and Mager, op. cit. Ch. 3.

However, in 1991 a survey by the Rand Corporation found that 57 per cent of those questioned favoured total withdrawal, although, not surprisingly, the bulk of these were to be found in the former East Germany.

Among politicians there were no such doubts. All four political parties in Germany saw the need for a continued American military presence in the country. In May 1991, the Social Democratic Party (SPD) Commission on Security Policy issued the following statement:

Substantially, Europe will no longer need the physical presence of the USA, following the retreat of the Soviet Union behind its own borders . . . Political and psychological factors, however, will militate in favour of a physical presence of the United States in Europe for some time to come.[34]

This was a view shared by statesmen across Europe, even in those quarters not traditionally enthusiastic about the dominant American position in the Alliance. Earlier in 1991, while the Gulf war was in progress, the German Foreign Minister Hans-Dietrich Genscher had persuaded his French colleague Roland Dumas to join him in calling for a permanent American military presence in Europe which they considered 'indispensable for European security and stability'.[35] Two years later at the Wehrkunde conference at Munich in February 1993, the European participants urged the United States not to cut her forces in Europe too deeply.

The recognition that the continued presence of American troops was essential to the future stability of Europe was one reason why few favoured their total withdrawal. The conflict in Yugoslavia, which commenced in 1991, soon provided evidence of this. The United States was slow to get involved, mainly for domestic political reasons, but by the summer of 1995 it became apparent that a more forceful approach was required and only the United States had the authority to resolve the conflict. After a period of hesitation on the international stage, which gave rise to fears of a return to isolationism, the United States was obliged to resume her post-war role as guarantor of European security. She brokered a peace settlement at Dayton, Ohio, and made a contribution of 22,000 troops, largely diverted from Germany, to the international Implementation Force dispatched under NATO auspices to police the agreement. However, a more fundamental reason for maintaining American forces in Europe was that it was difficult to envisage

---

[34] H. Pohlman, op. cit. 71.
[35] Haglund and Mager, op. cit. 136.

NATO without them and continued membership of NATO was the key to anchoring a reunited Germany into the collective security institutions of the West. Gorbachev had not been alone in viewing the prospect of a united Germany with alarm. Margaret Thatcher and François Mitterand had both fallen prey to similar fears. The need to reassure allies as well as adversaries remained as strong as ever, even though the theory of 'double containment' was no longer valid. In broader terms, there was a risk, with the fragmentation of the Eastern Bloc, that the collective security arrangements in Western Europe would also dissolve without firm American leadership. The American Defense Secretary Dick Cheney summarized this view in April 1991 saying 'A visible US military presence, though with reduced numbers, continues to be the glue that holds NATO's integrated structure together', but he added that 'One American corps, with support troops and air force units, should suffice for this purpose'.[36] Neither the United States nor the leading European members of NATO wished to see the 'renationalization' of defence. This was acknowledged by the Germans themselves, an SPD official commenting:

Our military has benefited greatly from participation in an integrated command structure which has had a socialising influence. NATO works against any tendencies towards renationalisation of the German military.[37]

The same point was made by NATO collectively. In June 1994, the North Atlantic Council, meeting in Istanbul, declared that a continuing American presence in Europe was 'fundamental not only to guarantee the alliance's core functions but also to enable it to contribute effectively to European security'.[38] This was also to become the rationale for the expansion of NATO to the East, despite the significant costs involved and the concern expressed by the Russians.

Thus, American forces remained in Europe, which effectively meant in the former West Germany, albeit in much reduced numbers. This was not entirely an act of altruism on the part of the United States. The security guarantee she had provided to Europe during the Cold War had given her a powerful voice in the political and economic affairs of the continent which she was reluctant to forego. Nevertheless, the withdrawal of American forces from Europe was dramatic. In 1990, the United States still had 213,000 troops in West Germany. President Bush

---

[36] Statement by R. Cheney, US Secretary of Defense. 12 April 1991. Cited by Haftendorn, op. cit. 34.

[37] Anderson and Goodman, op. cit. 42.

[38] Meeting of North Atlantic Council. June 1994. NATO Handbook. Brussels, 1995.

undertook to reduce these to 150,000 by 1995, of whom 92,000 would be US Army personnel. In the event, only 100,000 remained by this date and by 1997, total American forces in Germany numbered only 75,000, of which the US Army accounted for 60,000 and the US Air Force 15,000. By 1999, following the American commitment to Bosnia, the US Army in Germany had been reduced to only 43,000 personnel although 15,000 USAF personnel remained. The single corps remaining, V Corps, comprised only two divisions, one armoured and one mechanized infantry. Combat battalions had been reduced from 147 to 37 since the end of the Cold War. The most symbolic withdrawals were those of the Second Armoured Cavalry Regiment from Fürth near Nürnberg in 1992 and the Eleventh Armoured Cavalry Regiment from the Fulda Gap on the old inner German border the following year. 'It was here', said General Colin Powell, Chairman of the Joint Chiefs of Staff, that 'I first confronted the Warsaw Pact . . . as a second lieutenant platoon leader in 1959 and where I did the same thing as a lieutenant general and V Corps commander in 1986 . . . This chapter of history is reaching a peaceful conclusion'.[39] Likewise, Seventeenth Air Force retained only three major air bases in place of six. Units at Bitburg, Zweibrücken, and Hahn were disbanded or dispersed, leaving only a single Tactical Fighter Wing at Spangdahlem with 72 combat aircraft and support and airlift units at Rhein-Main and Ramstein.

The end of the Cold War and the reunification of the country allowed Germany to become a 'normal' nation for the first time since 1945. The reduction in American forces on her territory played an important part in this process. Although the Convention on the Presence of Foreign Forces dating from 1954 was retained, in an Exchange of Notes signed with the former occupying powers in September 1990, Germany felt sufficiently confident the following year to request a revision of the Supplemental Agreement to the NATO Status of Forces Agreement. This had been signed in 1961, in order to improve the terms on which allied forces remained on German soil and to reduce the environmental burden of allied training and exercises. Another sign of the return to normality was a growing willingness to play a full part in allied military missions abroad. The Basic Law of 1949 had been widely assumed to prohibit the use of West German troops in other countries. It was not until 1994 that the Constitutional Court in Karlsruhe ruled that the German armed forces could participate in international military oper-

---

[39] News Release. Office of the Assistant Secretary of Defense (Public Affairs). Washington, DC.

ations outside the NATO area within the framework of multilateral collective security arrangements, provided each operation was specifically approved by the Bundestag. But Germany, like Japan, had felt divided and isolated by the Gulf War with her role, like Japan's, limited to that of paymaster to the victorious coalition. (In January 1991, she had sent forces to Turkey for defensive purposes to safeguard a fellow member of NATO from attack by Iraq—but even this limited deployment had provoked strong criticism from the SPD.) 'Obsessed with regional stability since its emergence as a state, the country was unaccustomed to thinking in global terms.'[40] For historical reasons, the conflict in Yugoslavia posed particular difficulties for Germany but, in keeping with her view of herself as a 'normal' nation, she made a destroyer and a reconnaissance aircraft available in the Adriatic in 1992 to help monitor United Nations sanctions in Bosnia. Subsequently, token humanitarian deployments to UN missions in Cambodia and Somalia were authorized, and in mid 1995 a decision was taken to send Tornado reconnaissance aircraft to take part in Operation DENY FLIGHT enforcing the air exclusion zone over Bosnia. These aircraft were based at Piacenza in Italy with operations commencing in 1996. When NATO air operations were launched against Serbia in 1999 the German government under Gerhard Schröder gave full political support to these. Although Schröder remained opposed to military intervention in Serbia by ground forces the German army played a full part in the peace-keeping operation in Kosovo once Serbian forces had surrendered and withdrawn.

Conclusion

West Germany became the core of the United States post-war global security system not by design but through the unplanned confrontation of the Cold War. The garrison of some 250,000 troops stationed in West Germany on a permanent basis far exceeded US deployments elsewhere, and became the symbol of the American commitment to the defence of Europe. But these forces also served to reassure allies and adversaries that containment would apply to Germany no less than to the Soviet Union. Furthermore, they gave the United States an entrée into European affairs that she was reluctant to discard once the Cold War was over. As a result, Germany continued to play host to the three-quarters of the American forces retained in Europe in the 1990s, just as

---

[40] Anderson and Goodman, op. cit. 36.

Japan continued to provide the main platform for American power projection in Asia.

During the Cold War period, American forces were first stationed in West Germany for some ten years by right of conquest and occupation but remained in increasing numbers as the key element of the integrated NATO forces deployed to counter the threat from the East. The forces of occupation evolved into partners in an alliance with little outward sign of change and the terms on which American forces remained in Germany were sometimes referred to as the dual right of stationing. In this sense, West Germany was a host nation with limited room for manoeuvre who found it difficult to come to terms with the fact that she was wholly dependent on the United States for her security. Moreover, she resented the impact of history and geography which made her territory the most likely battleground for full-scale conflict between NATO and the Warsaw Pact, even though as a nation she was almost wholly responsible for the quandary in which she found herself.

While acutely concerned at the implications of a tactical or strategic nuclear exchange, West Germany also recognized that an all-out conventional conflict across the inner German border would be scarcely less devastating. She was therefore an ambivalent and understandably nervous subscriber to the NATO doctrines of forward defence and flexible response but at the same time easily alarmed at American schemes for force improvement, burden-sharing, or rapid reinforcement which threatened to decouple the United States from her defence. For these reasons, the American security relationship with West Germany was a good deal less harmonious than that with Britain, who had been an ally not an enemy during the war, was less directly threatened by the Warsaw Pact and could still play a global security role to which West Germany could not aspire. The concentration of American forces in West Germany, the military and social repercussions of Vietnam, the prolonged negotiations over offset, the various American initiatives to reduce or redeploy their troops, and the overarching debates on nuclear policy all made for a tense and unsettled partnership. Even where the strategic community of interest was strongest in the global security system and the host nation fully supported the American military mission, a series of conflicts and disputes impaired relations between two of the leading members of the Alliance.

However, with the end of the Cold War a less dependent and more evenly balanced security relationship has developed between the new Germany and the United States, no longer based on the defence of West German territory but on a shared interest in the stability of Central and Eastern Europe and the countries of the former Soviet Union. The last vestiges of post-war occupation were removed with the signature of the Final Settlement in Moscow in September 1990, and the withdrawal of the Four Power garrisons from Berlin in 1994. In 1992, President Bush invited Germany to become a partner in leadership with the United States while President Clinton has indicated that he regards Germany as America's principal partner in Europe, whom he would be prepared to support for a permanent seat on the UN Security Council. The hesitant steps taken by Germany towards playing a full part in international security operations outside her borders have helped to foster this new, more equal, partnership.

It is true that 75,000 American troops remain in Germany, a number six to seven times greater than that in any other European country, which suggests a residual element of containment. In theory, there is no overriding reason for the forces required to demonstrate America's continuing commitment to Europe to be concentrated predominantly in Germany, but in practice this is the only option likely to gain general acceptance. Despite the tensions of the Cold War period, there is now remarkably little hostility to the American military presence in Germany. At a ceremony at the Brandenburg Gate in Berlin in July 1994, Chancellor Kohl endorsed the role which American troops play in preserving the stability of Europe. In the words of one recent commentator:

Bonn's keen interest in preserving the stationing regime stems in part from the desire to dispel the fears of its neighbours; it also stems from a wish to maintain the security arrangements that guaranteed Germany's political, economic and even moral recovery after World War II, and its territorial integrity after the Cold War.[41]

Nevertheless, as Germany recovers her self-confidence as a 'normal' nation, there must be some doubt as to how long Europe's premier economic power will remain content to act as host to three-quarters of the United States forces stationed in Europe, when the purpose of these forces, besides underwriting stability in Central and Eastern Europe, is to preserve American influence on the continent and, tacitly, to exercise a residual element of restraint on the reunited Germany.

Italy

Italy's Strategic and Political Position

Occupying a key strategic position bisecting the Mediterranean and flanking the former territory of Yugoslavia, Italy might best be

---

[41] Haglund and Mager, op. cit., 276.

considered as fitting into the United States global security system along-side her other Mediterranean allies, Spain, Greece, and Turkey. However, in political and military terms, the deployment of American forces in Italy has more in common with the close security relationship which the United States established with West Germany, following the post-war occupation, than with the subsequent, less satisfactory arrangements she later developed with other Mediterranean countries, with whom she had no previous security links. In fact, the occupation of Italy dated from the Armistice signed with the Allied Powers on 3 September 1943. Thereafter, the Italians considered themselves co-belligerents against Germany and Churchill later commented that Italy had 'worked her passage home'. But once Germany was defeated, Italy too was treated as a conquered nation. The Peace Treaty imposed on her in September 1947 stripped her of her African colonies, gave the Dodecanese Islands to Greece, made Trieste a free territory under the UN Security Council, and placed restrictions on the size of her armed forces. Even so, less than two years later Italy was invited to become a founder member of NATO, well before West Germany. Both the United States and France saw advantages in drawing Italy into NATO, although their motives were somewhat different.

Post-war occupation and early membership of NATO do not fully explain the marked differences between America's security relationship with Italy on the one hand and Spain, Greece, and Turkey on the other. But these differences are significant. Italy was the only host nation in the Mediterranean not to expect military aid from the United States and, despite some forty changes of government during the Cold War period, the only one not to suffer from a political dictatorship or military government at some point. Despite a large, well-organized communist party in the country—or perhaps because of this—Italy never attempted to renegotiate her basing agreements with the United States during the Cold War or reduce the American military presence on her territory. Nor did she raise difficulties over nuclear weapons. Indeed, she was ready to accept a wide variety of nuclear weapons on her territory including Jupiter in the 1960s and ground-launched cruise missiles in the 1980s. In the late 1980s, Italy was also prepared to accept the transfer of F-16 aircraft from Torrejón near Madrid (albeit in the conventional mode) on the understanding that the NATO infrastructure fund would bear the costs. The United States therefore looked on Italy as her most reliable ally in the Mediterranean, maintaining some 11,350 troops there in 1979, at the height of the Cold War, compared with some 8,750 in Spain, 4,500 in Turkey, and 3,500 in Greece.

Moreover, there was, during the early stages of the Cold War, little evidence of the social or cultural friction between American troops and the host nation population which appeared elsewhere in the Alliance, not least in West Germany. In a report prepared for the President in November 1957, Frank Nash, the United States Assistant Secretary of Defense, commented:

The usual irritations associated with the presence of US forces in foreign countries have been conspicuously absent in Italy.[42]

This view was endorsed thirty years later in a report by the Congressional Research Service in 1986 which concluded:

Italy is a nation with which the United States has few outstanding politico-military differences of consequence.[43]

These later comments may have been slightly optimistic. Security relations between the United States and Italy remained harmonious during the 1950s and 1960s, but because of Italy's central strategic position in the Mediterranean and her need to maintain good relations with the Arab world, differences arose in the 1970s and 1980s over United States policy in the Middle East. In 1973, during the Yom Kippur War, Italy, in common with all other European members of NATO except Portugal, felt compelled to state that membership of the Alliance did not oblige her to assist the United States in her Middle East policy. In the 1980s, Italy played her part in international peacekeeping operations in the Middle East, contributing to United Nations operations in South Lebanon in 1980 and Sinai in 1981, and participating in the abortive Multinational Peacekeeping Force organized by the United States in the Lebanon in 1982. But the more assertive stance adopted by President Reagan in the Mediterranean caused difficulties for Italy. In 1985, she made a formal protest to the United States over American action following the hijacking of the cruise ship *Achille Lauro* and the following year she was to do the same over the American air strike on Libya.

Post-War Developments

The duration of allied occupation forces in Italy after the war was influenced by both the dispute with Yugoslavia over Trieste, which was

[42] United States Overseas Military Bases. Report to the President by F. C. Nash. Cited by L. Nuti, US Forces in Italy 1945–63. In *US Military Forces in Europe: The Early Years 1945–70*, S. Duke and W. Krieger (ed.) (Boulder: CO, Westview, 1993, Ch. 10).
[43] US Military Installations in NATOs Southern Region. Report by the CRS for the House Sub-Committee on Europe and the Middle East. 95th Congress, 7 October 1986.

not resolved until August 1948, and the presence of allied troops in Austria until 1955, for which Italy provided an important supply route. Furthermore, in the immediate post-war period there was considerable communist activity in Italy itself and a full-scale civil war in neighbouring Greece. Against this background, the Allied Commanders in Italy, Field Marshal Alexander and Rear Admiral Ellery Stone, urged that a significant number of allied troops be maintained in Italy until a stable, democratic system had emerged in the country. Despite these representations, the 1947 Peace Treaty stipulated that all occupation forces should be withdrawn from Italy in ninety days. By mid 1947, the Americans had only one tank battalion and one infantry division in the country, while the British had only 5,000 infantry and 8,000 support troops.

In December 1947, the Italian Prime Minister Alcide de Gasperi asked for allied assistance in quelling internal disturbances and begged that the departure of the occupation forces be delayed. Unmoved, President Truman announced the total withdrawal of American troops from Italy as required by the Peace Treaty. However, his statement implied that the United States acknowledged a residual commitment to Italy at a time when there remained a strong possibility of a communist takeover. The United States, he said, would be 'obliged to consider what measures would be appropriate for the maintenance of peace and security' in certain unspecified circumstances.[44] This somewhat Delphic utterance may have been prompted by an American intelligence assessment on Italy prepared three months earlier:

Withdrawal would seriously affect US interests and security in Italy by (a) throwing open to communist pressure the important area of Northern Italy where the proximity of Yugoslav communists makes it possible for the USSR to create a situation on the border similar to that prevailing in Northern Greece; and (b) leaving the entire country and the weak de Gasperi Government ill-prepared to cope with the powerful Communist Party in the national elections scheduled for April 1948.[45]

Allied occupation forces duly departed from Italy but residual contingents remained in both Austria and Trieste. The Italians were anxious to co-ordinate the military plans for their forces with those for these neighbouring occupation forces. Italy was not admitted to the Brussels Treaty in 1948 but in December that year General Marrass, Chief of

[44] *NATO and the Mediterranean*, L. Kaplan, R. Clawson, and R. Luraghi (ed.) (Wilmington, DE: Scholarly Resources, 1985, Ch. 2).

[45] Central Intelligence Group Special Evaluation No 30, 16 September 1947. Cited by Nuti, op. cit.

Staff of the Italian Army, visited Washington to discuss formal security links with the Western Alliance. The Americans suggested that military co-ordination could best be achieved by Italy joining either the Brussels Treaty or the North Atlantic Treaty then still under discussion. The prospect of Italy joining NATO provoked considerable debate among the Western allies, some of whom considered her more of a liability than an asset because of the restrictions on armaments which the Peace Treaty had imposed on her. France, herself a Mediterranean country, who was anxious to see Algeria included in the NATO boundaries, supported entry. But Britain, wary of diverting scarce military resources from the Atlantic, was less enthusiastic. However, the United States eventually forced the issue by inviting Italy to become a founder member of the Alliance. Dean Acheson explained the rationale for including Italy in the following terms:

Italy presented a perplexing problem. She was most decidedly not a North Atlantic state in any geography. Both European and American military opinion held that Italy would make little contribution to Western Europe's security against attack and might be a considerable drain on available military assets. Yet from a political point of view an unattached Italy was a source of danger. A former enemy state . . . Italy might suffer from an isolation complex and, with its large communist party, fall victim to seduction from the East.[46]

Once Italy was admitted to NATO, Headquarters Allied Forces Southern Europe (HQAFSOUTH) was set up at Naples in June 1951. The Korean War had demonstrated the importance of co-ordinating plans for all allied forces in the region but the French and British withdrew their forces from Austria and Trieste in 1953, leaving the American forces in Italy the only allied military presence in the theatre. (It was not until 1954 that the Trieste dispute was resolved by giving the northern zone to Italy and the southern zone to Yugoslavia.)

The first bilateral agreement between the United States and Italy was an Exchange of Notes on 7 January 1952. This made no reference to NATO or bases for American forces. It merely bound Italy to 'fulfil the military obligations which it has assumed under multilateral or bilateral agreements or treaties to which the United States is a party'.[47] No doubt caution was necessary because of the considerable communist presence in the Italian parliament. A secret Implementing Agreement was signed on 20 October 1954 but it is probable that, in building up her forces in

[46] D. Acheson, *Present at the Creation* (London: Norton, 1969, 279).
[47] TIAS 2611. Cited by Duke, op. cit.

Italy, the United States relied, as elsewhere, on the catch-all provision of Article III of the North Atlantic Treaty:

The parties, separately or jointly, by means of continuous and effective self help and mutual aid, will maintain and develop their individual and collective capacity to resist armed attack.[48]

Under these agreements the first steps to be taken were the development of the port of Leghorn (Livorno), together with a large supply depot nearby, named Camp Darby, to reprovision American troops in Austria. However, the signature of the Austrian State Treaty in 1955 brought the post-war occupation of Austria to an end and ensured the neutrality of the country. This opened up a gap in the Western defence system since Italy had no contiguous links to the Central Region. It was decided to redeploy the American troops withdrawn from Austria to north-east Italy, and a new NATO command was set up at Vicenza. Under this command, American and Italian ground forces were integrated in the Southern European Task Force designed to defend Italy from an attack over the Alps. Over time, this role was superseded by NATO plans for the reinforcement by allied forces of Turkey and Thrace.

Allied Military Facilities

Thus Italy played host to the only significant body of American ground forces on the southern flank of NATO. At a later stage an airborne battalion assigned to the mobile force of Allied Command Europe (ACE) was located at Camp Ederle near Vicenza. However, the United States initially regarded Italy primarily as a basing area for the units of the US Navy which had entered the Mediterranean in 1946 and were later to be designated the Sixth Fleet. Gaeta, near Naples, became the home port for many of the ships involved. In Sardinia, the island of La Maddelena was developed as a replenishment base for nuclear-powered attack submarines and Decimomannu served as an air combat training range for a number of NATO countries. At the same time, the airfield at Sigonella in Sicily became an important centre for anti-submarine warfare operations.

Despite the frequent changes of government experienced by Italy in the post-war period, no administration questioned the deployment of nuclear weapons on Italian territory. In 1955, it was agreed that American troops in Italy should be equipped with Honest John and

[48] Duke, Op. cit. 1996.

Corporal missiles. At times, the United States has suggested reducing her ground forces and relying more on the tactical nuclear weapons held in Italy. For example, in 1958 the Americans proposed to retain sufficient ground forces in Italy only for the safe custody of the nuclear warheads stored in the country. The Italians protested at this and the American reductions were limited.

In 1963, the United States again wished to reduce her ground forces and replace Corporal by Sergeant missiles. The Italians, keen to retain a significant US Army presence in Italy, agreed to purchase more American equipment to forestall the withdrawals. As a result, Sergeant replaced Corporal on a one for two basis and was operated by American servicemen until withdrawn in the 1970s. In addition, Nike Hercules, Lance, and nuclear artillery shells have all been made available to the Italian armed forces under American custody arrangements and Jupiter missiles were deployed to Italy in the 1960s. In northern Italy, the Air Force base at Aviano was made available for the forward deployment of American nuclear capable aircraft which were maintained on Quick Reaction Alert. Italy also undertook to accept 108 ground-launched cruise missiles at Comiso in Sicily in 1987 under NATO's Twin Track policy. However, in agreeing to accept the transfer of 72 F-16 aircraft from Torrejón in Spain to Crotone in Sicily after 1988, Italy made it clear that these aircraft would be deployed in conventional mode only. In the event, the transfer to Crotone fell victim to funding and political problems and in November 1993 a new agreement was reached allowing the F-16s to be permanently based at Aviano, where they had been deployed on a temporary basis since leaving Spain.

It is a measure of the confidence which the United States has in Italy as a reliable ally that several NATO and United States headquarters are located in the country, mostly at Naples which houses the headquarters of Allied Air Forces Southern Europe and Allied Naval Forces in Europe. The headquarters of Allied Land Forces Southern Europe is at Verona. The headquarters of the US Sixth Fleet is close to Naples at Gaeta and in the mid 1980s Commander in Chief US Navy in Europe (CINCUSNAVEUR) moved his headquarters from London to Naples.

The Achille Lauro *Affair*

The even balance of relations between the United States and Italy as a host nation were abruptly disturbed in October 1985 by the *Achille Lauro* affair. This was the first of two incidents under the Reagan

Ádministration, the second being the air strike on Libya the following year, where the use of bases in Europe for national as opposed to NATO operations gave rise to considerable controversy and caused the host nation to reconsider the uses to which bases on its territory could be put.[49]

On 7 October 1985, four members of the Palestine Liberation Front, a faction of the Palestine Liberation Organization (PLO), hijacked the Italian cruise liner *Achille Lauro* 10 miles off Alexandria in an attempt to secure the release of 50 Palestinians held in custody by Israel. In legal terms, this incident fell under the jurisdiction either of Italy, as owner of the cruise liner, or Egypt, in whose territorial waters the hijacking occurred. Over the next two days negotiations conducted by the Egyptian authorities resulted in the hijackers being disembarked at Port Said in return for a safe conduct being granted to another country. However, it was then revealed that an elderly American tourist, Leon Klinghoffer, had been murdered on the *Achille Lauro* on 8 October. Once this was known, the Italian authorities wished to extradite the hijackers, but Egypt had by now put them onto a Boeing 737 to be flown to Tunis. Tunisia declined to accept the hijackers and the aircraft was returning to Egypt when it was intercepted by four F-15 Tomcats from the American aircraft carrier USS Saratoga and forced to land at the airfield at Sigonella in Sicily. In effect, the hijackers had themselves been hijacked.

The Italian Prime Minister Bettino Craxi had agreed to the interception because he wished to bring the hijackers to justice in Italy. But when the Egyptian plane landed, custody of the hijackers was disputed between Italian troops and American commandos from Delta Force, an elite anti-terrorist unit, which had flown to Sigonella under General Carl Steiner with instructions to arrest the terrorists and remove them for trial in the United States. A stand-off ensued, with the Americans showing scant regard for the sovereignty of Italy at Sigonella, while questions of jurisdiction were debated between the two governments.

Craxi argued, correctly, that the United States had no jurisdiction over the hijackers, who were subsequently tried at Genoa and given long prison sentences. The United States was offended that one of the Palestinians, Abul Abbas, was allowed to go free for lack of evidence. It later emerged that he had masterminded the hijacking, but had not taken part

---

[49] This brief account of the *Achille Lauro* affair draws heavily on Antonio Cassesse, *Terrorism, Politics and Law: The Achille Lauro Affair* (Princeton, NJ: Princeton University Press, 1989).

in it and had flown with the hijackers in the Boeing 737 pretending to be a PLO negotiator. On their side, the Italians strongly resented the high-handed action by the United States at a base made available to them for NATO purposes. In November 1985, Craxi made it clear that 'NATO bases in Italy can only be used for specific NATO ends in conformity with existing accords.'[50] The following year, when it looked as though the United States might wish to use forces based in Italy during her dispute with Libya, Craxi, who had attempted to mediate in the dispute, took care to point out that NATO bases in Italy 'cannot be a starting point of war operations outside the NATO framework'.[51] His caution was justified since Colonel Gaddafi launched an ineffective missile attack on the Italian island of Lampedusa, situated midway between Malta and Libya, following the American air strike on Libya.

Conflict in the Balkans

Although these incidents caused some tension between the United States and Italy in the mid 1980s, the conflict in the Balkans which developed from 1991 onwards demonstrated the importance of Italy's strategic position and her standing as a dependable member of both the European and Atlantic communities. The air base at Aviano, close to the former Yugoslav border in north-east Italy, became the centre first for humanitarian food drops over Bosnia and later for Operation DENY FLIGHT, in which the United States played a full part, using F-15s deployed from Lakenheath and F-16s from Ramstein as well as F-18 Hornets detached from their aircraft carriers. At the same time other airfields were used by the air forces of other nations participating in the allied operations over Bosnia, notably Gioia del Colle by the British and Piacenza by the Germans. Following the reduction of US Air Force units in Germany, Aviano became the headquarters of Sixteenth Air Force, one of only two numbered Air Forces remaining in Europe (the other being Third Air Force in Britain). In 1994/95 an extra 1,000 USAF personnel were deployed to the base to support the missions over Bosnia, and in 1999, when NATO air operations were launched against Serbia and Kosovo, Italy made air bases available to all the allied air forces involved.

The enhanced strategic position of Italy was reflected in a new agree-

---

[50] CRS 1986, 23.
[51] *New York Times*, 23 March 1996. Cited in *The Sun Never Sets*, J. Gerson and B. Birchard (ed.), (Boston, MA: South End Press, 1991).

ment with the United States signed in February 1995 governing the use of military facilities by American forces. This agreement also marked a more balanced and mature security relationship between the United States and Italy which, as a former enemy power subject to endemic political instability, had been one of the more compliant and accommodating host nations in the global security system. Article 1 emphasized the bilateral nature of this relationship within the wider NATO alliance:

Common defense co-operation shall be accomplished at the bilateral level within the scope of the North Atlantic Treaty.[52]

At the same time, the agreement tacitly acknowledged the secret nature of previous bilateral arrangements. The preamble stated that the two countries had agreed 'to modernise their defense relationship and to implement the BIA'. Elsewhere in the text the BIA was described as an 'Agreement regarding Bilateral Infrastructure in implementation of the North Atlantic Treaty', signed on 20 October 1954 but never published. The new agreement provided for 'installations ceded in use to the United States of America' to remain under Italian command and required the US commander to notify the Italian commander 'of all significant US activities, with specific reference to operational and training activity', and to 'the movements of material, weapons and civilian/ military personnel'. It was also made clear that 'permanent increases of the operational component and relative support shall be authorised by the Italian National Authorities'. Although understandings on some of these points may have been reached previously, the text of the 1995 agreement reads as though the Italian government was asserting its sovereign rights for the first time and, in doing so, belatedly catching up with practice already adopted by other host nations in the global security system.

The weight which the United States continued to place on Italy as a reliable ally is reflected in the level of military forces she has maintained in the country since the end of the Cold War. Excluding the additional personnel deployed for missions in the Balkans, there were still 10,500 American servicemen in Italy in 1999. These were mainly US Navy and USAF personnel but ground forces were represented by 1,750 troops including an airborne infantry battalion. By comparison, American forces elsewhere in the Mediterranean numbered 2,500 in Turkey, 2,500

---

[52] Memorandum of Understanding concerning the Use of Installations/Infrastructure by United States Forces in Italy. Signed in Rome, 2 February 1995. TIAS 12317.

in Spain, and a mere 500 in Greece. With the rundown of the American military presence in other host nations, Italy remained a secure base for the Sixth Fleet and the only location for substantial American forces in the Mediterranean.

Nevertheless, there were signs at the end of the 1990s that cracks were opening up again in this harmonious relationship. In August 1994 Italy had been refused a place on the European Contact Group set up to find a political solution to the problems of the Balkans. The following year she chose to protest at this exclusion by banning American fighter air-craft from Italian territory for a time and imposing restrictions on the logistic support provided for NATO. This ban was lifted following the Dayton Peace Accords in December 1995. However, in 1996, a significant shift to the left occurred in Italian politics, bringing to an end the long dominance of the Christian Democrats. Professor Romano Prodi, Prime Minister of a centre-left coalition, found himself depend-ent on the support of the hardline Rifondazione Comunista in the Lower House. Armando Cossutta, the leader of this group, declared in December 1997 that there was no continuing justification for the American military presence in Italy and that there was no guarantee that the United States might not use the bases she occupied for pur-poses which were at odds with Italian foreign policy.[53]

The Italian government was obliged to consider a review of the secret agreements drawn up in the 1950s which had never been debated in Par-liament. In all probability, little action would have followed but early in 1998 a tragic accident in the Dolomites stirred up further anti-American feeling. On 3 February, an American EA-6B Prowler surveil-lance aircraft based at Aviano cut through the wire of a cable car at the ski resort of Cavalese killing twenty people of mixed nationalities. Since the cable car was only 300 feet above the ground it was evident that the accident was the result of reckless manoeuvring by the US Marine pilot and this was admitted by the United States authorities. The usual issues of jurisdiction arose with the US authorities declining to surrender juris-diction to Italy. The four-man crew were repatriated to North Carolina where charges of negligent homicide and involuntary manslaughter were brought against them at a court martial. Such was the sense of outrage in Italy that an emergency debate was held in which the Defence Minister was obliged to counter calls for the closure of the bases occupied by the United States on the grounds that this would be tantamount to

---

[53] *The Times*, 23 December 1997.

renationalizing the Italian defence system.[54] Feeling in Italy was further inflamed when the American pilot was acquitted of manslaughter and not much mollified when he was subsequently convicted of obstruction of justice for helping to destroy a videotape of the flight. He was sentenced to six months in prison and dismissed from the Marine Corps.

[54] *The Times*, 6 February 1998.

8

New Allies in the Mediterranean

Introduction

The Mediterranean was of critical strategic importance to the allies during the Second World War, providing the springboard for the first assault on the European mainland via Sicily and Italy. This strategic emphasis came from Britain, who had controlled the Mediterranean since the time of Nelson and had regarded the waterway as the lifeline to India since the opening of the Suez Canal in 1869. She persuaded the United States, with considerable difficulty, to defer a cross-Channel invasion of France in favour of landings in North Africa and an attack on the Italian peninsula. Under the concept of regional policing prevalent in Washington in the mid 1940s, the United States tended to assume that British influence would predominate in the Mediterranean after the war, and consequently made no plans for acquiring bases in the area, with the exception of Wheelus Field in Libya.

However, Soviet pressure in the Eastern Mediterranean immediately after the war, first on Greece during the civil war and then on Turkey, caused the United States to respond with a succession of naval visits. These started with the visit of the cruiser *USS Providence* to Greece in December 1945 which was followed in 1946 by the battleship *Missouri* which visited Istanbul and Piraeus in April and the aircraft carrier *Franklin D. Roosevelt* which visited Greece in September. James Forrestal, then Secretary of the Navy, was the chief architect of an American naval presence in the Mediterranean. In June 1946 he spoke to James Byrnes, the Secretary of State, 'about sending casual cruisers unannounced . . . in small units into the Mediterranean so that we may establish the custom of the American flag being flown in those waters'.[1] In September 1946, he followed this up with a public statement that the US Navy would continue to operate in the Mediterranean as a matter of course. But it was not until 1947, when Britain withdrew support for Greece and Turkey, and surrendered her mandate in Palestine, that the

---

[1] W. L. Millis (ed.), *The Forrestal Diaries* (London: Cassell, 1952, 186).

United States realized she would need to supplant Britain in the Mediterranean.

The Truman Doctrine formalized these new responsibilities and gave the United States a foothold in Greece and Turkey. But she had no significant bases in the Mediterranean at this time and, although Italy became a founder member of NATO, a series of bilateral agreements with Spain, Greece, and Turkey were necessary to build up her position. In these countries, the United States had none of the advantages of colonial power, wartime partnership, or right of conquest and subsequent occupation, described elsewhere. She was dealing with impoverished sovereign nations who, after the death of Stalin, saw less immediate threat to their own security and were increasingly prepared to drive a hard bargain for the use of their territory. In the Eastern Mediterranean, Greece and Turkey also saw economic and strategic advantages in keeping a door open to the Soviet Union. Both Turkey under Bülent Ecevit in the 1970s and Greece under Andreas Papandreou in the 1980s actively courted the Soviet Union for aid and investment while playing host to American troops. Moreover, with Spain, Greece, and Turkey under authoritarian governments for much of the Cold War period, the political as well as financial problems of the 'leasehold empire' were as acute in these three countries as anywhere in the global security system.

Despite the strategic importance of the Mediterranean during the Second World War and the subsequent Soviet pressure on Greece and Turkey, there were divided views on the area in the deliberations leading to the creation of NATO. France, herself a Mediterranean power with possessions in North Africa, urged that the Washington Treaty should cover the Mediterranean and pressed strongly for the inclusion of Italy in the Alliance. American officials, wary of the reaction in Congress, were initially less enthusiastic although they eventually took the lead in inviting Italy to join the negotiations. They preferred to deal directly with Spain, Greece, and Turkey, thereby avoiding the security guarantees in the North Atlantic Treaty until Greece and Turkey joined NATO in 1952 and Spain, following the death of Franco, in 1982. In part this reflected the fact that, for the United States, the Mediterranean was less significant in strategic terms as the southern flank of NATO than as a means of power projection in the Middle East. Her European allies consistently drew a sharp distinction between the Cold War and the Middle East conflict. But for the United States, the two increasingly overlapped as the Soviet Union countered American support for Israel with further support for the Arabs. However, what were known in

NATO as 'out of area' disputes were not the only difficulties faced by the United States in the Mediterranean. Problems arose in a number of other areas.

First, the new allies in the Mediterranean had a very patchy record on democracy. Spain was a dictatorship until 1975 and, because of General Franco's collaboration with the Axis Powers, could not be admitted to NATO until after his death. Greece fell under the rule of a military junta from 1967 to 1974 and in Turkey there were interventions by the armed forces in 1960, 1971, and 1980. These developments posed the same dilemma for the United States as she had already experienced in Portugal and was to experience, to a lesser extent, in South Korea, Panama, and the Philippines. The strategic importance of the territory controlled by these undemocratic governments was such that the United States felt obliged to make an accommodation with them. As a report for the Senate Committee on Foreign Relations commented in 1979:

For a number of years, United States policy generally accepted the stability of right wing regimes in some Southern European countries as preferable to the possibility of political chaos.[2]

But in making this accommodation, the United States became associated with illegitimate rule in the eyes of the people and this led to further difficulties for her when these governments were replaced. 'The newly emerging democracies', added the 1979 report, 'have witnessed in their midst a questioning of the wisdom of continued military association with the United States'.

Secondly, the impoverished nature of these countries in the early years of the Cold War led to demands for military and economic assistance which both sides recognized as rent for the bases, even though they were careful not to use this term. Once established, this pattern was difficult to break. In the late 1970s a ratio of 7:10 for US military aid to Greece and Turkey was instituted, and by the end of the 1980s period the United States was providing security assistance of $480 million per annum to Turkey and $343 million to Greece. These sums were higher than those for any other recipient country except Egypt and Israel under the Camp David Agreement. They were also significant sums in proportion to the national economies of the host nations which gave rise to an unhealthy dependency on American aid. The payments to Greece, for example, were equivalent to the whole of her healthcare

[2] United States Foreign Policy and Overseas Military Installations. Report for the SCFR. CRS April 1979.

budget. Lower sums were also paid over to Spain and Portugal, although military aid to Spain ceased from 1989 onwards.

Total military and economic aid from the United States amounted to $13 billion to Turkey and $9 billion to Greece over the period 1946–87. A report prepared by the Congressional Research Service in 1986 indicated that the aid payments amounted to rent in all but name:

With the exception of Italy, which receives no US security assistance, Portugal, Spain, Greece and Turkey have expected increased American security assistance in return for continued use of host country military facilities . . . Such assistance is viewed by most of these allies as a de facto quid pro quo for the privilege of continued use of their territories for military installations.[3]

Finally, the United States bilateral relationships with Greece and Turkey were bedevilled by the conflict between these two countries over Cyprus and the consequent disputes over territorial waters, drilling rights, and air traffic control in the Aegean. As early as 1955, Dulles wrote to Greece and Turkey urging them to put their NATO obligations before their bilateral antagonism, an approach which only irritated both countries and caused Greece to withdraw from NATO exercises. There were major crises over Cyprus in 1964 and more significantly in 1974, when Turkey invaded and annexed the northern part of the island. This conflict led at different times to the closure of most American installations in Turkey and the withdrawal of Greece from NATO-integrated command structures in the region.

Nevertheless, the Sixth Fleet, formed in February 1948, continued to operate from Spain, Italy, Greece, and Turkey without significant interruption throughout the Cold War period. In the early post-war years, when the United States had limited ground forces in Europe and the Soviet Union virtually no naval units in the Mediterranean, ship visits by the Sixth Fleet provided an impressive show of support not only for Greece and Turkey but also for Italy during the Trieste crisis and the critical election of 1947. The average strength of the Sixth Fleet during the Cold War was approximately forty ships comprising two carrier battle groups and one amphibious task force of between four and seven amphibious ships and some 1,800 assault troops. Between them, the two aircraft carriers could operate 150 aircraft and they were generally accompanied by some 14 surface combat ships, 4 nuclear-powered attack submarines, and 12 auxiliaries. This naval force was initially

[3] US Military Installations in NATO's Southern Region. Report for the House of Representatives Sub-Committee on Europe and the Middle-East 99th Congress. CRS 12 October 1986.

configured for power projection rather than control of the sea lanes, and until the mid 1960s the Mediterranean was a 'mare nostrum' for the United States.

The Soviet Navy first established a permanent presence in the Mediterranean in 1964 and increased this from 1967 onwards, following the Six Day War, by negotiating improved access at Port Said and Alexandria. However, the Soviet basing arrangement with Egypt was short lived. Egypt asked for some troops to be withdrawn in 1972 and closed her bases to the Russians completely in 1976. Thereafter, the Soviet Navy was forced to rely largely on anchorages in the Gulf of Sidra, as well as off Algeria and Tunisia. In contrast, the US Sixth Fleet was not seriously inconvenienced in the many operations it undertook in the Mediterranean over the Cold War period. These included support for Greece, Turkey, and Italy in the late 1940s, monitoring the Suez crisis in 1956, the reinforcement of Lebanon in 1958, the two Arab-Israel wars of 1967 and 1973, the deployment of US Marines to Lebanon in 1982–4, and confrontation with Libya in the Gulf of Sidra in 1981 and 1986.

Throughout the period of the Cold War it was the US Sixth Fleet that, in the British tradition established by Nelson, formed the most tangible evidence of American military power in the Mediterranean. But in building bilateral arrangements with her Mediterranean allies, the United States gave equal prominence to the need for air bases in the region, initially for strategic and later for tactical air operations. The desire to use these air bases for operations in the Middle East in pursuit of US national policy gave rise to a series of difficulties and disputes with host nations but, once the Cold War was over, the air bases in Italy and Turkey played an invaluable part in allied or coalition operations against the new threats which emerged to the collective security of the West. The air base at Aviano in north-east Italy became the centre for allied air operations over the Balkans and the air base at Incirlik in south-east Turkey was used, albeit with considerable misgivings by the host nation, for air operations by coalition forces both during the Gulf War and subsequently to monitor Iraq's compliance with United Nations Resolutions.

Spain

Background to the Agreements

Spain could not be admitted to NATO while General Franco was alive. Membership for Spain at this stage was scarcely compatible with the political aims of the Alliance, set out in the preamble to the North Atlantic Treaty, in which those joining pledged to preserve 'the freedom, common heritage and civilisation of their peoples, founded on the principles of democracy, individual liberty and the rule of law'. The European members of the Alliance were prepared to do business with Portugal under Dr Antonio de Oliviera Salazar, largely because of the strategic importance of the Azores. But Franco was far less acceptable than Salazar and the strategic assets which Spain could provide were not, in European eyes, of equal importance to the Azores. The entrance to the Mediterranean was guarded by Gibraltar, which was in British hands, and by 1953, when the Madrid Pact was signed, heavy bomber bases were available to Strategic Air Command (SAC) in Britain, very much closer to the Soviet Union than Spain. While there was some merit in spreading SAC assets over a wide geographical area, for defensive purposes, the United States had also established bomber bases in Morocco, still a French Protectorate at a time when France was fully committed to NATO, before constructing bases in Spain.

The land mass of Spain forms an appendage to Europe far from the threat posed by the Soviet Union and, although some American strategists, emulating the Duke of Wellington, may have contemplated a retreat beyond the Pyrenees in the face of a Russian attack,[4] Europeans could see few military advantages in bringing Spain into their collective security arrangements sufficient to offset the grave political disadvantages. The British Foreign Secretary Herbert Morrison made precisely this point in the House of Commons on 25 July 1951:

We have expressed our conviction that the strategic advantages which might accrue from associating Spain with Western defence would be outweighed by the political damage which such an association might inflict on the Western community of nations.[5]

In the early post-war years, when Franco's association with Hitler was still fresh in the minds of the international community, there was widespread support for the policy of isolating Spain. She was excluded from

---

[4] This disturbing possibility is mentioned by Ernest May in a chapter headed: American Forces in the Federal Republic of Germany in *The Federal Republic of Germany and the United States*, E. Kirchner and J. Sperling (ed.) (Boulder, CO: Westview, 1984). The JCS Emergency War Plan HALFMOON JCS1844/13 assumed that all Europe except the British Isles and the Spanish Peninsula would be overrun. The French were seriously concerned that American forces would retreat from the Rhine to the Pyrenees in the face of a Russian assault.

[5] Cited by A. Whitaker, *Spain and the Defense of the West*, (New York: Council on Foreign Relations/Harper/OUP, 1961).

the United Nations in 1945, and the following year the General Assembly passed a Resolution urging members to withdraw their Ambassadors from Madrid. Moreover, in March 1946 the United States, Great Britain, and France issued a Tripartite Declaration saying that they could envisage no 'full and cordial association' with Spain while Franco remained in power. Yet, by July 1951 Admiral Forrest Sherman, the US Chief of Naval Operations, was in Madrid for preliminary negotiations on setting up American bases on Spanish territory and a series of agreements, collectively known as the Madrid Pact, was signed in September 1953. What had happened to bring about this reverse course, which has been described as even more radical than those adopted in Germany and Japan where, in contrast to Spain, the enemy powers had been defeated and the wartime governments purged?

In October 1947, George Kennan, rather surprisingly, linked Spain with Japan as two countries on which the United States should change course. Although the reasons for reversal on Japan were largely economic, Kennan felt that 'the Mediterranean cannot be considered without considering Spain and the question of transit through the Straits of Gibraltar', and he consequently urged that American representatives at the United Nations should 'not join in any further attempt to discredit the present Government of Spain'.[6] By January 1949, the Joint Chiefs of Staff were pressing the strategic importance of Spain on the Secretary of Defense.[7] The following year, an American naval squadron visited El Ferrol on Spain's north-west Atlantic coast. It was apparent that the Pentagon was pushing hard for a rapprochement with Spain and, in political terms, the State Department had concluded that ostracism had strengthened rather than weakened Franco's regime. In January 1950, Dean Acheson had hinted at more cordial relations and in November the United States was active in persuading the UN General Assembly to reverse its Resolution on the recall of Ambassadors four years earlier. As with developments elsewhere in the global security system, American policy was greatly influenced by the outbreak of the Korean War in June 1950. In the words of one early commentator:

Strategy took the upper hand over ideology and more weight was given to the help Spain might give in the next war than to any hindrance she had offered in the last.[8]

---

[6] *The Forrestal Diaries*, op. cit. 316.
[7] JCS to Secretary of Defense 5 January 1949. Cited in L. Kaplan, R. Clawson, and R. Luraghi, *NATO and the Mediterranean* (Wilmington, DE: Scholarly Resources, 1985).
[8] Whitaker, op. cit. 32.

There was clearly a bargain to be struck. Franco was desperate for both political recognition and economic assistance. He had started fishing for American bases as early as July 1947. Isolation may have strengthened his personal position but the cost had been severe. Spain had been excluded from the Marshall Plan and economic productivity in 1951 was only 50 per cent of the level reached prior to the Civil War. There were acute economic crises in 1945 and 1949. For her part, the United States came to value Franco's anti-communist credentials at a time when communist parties were making significant gains in both France and Italy. The future of Morocco as a French Protectorate was uncertain and Spain appeared to offer greater stability than some other European allies, both as a strike base for deterrent operations against the Soviet Union and as a naval base for operations by the Sixth Fleet in the Mediterranean.

However, the negotiations were by no means easy. The United States wanted maximum operational flexibility for her own forces but minimum commitment to the defence of Franco's Spain. Franco wanted international recognition and economic succour without being obliged to concede domestic political reform in return. Both parties obtained their objectives but Truman was a reluctant convert to rapprochement with Spain and it was left to the Eisenhower administration to bring the negotiations to a conclusion. Surprisingly, religious factors played a significant part in delaying negotiations on both sides. Truman at one stage pressed unsuccessfully for greater tolerance towards Spanish Protestants as part of the negotiations and, once these were completed, Franco wished to conclude a Concordat with the Vatican before signing an agreement with the United States.

Britain and France, who had joined the United States in the Tripartite Declaration of 1946, were neither informed nor consulted on the American decision to open negotiations on basing rights. France made a formal protest and Herbert Morrison's reaction has been recorded above. However, the United States took the view that it was time to erode Spain's isolation. The American Ambassador James C. Dunn, who concluded the negotiations on the Madrid Pact begun by Lincoln MacVeagh, explained the administration's approach to the House Foreign Affairs Committee in May 1953:

We feel that this bilateral agreement with the United States may be the opening phase of getting Spain back into international co-operation and is certainly our purpose.[9]

[9] House Committee on Foreign Affairs. European Problems 1951–56. Vol. XV, 376. Cited in *US Bases Overseas*, J. W. McDonald and D. B. Bendahmane (ed.) (Boulder, CO: Westview, 1990).

However, on the military rationale for the agreement he remained vague and not wholly convincing:

We want to have bases in Spain. They fill a certain place in the general scheme of defense arrangements which are, according to our military people, essential if we can possibly obtain them.

Once the Madrid Pact was signed, Dulles chose, slightly disingenuously, to present this bilateral agreement between the United States and Spain as a means of strengthening NATO. Ignoring the distaste which his European allies felt for Franco he stated in April 1954:

The NATO defense system has been supplemented, so far as the United States is concerned, by a base arrangement with Spain. This will enlarge in an important way the facilities available to the United States air and naval craft in the Western Mediterranean area.[10]

Furthermore, Dulles developed the habit of calling on Franco in the late 1950s to debrief him on NATO meetings he had attended and in December 1959, Eisenhower bestowed on the Spanish dictator the mark of approval he was so anxious to obtain by making a formal visit to Madrid—the first Western leader to meet Franco since the border meeting with Hitler at Hendaye in 1940.

This subservience of the ideological to the strategic was not lost on American critics of Franco and a sense of unease persisted in some quarters. In April 1969, Senator Fulbright, taking evidence at the Senate Sub-Committee on US Security Arrangements and Commitments Abroad, criticized the relationship with Spain as an 'extension of NATO' and questioned the wisdom of the United States doing business with 'one of the oldest and most entrenched military dictatorships in the world'.[11]

The 1953 Agreements

The three executive agreements signed in parallel on 26 September 1953, collectively known as the Madrid Pact, comprised a Defense Agreement, an Economic Aid Agreement, and a Mutual Defense Assistance Agreement. The Defense Agreement, which covered the use of military facilities in Spain by the United States, was of 10 years' duration, to be automatically extended for two successive periods of 5 years unless terminated. The preamble spoke of the principle of 'maintaining

[10] Dulles, 5 April 1954. Cited in Whitaker, op. cit.
[11] SCFR. Sub-Committee on US Security Agreements and Commitments Abroad. Evidence taken on 14 April 1969, 2360.

international peace and security in the face of the danger that threatens the Western world'. Article I associated the two governments in the
policy of 'strengthening the defenses of the West' and authorized the
United States:

to develop, maintain and utilise for military purposes, jointly with the Government of Spain, such areas and facilities in territory under Spanish jurisdiction
as may be agreed upon . . .[12]

In return, the United States undertook to assist with Spanish air defence
and naval equipment subject to other demands and Congressional
appropriations.

Article III preserved Spain's rights to approve the use to which
the bases were put in wartime. It read 'the time and manner of wartime
utilisation of said areas and facilities will be as mutually agreed upon'.
No details of the numbers or locations of the bases were given, but
in separate Notes signed by the Spanish Foreign Minister and the
American Ambassador, which remained secret until 1974, conditions on
the use of the bases were spelt out in greater detail. A distinction was
drawn between a response to communist aggression and other emergencies. 'In the light of obvious communist aggression that threatens the
security of the Occident', American forces could use:

the areas and facilities situated in Spanish territory as bases for action against
military objectives, in such manner as may be necessary for the defense of the
West, provided that . . . both countries communicated to each other . . . their
information and intentions.[13]

In other emergencies, that is apart from communist aggression, use of
the bases would be 'subject to urgent consultation between both Governments and will be determined in the light of the circumstances of the
situation which has developed'.

This distinction between communist and non-communist aggression
is an interesting one, not found in any other security agreements negotiated by the United States at this time. It gave the United States a fairly
free hand to use the assets of Strategic Air Command to meet a Soviet
threat, subject only to informing the Spanish government. This put Spain
in exactly the position which Britain had been anxious to avoid—serving
as a launching pad for an atomic strike by the United States in a conflict
in which the host country might not be involved. But the wording

---

[12] Use of Military Facilities in Spain. Signed 26 September 1953. TIAS 2850.
[13] TIAS 2850. Cited in S. Duke, *United States Military Forces and Installations in
Europe* (Oxford: OUP, 1989).

on any other threats is not dissimilar to that of the Attlee–
Churchill–Truman understandings on bases in Britain, and there were
consultations from time to time on American requests to use the bases
for operations in the Middle East.

The provisions for military and economic assistance in the parallel
agreements made aid available to Spain in return for use of the bases,
thus establishing a link which the United States took care not to make
explicit with other host nations. It is difficult to quantify the exact extent
to which Spain benefited under these two agreements. A State Department press release at the time of signature indicated that $226 million
of military and economic aid would be provided for Fiscal Year 1954. A
subsequent agreement extended this to $350 million over the four-year
period 1953–7. Over the ten years 1953–63 it is estimated that military
aid totalled $504 million or the equivalent of one year's foreign ex-
change earnings from Spanish exports. In addition, Spain received an
additional $500 million in aid not stipulated in the agreements and some
$300 million through the Export-Import Bank. This was a substantial
investment by the United States in military basing facilities, which to
some extent compensated Spain for her exclusion from the Marshall
Plan. The agreements provided Spain with both political and economic
support but they contained no security guarantees for Spain, no veto on
SAC operations against a communist threat, and no control over the
introduction of American atomic weapons. The United States had
obtained the freedom of manoeuvre she had sought at minimum commitment to the host nation. In some ways, Spain had been treated rather
like Japan.

The Facilities Established

The three published agreements only represented the tip of the
iceberg. A further 22 agreements were concluded in the period 1954–60,
often in secret and on the authority of local military commanders. One
recent Spanish commentator has described the web of agreements
underpinning the Madrid Pact as 'a contractual pyramid involving one
major agreement and several subsequent understandings'. He goes on
to say:

An in-depth examination reveals a contractual labyrinth which emerged in the
aftermath of the 1953 accord. The plethora of minor agreements, the administrative confusion, the lack of intra-administrative communication and co-

ordination and unclear responsibilities created a lack of control, responsibility and enforcement capability.[14]

Under these agreements, construction began in 1953 on three major air bases for Strategic Air Command with runways of over 13,000 feet at Zaragoza, Torrejón (near Madrid), and Morón (near Seville). In addition, two minor air bases were established at San Pueblo near Seville and at Reus, 90 miles from Barcelona. Several radar stations were also set up, including one in Majorca. In contrast to the rapid construction programme carried out in Morocco in 1951–2, these bases were not finally completed until 1959, by which time some 7,000 American servicemen were stationed in Spain, of whom 6,000 were airmen and only 600 were naval personnel. The air bases were equipped with B-47s which were capable of reaching the Soviet Union from Spain and were protected by fighter aircraft based at Torrejón and Zaragoza. The B-47s remained in Spain until 1965, although, for these aircraft, Zaragoza and Torrejón were used primarily as recovery bases at the end of this period. Both Morón and Zaragoza were also used as support bases housing a number of refuelling tankers. By 1979, Zaragoza had a role as a fighter training base using the nearby firing range at Bardenas-Reales. Once the B-47s were withdrawn, the bases housed B-58 'Hustler' bombers until 1968 and thereafter F-4 Phantoms and F-100s for local area defence. (Some USAF assets and tasks were redeployed to Zaragoza from Wheelus Airfield in Libya following Colonel Gadaffi's coup in 1969.)

Torrejón, with a 13,400-foot runway, was the largest air base made available to the USAF in the Mediterranean. It served as the headquarters for Sixteenth Air Force which was set up in July 1957 to cover USAF assets in Morocco as well as Spain. The base was later equipped with a Tactical Fighter Wing of 72 F-16s, the USAF's primary delivery system for tactical nuclear weapons in the Mediterranean, which were rotated through Aviano in northern Italy and Incirlik in Turkey. Torrejón also housed a unit of Military Airlift Command (MAC) and a support group for Strategic Air Command. It was the MAC and support functions that were to cause most controversy in the future as the United States sought to use the bases in Spain as a staging and refuelling facility en route to the Middle East.

Altogether, $535 million was spent by the United States on the

---

[14] C. C. Seidal, US Bases in Spain in the 1950s. In *US Military Forces in Europe: The Early Years 1945–70*, S. Duke and W. Kreiger (ed.) (Boulder, CO: Westview, 1993, Ch. 12).

construction of military facilities in Spain between 1953 and 1963. Fifty per cent of this was devoted to the new naval base constructed at Rota, just west of the Straits of Gibraltar and not far from Cádiz. The US Navy also had minor facilities at El Ferrol on the Atlantic coast and Cartagena on the Mediterranean. But the huge base at Rota dwarfed these. Rota originally comprised a naval air station and a replenishment base for the Sixth Fleet. Among the facilities constructed there were a mile-long breakwater, a 1,000-foot pier, a fuel jetty which could take two tankers at a time, and a 12,000-foot runway used for anti-submarine warfare and reconnaisance operations. Rota also served as the starting point for a fuel pipeline stretching over 450 miles diagonally across Spain, linking the port with the three air bases of Morón, Torrejón, and Zaragoza. This extensive pipeline was needed since, according to one SAC source, 'A wing of B-47s consumes in an afternoon more fuel than the entire Spanish railroad tanker fleet can transport in a month'.[15] But the primary purpose of Rota, from the mid 1960s to the end of the 1970s, was to act as the second forward base in Europe for Polaris and later Poseidon submarines. It was here that the stability of the Franco regime and limited opportunity for political protest were important to the United States. Indeed, it is alleged that General Muñoz Grandes, Spain's Deputy Prime Minister at the time, took the decision to permit Polaris submarines to use Rota on his own initiative in December 1962, without consulting the Spanish Foreign Ministry.[16]

Further Negotiations under Franco

Once the ten years' duration of the initial agreements had passed, the two nations issued a Joint Declaration in 1963. The Americans regarded this as a necessary expedient to secure the Polaris base at Rota but they ensured that it contained no defence commitment to Spain by the United States. The most that the Americans were prepared to concede on this point was:

a threat to either country and to the joint facilities that each provides for the common defense, would be a matter of common concern to both countries and each country would take such actions as it may consider appropriate within the framework of its constitutional processes.[17]

However, there was some forward movement on consultation with regard to deployment changes in a parallel Exchange of Letters

---

[15] Whitaker, op. cit. 66.   [16] Seidal, op. cit.   [17] Duke, op. cit.

between Dean Rusk, the American Secretary of State, and the Spanish Foreign Minister:

Any major change in United States military equipment on Spanish territory and in the use by the United States of the facilities and areas of joint utilisation in Spain, will continue to be the subject of prior consultation between the appropriate authorities of both governments.

The 1963 declaration extended the 1953 agreements for a further five years but it was not until June 1969 that an Interim Agreement was signed, extending use of the bases by fifteen months to September 1970. This also provided a further $50 million in military assistance and $35 million in credits at the Export-Import Bank for the purchase of military equipment. By the 1970s, Spain was obtaining some 70 per cent of her military equipment from the United States, but both Zaragoza and Morón air bases were now on standby status with only an air–sea rescue unit at Morón. General Earle Wheeler, Chairman of the Joint Chiefs of Staff, informed the Senate Sub-Committee on US Security Agreements and Commitments Abroad that the bases in Spain were important because of France's withdrawal from NATO's military structure, restricted over-flying rights over France and Morocco, and increased Soviet activity in the Mediterranean. However, the Sub-Committee was not wholly convinced and referred in its report to the bases in Spain as 'a good example of a commitment which has not only creeped (*sic*), but which has also in the process generated new justifications as old ones become obsolete'.[18] There was much to be said for this view. The advent of ballistic missiles had made the concept of nuclear strikes by manned aircraft obsolete. SAC units had been withdrawn from both Britain and Spain to be replaced by Polaris submarines. But neither the United States nor Spain wished to see the bases run down, and alternative uses were found for them, first training, airlift, resupply and refuelling, and subsequently the deployment of F-16 aircraft at Torrejón in the tactical nuclear role.

This uncertainty over the use of the air bases was reflected within the Nixon administration, which took over a year to decide that it definitely wished to retain them. Negotiations resumed with Spain in 1970, with the Americans again insisting that they could extend no security guarantee to Spain and the Spanish asking for a large military equipment package in recompense. A deal was finally struck under which the United States agreed to 'support the defense system' of Spain, and Spain

[18] SCFR. Report of the Sub-Committee on US Security Agreements and Commitments Abroad. 21 December 1970.

reduced its demands to $20 million of direct grants and $125 million in loans from the Export-Import Bank. This deal was set out in the first Agreement of Friendship and Co-operation signed in August 1970, a wide-ranging document covering all forms of cooperation, civil as well as military. The military provisions, set out in a supplementary agreement signed in September 1970, extended use of the bases by the United States for a further five years. In return, the United States agreed to provide an air defence system compatible with NATO and to help with the modernization of Spain's defence industries.[19]

There was no overt distinction between communist and non-communist threats in these agreements. Article 34 of the Agreement of Friendship and Co-operation described the provisions for consultation on the use of American forces in Spain in broadly similar terms to those previously used in relation to non-communist threats:

In the case of external threat or attack against the security of the West, the time and manner of the use by the United States of the facilities . . . will be the subject of urgent consultations between the two Governments, and will be resolved by mutual agreement in the light of the situation created.

These consultations were to take place in a Joint Committee which was to be set up but, as a caveat, it was noted that 'Each government retains, however, the inherent right of self defense'. It was also agreed that the two governments were 'to determine by common accord' the facilities to be used by the United States 'as well as the US force levels in Spain'.

Post Franco Negotiations

The death of Franco in 1975 allowed a more constructive approach to negotiations on both sides. As a mark of approval for the return of democracy, the United States was, for the first time, prepared to consider a formal treaty relationship with Spain and, as a result, a new Treaty of Friendship and Co-operation of five years' duration was signed in January 1976.[20] This paved the way for Spain's eventual admission to NATO by providing that both nations should harmonize their bilateral relationship 'with existing security agreements in the North Atlantic

---

[19] Agreement on Friendship and Co-operation between the United States of America and the Kingdom of Spain. Signed 6 August 1970. TIAS 6924. Agreement implementing Chapter VIII. Defense—Use of Military Facilities in Spain. Signed 25 September 1970. TIAS 6977.

[20] Treaty of Friendship and Co-operation Between the United States of America and the Kingdom of Spain. Signed 24 January 1976. Supplementary Agreement No 6, Article III. TIAS 8360.

area'. The treaty repeated with minor variations the formula on consultation in the face of a threat to the security of the West which had already been used in the 1970 agreement.

However, Article III of Supplementary Agreement No. 6 covering military facilities added a significant proviso 'but when the imminence of the danger so requires, the two governments will establish direct contact in order to resolve the matter jointly'. Clearly, it was recognized that there might not be time for a formal meeting of the Joint Committee. A paper prepared by the Congressional Research Service shortly after confirmed the need for Spanish approval of any military operations from its territory by the United States:

Since Spain is not currently a member of NATO, the missions carried out by US military personnel at such facilities would have to be cleared by Spain as serving Spanish as well as US defense interests.[21]

Side agreements to the 1976 treaty recorded that the Poseidon submarine force would be withdrawn from Rota by July 1979. This withdrawal was consistent with United States planning, since the more advanced Trident system had a longer range and did not need to be based forward in Europe. Arrangements were being made to withdraw Poseidon from Holy Loch in Scotland at the same time. However, it was in 1976 that Spain made it clear that she no longer wanted nuclear weapons stored on her territory. A serious nuclear accident had occurred ten years before, in January 1966, when a B-52 bomber of SAC had collided in mid air with a KC-135 tanker over the village of Palomares with the loss of four nuclear bombs. There had been no follow-up under Franco, but the new democratic government was adamant that nuclear weapons could no longer be stored in Spain. It was noted, somewhat belatedly, that all four major bases were close to major centres of population—which Franco had encouraged for reasons of prestige. In line with the new policy Supplementary Agreement No. 6 to the treaty stated categorically 'The United States may not store nuclear devices or their components on Spanish soil'. This gave rise to problems, as elsewhere, over the US Navy's traditional policy of neither confirming nor denying that nuclear weapons were on board particular warships. With regard to aid, arrangements were made to pay Spain $1.22 billion in grants and credits over the five-year period. Not all of this was new money since $600 million represented

---

[21]   United States Foreign Policy Objectives and Overseas Military Installations. Report for the SCFR. CRS April 1979. Cited in A. Cottrell and T. Moorer, *US Overseas Bases*, Washington Paper No 47. (Beverly Hills, CA: Sage, 1977, 15).

under the Foreign Military Sales (FMS) Scheme loans and much of the rest covered a complex buy-back scheme for F-4 Phantom aircraft.

Entry Into NATO and Subsequent Negotiations

Spain joined NATO in May 1982 following negotiations conducted by the short-lived government of Leopoldo Calvo Sotelo, the centre-right Prime Minister who succeeded Adolfo Suárez in January 1981, but was himself replaced as party leader in mid 1982. The decision to join the Alliance was taken after the abortive military coup in February 1981, Calvo Sotelo seeing NATO membership as a means of democratizing the armed forces and giving them a new sense of purpose. In parallel, an Agreement of Friendship, Defence and Co-operation was signed with the United States in July 1982, again with a duration of five years. But this was not to enter into force until May 1983, because of the change of government in Spain. The text of this agreement underlined the change in Spain's status both as a democracy and a member of NATO. The preamble spoke of the two governments being 'united by a common ideal of freedom' and determined to fulfil their obligations 'both bilaterally and within the scope of the North Atlantic Treaty'. Article II further enhanced the control exercised by Spain over the bases by including the words 'prior authorisation' for the first time:

Spain grants to the United States of America the use of operational and support installations and grants authorisations for the use of Spanish territory, territorial sea and air space for purposes within the bilateral or multilateral scope of this Agreement. Any use beyond these purposes will require the prior authorisation of the Government of Spain.[22]

Moreover, on nuclear weapons the 1982 agreement was less negative than the 1976 treaty. Article IV.2 simply said 'The storage and installation on Spanish territory of nuclear or non-conventional weapons or their components will be subject to the agreement of the Spanish Government'.

On defence assistance, the United States undertook, in a complementary agreement, 'to use its best efforts to provide defense support for the Government of Spain on the best terms possible . . . in the highest amounts, the most favorable terms and the widest variety of forms . . . as may be lawful or feasible'. These heavily qualified pledges, which broadly correspond to those in other agreements negotiated by

---

[22] Agreement on Friendship, Defense and Co-operation Between the United States of America and the Kingdom of Spain. Signed 2 July 1982. Article II.2. TIAS 10589.

the United States in the 1980s, reflect the determination of Congress, faced with escalating budget deficits, to make commitments on military assistance entered into by the administration subject to annual author-izations and appropriations. In fact, the Spanish economy improved with the return of democracy as the budgetary position deteriorated in the United States and Spain was obliged to forego further tranches of mil-itary aid from 1989 onwards.

Within the newly democratic Spain there remained considerable opposition both to NATO and the American military presence. In June 1984, there were major demonstrations against NATO and President Reagan encountered some hostility when he visited Spain in 1985. Many Spaniards took the view that the United States had supported Franco, and at the time of his death 56 per cent of the population were opposed to retaining the bases. Those of this persuasion were also opposed to Spain's entry to NATO and one of these was the socialist politician Felipe González who became Prime Minister in October 1982, before the agreement signed in July had been ratified. A separate Protocol was signed which allowed the bilateral agreement between Spain and the United States to take effect, but the arrangements being made for Spain to join the integrated military structure of NATO were frozen, allowing Spain, like France, to enjoy 'NATO à la carte', obtaining the protection of the Alliance without making a full contribution to it. Throughout 1983–4 the socialist party in Spain also campaigned vigorously against INF deployments, arguing that Spain had not been a member of NATO when the 'Twin Track' decision was taken in 1979.

The political debate on NATO membership continued within Spain until a referendum was held on whether or not to remain in the Alliance. By this time, González had realized that withdrawal from NATO could prejudice Spain's application to join the European Economic Community. He therefore shifted his ground to advocate continued membership of NATO, subject to certain conditions which he spelt out in October 1984. Furthermore, the referendum was deferred until Spain had signed the Treaty of Rome in June 1985 and González could be reasonably sure of support. It eventually took place in March 1986, some three and a half years after the election. In the event, 60 per cent of the electorate voted and agreed to remain in NATO by a margin of 13 percentage points, but on the terms which González had laid down. These were that Spain should not take part in the integrated military structure of NATO, that no Spanish troops should be stationed abroad, that the ban on 'stockpiling, stationing or introduction of nuclear weapons on Spanish territory' (first established in 1976) should continue and that there should be a progressive reduction in American forces in Spain.

The intention to reduce American forces in Spain was confirmed in a Joint Communiqué issued in December 1985, which announced that the United States and Spain would negotiate adjustments to the American military presence. It was stated that 'these adjustments will involve a phased reduction of the US military presence in Spain based on the assumption by the Spanish armed forces of specific responsibilities and missions currently undertaken by US forces in Spain'.[23] The negotiations led to a further agreement, announced in principle in January 1988 and signed in December that year, which allowed the United States access to the bases for a further eight years but obliged her to withdraw the 401st Tactical Fighter Wing, comprising 72 F-16 aircraft, from the air base at Torrejón within 3 years.[24] The reason given for this move was partly the proximity of the base to Madrid and partly the configuration of the aircraft which could carry nuclear weapons. However, there was also a feeling, emphasized in the Joint Communiqué, that Spain should do more for her own defence. She planned to purchase F-18 aircraft of her own, which could be regarded as replacements for the American F-16s, although not available to NATO, and base them at Torrejón (thus belying the argument about proximity to Madrid). Meanwhile, the problem of nuclear weapons on board American warships visiting Rota was finessed by dropping the ban on the 'introduction' of nuclear weapons to Spain and replacing this with a ban on the transit of nuclear warheads through Spain. This allowed the United States Navy to maintain its policy of studied ambiguity on the presence of nuclear weapons on board its ships.

The 1988 agreement ran for eight years, covering a much reduced American military presence. In 1988, there were still 12,000 American troops in Spain concentrated at the four major bases but with detachments at several smaller installations. With the end of the Cold War these numbers declined dramatically. By 1995, total American forces in Spain numbered only 5,000, comprising 4,500 from the US Navy and 500 from the US Air Force. Two years later, in 1997, the numbers had fallen by a further 50 per cent. There were only 2,500 American service personnel in the country, of whom 2,200 were US Navy personnel at Rota. Torrejón had reverted to Spanish control while the other air bases at Zaragoza and Morón had been reduced to standby status,

[23] Communiqué of 10 December 1985. Cited in CRS 1986.
[24] Duke, op. cit. 263. The agreement has not yet been published. Duke cites reports in the *International Herald Tribune*, 16–17 January 1988.

used mainly for exercise purposes. The Trident submarines had been withdrawn from Rota but the base remained an important support facility for the Sixth Fleet, acting as a centre for intelligence collection and anti-submarine operations while covering the western approaches to the Straits of Gibraltar. The agreement was due to be renewed or re-negotiated in 1996, but discussions were interrupted by the election in October 1996 which brought to power a Conservative Prime Minister, José Maria Aznar, and it was not until late in the year that an accord was signed extending American access to the remaining bases until May 1998. The new government indicated that it wished to join NATO's integrated military structure, albeit on conditions which caused some difficulties for her allies. However, negotiations commenced which eventually led to Spain joining the military structure of NATO in December 1997.

Conclusion

With the exception of Italy, the host nations in the Mediterranean have all proved areas of considerable difficulty for the United States when negotiating basing rights. The problems in Spain were compounded by the need to avoid an American security commitment to the country during Franco's lifetime and the political sea-change following the death of Franco, which the United States may have been slow to appreciate. But it was evident that arrangements agreed at the start of the Cold War under a dictatorship would need to be revised with the return of democracy, a diminishing Soviet threat, and the advent of a socialist government. With basing arrangements concluded in general for five-year terms, negotiations were at times virtually continuous both before and after the death of Franco. On each occasion, Spain managed to extract slightly better terms from the United States both politically and, until aid was phased out after 1989, economically. In the words of one Spanish commentator:

With each successive renewal, Spanish diplomacy obtained better terms from the Americans: stricter control over the use of the bases by US forces, greater economic compensation, increased political co-operation, etc. The 1963 agreement included US assurances of Spanish security; the 1970 agreement ceded to Spain important installations built by the USA and strengthened Spanish control over US-held facilities; the 1976 agreement represented . . . American endorsement of the democratic process just about to be initiated and established an indirect link between Spain and the Atlantic Alliance; the 1982 agreement extended the NATO status of forces to American military in Spain and reinforced Spanish control over the movement of US units on the national territory, in Spanish airspace and in Spain's sovereign waters.[25]

In the 1980s, the United States faced similar problems in Spain and Greece in retaining access to the military facilities she had developed in these countries on reasonable terms. In both countries she faced socialist Prime Ministers acutely suspicious of the role she had played in supporting the undemocratic regimes which had previously held power. It is not surprising that González and Papandreou were initially anti-American and hostile to NATO, although both moderated their opposition when in office. But González was probably easier to deal with than Papandreou. He had rational, defensible aims, notably the removal of nuclear weapons and the reduction of American forces in Spain, and once these were achieved stability returned. Moreover, the revival of the Spanish economy from the mid 1980s onwards lanced the boil of ever larger demands for military assistance in marked contrast to negotiations with Greece and Turkey.

However, there was one issue on which Spanish sensitivity remained constant both under Franco and his successors. Spain had close links with the Arab world both geographically and economically and was not prepared to sanction the use of bases on her territory to support American operations in the Middle East. Under Franco, Torrejón was used for refuelling American transport aircraft during the Lebanon crisis of 1958 when France and Italy both declined assistance. But during the Six Day War in 1967, Spain allowed the bases on her territory to be used only for the evacuation of American servicemen, not for military operations. She also declined to allow American aircraft to stage through Spain during the Yom Kippur war in 1973 and in 1974 she let it be known that this ban extended to tankers from Torrejón refuelling American aircraft on their way to the Middle East. With the advent of democracy, Adolfo Suárez refused permission for F-15 aircraft to be refuelled from bases in Spain en route to Saudi Arabia during the crisis in Iran in 1979. Furthermore, Spain refused the United States overflying rights for the air strike on Libya in 1986, protesting that tankers based in Spain had been redeployed to Britain for the operation, and only agreed with reluctance to allow an emergency landing at Rota by one of the F-111 aircraft on the return journey. An exception to this pattern emerged with the Gulf War during which, although plans for the

[25] A. Sanchez-Gijon, On Spain, NATO and Democracy. In *Politics and Security in the Southern Region of the Atlantic Alliance*, D. Stuart (ed.) (London: Macmillan, 1988, Ch. 5).

rundown of the air bases were well advanced, the Spanish government agreed to the use of Torrejón for staging purposes and, after some hesitation, to the use of Morón for B-52 bomber flights. Morón was also made available for further air operations against Iraq in late 1998 following the withdrawal of the United Nations Special Commission.

Greece

Greece and NATO

Greece was the *casus belli* for the Truman Doctrine, enunciated on 12 March 1947 following Britain's decision that she could no longer provide support against the communist insurrection that had plunged the country into civil war in 1944. Following Britain's withdrawal, the United States set up the Joint US Military Aid Group in Greece. This played a critical part in securing the country against a communist takeover and provided a strong American military presence which remained in place once the civil war ended in October 1949. Truman also used the US Navy to demonstrate American support for the constitutional forces in Greece. On 12 August 1947, he agreed a directive, which remained secret at the time, calling for:

A quiet, but considerable increase in American naval strength in Greek waters and an intensification of the show of the flag and the American uniform in Greek parts.[26]

A bilateral agreement between the United States and Greece signed in February 1949 allowed American troops to undertake exercises on the Greek mainland and in Greek territorial waters, permitting the US Navy 'to carry out limited shore training in Crete and other islands from time to time'.[27] During this period, the Greek armed forces were largely dependent on the United States for training and equipment. Assistance on the ground was backed by substantial economic and military aid under the Truman Doctrine, amounting to $2 billion over the period 1947–69. The purpose of this assistance was to block Soviet expansion towards the Mediterranean, but Greece was not immediately admitted to NATO when she first applied to join in April 1950. Those members of the Alliance bordering the Atlantic, Britain, France, Norway, and Denmark, were concerned at the potential diversion of resources to the

---

[26] E. J. Sheehy, *The US Navy, the Mediterranean and the Cold War 1945–47* (Westport, CT: Greenwood 1992, 98).
[27] TIAS 1972. Cited by I. Lagani in Duke and Krieger, op. cit.

Eastern Mediterranean. As a result, Greece was only given associate status in September 1950 and was not admitted to full membership until 1952, along with Turkey. By this time, the impact of the Korean War had persuaded NATO planners that the Alliance needed to cover the Eastern Mediterranean as well as the North Atlantic and the Central European land mass.

Once Greece had become a full member of NATO, the United States signed a bilateral Military Facilities Agreement with her on 12 October 1953 which, unusually, was to remain in effect 'during the period of the validity of North Atlantic Treaty'. This short document, only three and a half pages in length, placed American use of military installations in Greece firmly in the context of NATO plans and commitments. The preamble mentioned that both nations were parties to the North Atlantic Treaty and Article I authorized the United States to:

construct, develop, use and operate such military and supporting facilities in Greece as the appropriate authorities of the two governments shall from time to time agree to be necessary for the implementation of, or in furtherance of, approved NATO plans. The construction, development, use and operation of such facilities shall be consistent with recommendations, standards and directions from NATO where applicable.[28]

Bases and Nuclear Weapons

Under this agreement a number of military facilities were constructed in Greece by the United States. On the mainland, the most significant of these was Hellenikon Air Force Base, completed by May 1955 adjacent to the civil airport at Athens, which was used predominantly by Military Airlift Command. This was to house some 2,000 American servicemen in the 1960s and the visibility and central location of the base made successive Greek governments uneasy. (An agreement to close Hellenikon was first reached, but not implemented, in 1975 and in the event the base was not to close until June 1991, after the Gulf War.) The second important facility on the Greek mainland was a communications centre for the Sixth Fleet set up in September 1963 at Nea Makri on the Gulf of Marathon. This was linked to Naples and Morón in Spain as part of the worldwide US Defence Communications System. On the island of Crete there were two important facilities used by the United States. The air base at Iraklion, established in October 1954, was primarily an

---

[28] Agreement Between the United States of America and the Kingdom of Greece Concerning Military Facilities, 12 October 1953. TIAS 2868.

intelligence-gathering centre operated by the USAF Security Service. The other facility in Crete was the major logistics base for the Sixth Fleet at Souda Bay which opened in June 1959. This provided an anchorage large enough for the whole of the Sixth Fleet, together with extensive storage of fuel and ammunition. It was the main support base for the Sixth Fleet in the Eastern Mediterranean and was covered by a secret agreement allowing the storage of nuclear weapons, both for the US Navy and the US Air Force. The base also housed P-3 Orion aircraft tasked with reconnaissance duties in the region.

The introduction of nuclear weapons was to prove controversial in Greece, as elsewhere in the Alliance. The issue first provoked debate in the 1958 elections following American proposals to counter the threat from Soviet ICBMs with the deployment of Jupiter IRBMs. In the event, the government of Constantine Karamanlis decided not to accept Jupiter, although Italy and Turkey had agreed to do so. In taking this decision, Greece may have been motivated as much by temporary dissatisfaction with the United States over Cyprus and the level of military aid she was receiving as with concern over nuclear weapons on her territory. However, discussions continued between the United States and Greece on the nuclear issue and on 6 May 1959 an agreement was signed on the exchange of nuclear information. This was followed on 30 December by a secret agreement to store American nuclear weapons at Special Ammunition Storage Sites. Subsequently, Nike Ajax surface-to-air missiles were supplied to the Greek Air Force by the United States in 1960 and Honest John to the Greek Army, both in the conventional mode. It was not until 1963 that Nike Ajax was replaced by Nike Hercules which had a nuclear capability. As usual the warheads remained strictly under American custody.[29]

Summarizing the close relations that developed between Greece and the United States, first during the civil war and subsequently as fellow members of NATO, a memorandum for the Senate Sub-Committee on US Security Agreements and Commitments Abroad described the position in these terms in December 1970:

The close collaboration between the Greek and American military establishments which originated at the time of the civil war has been of primary importance in Greece's active role in the NATO alliance. At the same time, our reciprocal commitment in support of European defense has been instrumental in Greece's making available installations and facilities vital to US and NATO forces in the Eastern Mediterranean.[30]

[29] Langani, op. cit.
[30] SCFR. Sub-Committee on US Security Agreements and Commitments Abroad. 91st Congress, 1969–70.

The Military Junta and the Turkish Dimension

At the time this statement was made in 1970 Greece had been under military rule since the colonel's coup in April 1967. This regime was to last for seven years and pose an acute dilemma for the United States. Many Greeks believed that the United States either instigated the coup or could, had they wished, have done more to prevent it. The impression that the United States supported the colonels was enhanced by visits to Greece by the Secretary of Defense Melvin Laird and the Secretary of State William Rogers. The Greeks also noted that the arms embargo imposed by the United States after the coup was confined to heavy weapons only (with no restriction on light weapons), and was lifted in September 1970, long before Greece returned to democratic rule. But the problem for the Americans was how to reconcile the retention of vital strategic assets in the country with the unrepresentative nature of its government. A note to the same Senate Sub-Committee in 1970 set out the dilemma in the following terms:

We disagree with the political system which prevails in Greece and consider a return to parliamentary rule essential to the long term stability and prosperity of Greece. At the same time we must preserve our important strategic interests in Greece as a valuable geographic area in the critical East Mediterranean region.[31]

The military junta in Athens collapsed in July 1974 after a coup they had organized in Cyprus against President Makarios prompted an invasion by Turkey and the occupation of the northern part of the island. With the restoration of democracy in Greece, Constantine Karamanlis became Prime Minister once more. Subscribing to the popular view that the United States had backed the military regime, he initiated a difficult series of negotiations on the future of the bases, notwithstanding the terms of the 1953 agreement which was to remain in being during the validity of the North Atlantic Treaty. One outcome was that arrangements made in 1972 to home-port six destroyers at Elefsis near Athens were cancelled. The United States was prepared to close Hellenikon but tried without much initial success to retain Nea Makri, Iraklion, and Souda Bay in return for a larger aid package. After torturous negotiations, conducted against a background of intense anti-American feeling in Greece, an agreement was initialled in 1977 allowing all four bases to remain, provided they were brought under Greek command and

---

[31] State Department Note dated 9 June 1970. Cited by Duke, op. cit. 162.

control, in return for a military aid package of $700 million over four years.

Final negotiations on this agreement were deferred until 1977 to take account of a settlement which the United States had reached with Turkey shortly before, allowing a number of military installations which had been closed for some time to reopen, and providing military aid of $1 billion over four years. Hearing of this, Karamanlis instructed his officials to assess the amount of US military aid given to both countries since 1947. This exercise came up with figures showing a ratio of 7:10 in favour of Turkey. A convention was thereby established in the draft agreement of 1977 under which US military aid to Greece was maintained at seven-tenths of that made available to Turkey and in subsequent negotiations the Greek lobby in Congress ensured that the administration was not tempted to depart from this ratio. However, the agreement reached in 1977 was neither signed nor ratified and, although negotiations commenced again in January 1981, the future of the bases remained unresolved at the time of the general election held in October 1981.

Meanwhile, Greece had withdrawn from NATO's military command structure in 1974 in protest at the Turkish invasion of Cyprus and was to remain absent from it until 1980. Under NATO arrangements, air defence of the Aegean was vested in Sixth Allied Tactical Air Force (ATAF), commanded by an American officer based in Izmir. He had three subordinates working for him at Izmir, two Greeks and one Turk. The Greeks found it impossible to continue with this arrangement after the Turkish invasion of Cyprus and it became out of the question for them to return when a Turkish officer took over command of Sixth ATAF in 1978. The problem was compounded by a parallel dispute over exploration licences in the Aegean and it was not until October 1980, following painstaking negotiations by General Bernard Rogers, Supreme Allied Commander Europe, that a solution was proposed, although not implemented, involving the creation of a new NATO command for Greece at Larissa.

Negotiations with Papandreou

This was the background to the general election in October 1981 which resulted in victory for Andreas Papandreou's Pan Hellenic Socialist Movement, PASOK. Where Karamanlis had beaten the Americans with whips, Papandreou applied scorpions. Although formerly an American citizen, who had married an American wife, Papandreou held strong anti-American views. He portrayed the junta years as an American occupation by proxy and had campaigned on an election platform advocating the removal of the American bases and the complete withdrawal of Greece from NATO. He was to draw back from both these threats once in office, but it is significant that he retained the defence portfolio for himself in his first two administrations. Monteagle Stearns, the American Ambassador to Greece in the early 1980s, has characterized Papandreou's policy towards NATO in the following terms:

Between 1981 and 1989 the Papandreou Government, although it did not carry out its campaign threat to withdraw Greece from NATO, sought in every way possible to differentiate its foreign and security policies from those of the Alliance.[32]

PASOK was opposed to military blocs of any kind. In pursuit of this policy, Papandreou, following up a visit made by Karamanlis to Moscow in 1979, invited Nikolai Tikhonov, the Soviet Prime Minister, to Athens in 1983 and together they issued a joint communiqué, advocating a nuclear-free zone in the Balkans. Papandreou made a return visit to Moscow in 1985 and he later urged a non-aggression treaty between NATO and the Warsaw Pact. At other times he expressed support for the Palestine Liberation Organization and opposed the deployment of cruise missiles by NATO. Despite this anti-nuclear rhetoric by the Prime Minister, opposition to the storage of nuclear weapons on Greek territory never became the deep-rooted political issue in Greece that it did in Spain, since the United States had withdrawn nuclear warheads from Greece in 1974 on her own initiative and no Greek government had acknowledged the presence of nuclear weapons on Greek territory while they were there.

Protracted and difficult negotiations followed the 1981 election, but Papandreou showed that he was not one to be bound by election promises, provided he could obtain sufficient political advantage from taking an aggressively anti-American line in public. Moreover, he may have appreciated that cutting Greece's links with NATO and the United States would play into the hands of the Turks. As a report from the Congressional Research Service put it in 1986, 'were Greece to withdraw from NATO, alliance leaders could well decide to expand Turkey's role in NATO to compensate for the military assets lost in Greece'.[33]

---

[32] M. Stearns, *Entangled Allies: US Policy Towards Greece, Turkey and Cyprus* (New York: Council on Foreign Relations, 1992, 22).
[33] Report. US Military Installations in NATO's Southern Region. CRS 7 October 1986.

In February 1983, Papandreou declared that the bases used by the United States in Greece 'do not strengthen the country's national security and defence potential, nor are they related to our NATO obligations'.[34] Yet by the end of the year, Greece had signed the 1983 Defense and Economic Co-operation Agreement with the United States, which allowed the bases to continue for a further five years in return for an aid package in accordance with the 7:10 ratio, made up of $500 million in financing for Foreign Military Sales in the first year, and security assistance of $343 million in subsequent years. In Article VIII 'the provision of defense support' was promised by the United States 'consistent with its constitutional procedures' and it was acknowledged that this support would be 'guided in principle' by US law calling for preservation of the 'balance of military strength in the region'.[35]

The emphasis on NATO, which had been so prominent in the 1953 agreement, was removed, largely because the Greeks wished to have a free hand to abrogate the agreement at a later date without involving NATO if they so wished. During the negotiations Papandreou had asserted in July 1983 that the agreement was 'completely disassociated from the concept that the bases serve NATO interests, that they are NATO bases or that they serve the mutual defence interests of the two countries'.[36] The text of the agreement consequently stated, somewhat obscurely, that use of the bases was confined to 'missions and activities at these facilities for defence purposes in accordance with the provisions of this agreement'. This wording was deliberately circular since the purposes of defence cooperation were not spelt out elsewhere in the text. Greece maintained that this clause precluded American operations against countries in the Middle East which were friendly to Greece and stated publicly that the agreement required the United States to use the bases only for defensive purposes. In addition, Article VII.1 of the agreement allowed the Greek government 'to take immediately all appropriate restrictive measures required to safeguard its vital national security interests in an emergency'. Although the meaning of this clause was not spelt out, the Greeks regarded it as allowing them to control activity on the bases if they wished.

The United States considered this a favourable agreement permitting continued operation of the bases. Her negotiators had been at pains to

---

[34] J. C. Snyder, *Defending the Fringe: NATO, the Mediterranean and the Persian Gulf* (Boulder, CO: Westview. 1987, 60).

[35] Defense and Economic Co-operation Agreement. Signed 8 September 1983. TIAS 10814.

[36] CRS October 1986.

prepare an English text which said that the agreement was 'terminable after five years upon written notice by either party', implying that the agreement would continue unless this notice was given. But the Greeks chose to interpret the agreement as foreshadowing closure of the bases when the initial term ended in December 1988. Writing some years after the event, the American Ambassador, Monteagle Stearns, noted 'Americans were astonished to find the document described triumphantly by the Greek Government press as an agreement to terminate the bases'.[37]

Papandreou secured re-election in 1985 and expressed the hope that relations with the United States would enter 'calmer seas'. But he had unleashed forces which he could not wholly control. In November 1986, 100,000 Greeks demonstrated outside the United States Embassy calling for closure of the bases and withdrawal of Greece from NATO. This went further than Papandreou intended. He knew that he could ill afford to lose the military aid provided as a quid pro quo for use of the bases and he was at this time negotiating with the United States for the purchase of 40 F-16 fighter aircraft. A master of political ambiguity, he declared in January 1987 that Greece had to remain in NATO otherwise war with Turkey 'might be unavoidable'. But in May, mindful of his promise to remove the bases at the end of 1988, he proposed a referendum on their future. In September, negotiations commenced between the Greek Foreign Minister and the American Ambassador but these made little progress and in July 1988 Papandreou issued the United States with a formal notice to quit all four bases. However, this notice to quit nevertheless allowed the United States seventeen months to withdraw, during which further negotiations would continue. These manoeuvres were clearly devices to circumvent the pledge to remove the bases at the end of 1988 and hold the position open until after the next general election in June 1989.

After the Cold War

Papandreou, by now beset by financial and matrimonial scandals, failed to gain re-election and, after a period of instability with no clear majority in the Greek Parliament, Constantine Mitsotakis, leader of the New Democratic Party, became Prime Minister in April 1990 at the head of the first single-party government since 1981. Mitsotakis promised

---

[37] M. Stearns, *Talking to Strangers* (Princeton, NJ: Princeton University Press, 1996, 137).

stability and improved relations with the United States. He had pledged to maintain the 1983 agreement with the United States which, during the period of instability immediately before and after the 1989 election, had continued through a series of six-month extensions. But by now the United States, faced with a declining Soviet threat and the need to economize worldwide, had herself announced in January 1990 that she would be withdrawing from Hellenikon and Nea Makri.

This put a different slant on the negotiations which resumed under Mitsotakis, leading to a further Mutual Defense Co-operation Agreement which was concluded in May 1990. For the first time since 1983, this agreement reinstated NATO in the text by saying in the preamble that the two nations 'resolve to act in accordance with the North Atlantic Treaty'.[38] The agreement also maintained the 7:10 ratio for military aid with Turkey by providing Greece with $345 million a year for the two remaining bases and made these available to the United States for another eight years. In addition, destroyers and military aircraft worth $1 billion were made available to Greece. However, with plans already in train to transfer US military facilities from mainland Greece to Crete, Souda Bay and Iraklion were identified in the agreement as the only bases of any significance remaining available to American forces. The agreement made it clear that, once American forces had withdrawn from Hellenikon and Nea Makri, 'the number of US military personnel in Greece will be reduced significantly'. Furthermore, the rundown of American forces in Greece accelerated with the reduction of tension in Europe. In March 1993, the United States announced that all eight sites at Iraklion were to close and by 1999 there were only 500 American troops left in Greece, of whom over half were US Navy personnel at Souda Bay.

In summary, the United States experience in Greece has underlined all the disadvantages and difficulties of the 'leasehold empire'. Substantial sums were expended in the form of economic and military aid to maintain the bases, but the domestic and international political posture of the host nation made for an exceptionally difficult environment. First, the rule of the military junta compromised the United States in the eyes of the Greek people, then in the 1970s the conflict with Turkey called the future of the bases into question and weakened Greece's role in NATO. In the words of one Greek commentator 'PASOK drifted into anti-Americanism because of United States

---

[38] Mutual Defense Co-operation Agreement. Signed Athens 8 July 1990. TIAS 12321.

support for the Greek junta and its role in Cyprus'.[39] Finally, the 1980s were largely taken up with a series of negotiations and manoeuvres initiated by the socialist government under Papandreou which were primarily designed to serve domestic political ends. The patience of the United States and NATO was tested to the limit and American requests to use the facilities for operations in the Middle East was twice declined, during the Yom Kippur War in 1973 and, ten years later, in resupplying the US Marines in Beirut. Although the bases in Greece were made available to the United States and her allies for transport operations during the Gulf War, it is indicative of the continuing sensitivity of the bilateral security relationship that, when President Bush visited Greece in July 1991, in part to thank his hosts for their support, there were student demonstrations in protest against America's ambivalent attitude to the dispute with Turkey over Cyprus.

Turkey

Turkey's Strategic and Political Position

Turkey has always been of greater strategic importance than Greece, both to the United States and to NATO as a whole. She controls the Dardanelles, borders the Black Sea, where a substantial portion of Soviet naval assets were previously based, and, in the days of the Soviet Union, shared a land frontier with her. She still shares a land frontier with Iran, Iraq, and Syria and has long been recognized as forming a land bridge between Europe and the Middle East. Because of her geographical position, it was inevitable that competition for influence and basing rights would arise between the Soviet Union and the United States at the end of the Second World War. Turkey had a long history of resistance to Russian expansion and this was renewed in 1945 when the Soviet Union applied pressure to persuade her to cede the border provinces of Kars and Ardahan which had been transferred to Turkey in 1918. The Soviet Union also pressed for 'joint defence' of the Turkish Straits which would have involved Russian bases being established on the Bosporus and Dardanelles.

This approach was rebuffed but Soviet pressure continued with threatening troop movements in Bulgaria and in April 1946, the United

---

[39] T. Veremis, Greece. In *Politics and Security in the Southern Region of the Atlantic Alliance*, D. T. Stuart (ed.) (London: Macmillan, 1989, Ch. 7).

States took the opportunity to demonstrate support for Turkey by arranging for the *USS Missouri* to visit Istanbul, accompanied by two destroyers. The ostensible purpose of this visit was to return the body of the Turkish Ambassador to Washington, who had died at his post during the war. But the symbolism of the visit was potent. It was on the *USS Missouri* that General MacArthur had received the surrender of Japan in Tokyo Bay at the end of the war. Furthermore, it is interesting that this visit took place almost a year before the United States formally committed herself to the defence of the Eastern Mediterranean in March 1947 and American military aid for Turkey commenced under the Truman Doctrine. James Forrestal, at this time still Secretary of the Navy, intended that the visit should pave the way for regular visits to the Mediterranean by the US Navy and in September 1946 he was able to issue a statement confirming that units of the American Fleet would remain in the Mediterranean to support American forces in Europe and 'carry out American policy and diplomacy'.

In this respect and certain others, the American security relationship with Turkey echoed that with Greece. Neither country was admitted to NATO initially but the outbreak of the Korean War and the contribution of 4,500 Turkish troops to the United Nations force (the third largest contingent) caused a significant change in American perceptions—just as the Turks intended. It was also appreciated that the admission of Turkey would reduce the shortfall against NATO's over-ambitious targets for ready forces, which were already under discussion and were formally adopted at the Lisbon meeting of the North Atlantic Council in February 1952. As a result, both Greece and Turkey joined NATO and both subsequently signed bilateral Military Facilities Agreements with the United States. Neither played host to an excessive number of American troops. At the end of the Cold War there were some 7,000 American troops in Turkey and some 3,700 in Greece. But the hostility between the two countries meant that, from the mid 1970s onwards, the United States was locked in a triangular relationship with Greece and Turkey over the Cyprus crisis, the knock-on effects of this on NATO, disputes over territorial waters and air traffic control in the Aegean, and the 7:10 ratio for American military aid to the two countries.

Like Greece, Turkey was subjected to military government during the Cold War with coups taking place in both 1960 and 1980 and a further military intervention in 1971. However, Turkey was the less stable of the two countries with twelve minority or coalition governments between 1971 and 1977. The country has been described during the Cold War period both as 'a developing democracy with interludes of military rule',[40] and as 'a Parliamentary system that functions on the sufferance of the Turkish military'.[41] In both Greece and Turkey the demand for ever larger programmes of economic and military aid, coupled with considerable political sensitivity over the American military presence, led to frequent renegotiation on the bases in the late 1970s and 1980s. As a result, military aid to Turkey from the United States increased threefold over the 1980s.

But, for the United States, there were also important differences between Turkey and Greece. First, Turkey was a more enthusiastic ally than Greece. It was she rather than Greece that pressed to join NATO, partly as a safeguard against Soviet pressure but also as a means of gaining acceptance, following Kemal Atatürk's policy, as a Western European nation. Turkey also took a much more robust line than Greece over the deployment of nuclear weapons on her territory. She was prepared to accept Jupiter missiles on her territory when Greece declined to do so, but felt that the United States should have done more to consult her about these weapons—especially when removing them. Secondly, the security relationship between the United States and Turkey was at first much less open than that with Greece, partly because of intelligence-gathering facilities at the bases and partly because of the military flavour to successive governments in Turkey.

Finally, Turkey was of much greater potential value to the United States than Greece as a basing area for non-NATO operations in the Middle East. But, as a Muslim nation, closely tied to the Arab world in economic and political terms, Turkey could not afford to authorize any American operations from her territory in support of Israel. Although Turkey had been one of the first nations in the Middle East to recognize Israel in March 1949, by the mid 1970s her political and economic links with the Arab world were paramount. In political terms, Turkey established relations with the PLO in 1975 and recognized the organization as the legitimate representative of the Palestinian people in 1979. Economically, Turkey was heavily dependent on trade with the Arab world, particularly after the oil crisis of 1973/74 and the construction of the oil pipeline with Iraq, which was completed in 1977. There was consequently an inbuilt conflict of interest in the American security relationship with Turkey, which led to disagreements over the use

---

[40] D. A. Rustow, *Turkey: America's Forgotten Ally* (New York: Council on Foreign Relations, 1987).

[41] Stearns, *Entangled Allies* op. cit. 21.

of the bases for American operations in the Middle East and renewed emphasis on NATO by Turkey during negotiations on the bases.

Nature of the Agreements and Facilities

The only security agreement between the United States and Turkey in the 1950s made public was an Exchange of Letters on 7 January 1952, in similar terms to that concluded with Italy, under which Turkey undertook to 'fulfil the military obligations which it has assumed under multilateral or bilateral agreements or treaties to which the United States is a party'.[42] These further agreements were not made public at this stage, although it is known that a secret Military Facilities Agreement was signed in June 1954, alongside a Status of Forces Agreement which was published. George Harris, who served in the American Embassy in Ankara from 1957 to 1962, has described the position in the following terms:

> The NATO agreement was soon complemented by bilateral understandings dealing with specific facets of Turkish-American military co-operation. Some of these understandings were . . . openly published and ratified by the Turkish Parliament, for example the Status of Forces Agreement of June 1954 . . . But in addition there were secret exchanges of notes and executive agreements concerning such matters as the deployment of weapons systems and . . . activities of a military or intelligence nature . . . Most basic of these was the Military Facilities Agreement of June 1954 . . .[43]

Because of the long border along the Black Sea and the high mountains in the east of the country, Turkey was ideally situated for intelligence gathering and a number of important facilities were set up by the United States for this purpose. Belbasi near Ankara was established to record seismic data from the Soviet Union, providing valuable information on her nuclear testing programme. In eastern Turkey, Diyarbakir and Karamürsel were used to monitor the Soviet missile testing programme. Other sites were developed to gather intelligence on the Soviet Navy, to monitor activity in space and provide early warning of attack from the Soviet Union. Apart from intelligence facilities, naval storage depots were established at Yumurtalik and Iskenderun on the Mediterranean for the Sixth Fleet, providing contingency stocks of fuel and ammunition. But in operational terms the most valuable facilities in Turkey were the NATO air base at Izmir, which housed the Sixth Allied Tactical Air Force from 1957 onwards, and the air base at Incirlik, on the south-east

---

[42] Exchange of Letters on Mutual Security, 7 January 1952. TIAS 2621.
[43] G. Harris, *Troubled Alliance: Turkish/American Problems in Historical Perspective 1945–1971* (Washington, DC: ACE–Hoover Policy Studies, 1972, 54).

coast of Turkey. Incirlik was originally constructed with military aid under the Truman programme for Strategic Air Command, but the US Air Force later deployed U-2 reconnaissance aircraft from the base and used it as a forward base for Tactical Fighter Wings rotated from Aviano in Italy and Torrejón in Spain. A report for the Senate Committee on Foreign Relations in 1979 acknowledged that Incirlik was 'capable of launching a tactical nuclear strike in the event of conflict in the region'.[44]

By the late 1960s the unsatisfactory nature of these agreements was giving rise to considerable disquiet in the Turkish Parliament. Concern first arose over the U-2 incident in 1960. Although the aircraft shot down over the Soviet Union had taken off from Peshawar in Pakistan, the fact that the aircraft was based at Incirlik implicated Turkey in the violation of Soviet air space. However, matters were brought to a head in December 1965 when an American RB-47 reconnaissance aircraft crashed in the Black Sea, allegedly in international waters but nevertheless provoking strong protests from the Soviet Union. Turkey asked for reconnaissance flights to be discontinued and the Prime Minister Suleyman Demirel initiated a thorough review of the basing agreements early in 1966. Negotiations continued for over three years until the first Defense Co-operation Agreement was signed in July 1969. Once again, Demirel wished to keep the full text of this agreement secret, even though the opposition claimed it would be invalid without parliamentary approval. To square this circle Demirel gave an extensive briefing to Parliament in January 1970 and followed this with a press conference on the agreement in February. In the course of the press conference he maintained that the main purpose of the agreement had been to rationalize and codify 'scattered agreements concluded by several authorities not based on any principles'. He cited some 54 separate agreements concluded prior to 1969 and made it clear that:

The control of the Turkish Government over the joint defence installations and the activities from them will be full and absolute. Turkey will inspect all these installations . . . to ensure that they are used in accordance with the agreements.

He also added that:

The Turkish Government will allow the US Government to engage in any of the joint defence activities in Turkey only after it has full and detailed knowledge of them.[45]

---

[44] United States Foreign Policy Objectives and Overseas Military Installations. Report for the SCFR. CRS April 1979.
[45] Report of Demirel's Press Conference, 7 February 1970. Set out in Harris, op. cit. Appendix 5, 229.

These comments by Demirel underlined the concern of the Turkish government over the possible use of the bases, both for non-NATO operations and, more generally, for other operations that might give offence to the Soviet Union. In 1958, support was provided from Incirlik for the landing of United States Marines in Lebanon. The Turkish government was notified of this rather than consulted, and this had caused considerable resentment. Consequently, during the Six Day War in 1967 and the Yom Kippur War in 1973, Turkey made it quite clear that the United States could use the facilities on her territory for communications purposes only and that no refuelling or resupply operations would be permitted. Later, in 1979, the Turkish government stipulated that the Soviet Union would have to agree to U-2 aircraft flying over her territory from bases in Turkey in order to monitor compliance with SALT II. In 1983, restrictions were placed, under a new agreement, on the resupply of the United States Marines in Beirut from Incirlik. The Transit Terminal Agreement, specifically negotiated to cover this, allowed Incirlik to be used as a base for the supply of personnel and medical stores and other non-military provisions, but precluded the supply of any warlike stores. And to avoid offending the Soviet Union, the Turkish authorities declined to allow the Americans to inspect a Mig-29 which had been flown to Turkey by a defecting Soviet pilot.

The United States fully appreciated the sensitivity of Turkey's position, although she did not always welcome these restrictions. In June 1970, Rodger Davies, Deputy Assistant Secretary of State for Near East and South Asian Affairs, told the Senate Sub-Committee on US Security Agreements and Commitments Abroad:

The Turkish Government takes the position, as does its parliament, that our joint defense efforts are directed against an attack from the Soviet bloc . . . The Turks are very anxious to have our military relationship clearly rest on the NATO Agreement.[46]

Perhaps because of this, Turkey was less concerned than some other host nations about the deployment of nuclear weapons. In 1959, Jupiter Intermediate Range Ballistic Missiles were stationed in Turkey as part of a programme which also placed Jupiter missiles in Italy and Thor missiles in Britain. However, in the course of the Cuban missile crisis in October 1962, the United States secretly agreed that the Jupiter missiles in Turkey would be withdrawn as a quid pro quo for the withdrawal of

⁴⁶ SCFR. Sub-Committee on US Security Agreements and Commitments Abroad. Evidence, 9 June 1970, 1862.

Russian missiles from Cuba. An announcement on the withdrawal plan was made in January 1963 and the missiles were removed in April. Turkey had not been consulted on the proposed withdrawal and first heard about it from the Soviet Ambassador in Ankara. Although assurances were given that the same targets would be covered by Polaris, she felt, with some justification, that her security had become a pawn in a wider game between the United States and the Soviet Union. Turkey never renounced the deployment of nuclear weapons on its territory, as Spain did in 1976. However, she was not considered for the deployment of cruise or Pershing missiles as part of NATO's Twin-Track policy in 1979.

The Cyprus Conflict

The first crisis in relations between the United States and Turkey over Cyprus occurred in 1964. On 5 June, President Johnson, fearing a Turkish invasion of Cyprus, wrote to President Inonu saying that 'the United States cannot agree the use of any US-supplied military equipment for a Turkish intervention in Cyprus under present circumstances',[47] and adding that any move by Turkey which provoked a Soviet intervention might cause NATO to reconsider her obligations to Turkey. This warning has been recognized as a clumsy and ill-conceived threat even by American commentators. One has called it 'a startling specimen of diplomatic over-kill',[48] and George Ball later described it as 'the most brutal diplomatic note' he had seen.[49] The message infuriated the Turks, who published Johnson's letter and their own reply, complaining of 'a wide divergence of views as to the nature and basic principles of the North Atlantic Alliance', but it may have had the desired effect. For whatever reason, Turkey held back from invasion, despite some isolated air strikes as the situation on the island deteriorated, and the crisis passed, only to return in more acute form ten years later.

In July 1974, Archbishop Makarios was removed as President of Cyprus in a coup of singular ineptitude instigated by the military junta in Athens. In the chaotic conditions that followed under the inexperienced leadership of Nikos Sampson, Turkey feared that the new government of Cyprus would proceed with Enosis (union with Greece)

---

[47] Snyder, op. cit. [48] Stearns, *Estranged Allies* op. cit. 36–37.
[49] G. Ball, *The Past Has Another Pattern* (New York: Norton, 1982, 350). Cited by Stearns, op. cit.

and that Turkish Cypriots living predominantly in the north of the island would be at risk. The Turkish government therefore launched the invasion of Cyprus from which they had held back in 1964, on the pretext that the Treaty of Guarantee between Britain, Greece, and Turkey in 1960 gave each party the right to intervene, jointly or separately, if the constitutional settlement at the time of independence was violated. By the end of July, she had overrun the north of the island. Sampson was dislodged and the military junta in Athens collapsed. But the 1960 Treaty gave the guaranteeing powers the right to intervene 'with the sole aim of re-establishing the state of affairs created by the present treaty'. The Turks went well beyond this, making a further advance in mid August to occupy some 40 per cent of the island—a proportion far in excess of the area previously occupied by the Turkish Cypriots or justified in terms of population ratios.

In response, the United States Congress imposed an arms embargo in October 1974 on Turkey which had, in defiance of President Johnson's warning ten years earlier, used arms and equipment supplied by the United States during the invasion. The implementation of this embargo was deferred until February 1975 to allow time for negotiation but, once it came into effect, Turkey retaliated by suspending military activity at all non-NATO facilities used by the United States except Incirlik. She declared that the various bilateral agreements consolidated in the 1969 Defense Co-operation agreement had 'lost their legal validity' and that the bases had been brought under the 'control and custody of the Turkish armed forces'.[50] For their part, the United States maintained that the 1969 Agreement remained operative pending renegotiation but work at the important monitoring stations at Belbasi, Karamürsel, and Diyarbakir was undoubtedly hampered. At this time, however, information could still be obtained from monitoring stations in Iran, which were available to the United States until the fall of the Shah in 1979.

The arms embargo on Turkey had been imposed by Congress against the wishes of the US administration. Henry Kissinger, Secretary of State during the difficult transition period following the resignation of President Nixon, later summarized the situation in the following words:

A free-wheeling Congress destroyed the equilibrium between the parties we had previously maintained; it legislated a heavy-handed arms embargo against

---

[50] US Military Installations in NATO's Southern Region. Report. CRS 1986.

Turkey which destroyed all possibility of American mediation on the Cyprus issue.[51]

Negotiations continued during 1975 and 1976 to resolve the crisis and agreement was reached on the terms of a Defense and Economic Co-operation Agreement in 1976. Under this, the bases were to reopen in return for an aid package of $1 billion over four years and the arms embargo was to be lifted. The Turks also took the opportunity to re-emphasize that the bases were to be used for NATO operations and that anything else required their consent. Article II of this agreement stated 'the extent of the defense co-operation envisaged in this agreement shall be limited to obligations arising out of the North Atlantic Treaty, per-mitting out-of-area operations only with prior consent from Turkey'.[52] However, Congress initially declined to approve this agreement or lift the arms embargo, and it was not until October 1978 that President Carter managed to break the deadlock. The arms embargo was eventu-ally lifted in February 1979, the bases were reopened, and negotiations on the new Defense and Economic Co-operation Agreement were resumed. The Iranian revolution in January 1979 and the Soviet inva-sion of Afghanistan in December provided a powerful incentive to both countries to resolve their differences. Nevertheless, the Turkish Prime Minister, Bülent Ecevit, speaking to the International Institute of Strategic Studies in London, had made it clear that continued use of the bases was dependent on long-term economic assistance to Turkey from the United States.[53]

Agreements During the 1980s

The results of these further negotiations were set out in an Agreement for Co-operation on Defense and Economy which was signed in March 1980.[54] The text reflected continuing Turkish enthusiasm for NATO coupled with concern about American use of the bases for non-NATO operations. In sharp contrast to the 1983 agreement with Greece, the preamble alone contained four references to NATO. The full title of the agreement included the words 'in accordance with Articles II and III of the North Atlantic Treaty' and Article V, section stated that 'the defense co-operation envisaged in this agreement shall be limited to obligations arising out of the North Atlantic Treaty'. The agreement was to run for

[51] H. Kissinger, *Years of Upheaval* (London: Weidenfeld & Nicolson, 1982, 1192).
[52] Duke (1990), op. cit.   [53] Snyder, op. cit.
[54] Agreement for Co-operation on Defense and Economy. TIAS 9901. Signed 29 March 1980. Entered into force 18 December 1980.

five years but would continue from year to year thereafter. Under Article III, the United States was 'committed to use its best efforts to provide defense support' for the Turkish government 'on the best terms as may be possible . . . in order to achieve the objectives of its modernisation and maintenance programme'. Various supplementary agreements were attached to the main agreement. The first of these set up a joint US-Turkish Defense Support Commission, and the third supplementary agreement permitted the United States to 'participate in joint defense measures' at twelve specified locations. This wording underlined that the bases were under Turkish jurisdiction and the Turkish authorities had the primary responsibility for security. The supplementary agreement also acknowledged that at certain installations, where the 'primary purpose is intelligence collection, nodal communication or radio navigation', technical and maintenance services were to be carried out jointly by American and Turkish personnel, with all intelligence information being shared between the two governments. The Congressional Research Service considered that the agreement reflected 'both the Turkish concern with maintaining sovereignty over the use of its territory and the American concern with continuity of access to and some flexibility in the use of Turkish installations'.[55]

In November 1982, Turkey adopted a new Constitution marking the return to civilian rule after the military coup in 1980. This vested the right 'to allow foreign forces to be stationed in Turkey' in the Grand National Assembly,[56] at last making the basing agreements subject to the parliamentary approval which had long been circumvented. In October that year, following a visit to Turkey by Richard Perle of the US Department of Defense, a Memorandum of Understanding was signed on co-located operating bases. This allowed for ten Turkish airfields to be modernized in order to take American aircraft during a period of reinforcement, and three new bases to be constructed at Batman, Muş, and Erzurum. The memorandum stated that these bases were to be constructed for 'missions within the framework of NATO', but it was noted that they were all situated in the east of the country which would be convenient for operations in the Middle East. A report by the Congressional Research Service in 1986 commented:

These eastern Turkish bases are all viewed as important in deterring Soviet military activities in the Persian Gulf and the Middle East because aircraft

    [55] CRS April 1986, 53.
    [56] J. Woodliffe, *The Peacetime Use of Foreign Military Bases* (Dordrecht: Martinus Nijhoff, 1992).

deployed from them could cover the entire Turkish-Iranian Transcaucasian border region without refuelling. Planes based at Mus would be about 500 miles from Teheran and about 700 miles from the Iranian port of Abadan.[57]

Shortly after the memorandum was signed, there were reports in the Turkish press that Hayrettin Erkmen, the Turkish Foreign Minister, had said 'when the need arises the Rapid Deployment Force could use not only the new bases, but the old ones as well'.[58] This comment seemed at the time to be at variance with the strong line Turkey had been taking against the use of bases on her territory for national operations by the United States in the Middle East. And to be fair, the report by the Congressional Research Service went on to emphasize:

Turkish public opinion has been sensitive to the possible use of these eastern bases for US contingencies outside the NATO area. Moreover the Turkish Government has publicly stated that the bases have no connection with such contingencies and that they are being constructed solely within the framework of NATO defense plans.

In fact, these bases were never used for US national operations but the airfield at Batman, close to the Iraqi border, came into its own during the Gulf War as a refuelling base for allied aircraft flying from Incirlik.

The 1980 agreement became due for renewal at the end of 1985. In September, the Turks asked for a new agreement rather than an extension of the 1980 agreement but this was resisted by the United States and in December 1985, agreement in principle was reached to continue the existing arrangements for a further five years. However, it proved difficult to reach agreement on the aid and trade concessions demanded by Turkey and it was not until early 1987 that this provisional agreement was confirmed in an Exchange of Letters between George Shultz, the United States Secretary of State, and Vahit Halefoğlu, the Turkish Foreign Minister. In his letter of 16 March 1987, Shultz proposed a high level of support 'commensurate with Turkey's important contribution to the common defense', but made no promises on any particular sum.[59] The reason for this caution was partly that the United States administration did not wish to create a direct link between retention of the bases and the provision of economic and military aid, and partly that they were experiencing increasing difficulty in obtaining authorization from Congress for any sums promised to host nations.

Turkey had hitherto enjoyed a substantial level of economic and military assistance on a fairly regular basis. As one commentator has

---

[57] CRS October 1986, 46.   [58] Snyder, op. cit.   [59] Duke (1989), op. cit.

observed 'developmental goals are central to Turkish-US relations. The emphasis placed on economic matters in the Defence and Economic Co-operation Agreements is therefore not surprising'.[60] Between 1950 and 1974, payments averaged $165 million per annum, with some $3 billion being paid between 1949 and 1969. These payments dropped only marginally during the four-year period from 1974 to 1978, when activity at most of the bases was suspended for three years. Over these four years average payments were $130 million instead of $165 million. However, the 1980 agreement reflected the reluctance of the United States administration, under growing pressure from Congress, to make firm commitments to any particular level of aid. It contained only an undertaking to use 'best efforts' to obtain military aid of $450 million per annum. In fact, this figure was achieved up until 1987 with an increase to $480 million in 1988. But Turkey's needs were escalating and her foreign debt had by now reached a figure of $38 billion. Following an Exchange of Letters in 1987, the United States administration sought an annual aid allocation of $913.5 million, but this was reduced by Congress by some 40 per cent, leaving only $569.5 million. The Turks were displeased by this, as the Portuguese had been in similar circumstances. Nevertheless, this sum represented a considerable increase on the figures prior to 1980 and Turkey was by now the third-ranking recipient of United States military aid after Egypt and Israel, for whom special arrangements had been set up following the Camp David Agreement.

The Gulf War

The extension of the 1980 agreement for a further five years from 1985, finally agreed in 1987, was due to run until December 1990. However, this timetable was overtaken by the Iraqi invasion of Kuwait in August 1990 and the rapid build-up of coalition forces in the Middle East under American leadership. Turkey took a firm stand against Iraqi aggression despite her considerable economic ties with her neighbour. One of her first acts was to close the oil pipeline which ran from Iraq to the Mediterranean through Turkish territory, even though this caused her extensive economic hardship. The 1980 agreement was rapidly rolled forward in September 1990, allowing the United States to continue using the facilities available to her in Turkey. However, the conduct of

[60] S. Deger, The Economic Costs and Benefits of US—Turkish Military Relations. In *Europe After an American Withdrawal*, J. Sharp (ed.), (Oxford: OUP, 1990, Ch. 13).

military operations from these bases raised acute political difficulties for Turkey who declined to deploy any of her own armed forces against Iraq. The air base at Incirlik, on the Mediterranean coast close to Syria, was ideally situated for operations against northern Iraq and the United States wished to use the base to mount Operation PROVEN FORCE. This operation comprised attacks by approximately 100 aircraft on air defence installations, military supply depots, and industrial buildings in northern Iraq in order to divert elements of the Iraqi Air Force from operations in the south of the country opposite Kuwait and Saudi Arabia. These proposals proved controversial. Turgat Özal, the Turkish President, was obliged to handle the negotiations on a personal basis, since his Foreign and Defence Secretaries both resigned over the issue in October 1990 and the Chief of the Defence Staff followed them in December. As a result, parliamentary approval for the use of Incirlik by coalition forces was given on 17 January 1991 only days before air operations were due to commence.

With the defeat of Iraq, Turkey faced further problems at Incirlik. The leading Western members of the coalition, the United States, Britain, and France, wished to continue using the base both to monitor the air exclusion zone established by the United Nations over northern Iraq (Operation NORTHERN WATCH) and as a base camp from which to protect the safe havens set up in the area for Kurdish refugees (Operation PROVIDE COMFORT). The United States inevitably played the dominant part in these post-war operations, initially retaining nearly sixty aircraft at Incirlik, a mixture of F-15s, F-16s, and F-111s, with over 2,000 military personnel on site. Britain provided eight Harriers supported by 250 servicemen and France contributed four Mirage and four Jaguar aircraft with over 100 servicemen. New arrangements were required to authorize the continued use of Incirlik by coalition forces. In September 1991, the initial agreement reached at the start of the Gulf War was extended by a year and a series of six-month extensions was agreed by the Turkish Parliament thereafter. However, the renewal process was attended by considerable political debate and uncertainty. In May 1994, the United States Congress withheld 25 per cent of the foreign aid due to Turkey in an attempt to obtain concessions from the Turkish government on human rights and the conflict in Cyprus. In response, the Turkish Parliament threatened not to renew the agreement and voted to do so only in June after further negotiation. The following year, an inconclusive election in December 1995 eventually brought Necmettin Erbakan, the leader of the fundamentalist Welfare Party, to power as Prime Minister of a coalition government in June

1996. Once more, the use of Incirlik was called in question. In March, it was stated that operations to support the safe havens from the base would only be permitted for a further three months, although this was later extended until the end of the year. In October, a dispute over the weapons carried by American aircraft led to the suspension of operations for ten days and in December there were further threats not to renew the agreement.

Although Turkey had little difficulty with allied forces monitoring the air exclusion zone, the provision and protection of safe havens for the Iraqi Kurds raised more complex issues. Faced with a huge influx of Turkish refugees from Iraq at the end of the war, Turkey was initially supportive of the safe haven proposals. However, the eastern provinces of Turkey had long been plagued by a well-established Kurdish separatist movement which maintained a campaign of violence and disruption against the central authorities with frequent resort to terrorism. This campaign, which involved some 150,000–200,000 Turkish troops in the area, was directed by the Kurdish Workers Party (the PKK) from over the Iraqi border. Thus, while reluctantly supporting Operation PROVIDE COMFORT, the Turkish government took advantage of the restrictions placed on Iraq after the Gulf war to launch a series of raids on PKK bases inside Iraqi territory. Cross-border attacks were launched in August and October 1991. In March 1992, the PKK mounted an offensive inside south-east Turkey and the Turkish government responded later in the year with both air attacks and ground operations, deploying a total of 20,000 Turkish troops within northern Iraq at one stage. This was followed by further air attacks in August 1993 and a further air and ground offensive in March 1995 involving 35,000 troops.

The aggressive stance adopted by the Turkish government inevitably posed a serious conflict between the policies of the major Western powers led by the United States and those of the host nation on whom these powers relied for support. The complexity of the situation was aggravated by disputes between the different Kurdish factions in Iraq which, in August 1996, allowed Saddam Hussein to send 30,000 troops into northern Iraq to support one faction against another, thereby mounting a temporary threat to the safe havens established by the Western powers. On this occasion Turkey, who increasingly saw the safe havens as bases for the Kurdish separatist movement, refused to allow allied operations to protect them to be mounted from her territory. The growing divergence between Turkish and allied policies in the area applied not only to support for the safe havens but also to the implementation of UN resolutions on Iraq. At the end of the year, when

Saddam's intransigence raised once more the prospect of military action by the Western powers, Turkey specifically ruled out the use of Incirlik for air strikes against Iraq. Meanwhile, Turkey launched further offensives against suspected PKK bases in northern Iraq in May and September 1997 and again in February and April 1998. In December 1998 the decision by the United States and Britain to launch further air strikes on Iraq, following the withdrawal of the United Nations Special Commission, caused renewed problems for Turkey. Nevertheless authority was given for American and British aircraft to use Incirlik both for Operation DESERT FOX and, on a six monthly review basis, for subsequent air operations over Iraq.

Conclusion

The geographical position of Turkey, the intelligence facilities set up on her territory, and the close relationship between the American and Turkish armed forces following the Truman Doctrine, all made for an informal and initially secretive association between Turkey and the United States. But this increasingly led to complaints from opposition groups in Parliament that Turkey had no real control over American military activity on her territory and the unfounded suspicion that the Americans were meddling in domestic politics. The 1969 Defense Co-operation Agreement went some way towards clearing the air but suspicions remained since the full text was neither published nor debated in Parliament. Hostility towards the United States increased as the Cyprus crisis unfolded during the 1960s and 1970s, with the Johnson letter of 1964 and the arms embargo of 1974 adding fuel to the flames. Even before the 1974 crisis, George Harris, writing in 1972, commented on the extent of anti-American feeling:

Port calls by the Sixth Fleet have become chancy affairs, they no longer serve to display the strength of the Alliance but rather add to divisiveness within Turkish society, embarrass the Turkish Government and focus discontent against the United States.[61]

Nor was this all. The Cyprus crisis of 1974 put an end to the broad measure of support for the United States military presence to which the major political parties had previously subscribed. From this point onwards left-wing parties and student groups became consistently anti-American and over the period from 1975 to 1978 Turkey became only the second NATO nation, after France, to suspend American military

[61] Harris, op. cit. 171.

activity at most of the bases on her territory. Nevertheless, the 1980s saw an improvement in relations between Turkey and the United States, prompted in part by the Soviet invasion of Afghanistan and cemented by substantial amounts of American military aid. The 1980 Agreement for Co-operation on Defense and Economy met the legitimate demands of Turkey for greater control over the facilities made available to the United States and tied the use of these facilities firmly to the needs of NATO. This agreement was carried forward in 1985, even though the United States administration was unable to make firm commitments on the amount of aid which Congress would be prepared to authorize. The same agreement was renewed in September 1990, despite the subsequent controversy over use of the bases for military operations during the Gulf War. Notwithstanding extreme Turkish sensitivity on this issue, the base at Incirlik was eventually made available to the coalition partners for operations against Iraq in 1991. Following the Gulf War, Incirlik continued to be used by United States, British, and French forces for a variety of follow-up missions. These were increasingly constrained, after several threats of withdrawal, by the divergent policies of Turkey and the leading Western powers towards both the Kurds and Iraq. But Turkey agreed that Incirlik could be used for operation DESERT FOX at the end of 1998 and for follow-on air operations over Iraq in 1999.

9

Resistance in the Middle East

Rivalry with Britain

The one region in which the United States developed substantial strategic interests following the Second World War but was unable to obtain permanent access to forward bases was the Middle East. This was also the area in which rivalry between the traditional colonial and 'informal' empire of Britain and the new 'leasehold empire' of the United States lingered longest. The interests of the United States in the Middle East, as they developed during the Cold War, involved support for Israel and security of oil supplies, with the rider that the Soviet Union should not be allowed to interfere with either or gain a foothold in the region for herself. However, in the early post-war years, despite access to bases at Wheelus Field in Libya and Dhahran in Saudi Arabia, the Middle East was not a priority area for forward basing by the United States. The region was not integral to the key military transport routes across the Atlantic or the Pacific which were the initial preoccupation of the Washington planners. Nor was the Middle East regarded as central to the policy of containment since the dangers of communist expansion at first seemed far more pressing in Europe and the Far East. Moreover, the United States had no easy entrée to the region of the kind which enabled her to gain access to military facilities elsewhere. She had no colonial or quasi-colonial connections in the area, only limited experience of wartime partnership (in Iran and Saudi Arabia which were used as supply routes to the Soviet Union) and no established military presence as a result of post-war occupation. She also found it difficult in the long term to set up bilateral security arrangements in return for military assistance in the Middle East as she had in the Mediterranean.

Many of the Arab nations of the Middle East remained within the orbit of Britain's 'informal empire' in the early post-war years. Those that were not, in particular Saudi Arabia, had no wish to be drawn into a parallel relationship with another Western power, particularly one that was a committed supporter of Israel. Saudi Arabia was anxious to obtain military equipment from the United States and reach an understanding with her on security. But with the rise of Arab nationalism she was reluctant to accept an operational American military presence on her territory from the 1960s onwards. This reluctance was reinforced by deep-rooted political, religious, and cultural factors. But most of the other Western-inclined Arab nations took the same line once free of British influence, even when faced with a direct threat from Iraq in 1990/91.

The main problem for the United States was that the Middle East had traditionally been a British sphere of influence. Anglo-American relations in the area had been characterized by commercial competition since the discovery of oil in the 1930s, and in the early post-war years the United States hoped to supplant Britain in commercial terms without shouldering her political and security responsibilities. For a time she was torn between reliance on Britain and rivalry with her. The Middle East had long been of vital strategic importance to Britain as the lifeline to India, secured by her interest in the Suez Canal and her colony at Aden. At the end of the nineteenth century, the British government in India had entered into special treaty relationships, characteristic of her 'informal empire', with various local rulers in the Persian Gulf in order to safeguard the trade routes to India, as well as to suppress piracy and, in the case of Oman, slavery. Following the First World War, Britain, along with France, had been responsible for carving new states out of the defeated Ottoman Empire. Both Jordan and Iraq were nations created by Britain and in these new nations she installed as rulers her Hashemite allies who had helped her to drive the Turks out of Saudi Arabia and Palestine.

After the Second World War, Britain retained a substantial military presence in Egypt with some 80,000 troops in the Canal Zone. She still exercised control over the foreign and defence policy of Iraq, where she had put down a coup in 1941 and retained a major air base at Habbaniya. In Jordan, a British officer, Glubb Pasha, commanded the nation's army, the Arab Legion. Britain also maintained a dominant position in most of the sheikdoms of the Gulf, retaining responsibility for their defence and the conduct of their foreign relations through a Political Resident based in Bahrain and a series of Political Agents in the other Gulf States. This was not a role she was prepared to surrender lightly even though by 1947 she was planning independence for India, the return of the Palestine mandate to the United Nations, and the transfer of her post-war security responsibilities for Greece and Turkey to the United States.

Access to Bahrain and Saudi Arabia

Anxious to obtain a foothold in the Gulf area after the war, the United States was not averse to capitalizing on British overseas connections in pursuit of her strategic interests. In keeping with this policy, the United States negotiated in 1948 an informal arrangement with Britain, as the protecting power, which allowed elements of the US Navy, generally a flagship and two destroyers, occasional access to Bahrain. The following year, the post of Commander US Middle East Force was set up under a US Navy Captain based in Bahrain and in 1951 this command was upgraded to Rear-Admiral. Elsewhere in the Middle East, given Britain's dominant position, the United States could only look to Saudi Arabia as an area in which to obtain some commercial and military influence. In commercial terms Britain had controlled the oil fields of Persia since the beginning of the century. The Anglo-Persian Oil Company had been established in 1909 and in 1914 the British government had taken a controlling interest in the company when the Royal Navy, at the instigation of Winston Churchill and Admiral Sir John Fisher, respectively First Lord of the Admiralty and First Sea Lord, had switched from coal to oil burning. However, it was Standard Oil of California which discovered oil in Bahrain in 1932 and subsequently gained the prospecting concession for Saudi Arabia where oil was discovered in the Eastern Province in 1938.

American military influence in the Middle East had first been established in a modest way during the Second World War when 30,000 troops were deployed to Iran to secure the supply routes to the Soviet Union. (It has been estimated that a quarter of all wartime Western aid reached the Soviet Union via this route.) To assist this supply operation the United States declared Saudi Arabia to be eligible for lend–lease in 1943 and Cordell Hull, explaining this move to the lend–lease administrator, informed him that the US Army 'may at any time wish to obtain extensive air facilities in Saudi Arabia'.[1] This wish did not materialize, but a United States Military Mission was established in the country and in August 1945 the two governments agreed to the construction of an airfield at Dhahran by the US Army Corps of Engineers. This was conceived as a staging post between Cairo and Karachi, at a time when the Americans were planning to redeploy their forces from Europe to the Far East, and the agreement provided for the airfield to be handed over

---

[1] D. Long, US–Saudi Military Relations. In *The United States and Saudi Arabia: Ambivalent Allies* (Boulder, CO: Westview, 1985, Ch. 3).

to Saudi Arabia three years after the conclusion of hostilities with Japan. The United States recognition of Israel in 1948 delayed discussions on the future of Dhahran but in 1949, a new agreement allowed the US Air Force continued access and in 1951 a further agreement extended access for a period of five years. In parallel, a Mutual Defense Assistance Agreement was signed which established a framework for military training and arms deliveries by the United States. This led to a US Military Training Mission being set up in 1953. By now Dhahran was being used on an occasional basis by Strategic Air Command (SAC), and in 1957 President Eisenhower and King Saud concluded a new agreement which extended access for a further five years. At the same time, the United States undertook to provide grant aid of $45 million over the period with an additional $5 million for building a civil air terminal and a further $20 million for the construction of a pier at Damman.

So far, the pattern of access for American forces in return for military assistance, deliveries of equipment and training differs little from similar arrangements elsewhere in the 'leasehold empire'. But in 1961, the United States took the initiative to bring this arrangement to an end. Robert McNamara, the American Secretary for Defense, decided that, with the advent of Intercontinental Ballistic Missiles, forward bases for SAC were no longer needed. The United States initially prepared a draft joint statement saying that the agreement would not be renewed but then decided to pre-empt the Saudis by making a unilateral announcement. The arrangement formally came to an end in April 1962. Thereafter, Saudi Arabia, which had attracted some criticism from the radical nationalist regimes in Egypt and Iraq, declined to accept the deployment of operational forces from Western nations on her territory. However, she remained keen to preserve a security relationship with the United States and this was subsequently developed on the basis of contracts for substantial arms sales and infrastructure projects, with associated training provided by military missions. The Saudis were prepared to accept a US military mission to the National Guard and to pay the Americans to build them military facilities on a lavish scale, possibly with an eye to American reinforcement in time of trouble. But they preferred United States forces to remain well over the horizon in peacetime. In 1965, an Engineer Assistance Agreement was concluded between the United States and Saudi Arabia and, on the strength of this, the US Army Corps of Engineers was kept working in Saudi Arabia continuously until 1988.

The Decline of British Influence

Meanwhile, British influence in the Middle East was on the wane, initially because of Arab nationalism, an awakening of political consciousness which came to a head with the Suez crisis of 1956, and the Iraqi revolution of 1958; but also, from the mid 1960s onwards, because of recurring economic difficulties that required Britain to relinquish her dominant role in the region and withdraw her armed forces from East of Suez. The American reaction to these developments was ambivalent. Initially, the United States appeared content to compete with Britain in the area commercially without challenging her political position, even though she realized that the security of the Middle East relied on a system of imperial control which she regarded as outdated. For example, in October 1944, Lincoln MacVeagh, at that time American Ambassador to the Greek government in exile in Cairo, wrote to Franklin D. Roosevelt saying 'I doubt if in any other part of the world it can appear so clearly as here . . . that, militarily speaking, the British Empire is anachronistic, perfect for the eighteenth century, impossible for the twentieth'.[2] But by the time that a British withdrawal became inevitable in the late 1960s, the United States, by then suffering the political and economic strains of the Vietnam War, realized that she could not herself fulfil Britain's traditional role in the Middle East and became concerned that her departure would lead to greater instability in the region.

In the early 1950s, self-doubts of this kind were still some way off. At this stage, the United States was beginning to question whether the British presence in the Middle East was strong enough to protect American commercial and military assets in the region. In 1951, a State Department official wrote:

The United Kingdom, which has the primary responsibility for defense of the area, lacks both the manpower and resources successfully to defend the area and has no plans for the defense of the Saudi Arabian oil fields and the Dhahran Air Base.[3]

For their part the British detected an American desire to supplant them in the Middle East, not only commercially but politically.

---

[2] Lincoln MacVeagh to President Roosevelt 15 October 1944. Cited in M. A. Palmer, *Guardians of the Gulf. A History of America's Expanding Role in the Persian Gulf 1833–1992* (New York: The Free Press, 1992).

[3] G. C. McGhee. Assistant Secretary of State for the Near East, South Asian and African Affairs. FRUS 1951, Vol. 5, 6–11. Cited by Palmer, op. cit. 58.

In 1954, the British Ambassador in Washington, Sir Roger Makins, reported:

There is on our side a very considerable suspicion that the Americans are out to take our place in the Middle East. Their influence has greatly expanded there since the end of the Second World War and they are now established as the paramount foreign influence in Turkey and Saudi Arabia.[4]

Evidence of the American desire to play a greater role in the Middle East first became apparent in Iran. During the war, Britain had occupied the south of Iran and the Soviet Union the north in order to safeguard allied oil supplies and prevent encroachment by Germany. The Anglo–Soviet–Persian Treaty of 1942 had provided retrospective authority for the joint occupation but guaranteed the integrity and independence of the country after the war. Under the treaty, the Soviet Union had undertaken to withdraw her forces from Iran six months after the end of the war but in March 1946 the Soviet Union took steps to consolidate her position in Azerbaijan, the northern province of Iran, in parallel with the pressure exerted on Turkey over her border provinces and the Straits. The United States was able to send the *USS Missouri* to Istanbul but had no military forces available in the Middle East, the 30,000 troops deployed during the war having long since been withdrawn. She was obliged to rely on diplomatic pressure to persuade the Soviet Union to honour her wartime undertaking to withdraw her troops from northern Iran.

The United States was also compelled to resort to political expedients of a less open nature to resolve the Iranian oil crisis of 1951–3. Not only had she no forces in the area, apart from the few ships based in Bahrain, but military intervention might have prompted Soviet troops to return to Iran under the provisions of an earlier treaty signed between Iran and the Soviet Union in 1921. In March 1951, Mohammed Mossadegh, the radical Iranian Premier, nationalized the Anglo-Iranian Oil Company and appeared likely to offer a commercial interest to the Soviet Union. The Eisenhower administration, under pressure from Britain who had seen her assets appropriated and alarmed at the renewed threat of Soviet penetration, collaborated with Britain in engineering a coup in August 1953 which removed Mossadegh and transferred power to the young Shah of Iran. The United States had felt obliged to take the lead in this operation since, in the words of an assessment made by the National Security Council:

---

[4] William Roger Louis, American Anti-colonialism. In *The Special Relationship*, W. R. Louis and A. Bull (ed.), (Oxford: OUP, 1986, Ch. 16).

It is clear that the United Kingdom no longer possesses the capability unilaterally to assure stability in the area. If present trends continue unchecked, Iran could effectively be lost to the free world.[5]

Nevertheless, there were also commercial advantages from playing a more assertive role in the Middle East. In the subsequent settlement American oil companies, hitherto excluded from the Iranian oilfields, acquired a 40 per cent share in the new international consortium.

American Policy under Eisenhower

Under President Eisenhower, the United States grew increasingly concerned at the perceived gap in her global security system in the Middle East. John Foster Dulles, the American Secretary of State, first contemplated a group of nations forming a barrier to Soviet expansion which he characterized as the Northern Tier. This was to include Syria, Iraq, Turkey, and Pakistan with the possible later addition of Iran. Turkey and Iraq were the first to sign an agreement in February 1954 and, under pressure from Dulles, Britain took the initiative in 1955 in persuading Pakistan and Iran to join what became known as the Baghdad Pact. The United States declined to join the Pact herself, possibly because of her commitment to Israel, but in asking Anthony Eden to take the lead, she appeared still to see a role for Britain in the security of the Middle East. However, this proved to be something of a poisoned chalice. The Baghdad Pact was a short-lived affair since it was seen by the radical Arab nationalists, especially Colonel Nasser of Egyrot, as perpetuating the Western colonialism that Dulles was determined to eradicate and for this reason Syria refused to join. Moreover, containment was not a priority for the Arabs who saw no imminent Soviet threat to their territories and in many cases preferred to play the superpowers off against each other. As Henry Kissinger has noted 'the divisions and animosities among the nations in the area were greater than their mutual fear of Soviet expansion'.[6] The Pact was not to survive the Iraqi revolution of 1958 which brought a radical nationalist regime to power in the city after which it was named.

Although Dulles saw a continuing role for Britain as sponsor of the Baghdad Pact, this did not extend to the retention of colonial garrisons on Arab territory. In 1954, shortly after engineering the coup in Iran and while working up the concept of the Northern Tier, the United States

---

[5] NSC 136/1 20 November 1952. Cited by Palmer, op. cit. 65.
[6] H. Kissinger, *Diplomacy* (London: Simon & Schuster, 1994, 517).

was pressing Britain to withdraw her forces from the Suez Canal Zone following the revolution which had deposed King Farouk in 1952. Britain agreed to withdrawal by 1956 but this plan was overtaken by the Suez crisis, which, together with the Iraqi revolution two years later, effectively put an end to the British military presence in the Arab heartland, although this was to live on for some years in the peripheral areas of Aden and the Gulf sheikdoms. In 1961, the special treaty relationship between Britain and Kuwait had been ended by mutual agreement. With the apparent withdrawal of British protection, Kuwait was promptly threatened with invasion from Iraq, to be deterred only by the temporary return of British forces assembled from Kenya, Aden, and Bahrain. This proved to be the last occasion on which Britain was able to take independent action to influence events in the Middle East. In Aden, a bitter internal struggle between different ideological groups obliged Harold Wilson's government, faced with increasing economic difficulties, to withdraw in 1966, leaving a Marxist regime in South Yemen. It was also economic weakness which caused Britain to announce in January 1968 that she would be completing her withdrawal from the Gulf by 1971.

By now, however, the United States was having second thoughts. In the course of the Suez crisis Eisenhower and Dulles had backed the emerging forces of Arab nationalism in preference to the European colonial powers and Israel. The Eisenhower Doctrine formulated shortly after Suez, in January 1957, had represented a clear bid for the allegiance of the moderate, pro-Western Arabs, promising a threefold programme of economic aid, military assistance, and protection against communist aggression. Following the Iraqi coup in July 1958, it looked as though the moderate Arab states would fall in with American aspirations as both President Chamoun of Lebanon and King Hussein of Jordan sought military assistance from the West. With the dispatch of a contingent of US Marines to Lebanon, the United States took the lead for the first time in orchestrating a Western military intervention in the Middle East, even though British forces played the major role in Jordan. But this was a temporary phenomenon. By October 1958, the Anglo-American intervention forces had withdrawn from the region and the United States found that the Arab states who had only recently escaped the colonial administration or protection of one Western power were in no hurry to submit to the political dominance of another. They remained wary of American support for Israel in the early 1960s and predominantly hostile to the United States in the aftermath of the Six Day War in 1967.

The Nixon and Carter Doctrines

For her part, the United States, deeply embroiled in Vietnam during this period and increasingly isolationist once the war was over, now had little enthusiasm for the new regional responsibilities to which she had earlier aspired. Having given a firm push to Britain's withdrawal from the Middle East, the United States found that she was not well placed to step into her shoes when the opportunity arose. The new mood was summed up in the Nixon Doctrine formally set out in 1970 which looked to major regional powers to take the lead in maintaining stability:

The nations of each part of the world should assume primary responsibility for their own well-being; and they themselves should determine the terms of that well-being. [7]

Furthermore, the United States had virtually no military facilities available to her on a permanent basis in the Middle East. At the time of Britain's final withdrawal from the Gulf in 1971, she could rely only on the informal arrangements for naval access to Bahrain negotiated with the former protecting power in 1948. Steps were taken to put this on a more formal footing. In December 1971, the United States concluded an executive agreement with Bahrain allowing continued access by US naval forces on an occasional basis for payment of $4 million a year. No military construction was involved but access to commercial piers, warehousing, and other facilities such as cold storage was permitted under a leasing arrangement.

Following the Yom Kippur War in 1973, Bahrain became less well-disposed towards the American military presence and initially announced that the lease would be terminated. However, a new agreement was concluded in 1977 under President Ford which reduced the facilities extended to the US Navy. The headquarters of US Middle East Forces was obliged to move on board ship and US warships were no longer home-ported at Bahrain, although sixty-five personnel remained ashore to man a support unit. In an interview with the *Washington Post*, the Bahraini Foreign Minister made the position quite clear:

We don't want the United States presence in such a way that it could be construed as a base and give other Persian Gulf or Indian Ocean countries an excuse to allow foreign powers to put in military bases.[8]

---

[7] State of the Union Address by President Nixon. 22 January 1970.
[8] A. Cottrell and T. Moorer, *US Overseas Bases*, Washington Paper No 47-2 (Beverly Hills: Sage, 1977, 33).

The United States also had some success in gaining access to facilities in Oman when the British finally withdrew, later than from the Gulf itself, in 1977. The airfield on the island of Masirah had long been used by Britain, along with Gan in the Maldive Islands, as one of a series of staging posts to her possessions in the Far East. The United States enjoyed occasional access to Masirah when it was in British hands and was able to retain this, together with access to other airfields at As Sib and Thumrait, when British forces left the country. She also gained occasional access to the naval bases at Muscat and Salalah. Oman had always taken a more positive attitude towards the West than her Arab neighbours and, apart from Bahrain, she remained the only country prepared to sign a formal access agreement with the United States prior to the Gulf War.

The Facilities Access Agreement, concluded in June 1980, allowed the United States to upgrade the various military facilities available to her in Oman at a total cost of $255 million and to use Masirah for staging purposes, mainly for P-3C Orion aircraft.[9] But it did not permit the permanent deployment of American troops in Oman. Moreover, use of the facilities available in Oman was not always straightforward. Sultan Qaboos had reservations over American C-130 transport aircraft, refuelling in Oman during President Carter's abortive attempt to free the American hostages in Iran in April 1980. A threat to withdraw the access arrangements was averted and in December 1981, American troops were permitted to land in Oman as part of exercise BRIGHT STAR. In addition, a development programme of $200 million was authorized by the United States for the period 1981–3 to improve military facilities in Oman and this was later increased to $300 million. But in 1985, Oman insisted that her approval would in future be required before the United States used these facilities in an emergency, and that she would need to approve the military goods and equipment moving in and out of the bases.

Initially, the United States was not too concerned at her inability to establish a military presence in the Middle East comparable to that relinquished by Britain. Under the Nixon Doctrine, she was prepared to rely on major regional allies instead of establishing further forward bases of her own to shore up her global security system. In the Middle East she placed her faith primarily in the Shah of Iran whom she had returned to the Peacock Throne as a young man in 1954. With the oil price increases of 1973 and 1976, the latter a direct consequence of the Yom Kippur War,

<hr />

[9] The Facilities Access Agreement. Signed 4 June 1980. TIAS 9791.

the Shah was able to embark on a massive programme of arms purchases, spending petrodollars, as one critic put it, 'like a drunk in a liquor store'.[10] He spread his largesse liberally round all the major Western nations but inevitably it was to the United States that he looked to meet most of his needs. Estimates of his arms purchases from American companies range from $12 billion to $20 billion, and at one time there were some 25,000 American advisers, technicians, and dependants in Iran. In the decade spanning the start of the Nixon administration in 1969 and the Iranian revolution in 1979, the Shah's defence budget increased by 600 per cent, finally accounting for one-third of all government expenditure. Across the Gulf, much the same was happening in Saudi Arabia, the second of the Twin Pillars supporting security in the Gulf under the Nixon Doctrine, although the United States probably placed less confidence in the cautious and conservative regime there to play the role of regional security guarantor. Moreover, the reservations entertained by Congress over the supply of advanced military technology to an Arab country hostile to Israel allowed other Western nations, notably Britain and France, to secure some substantial defence contracts from Saudi Arabia.

Although the United States had to be content with limited access to her allies in the Middle East and was prepared to rely on Iran and, to a lesser extent Saudi Arabia, as regional power-brokers, she could not afford to ignore the threat of Soviet expansion. Under Admiral Gorshkov, the Soviet Navy had succeeded in leapfrogging the containment strategy of the 1950s and the early 1960s. In March 1968, shortly after Britain had announced her withdrawal from the Gulf, Soviet warships first appeared in the Indian Ocean, initially relying on anchorages off Socotra, the Seychelles, and the Chagos archipelago. By the 1970s, the Soviet Fleet was operating extensively in the Indian Ocean, mustering twenty-three warships for a major naval exercise known as OKEAN in April 1975. By this time, its access to littoral bases was a good deal better than that of the US Navy. It was the Soviet Union which signed an agreement with Aden in 1968 and later set up port facilities at Socotra and Berbera. By contrast, the United States was largely dependent on the British territory of Diego Garcia, 2,500 miles from the Gulf.

As a consequence, competition developed during the 1970s between the United States and the Soviet Union for *ad hoc* access arrangements among the states bordering the Indian Ocean and the Gulf. In some countries bases would change hands from one superpower to the other as alliances altered along with the complexion of the host nation

[10] T. J. McCormick, *America's Half Century* (Baltimore, MD: Johns Hopkins University Press, 1993, 187).

government. For example, Egypt curtailed her arrangements with the Soviet Union in 1972 and asked all Russian forces to leave the country in 1976. Shortly after, she permitted American AWACS aircraft to operate out of Upper Qena and granted access for the US Navy on an occasional basis at the port of Ras Banas in the Red Sea. Similarly, although the Soviet Union gained access to the port of Berbera in Somalia during the 1970s, by 1980 she had been supplanted by the United States, which was able to use the facilities there, in return for a modest aid package, while avoiding commitment to Somalia over the Ogaden dispute. Further down the African coast, Kenya agreed to visits to Mombassa by the US Navy during the 1980s, but this carried little strategic benefit since the port was no closer to the Gulf than Diego Garcia.

On the surface it appeared that access arrangements in the Middle East and the Indian Ocean enabled the United States to maintain a presence in the region which, while not fully compensating for Britain's withdrawal from Aden and the Gulf, was sufficient to warn the Soviet Union of American commitment to the area. A report by the Congressional Research Service in 1979 concluded that 'despite the absence of any major military bases in the Indian Ocean, the United States has maintained the appearance and reality of a major Indian Ocean power'. But this report also acknowledged the difficulties of persuading countries in this area to accept the permanent deployment of American forces on their territory:

Due to the circumstances that led to the withdrawal of the European colonial powers from the Indian Ocean littoral states . . . most local states are strongly opposed to a permanent shore presence by an outside military power.[11]

However, the shortcomings of the Nixon Doctrine were exposed in 1979 which proved to be a traumatic year for the United States. January saw the fall of the Shah and the Iranian revolution, followed in November by the seizure of American Embassy staff in Tehran as hostages. December brought the Soviet invasion of Afghanistan. These two events effectively removed Iran as one of America's Twin Pillars, for whom a major regional security role was envisaged under the Nixon Doctrine, and revived fears of a Soviet threat to the oil fields of the Gulf. They led to a renewal of interest by the United States, and also by Britain, in supporting the Arab states in the Gulf through the supply of defence equipment and the provision of military advice. They also prompted President Carter to set up the Rapid Deployment Force (RDF) in October 1979

[11] United States Foreign Policy Objectives and Overseas Military Installations. Report for the SCFR. CRS April 1979, 7.

and enunciate the Carter Doctrine in January 1980. This policy state-ment, set out in the President's State of the Union message, was a forth-right declaration of American interests in the Gulf area:

An attempt by an outside force to gain control of the Persian Gulf region will be regarded as an assault on the vital interests of the United States of America, and such an assault will be repelled by any means necessary, including military force.[12]

But the United States did not have the forces permanently deployed in the region to enforce this declaration. The headquarters of the RDF was set up at MacDill Air Force Base at Tampa in Florida and, as one con-temporary commentator accurately observed:

The United States possesses none of the critical operational and logistics benefits that it enjoys in comparative abundance in Europe, where large mil-itary forces are firmly ensconced ashore and can count on the support of pow-erful and reliable allies.[13]

The Iran-Iraq War

The Arab nations of the Gulf were intensely suspicious of the RDF and they were not reassured when in January 1983 President Reagan created Central Command (CENTCOM), the first new geographical command set up by the United States for thirty-five years, which embraced a wedge-shaped slice of the Indian Ocean between the Horn of Africa and the Gulf. Despite the outbreak of the Iran–Iraq war in the summer of 1980, most of the Arab states saw no reason for an increased military presence in the region by the United States during the early stages of the conflict. Saudi Arabia, in particular, remained opposed to a perman-ent American military presence on her territory. However, the attacks on neutral oil tankers, a desperate ploy adopted first by Iraq and then Iran in the mid 1980s, and the discovery of mines in the Gulf over the same period, caused a gradual change in attitudes. Saudi Arabia allowed American AWACS aircraft to be stationed on her soil and purchased similar aircraft for herself. Oman, which had always taken a more inde-pendent line on these matters, permitted the United States to operate maritime patrol and refuelling aircraft from her territory to carry out surveillance of tanker movements in the Gulf. In April 1987, the US Navy, which had been escorting American-flagged tankers for some

[12] State of the Union Message by President Carter. 23 January 1980.
[13] J. Record, *Projection of Power. Perspectives, Perceptions and Problems* (Archon, CT: Hamden, 1982). Cited in J. C. Snyder *Defending the Fringe* (Boulder, CO: Westview, 1987).

time, agreed to reflag Kuwaiti tankers and thereby extend the protection of the United States to these vessels. This rapidly became an international operation, involving ships of the British, French, and other allied navies until, at the height of the tension in the Gulf, there were some sixty allied warships engaged on escort and mine-clearance duties, of which approximately half were American. This large international force, protecting Arab as well as Western interests, inevitably eroded Arab reservations over reliance on military assistance from the United States and her allies. Access to ports up and down the Gulf became more acceptable, host nation support became more readily available and Kuwait, which was the nation most vulnerable to the interruption of tanker traffic, assisted Western navies with the cost of fuel.

At the same time, the sensitivity shown by the Arab nations of the Gulf to an American military presence on their territory, despite the dangers of the Iran-Iraq war, pushed the United States towards a more flexible and economic global security system in the mid 1980s. Plans for a reduced permanent presence in Europe, supplemented by massive reinforcement at short notice, led to a similar approach in the CENTCOM area. The concept of permanent bases, which had dominated American thinking in the early post-war period, was replaced in the Gulf and Indian Ocean by a strategy based on mobile forces and the pre-positioning of military equipment. This strategy was made possible by advances in the range and capacity of military transport aircraft but was dictated primarily by political considerations. Nations who still wanted the reassurance of American protection were less disposed to accept a permanent military presence on their territory. Permanent basing arrangements had worked best where the United States could rely on her own overseas possessions or those of her allies, where wartime arrangements had built up a relationship which could be developed, or where the communist threat and the collective defence arrangements necessary to meet it made permanent bases essential. They were less satisfactory where sovereign nations with no previous defence relationship with the United States felt that the threat was not sufficiently close to outweigh the disadvantages of playing host to United States forces or, as in the Middle East, there were strong religious, cultural, and historical reasons for avoiding the permanent deployment of American troops.

The Gulf War and After

The Arab preference for limited and occasional access by the American forces rather than permanent deployments largely survived the Iraqi invasion of Kuwait in August 1990 and the Gulf War that followed in the first months of 1991. Although some 500,000 American troops were deployed to Saudi Arabia, approximately the same number as were engaged in Vietnam and twice the number stationed in Europe at the height of the Cold War, it was made very clear that these should not outstay their welcome and that all the coalition's Western forces, which included 35,000 British and 13,500 French troops, should be withdrawn once Iraq had been driven out of Kuwait.[14] However, the difficulty of enforcing the United Nations conditions for ending the war and the introduction of an air exclusion zone south of the 32nd Parallel required Western forces to return to the Gulf for extended duty. Moreover, the further feints by Iraq towards the Kuwaiti border in 1994 and 1996 prompted the temporary return of Western ground troops in significant numbers. In response to the threat posed by the movement of two Iraqi Republican Guards divisions towards Kuwait in October 1994, the United States deployed 6,000 troops to Kuwait in three days and sent a US Air Force detachment to Saudi Arabia. A detachment of Royal Marines was also sent out from Britain. A lesser threat in 1996 was countered by the deployment of 3,500 American ground troops to the Gulf.

The frequency with which Iraq continued to provoke Kuwait and her allies began to lend an air of semi-permanency to the deployment of Western forces in the Gulf area. In July 1995, the US Fifth Fleet was established to take charge of American naval operations in the Gulf and the headquarters for US Naval Forces Central Command was set up in Bahrain. The presence of significant numbers of American troops in Saudi Arabia was highlighted in June 1996 when a bomb attack on a barracks in Dhahran killed nineteen servicemen. As a precaution, 4,500 troops out of a total of 6,000 in country were moved to the more secure area of al-Kharj in the desert. In April 1997, the American Secretary of Defense's Annual Report recorded the 'continuous presence of an Army heavy battalion task force in Kuwait and Patriot air defense artillery task forces in Kuwait and Saudi Arabia',[15] as well the deployment of land-based aircraft in the Gulf region for Operation SOUTHERN WATCH (monitoring the air exclusion zone). The DOD later confirmed that an average of some 15,000 American troops remained in the Middle East during 1998, a year which saw a series of confrontations between Iraq and the United Nations Special Commission charged with locating and destroying weapons of mass destruction

---

[14] For Saudi sensitivity over Western forces on her territory see Sir Alan Munro, *An Arabian Affair* (London: Barssey's, 1996).

[15] Annual Report by the Secretary of Defense to the President and Congress for FY 1998. April 1997 (RSD FY 98) USGPO.

and related manufacturing facilities in Iraq. The Special Commission finally withdrew from Iraq in December 1998 and the withdrawal was followed by Operation DESERT FOX, a short-lived series of intensive air strikes by the United States and Britain designed to degrade any remaining weapons of mass destruction or manufacturing facilities in the country. Operation DESERT FOX and subsequent lower level air operations over Iraq throughout 1999 made use of air bases in both Saudi Arabia and Kuwait as well as Incirlik in Turkey and naval units in the Gulf.

Nevertheless United States policy in the Middle East continued to rely on the pre-positioning of military equipment in a number of countries to allow rapid reinforcement by American troops in an emergency. By the late 1990s equipment had been pre-positioned for a heavy brigade in Kuwait and a heavy battalion task force in Qatar. There were also plans for pre-positioning equipment for a second heavy brigade in the region and for a divisional base in Qatar.

The policy of pre-positioning, backed up by frequent exercises, suited both the United States and her Arab allies alike. The Arabs, particularly the Saudis, remained acutely sensitive to the prospect of American forces permanently based on their territory, no matter what the danger from Iraq. The United States, for her part, was reducing her permanent deployments in the aftermath of the Cold War and, while retaining a substantial military presence in both Europe and the Far East, no longer wished to add to this in the Middle East. Consequently, the years immediately following the Gulf War saw the United States negotiating a series of arrangements with the Gulf states which in general allowed for the stockpiling of equipment in country and occasional access for her forces, but not for permanent basing facilities.

In September 1991, a ten-year agreement was concluded with Kuwait, permitting the pre-positioning of equipment and allowing for joint exercises but no permanent bases. The following month a Defense Co-operation Agreement was signed with Bahrain which allowed the United States limited use of certain military facilities and made arrangements for stockpiling equipment. A further Defense Co-operation Agreement was completed with Qatar in June 1992 which provided for pre-positioning but not permanent basing. This allowed the United States to stockpile a substantial amount of army equipment in the country sufficient for a tank battalion, a heavy brigade, and a divisional base. Finally, an agreement was also concluded with the United Arab Emirates in 1992 permitting the pre-positioning of equipment and access to some military facilities on a temporary basis. The United States took advantage of these agreements not only to stockpile equipment but also to exercise the new Air Expeditionary Forces which had been developed for quick reaction to emergencies overseas. Temporary deployments were made to Bahrain and Qatar in 1996 and again to Qatar in February 1997.

Driven largely by Arab sensitivity, but reinforced by changing strategic requirements and the need for economy, access arrangements became the predominant pattern for the deployment of American forces in the Middle East and Indian Ocean region, rather than permanent basing. This pattern extended as far as Singapore, where an agreement providing increased access for US warships and military aircraft on an *ad hoc* basis was concluded in November 1990. However, this agreement permitted training not operational deployments and it allowed only ninety-five American servicemen to be stationed at Singapore on a permanent basis. Moreover, in adjusting to the end of the Cold War, the US Department of Defense saw a wider application for access and stockpiling arrangements as a means of projecting power in areas where, for reasons of either economy or local political sensitivity, permanent bases could not be secured. The Secretary of Defense's Annual Report for 1993, published in February 1992, recorded that the United States had access agreements with Djibouti, Gambia, Kenya, Liberia, Senegal, and the Seychelles and stated that these were 'indicative of a new approach'.[16] The Annual Report for 1996, published in February 1995, stated that 'Pre-positioning heavy equipment and supplies ashore and afloat can greatly reduce both the time required to deploy forces to distant regions and the number of airlift sorties devoted to moving such supplies'.[17] The report went on to illustrate the role which stockpiling equipment had played in the rapid reinforcement of Kuwait in October 1994, estimating that only one-third of the forces dispatched could have been operational in the same time-frame without pre-positioning. The following year, the Annual Report indicated that pre-positioning was now accepted policy worldwide. 'Strong deterrence', it said, 'requires us to maintain pre-positioned equipment in the Persian Gulf, the Indian Ocean, Korea and Europe'.[18] The new approach was also underlined by the 1998 report which listed permanently stationed forces as only one element amongst eight designed 'to maintain a robust overseas presence'. The other seven included temporarily deployed forces, combined exercises, security assistance activities, and pre-positioning of military equipment and supplies.

[16] RSD FY 93. February 1992.   [17] RSD FY 96. February 1995.
[18] RSD FY 97. March 1996.

Conclusion

In summary, the United States was at first prepared to accept the dominant position of Britain in the Middle East after the Second World War but increasingly came to challenge this for commercial as well as strategic reasons. British power in the region declined more rapidly than expected, particularly after the Suez crisis during which Eisenhower and Dulles had backed the emerging forces of Arab nationalism in preference to the colonial pretensions of their European allies. But by the time Britain's withdrawal was complete in the 1970s, the United States was in no position to replace her. Moreover, the Arab nations which had escaped from Britain's sphere of influence had no wish to succumb to American dominance. Under Nixon and Carter, the United States relied first on regional self-help and then on long-distance intervention to meet the perceived Soviet threat to the Gulf. But the Arabs did not share the American fear of Soviet intentions and, anxious to preserve their independence as well as their social and religious traditions, preferred United States forces to remain well over the horizon. As a result, the United States encountered greater resistance to the permanent deployment of her troops in the Middle East than in any other region in which she attempted to establish forward bases.

In the event, it was the outbreak of regional conflict rather than the threat from the Soviet Union that persuaded the Arab nations of the Gulf to overcome their scruples and accept military assistance from the United States and her Western allies. As a result, the United States is now more deeply involved in the security of the Middle East than at any time since the Second World War. The position she sought in order to contain communist expansion was finally granted to enable her to check the ambitions of Saddam Hussein. Even so, the Middle East remains the one area in the United States global security system where host nations have kept American forces at arm's length and successfully resisted permanent deployment.

10

The End of Empire?

Rundown and Consolidation

Growing Economic and Political Pressures

By the mid 1980s, the 'leasehold empire' of the United States was showing signs of strain. The threat from the Soviet Union was diminishing but so too was the economic predominance of the United States which had sustained her global security system since the Second World War. The gradual erosion of the exceptional position occupied by the United States in 1945 was inevitable, but this process was compounded by those actions of the Reagan administration designed to face down the Soviet threat. The budget of the Department of Defense had increased by $1 trillion during Reagan's first term until it accounted for 8 per cent of US GNP and in 1985 the United States, having long been the world's major lending nation, became its largest borrower. A foreign debt of $3 trillion rapidly accumulated. The increase in defence spending, coupled with reductions in taxation, was mainly responsible for this debt, which was largely funded by the Japanese and other surplus nations purchasing US Treasury bonds. The twin deficits on the federal budget and national trade account both soared during Reagan's first administration. The annual trade deficit rose from $30 billion to $130 billion, while the federal budget deficit expanded from $60 billion to $200 billion.

It was suggested that the United States was suffering from imperial overstretch in the same way that other empires had suffered before. As long ago as 1971, the Senate Committee on Foreign Relations, surveying America's military commitments round the world, had concluded that 'the United States eventually would not be able to continue bearing the financial burden of all these activities'.[1] In 1983 the Chairman of the Joint Chiefs of Staff was reported as saying that the mismatch between the United States forces and strategy 'is greater now than ever before'.[2]

---

[1] SCFR. Report of the Sub-Committee on US Security Agreements and Commitments Abroad. 91st Congress, 1969–70, 2415, Vol. 6, 1970.
[2] *New York Times*, 10 August 1983. Cited in P. Kennedy (see note 3).

But the theory of overstretch was most cogently expressed by the historian Paul Kennedy in the *The Rise and Fall of the Great Powers*, published in 1988. In his concluding chapter he wrote:

Given the worldwide array of military liabilities which the United States has assumed since 1945, its capacity to carry these burdens is obviously less than it was several decades ago, when its share of global manufacturing and GNP was much larger, its agriculture was not in crisis, its balance of payments was far healthier, the government budget was also in balance, and it was not so heavily in debt with the rest of the world.[3]

However, the immediate manifestations of imperial overstretch were political rather than economic. Where the United States was obliged to reduce her overseas commitments or redeploy her forces, this was caused not so much by economic necessity as by host nation pressure abroad or political reappraisal at home. As the communist threat diminished, some nations not directly in the front line felt that the close convergence that had earlier existed between their security interests and those of the United States no longer applied. These nations increasingly began to exercise their sovereign rights in the renegotiation of basing agreements. This was particularly noticeable in the Mediterranean where Spain asked for F-16 aircraft to be withdrawn from Torrejón, only to replace these with F-18 aircraft of her own at the same base. Further east, Greece insisted on reductions in American forces and the United States, for her own reasons, decided to withdraw from the mainland, leaving forces only in Crete. The same process was to apply in the Philippines where the replacement of President Marcos by Cory Aquino made negotiations no easier and the United States was obliged to withdraw her forces altogether in the early 1990s. In Panama the United States had undertaken under President Carter to withdraw her forces by 1999. This decision, although strongly contested within the United States, reflected the view that the quasi-colonial relationship between the United States and Panama was no longer appropriate at the close of the twentieth century. Belatedly, 'the leasehold empire' of the United States was experiencing many of the political pressures that Britain's territorial empire of had encountered in the post-war years. Writing in 1990, James Blaker summarized the situation as follows:

Once, perhaps 20 years ago, the United States was in a position to convince a wide range of nations that their security interests were widely shared. That is no longer the case and the United States must increasingly recognise that its

[3] P. Kennedy, *The Rise and Fall of the Great Powers* (London: Unwin Hyman, 1988, 529).

foreign bases provide two way links tying the host country to US policies and interests and the US to the policies and interests of the host country.[4]

The Reagan and Bush administrations were slow to recognize this divergence in interests and a series of incidents in the late 1980s caused growing concern over the use of American forces stationed in other countries. The *Achille Lauro* affair in 1985 and the air strike on Libya in 1986 demonstrated that President Reagan was fully prepared to use American forces stationed for collective security in Europe on anti-terrorist operations of a national nature. The invasion of Panama in 1989, although fully justified by the excesses of the Noriega regime, sent a clear message to host nations that American troops based in their countries could still be used *in extremis* to intervene in their domestic affairs.

During the 1980s, some host nations attempted to limit American freedom of manoeuvre by progressively revising and renegotiating the appropriate basing agreements. But many of the less advanced countries were concerned more with increasing the flow of aid from the United States than restricting American activities at the bases. The mutual dependency that had developed between the United States and host nation governments, in some cases run by corrupt and unrepresentative leaders, proved difficult to break. In Fiscal Year 1988, security assistance in various forms totalling $2.3 billion was dispersed to thirteen countries hosting United States forces—80 per cent of this was allocated to Greece, Turkey, Spain, and Portugal in the Mediterranean and the Philippines in the Pacific.[5] The increasing demands of these countries led to difficulties between the United States administration and Congress at a time of mounting deficits and increasing budgetary pressure within the United States. Congress would reduce requests for aid from the administration by as much as 50 per cent, and this frequently led to further dissatisfaction on the part of host nation governments who felt they had been let down. The dilemma faced by the United States was spelt out in some detail in the Department of Defense (DoD) report to the President and Congress for Fiscal Year 1991:

Although many countries in which United States forces are stationed have sought increased foreign aid in exchange for basing rights, the United States does not view foreign assistance as 'rent' or compensation for base access, but

---

[4] J. R. Blaker, *United States Overseas Basing: An Anatomy of the Dilemma* (London: Praeger, 1990, 143).
[5] J. Woodliffe, *The Peacetime Use of Foreign Military Bases* (Dordrecht: Martinus Nijhoff, 1992).

rather as one element of US participation in mutual defense efforts with its allies. There are of course clear fiscal limits to what the United States can provide. If mutually satisfactory arrangements cannot be achieved with various countries hosting US forces currently, the United States must be prepared to make alternative arrangements.[6]

Nuclear Weapons

The area in which host governments did most to assert their sovereignty and restrict American activity concerned the deployment of nuclear weapons on their territory. Several host nations, including some members of NATO, had excluded nuclear weapons from their territory in their initial basing agreements with the United States. France had insisted on the withdrawal of nuclear weapons from her territory in 1959 and the continuing dispute over nuclear policy precipitated her withdrawal from NATO's military structure in 1966. From 1960 onwards, Japan required consultation before nuclear weapons were deployed on her territory and this requirement extended to Okinawa after reversion came into effect in 1972. In the 1970s and 1980s, other host nations took a hostile line on the presence of nuclear weapons within their borders. In 1976, the new United States agreement with Spain precluded the introduction of nuclear weapons and in 1977 they were banned from Panama under the Supplementary Notes to the Canal Treaty. Iceland had insisted in 1951 that her approval should be obtained before nuclear weapons were stationed on her territory and this was confirmed in 1984. In the same year, the Technical Agreement between the United States and Portugal on the Azores limited the right of the United States to store and maintain weapons there to conventional munitions and explosives. Two years later, the Philippines adopted a Constitution that banned nuclear weapons.

These measures further reduced the options available to the United States. They also caused difficulty over the traditional policy that the United States would 'neither confirm nor deny' whether her warships were carrying nuclear weapons when visiting foreign ports. Refusal to modify this policy led to difficulties with New Zealand which passed legislation in 1987 banning warships carrying nuclear weapons from her territory, with the result that the United States thereafter regarded the ANZUS Treaty of 1951 as no longer applicable to New Zealand. There

[6] Report of the Secretary of Defense to the President and the Congress for Fiscal Year 1991. January 1990. (RSD FY 91). USGPO.

also remained considerable concern that, notwithstanding agreements with host nations forbidding the introduction of nuclear weapons, the knowledge of whether nuclear weapons were present or not was limited to very few people. In 1970, the Senate Committee on Foreign Relations disclosed that many US Ambassadors were not aware that tactical nuclear weapons were deployed in their host country and commented 'most people . . . are unaware of the fact that US tactical nuclear warheads have been and are stationed in countries all around the world'.[7] The difficulties over the carriage of nuclear weapons on American warships were not finally resolved until the conclusions of the Nuclear Posture Review, announced in October 1994, confirmed the withdrawal of nuclear weapons from all surface ships and aircraft carriers in the US Navy.

Adjusting to the End of the Cold War

These problems should not be exaggerated. The United States was able to carry out a planned rundown of her post-war global security system in much the same way as Britain started to dismantle her colonial empire after 1945. Both nations, it has been said, embarked on 'decline by design'. The end of the Cold War and the collapse of communism allowed orderly reductions and realignments which might otherwise have been forced on the United States by political and perhaps later economic pressures. In effect, the United States was able to make a virtue out of necessity.

In January 1988 an elite study group set up by the DoD issued a report entitled 'Discriminate Deterrence'. The title itself suggested some retrenchment in American overseas deployments. However, the report recommended that the United States should remain a global power exercising control over the Gulf, the Pacific, and the Mediterranean, and it concluded that bases overseas would remain important for power projection and the concentration of power.[8] At the same time the annual DoD report for 1989, published in February 1988, made the same point:

A continuing element of American power projection is our superior worldwide basing network. Our forward deployments require sea and air links to the overseas bases supporting these tasks.[9]

---

[7] SCFR 1970.

[8] Discriminate Deterrence: Report of the Commission on Integrated Long Term Strategy. January 1988. USGPO.

[9] RSD FY 89. February 1988, 41.

But the growing concern over matching resources to commitments was reflected in a further report made public in August 1988. This was the report of the Defence Burden Sharing Panel, chaired by Representative Pat Schroeder. It too recommended that 'forward deployment of US troops should remain the cornerstone of US military strategy in the near term', but urged that America's allies should make a greater contribution to burden sharing if they wished to retain the protection of the United States.[10]

The mood during the first half of 1988 was clearly a troubled one in the United States, but the problems faced by the Soviet Union were far more severe. On 7 December 1988, President Gorbachev, in a speech to the United Nations, announced extensive withdrawals of Soviet troops from Eastern Europe, including some 10,000 tanks—half those facing NATO—and a unilateral reduction of half a million men in the Soviet armed forces. One year later, the Berlin wall had fallen and it was clearly the 'evil empire' of the Soviet Union that was unravelling, whereas the United States global security system was engaged in an orderly rundown.

The government of the United States was quick to respond to the reduction of tension in Europe. A drawdown of American forces had commenced prior to 1989 but in January 1990 it was announced that fourteen American bases in Europe would close, including four air bases in Britain and the submarine base at Holy Loch. The annual DoD report to the President and Congress published in January 1990 included an introductory statement by Dick Cheney, Secretary of Defense, which balanced optimism with caution:

The events of 1989 have reduced the threat of a sudden Soviet attack in Europe; they clearly call for a review of United States defense policy priorities in the 1990s.[11]

But the statement added that the United States must not 'get ahead of events'. 'The opportunities are great', Cheney said, 'but so are the uncertainties and risks'.

Planning proceeded within the United States government with considerable despatch. In August 1990, President Bush outlined a new strategy for the United States in Aspen, Colorado. While concluding that 'a forward presence will remain an indispensable element in our strategy' and that the United States 'must possess forces able to respond to threats in whatever corner of the globe they may occur', Bush concluded

---

[10] Report of the Defense Burden Sharing Panel. House of Representatives, 100th Congress, August 1988.

[11] RSD FY 91. January 1990.

that the security needs of the United States by 1995 could be met by an active force 25 per cent smaller than in 1990.[12] By September that year, the United States was ready to announce an end or reduction in operations at 151 military sites in 10 countries. These were primarily in Europe but reductions were also envisaged in Korea and Japan with American forces in East Asia being cut back from 135,000 to 120,000 by 1993. By January 1991, Cheney's annual report spelt out the detailed implications for US forces worldwide. Over the period 1990–5 Army divisions would be reduced from 28 to 18 (18–12 active divisions), Tactical Fighter Wings of the US Air Force would be reduced from 36 to 26 (24–15 active Wings), and the goal of a 600-ship Navy (which had peaked at 547 ships) was formally reduced to the more realistic figure of 451.[13]

The Gulf War

However, Bush's statement in Aspen was made by chance at the very moment that Saddam Hussein invaded Kuwait. The subsequent military operations to safeguard Saudi Arabia and liberate Kuwait, led by the United States, emphasized the continuing need for forward basing despite the end of the Cold War and marked a rapprochement between host nations and the United States in the face of a common danger. With the erosion of the communist threat after the fall of the Berlin Wall, pressures had begun to build up within the global security system. The need for containment seemed to be over and there was a feeling in some areas that the United States was retaining overseas bases more for her own national interests than for collective security. The Gulf War showed how quickly political differences could be set aside when a new danger threatened and collective action was required. The invasion of Kuwait in August 1990 brought the United States and her allies together again with a common sense of purpose and enrolled in the coalition against Iraq a number of countries not normally considered natural partners of the Americans. In all, some 600,000 troops from 30 nations took part in the coalition.

To prosecute the war the United States had to draw on the wide network of overseas bases established for NATO and other purposes. On this occasion, consent for American military operations was freely given by the host countries concerned without exception. British bases in Cyprus and Diego Garcia were used, but more remarkably, Spain

[12] Statement by President Bush at the Aspen Institute Symposium. 2 August 1990.
[13] RSD FY 92. January 1991.

gave permission for the use of Torrejón, and Greece for the use of Hellenikon for transit purposes, even though the host nation had in each case asked for the withdrawal of American forces from these bases. A resupply route was quickly established between the United States and the Arabian peninsula on a blanket approval basis using Lajes in the Azores, Cairo West, Torrejón, and Hellenikon. The only exception to this ready approval was that some host nations were initially reluctant to allow B-52s to be flown from their territory because of the nuclear connotations. The British government promptly agreed to these aircraft flying from Fairford for conventional missions over Iraq but it took longer to negotiate similar facilities at Morón in Spain.

The United States readily acknowledged the assistance provided by her allies on this occasion in contrast to the disputes which had arisen in the past when security perceptions had diverged. The DoD annual report published in January 1991 stated that 'bases and access to facilities in Portugal, Greece, Turkey, the Philippines and elsewhere have proved important to our ability to project power to the region'.[14] The 'US Gulf War Air Power Survey', published in 1993 commented:

Unlike American experience in the 1973 Arab-Israeli War and the 1986 raid on Libya, the United States encountered few difficulties in securing overflight rights and obtaining access to bases within and leading to the theater.[15]

More remarkable still was the role played by Turkey, which had traditionally proved most reluctant to allow bases on her territory to be used for American operations in the Middle East and had close economic ties with Iraq. She declined to deploy her own armed forces against Iraq but eventually agreed to the use of Incirlik by the coalition, just as the air war was about to begin, even though this decision was strongly contested within the Turkish government and led to a number of ministerial resignations.

Victory in the Gulf War gave a boost to American self-confidence after the traumas of the Vietnam War, the abortive attempt to free the American hostages in Iran in April 1980, and the failure of the peacekeeping force in the Lebanon in October 1983. 'By God we've kicked the Vietnam syndrome once and for all' declared President Bush.[16] The United States emerged from the war as the sole surviving superpower in a position of influence unrivalled since 1945. Yet the promise of

[14] Ibid.

[15] T. Keaney and E. Cohen, *Gulf War Air Power Survey: Summary* Report. 1993. USGPO.

[16] T. J. McCormick, *America's Half Century* (Baltimore, MD: Johns Hopkins University Press, 1995, 249).

President Bush's New World Order went largely unfulfilled, despite an attempt to revitalize the Middle East peace process and the first steps towards a new relationship with Russia and eastern Europe. In November 1992, Bush lost the presidential election to Bill Clinton, a candidate who deliberately turned his back on foreign policy in order to focus on domestic issues and the economy. The early years of the first Clinton administration confirmed this switch of emphasis. For a time, the United States appeared to be withdrawing from the security responsibilities she had assumed since the Second World War and there were real fears among her allies that she might return to a policy of isolation. The new mood was underlined by the humiliation of American troops engaged in the United Nations operation in Somalia in October 1993 and the initial reluctance of the United States to get involved in the unfolding conflict in Yugoslavia.

Overseas Withdrawals

President Clinton believed that Bush's rundown of the American armed forces did not go far enough. His administration consequently embarked on a further series of reviews conducted by the new Secretary of Defense, Les Aspin. The 'Bottom-Up Review' made public in October 1993 based future American strategy on the capacity to fight and win two major regional conflicts 'nearly simultaneously'. It reaffirmed the commitment of the United States to her allies around the world but stressed the need to reduce costs and fixed new force levels of 100,000 troops for both Europe and the Far East. A key summary passage read:

Our strategy envisions that the United States will remain the leading security partner in Europe, East Asia, the Near East and South West Asia. However, we must find ways to sustain our leadership at lower cost.[17]

The overseas military presence of the United States was to take various forms—permanent or long-term deployments, periodic and temporary deployments, and pre-positioning of military equipment and supplies to facilitate a rapid response. The move away from permanent basing towards periodic deployments relying on pre-positioned equipment was underlined by details given in the review. A brigade-sized set of equipment was to be kept in Kuwait and, at Diego Garcia, in addition to a brigade-sized set of equipment for the Marine Corps, seven afloat pre-positioning ships were maintained with equipment for all three Services. This policy was not confined to the Middle East and the Indian Ocean.

[17] Report of the Bottom-Up Review. October 1993, 3. USGPO.

Equipment was also stockpiled in Europe on pre-positioning ships stationed at Antwerp and Livorno.

Aspin kept up a regular series of announcements on withdrawals from overseas bases while Secretary of Defense. In part, his running tally of overseas withdrawals was designed to ease the political problems surrounding domestic base closures which had been remitted to the Base Closure and Realignment Commission whose recommendations had to be either accepted or rejected as a whole. In July 1993, he announced that United States military sites overseas had been reduced by 50 per cent since January 1990, with operations either reduced or terminated at 840 separate locations, of which 773 were in Europe.[18] These figures included a large number of minor installations and small detached sites but there were some major withdrawals among them. This and subsequent announcements covered plans for total withdrawal of American forces from Hellenikon and Nea Makri in Greece and Comiso in Italy, with reductions also at Aviano. In Germany a wide range of reductions and withdrawals was planned beginning with Zweibrücken air base which was scheduled for closure together with US Army facilities guarding the Fulda Gap. Total withdrawal was planned from Florennes in Belgium, and in Spain withdrawal from Torrejón and Zaragoza was completed in 1992.

In Britain, the greater range of the Trident submarine system had already permitted withdrawal from the Polaris base at Holy Loch, while the INF Treaty allowed withdrawal from Greenham Common and the end of the requirement for massive reinforcement of continental Europe in time of war saw the US Air Force leaving Upper Heyford and Woodbridge–Bentwaters. In addition, American forces left Burtonwood and Caerwent (both storage depots), the communications facility at Chicksands, and the co-located operating base at Sculthorpe. Outside Europe United States forces were to withdraw completely from the Philippines, once regarded as indispensable to American operations in the Pacific, with naval and air units relocated elsewhere. There were to be reductions at over fifteen sites in South Korea, even though the 'Bottom-Up Review' had frozen American troop levels there, and American forces were to withdraw from the naval air station and annex at Bermuda.

William Perry, who succeeded Aspin as Secretary of Defense, was able to report in February 1995 that it was planned to reduce American active duty servicemen from 2.2 million in the late 1980s to 1.4 million by 1999, and that the US defence budget had been reduced by 40 per

---

[18] News Release. Office of Assistant Secretary of Defense (Public Affairs). 1 July 1996.

cent in real terms between the mid 1980s and the mid 1990s. The number of American forces stationed overseas had been reduced from 510,000 in Fiscal Year 1989 to 238,000 in Fiscal Year 1995—a reduction of more than 50 per cent. As was to be expected, the greatest reductions were seen in Germany, the remainder of Europe and the Philippines, but reduced force levels were recorded in all theatres.[19]

The rapid steps taken by the United States to realign her forces stationed overseas to levels commensurate with the changed security environment did much to ease the tension that had been building up in some host countries during the 1980s. At the same time, the United States made it clear that she intended to maintain forces at reduced levels both in Europe and the Far East and reassured those allies still facing a direct threat, in particular South Korea, that they could count on American protection. President Clinton reaffirmed early in his administration that American troops would stay in South Korea as long as the local people needed them and in February 1995, after a period of some uncertainty, he reaffirmed the leading role which the United States had assumed on global security issues since 1945. In his 'National Security Strategy of Engagement and Enlargement',[20] Clinton declared:

First and foremost we must exert global leadership. We are not the world's policeman, but as the world's premier economic and military power, and with the strength of our democratic values, the United States is indispensable to the forging of stable political relationships. . . .

However, there was a cautionary note in this policy document at odds with the ringing global undertakings voiced by Truman, Eisenhower, and Kennedy. On the one hand it claimed 'never has American leadership been more essential'. On the other it made clear that intervention overseas would be judged against more restrictive criteria in future. 'We therefore will send American troops abroad', it stated, 'only when our interests and our values are sufficiently at stake'.

Conflict in the Balkans

Thus it was that, having negotiated the Dayton Peace Accords on Bosnia in November 1995, the Clinton administration found it necessary to persuade Congress that an American military contribution to the Implementation Force (IFOR), an operation under NATO command and control, was in the interests of the United States. The debate was a

[19] RSD FY 96. February 1995.
[20] A National Security Strategy of Engagement and Enlargement. The White House. February 1995.

close-run thing but the President obtained the authority he needed and the US First Armoured Corps was deployed to Bosnia from Bavaria over December 1995 to January 1996. The United States contribution of 22,000 troops to IFOR was twice that of the next largest contingent, from Britain, and she also made substantially the largest contribution of 8,500 troops to the subsequent Stabilisation Force (SFOR). The European allies of the United States welcomed this renewed involvement in their security concerns, recognizing that the brief flirtation with isolation was over.

IFOR, and its successor SFOR, were the first peacekeeping operations undertaken by the Atlantic Alliance. They were followed in March 1999 by the concerted NATO air strikes on Serbia and Kosovo. Consequently, military bases in Europe, which had not been used in anger during the Cold War, were actively involved in NATO operations for the first time. Aviano in north-east Italy was the base most affected, becoming the centre for air operations over Bosnia and subsequently Serbia and Kosovo. At the same time Incirlik in eastern Turkey was used following the Gulf War first to provide protection for the Kurds of northern Iraq, and subsequently as a base for air strikes on Iraq from December 1998 onwards, following withdrawal of the United Nations Special Commission, even though both operations remained controversial within Turkey. The use of these bases in the Mediterranean demonstrated that the United States, and her allies, would continue to need access to overseas bases set up during the Cold War to discharge their new security responsibilities in a less certain world.

The Way Ahead

It therefore seems likely that the United States 'leasehold empire' will continue albeit on a reduced scale. President Clinton has undertaken to maintain 100,000 troops in both Europe and Asia and American defence policy remains predicated on the need, reiterated in the DoD report for 1998, 'to deter and, if required, decisively defeat aggression . . . in two nearly simultaneous major regional conflicts'.[21] The armed forces of the United States have been reduced and reshaped since the end of the Cold War. Reductions of over 30 per cent have been made overall, spread evenly among the US Army, Navy, and Air Force. However, the US Marine Corps has remained least affected by the drawdown, retaining three Marine Expeditionary Forces, and both the Army and Navy have

---

[21] RSD FY 98. April 1997.

been reshaped to rely less on overseas bases and more on rapid intervention on a more flexible basis. The US Air Force has developed the concept of the Air Expeditionary Force designed to demonstrate that 'we can deploy fighter aircraft at very short notice to meet contingencies around the globe'.[22] The US Army has acknowledged that it is 'now a power projection army based largely in the United States'.[23] These developments are consistent with a more mobile military doctrine, relying on pre-stocked equipment in allied nations rather than permanent overseas garrisons.

In keeping with this doctrine, the more controversial elements of the 'leasehold empire' have been dismantled. American forces have withdrawn from the neo-colonial bases in Panama and the Philippines. Major reductions have been made in the Mediterranean countries of Greece and Spain. Despite a continuing military presence in the Middle East following the Gulf War, the United States has established few permanent facilities in the region, relying largely on naval power, supplemented by temporary deployments of air and ground forces. Elsewhere, however, the United States has clung tenaciously to elements of her 'leasehold empire'. She has shown little inclination to withdraw from her own overseas territories where these play an important role in her global security system. She has retained a significant presence in Britain and some of her overseas territories. She continues to use Lajes in the Azores as an Atlantic staging post and maintains substantial forces in each of the countries conquered and occupied at the end of the war, with those in Germany and Italy playing a major part in NATO's efforts to bring stability to the Balkans.

Moreover, in economic terms the United States experienced a remarkable revival in the mid 1990s. The nation which in the 1980s had appeared to be suffering from irreversible decline, with unmanageable budgetary and balance of payments deficits covered by massive borrowing from overseas, was riding the crest of a wave by the end of the century. In 1998, the American economy was enjoying its eighth successive year of sustained growth, a longer period than that achieved in either the German or Japanese economic miracles. Inflation was at a thirty-year low at less than 2 per cent and, despite an extensive shake-out of employment, a net total of 30 million new jobs had been created since 1980. Unemployment at less than 5 per cent was at its lowest level for twenty-five years. Above all, the chronic fiscal deficit, which had been

[22] General J. Bury, USAFE Director of Plans and Programs. *Janes Defence Weekly*, 24 September 1997.
[23] RSD FY 98. April 1997, 249.

the subject of bitter political manoeuvring with the Republican Congress in Clinton's first term, was remedied in his budget for 1999. Announcing a projected budget surplus of $9.5 billion in February 1998, the first in thirty years, the President predicted continuing surpluses 'as far as the eye can see',[24] amounting to $200 billion over the following years and $1,000 billion for the decade ahead. Economic commentators tended to agree with this assessment, one declaring that 'The era of the deficit is over, assisted by the slowdown in military spending since the end of the Cold War'.[25]

By contrast, the United States economic competitors seemed to have lost their way. Growth and competitiveness in Europe remained sluggish, while Japan, although still running a substantial export surplus, achieved little or no growth during the 1990s, and suffered a 2.6 per cent contraction of GNP in 1998. Public confidence in Japan was undermined by a series of bank failures, underfunded pension liabilities, and other financial scandals exposing the pitfalls of 'crony capitalism'. Meanwhile the bubble economies in South-East Asia, long held up as examples for the West to follow, began to burst one after the other. In 1997, the stock markets of Indonesia, Malaysia, South Korea, Thailand, and the Philippines collectively lost three-fifths of their value in dollar terms and by the end of the year Indonesia, South Korea, and Thailand were all receiving assistance from the International Monetary Fund.

These contrasting economic developments appeared to confirm the underlying superiority of the American economic model after the traumas of the 1970s and 1980s. Taken together with the United States role as the sole surviving superpower and the resumption of her post-war security responsibilities in the mid 1990s, they caused some to predict a period of renewed American pre-eminence characterized as 'A Second American Century'.[26] Although this may prove over-optimistic it is evident that, after a long period of mismatch, the demands of the United States global security system and the resources to sustain these are now back in equilibrium. In January 1999, President Clinton, confident of continuing budget surpluses, was able to announce the first increase in US defence spending for a decade, proposing a rise of 4.2 per cent to $296 billion for Fiscal Year 2000 with further increases planned for the following six years. On this basis, there is no reason to suppose that the system of forward basing overseas, characterized here as the leasehold empire, should not continue on the present reduced scale well into the twenty-first century.

[24] *The Times*, 3 February 1998.
[25] M. A. Zuckerman. *Foreign Affairs*, May/June 1998.   [26] Ibid.

Conclusions

The Imperial Tradition

The United States global security system initiated after the Second World War was primarily but not exclusively designed to counter the threat of communist expansion by the Soviet Union and later China. However, the network of bases underpinning the system was planned long before the full extent of the communist threat became apparent and, notwithstanding powerful American opposition to the European colonial empires during the Second World War, the wartime planning process in the United States was partly driven by traditional imperial concerns of her own. These concerns included commercial and political rivalry with Britain, particularly in the Middle East, the desire to establish a dominant position for the US Navy first in the Pacific and subsequently in the Mediterranean, and the sense, once Roosevelt's concept of the 'Four Policeman' had collapsed, that the role of global policeman previously fulfilled by Britain should now be assumed by the United States. To fulfil this role the United States sought to use her own overseas possessions, the bases she had constructed elsewhere during the war, and any others that could be acquired by a variety of different means. The American global security system was therefore an empire of a kind and as such it has outlived the Cold War, ostensibly for the continued containment of China and North Korea in Asia and the preservation of stability in Europe and the Middle East, but in reality to underline the global dominance which the United States has seen as her role since the demise of the British Empire.

Since the end of the Cold War the Department of Defense has spelt out the continued need for forward basing in its annual reports in terms which would be familiar to the European colonial powers:

US forces must be forward deployed or stationed in key overseas regions in peacetime to deter aggression, demonstrate US commitment to allies and friends, underwrite regional stability, gain familiarity with overseas operating environments, promote joint and combined training among friendly forces and provide initial capabilities for timely response to crises.[27]

But if the American global security system is seen as a successor to the European colonial empires which the United States was quick to criticize, it has clearly been an empire of a quite different kind, depending not on the acquisition of territory by force, but on the negotiation of basing rights with independent sovereign nations. The extent to which

[27] RSD FY 96. February 1995, 19. Also RSD FY 98. April 1997, 5.

these negotiations have been freely conducted between equals has varied according to whether the host nation was a wartime ally of independent standing, a former enemy power which had been occupied, a colony or former colony of the United States, or a sovereign state anxious for political recognition and economic support. But in no instence, apart from the use of her own colonial possessions, has the United States had an entirely free hand in negotiating overseas basing rights. On the contrary, some host nations, conscious of the importance of their strategic position, have been able to exercise the tyranny of the weak by driving an ever harder bargain for the facilities on offer. It is therefore appropriate to describe the American global security system as the first 'leasehold empire' rather than an all-embracing 'hegemonic project' on traditional imperial lines,[28] an 'empire by invitation' or an 'informal empire' of the kind developed in some areas by Victorian Britain, even though there were informal elements to the position which the United States established for herself.

The concept of the 'leasehold empire' was not entirely novel in the post-war period. At the turn of the century both Britain and the United States had signed leases for small tracts of territory within another sovereign nation, Britain for the New Territories facing Hong Kong island and the United States for Guantánamo Bay in Cuba. Half a century later, at the approach of the Second World War, the United States signed ninety-nine year leases with Britain in 1941 for military facilities in the Atlantic and Caribbean. What was novel about the arrangements that the United States entered into after the war was the development of a worldwide system of military bases in, for the most part, independent sovereign states, where the role and status of American forces were subject to far greater political sensitivity than the garrisons established in traditional colonial possessions. This crucial distinction was not always fully recognized by the forces concerned and, in undertaking the role of global policeman in the post-colonial world, the United States frequently attracted the same hostility as her colonial predecessors. Having striven so hard to displace the European colonial powers, the United States often found herself tarred with the same brush by local nationalist sentiment. The cry of 'Yanks Go Home' succeeded the slogans of the 'Quit India' movement.

It is therefore appropriate in concluding this study to consider how far the 'leasehold empire' of the United States emulated the traditional colonial empires of the European powers and to what extent the very

---

[28] McCormick, op. cit.

real differences were observed in practice. These differences centred on the status of the countries playing host to American forces, which were in most cases sovereign independent nations. Traditional empires had been built on a master–servant relationship between the sovereign colonial power and the subject peoples they controlled, even though this relationship was modified over time to embrace various degrees of self-government and, under the British model, Dominion status. The 'leasehold empire' relied for the most part on a much more complex relationship between hosts and guests with the added sensitivity that the hosts were largely dependent on their guests for preservation of their national security. This created a whole series of difficulties and dependencies in the bilateral relationships between the United States and the nations on which she relied for forward bases overseas. Consequently, the *Pax Americana* faced problems never encountered by the *Pax Britannica*. As Ronald Steel commented somewhat ruefully in 1967:

Although we consciously seek no Empire, we are experiencing all the frustrations and insecurities of an imperial power . . . In many of the new states we performed the tasks of an imperial power without enjoying any of the economic or territorial advantages of Empire.[29]

There were those in Washington who fully appreciated the historical precedents for the United States as she embarked on her responsibilities as global policeman. The term '*Pax Americana*' had first been used by Charles E. Hughes, Secretary of State 1921–5,[30] but it was not until the late 1940s that the United States was unequivocally obliged to address this role. Surveying the tasks before him at this time, President Truman spoke in distinctly imperial terms to James Forrestal, his first Secretary of Defense:

We are faced with the most terrible responsibility that any nation has ever faced. From Darius I's Persia, Alexander's Greece, Hadrian's Rome, Victoria's Britain, no nation or group of nations has had our responsibilities.[31]

America's Global Outlook

It was perhaps inevitable that, driven by her own ambitions as well as the need to contain the threat from communism, the United States should have developed a global security system with marked imperial

[29] R. Steel, *Pax Americana* (New York: Viking, 1967, 19, 24).
[30] McCormick, op cit. 25.
[31] Geir Lundestadt, *The American Empire and Other Studies in US Foreign Policy* (Oxford: OUP/Oslo: Norwegian University Press, 1990).

features. Many of the bases occupied by American forces were built and maintained either by the US Army Corps of Engineers or the 'Seabees,' and the practice of home-porting American warships overseas gave an air of quasi-colonial permanence to US Navy deployments. As a result, the facilities made available to the United States were characteristically described as 'American bases' or 'US installations' even though the Congressional Research Service took pains to spell out the true position in a report issued in 1986:

A host nation does not as a rule waive its sovereignty over installations and facilities that it has permitted the United States to establish or utilise within its territorial boundaries . . . Rather host countries grant operating rights through specific base use agreements that are usually subject to conditions spelt out in associated agreements.[32]

The essential limits to American sovereignty were not always appreciated by American officials in Washington or even some occupants of the White House. The US Justice Department attempted to claim that the United States had retained title to the bases in the Philippines following independence and a similar claim was made after the war for the bases leased to the United States by Britain in the Atlantic and Caribbean. During the Cold War, the authorities in Washington tended to take an imperial view of the bases made available to the United States, using them to further either allied or national interests as they thought fit, with little regard for the views or sensitivities of the host nation. When deploying military assets overseas in an emergency the Pentagon was inclined to overlook the differences between bases at Guam (an American possession), Diego Garcia (a British colony), or the Azores (an integral part of Portugal). An indication of this attitude appears in a passage in a report prepared by the Congressional Research Service in 1979 which noted that the United States 'maintains 199 military facilities . . . in Mediterranean countries', and then added that 'Although these bases are scattered throughout a number of countries, they are linked together through a US military command structure'.[33] Furthermore, the United States tended to speak of closing the bases she occupied when these were no longer required at the end of the Cold War, whereas in reality she was obliged to hand them back to the host nation.

---

[32] US Military Installations in NATO's Southern Region. Report for House Committee on Foreign Affairs. CRS October 1986.
[33] United States Foreign Policy Objectives and Overseas Military Installations. Report for the SCFR. CRS April 1979.

The United States military command structure reinforced this tendency to treat all overseas bases alike. It was to be expected that the major US military commands should be organized on a geographical basis covering American forces stationed in a number of different countries. But these host nations did not always have a great deal in common. Pacific Command, for example, was responsible for American forces in a range of independent nations, Japan, South Korea, and the Philippines, linked by no formal treaty agreements between them, in addition to the American overseas territories of Hawaii, Guam, and Wake Island, and the British dependent territory of Diego Garcia. European Command covered American forces assigned to the NATO Alliance in Europe but was also responsible for American operations in the highly contentious area of the Near East. Consequently, General Bernard Rogers while SACEUR was closely involved in the controversial air strike on Libya in April 1986 in his capacity as Commander-in-Chief Europe. Moreover, the smaller geographical commands were more overtly interventionist. Southern Command located in Panama was specifically charged with the co-ordination of United States military operations throughout Central and South America, while Central Command, with virtually no American forces deployed in the area, was set up in Florida to safeguard United States interests in the Indian Ocean and the Middle East.

Apart from the major tri-Service geographical commands, the United States Air Force, because of the unique nature of air power, embraced a number of functional commands with worldwide responsibilities. Foremost among these was Strategic Air Command, set up in March 1946 with a remit 'to conduct long range operations on a world-wide basis'. In the late 1940s and early 1950s, SAC obtained access to overseas bases in Britain, Morocco, Okinawa, and Guam. In the mid 1950s access was gained to additional overseas bases in Spain, Newfoundland and Labrador in Canada, and Thule in Greenland. Operations at all these bases, mainly on a rotation system, were directly controlled from SAC Headquarters at Offutt Air Force Base at Omaha, Nebraska, via two subordinate Air Forces, the Eighth and the Fifteenth, both located in the United States. As *Air Force*—the magazine of the US Air Force Association—put it in 1957, expressing a common military misconception on the ownership of overseas basis, 'SAC's direct control over its major overseas bases gave it a completely global character befitting its mission'.[34] The other major functional command of the USAF with global responsibilities was Military Airlift Command

[34] A. Goldberg, A History of the United States Air Force, 1907–1957. *Air Force Magazine*, August 1957, 245.

(MAC) established in January 1966. This command was the lineal successor to the Air Corps Ferrying Command, set up to fly aircraft to Britain under the lend–lease programme in May 1941, which was renamed Air Transport Command in June 1942, and became the Military Air Transport Service in 1948, when it played the key role in the Berlin airlift. By 1989, MAC operated more than 1,000 aircraft from twenty-four different countries under the control of three numbered Air Forces. Twenty-First Air Force, from its Headquarters at McGuire AFB, New Jersey, was responsible for units overseas in the Azores, Britain, West Germany, Spain, Turkey, and Panama; Twenty-Second Air Force, from its Headquarters at Travis AFB, California, for units overseas in Hawaii, Japan, South Korea, the Philippines, and Guam; Twenty-Third Air Force, with its Headquarters at Hulbert Field, Florida, mainly comprised units in the United States but was also responsible for Special Operations Squadrons in West Germany and the Philippines.

Conflicts with Host Nations

It was natural for NATO commands, within the framework of the Alliance, to span a number of different countries and embrace military forces from several member nations. But United States national commands ran parallel to those of NATO with many senior officers combining national and NATO responsibilities. This caused difficulties when the United States was tempted to equate American foreign policy with Alliance foreign policy, using what she regarded as American bases in the pursuit of national objectives. The resupply of Israel during the Yom Kippur War, the *Achille Lauro* incident in 1985, and the 1986 air strike on Libya all showed the United States acting forcefully in pursuit of national policies in Europe, while the invasion of Panama in 1989 demonstrated the same tendencies in Latin America. The United States assumed that the bases made available to her on the territory of other nations could be used as she wished and seemed taken aback when the host nations chose to exercise their sovereign rights either on use of the bases or on overflying rights. Henry Kissinger was moved to complain that 'Europe avoided facing reality'[35] during the Yom Kippur War in 1973 by the use of legalistic arguments on NATO responsibilities, but he later acknowledged that in general terms 'Washington took the uniformity of interests among members of the Western alliance for granted'.[36] By 1986, a report from the Congressional Research Service,

[35] H. Kissinger, *Years of Upheaval.*(London: Weidenfeld & Nicolson, 1982, 711).
[36] H. Kissinger, *Diplomacy* (London: Simon & Schuster, 1994, 603).

commenting on the *Achille Lauro* affair and the air strike on Libya, recognized the problem, stating that these events demonstrated:

the on-going potential for serious problems with allied governments . . . should the US Government fail to display sufficient sensitivity to public perceptions and opinion in these NATO countries regarding the use of bases there for non-NATO operations.[37]

It was this lack of sensitivity to host nation concerns, customs, and cultures that caused many citizens of these countries to consider the American global security system as little different to the traditional colonial empires. The more discerning Americans were conscious that global supremacy could foster the 'arrogance of power'—a besetting sin of imperialists old and new—and were well aware of the social and legal problems that would occur when large numbers of American troops were stationed in an alien environment. One American commentator, surveying the plans of the United States to develop a worldwide network of bases after the Second World War, concluded that 'enveloped in the aura of a special sense of mission and virtue, Americans were often blind to the sensitivities of others'.[38] Writing in the late 1970s, Alan Cottrell and Thomas Moorer noted the importance of good relations with the host nation. 'These forces and bases depended upon the hospitality and viability of the host nations on whose territories they were employed.' But they were obliged to acknowledge that:

In the heyday of the US overseas deployments in the 1950s and 1960s there was little sensitivity to the delicate interaction of military and political factors that sustained expansion.[39]

Political and cultural conflicts were most evident outside Europe, especially in the quasi-colonies of Panama and the Philippines, but they were also to be found in Japan, where the concentration of American forces in Okinawa gave rise to particular tensions, the poorer Mediterranean countries of Greece and Turkey, where resentment of the American military presence was exacerbated by the role of the United States in the Cyprus dispute, and in West Germany, where, paradoxically, it was the relative wealth not the poverty of the host nation, in comparison with American forces stationed in the country, that led to social

[37] CRS October 1986, 59.
[38] E. Converse, United States Plans for a Post-War Overseas Military Base System, 1942–1948. Unpublished PhD thesis, Princeton University, January 1984, 262.
[39] A. Cottrell and T. Moorer, *US Overseas Bases*, Washington Paper No 47 (Bevelty Hills, Sage, 1977, p. 7).

problems. Taking the major nations playing host to American troops, only Britain, Italy, and to a lesser extent Spain and Portugal were largely free of social tensions of this kind, although there were periodic political disputes with the United States even in these countries.

These social and cultural problems took many forms and have attracted a good deal of adverse comment, often by concerned American observers. In West Germany it was indiscipline, drug abuse, and crime fostered by the Vietnam War and the civil rights movement in the United States that alienated the local population. Daniel Nelson noted in 1987 that 'Periods of heavy drug abuse and rampant criminality have badly tarnished the image of American forces in the German mind'.[40] The *Stuttgarter Nachrichten* commented in August 1972 that 'One lives dangerously in the vicinity of American garrisons'.[41] In Turkey high-handed behaviour by the United States, coupled with running sore of the Cyprus dispute, generated considerable ill-feeling which was recorded in an article for the *Journal of the US Army War College* in 1980. 'It has long been Turkey's contention', wrote the American author, 'that since the mid 1960s the United States has employed a paternalistic and condescending attitude in relations with its NATO ally'.[42] In the Philippines, the huge bases at Subic Bay and Clark Field spawned a rash of seedy establishments catering to the off-duty entertainment needs of American troops in the neighbouring townships of Olangapo and Angeles. A publication by the Library of Congress commented in 1993 'The so-called deformed communities outside the gates were seen as a national disgrace'.[43] In South Korea the black market in PX goods and the influence of the Armed Forces in Korea Radio Network were greatly resented, leading one Korean commentator to assert that the impact of American forces in the country was more damaging to Korean culture than the thirty-five years of colonial rule by the Japanese.[44] In Japan itself it was the aftermath of the occupation and the feeling that American forces had remained in Japan primarily to

[40] D. Nelson, *Defenders or Intruders? The Dilemmas of US Forces in Germany* (Boulder, Co: Westview, 1987, 203).

[41] *Stuttgarter Nachrichten*. 14 August 1972. Cited by D. Nelson, *A History of US Military Forces in Germany*.(Boulder, Co: Westview, 1987).

[42] F. P. Butler, Reassessing Turkey. A Faithful Ally Disillusioned and in Trouble. *Journal of the US Army War College*, 1980. Cited by N. B. Criss, US Forces in Turkey. In *US Military Forces in Europe*, S. Duke and W. Krieger (ed.), (Boulder, Co: Westview, 1993, Ch. 14).

[43] The Philippines—A Country Study, 234. Federal Research Division. Library of Congress. 1993.

[44] L. S. Bok, *The Impact of US Forces in Korea* (Washington, DC: National Defense University Press, 1987).

serve United States interests that generated opposition. In 1984, Richard Barnet summarized this perception in the following terms:

As the shock of defeat was wearing off, the presence of large numbers of American troops on the home islands was becoming an increasingly distasteful reminder that Japan's fate was not yet completely in her own hands . . . The rapes, homicides and traffic accidents that are an inevitable by-product of even well-behaved armies—and the US garrison in Japan . . . was not particularly well-behaved—now began to fan old feelings of nationalism and hurt pride.[45]

In Japan these feelings came to a head in 1995 when the rape of a schoolgirl on Okinawa by three American soldiers caused an outcry among the islanders who felt that they had borne more than their share of American troops with consequent overcrowding and environmental damage.

Jurisdiction

Many of these social and cultural problems were exacerbated by misunderstandings over jurisdiction, which is central to the concept of sovereignty. Under traditional territorial empires, sovereignty, and hence jurisdiction, rested with the colonial power. But within the 'leasehold empire' the host nation is sovereign and, under the normal rules of territorial law, would expect to exercise unfettered jurisdiction within its boundaries. On the other hand the armed forces of another nation are an instrument of that nation's sovereignty and the maintenance of military discipline within these armed forces depends on the military law of the nation concerned. Britain had recognized this during the Second World War by conceding exclusive jurisdiction to the American military authorities over their own armed forces first at the Atlantic and Caribbean bases leased to the United States in 1941, and subsequently by passing the United States of America (Visiting Forces) Act 1942 to cover the influx of American troops into Britain itself.

With the widespread deployment of American forces in different countries after the war, more evenly balanced arrangements were needed. On the one hand Congress felt that American servicemen and their dependants stationed overseas should have the same legal rights as they enjoyed at home and was not prepared to subject them to a variety of local legal systems, some of them exceptionally harsh and authoritarian. On the other hand the extended duration of these

[45] R. Barnet, *Allies* (London: Jonathan Cape, 1984, 182–3).

deployments in time of peace, involving civilian officials and dependants as well as servicemen, involving far greater potential for legal disputes with citizens of the host nation, clearly required a more complex system of shared authority. The compromise solution reached in the 1951 NATO Status of Forces Agreement, which was progressively extended in bilateral agreements between the United States and other host nations, was one of concurrent jurisdiction. This allocated the primary right of jurisdiction to either the host nation or the visiting force according to the circumstances of the alleged offence, with the proviso that either party could ask the other to waive its primary right in individual cases. 'The distinctive feature of a Status of Forces Agreement', wrote John Woodliffe in 1992, 'is that it allows one state, in time of peace, to exercise on the territory of another state extensive jurisdictional powers that include the transplantation of its own system of criminal justice'.[46]

These arrangements generally worked well within NATO, although they came under considerable strain in the 1980s when, despite the primary responsibility of the host nation for base security, there was a risk that American servicemen would seek to defend the bases they occupied against large-scale anti-nuclear demonstrations. However, they embodied several features which gave the impression, especially in non-NATO countries jealous of their sovereign rights, that American servicemen were above the law. First, the United States retained primary jurisdiction over 'offences arising out of any act or omission done in the performance of official duty'. But official duty was not clearly defined and was usually left to the American commanding officer to determine by issue of a certificate. Secondly, visiting servicemen were exempt from normal immigration and passport controls with the result that, in cases where primary jurisdiction lay with the host nation, they were often flown home before they could be brought to trial. Thirdly, the United States insisted on retaining custody of an American serviceman suspected of an offence falling under host nation jurisdiction until he was formally charged.

Although there were sound reasons for these arrangements, they caused considerable ill feeling in host nations, notably in Okinawa over the rape in 1995 and in Italy over the ski-lift incident in 1998. Furthermore, they were undoubtedly abused by the US military authorities anxious to protect their personnel from the vagaries of local justice in certain host nations. John Woodliffe has concluded that:

[46] Woodliffe, op. cit. 169.

The United States . . . has consistently pursued policies calculated to reduce the scope of the receiving state's jurisdiction over US service personnel to as narrow an area as possible.[47]

Nevertheless, American servicemen were occasionally brought to trial in the host country, sometimes at a senior level. In 1964, the American authorities in Turkey were obliged to try an American colonel who had killed two Turkish soldiers while driving under the influence of alcohol, and in 1970 a court in the Philippines cited Colonel Holman, the base commander at Clark Field, for contempt for permitting an airman charged with rape to leave the country. He obtained a duty certificate from his General and declined to appear before the court but was convicted *in absentia* and obliged to remain on base for the remainder of his tour of duty.

The Need to Negotiate

Although the host nation exercised primary jurisdiction in many cases, the impression that American servicemen and the bases they occupied fell outside the law of the host nation, coupled with a widely perceived lack of sensitivity to local customs and political conditions, combined to paint a picture of Americans, in their role as global policemen, behaving in a way virtually indistinguishable from traditional European imperialists. But the reality was a great deal more complex than this, for the key features of the 'leasehold empire' were first that the United States was able to deploy her forces overseas only on the sufferance of independent host nations, and secondly that she was obliged, for strategic reasons, to associate with some host nation governments of very questionable standing. The problems faced by traditional empires in holding on to their possessions in the face of local nationalist movements had been replaced for the United States by the difficulties of retaining access to important military facilities by negotiation with proud and often unscrupulous nationalist governments. As has been said of the tortuous negotiations on military bases in the Philippines 'Small countries in the shadow of great powers commonly feel required to demonstrate their independence of the shadow casters'.[48]

Overall, the United States proved remarkably successful in retaining access to the bases she needed. She was only obliged to withdraw from France, Morocco, Libya, and, at the end of the Cold War period, the Philippines. The agreement to pull out of Panama at the end of the

[47] Ibid.   [48] H. W. Brands, *Bound to Empire* (Oxford: OUP, 1992).

century was reached on American initiative. This was a creditable record during a period when nationalist feeling was running high and the traditional colonial empires were in prolonged retreat, a process often accompanied by considerable bloodshed. However, in certain areas retention was achieved at a significant cost in negotiation and concession. Although there was no pressure for withdrawal from host nations such as Britain, Italy, or Germany, and South Korea lobbied vigorously against troop reductions proposed in Washington, the United States faced repeated demands elsewhere for higher rent (thinly disguised as aid), reductions in forces, fewer bases, and greater host nation control.

In the Mediterranean, apart from Italy, five-year agreements became the norm, with one set of negotiations running into another punctuated by delays due to changes of government or suspensions when irreconcilable differences could not be bridged. The same pattern developed in the Philippines and at one stage it was suspected that national negotiators in Spain and the Philippines were comparing notes. At the same time the 7:10 ratio of aid for Greece and Turkey meant that negotiations with these two countries had to be co-ordinated by the United States. With Spain under González and Greece under Papandreou pressing for the closure of bases and the Philippines trying to reduce both the number and area of those on her territory, the United States sometimes found herself paying more for fewer facilities. There were also political disputes with Turkey, which caused the temporary suspension of American operations at a number of key installations in the mid 1970s, and with Japan over the status of Okinawa, which was only resolved in 1969. Even in Iceland, which had entrusted her sovereign responsibility for defence to the United States, there were discussions over the maximum number of troops to be allowed into the country for this purpose.

Damage by Association

The need for negotiations of this kind illustrate one essential difference between the 'leasehold empire' and traditional colonial regimes. A second significant difference was the extent to which the United States was obliged, for overriding strategic reasons, to associate with undemocratic and authoritarian governments over which she had little or no control. Association with these regimes was inevitably interpreted as support for them both at home and abroad. This led to difficulties with Congress, which became increasingly concerned with human rights, and also provoked intense suspicion of the American military presence on the part of more liberal governments when they eventually gained power in host nations previously under authoritarian regimes. In the Mediterranean, fascist dictatorships ruled in Portugal until 1974 and Spain until 1975, with Portugal's repressive policy in Africa becoming a source of grave embarrassment to the United States towards the end of this period. In addition Greece was governed by a military junta from 1967 to 1974 and Turkey was subject to military coups or interventions in 1960, 1971, and 1980. In South Korea, virtually the whole of the Cold War period was characterized by military or quasi-military governments, brutal repression, and blatant manipulation of the Constitution. Martial law was imposed for varying periods in both South Korea and the Philippines in the early 1970s, and the 1980s were to see the worst excesses of President Marcos in the Philippines and Colonel Noriega in Panama, involving the assassination of political opponents in both countries.

The United States could do little to instil acceptable democratic practices in host nations ruled by regimes determined to ignore these. But her leaders often seemed to go further than was necessary in identifying themselves with governments which were clearly unrepresentative. Eisenhower's visit to Spain in 1959 was an early case in point but the Reagan administration was particularly prone to gestures of this kind. Reagan himself invited President Chun of South Korea to Washington shortly after his inauguration in 1981 and the same year Vice-President Bush attended the inauguration of President Marcos in the Philippines, openly praising his 'adherence to democratic procedures and democratic principles'.[49] A similar seal of approval was conferred on Manuel Noriega by George Shultz when he attended the inauguration of Nicolás Barletta as President of Panama in October 1984, after Noriega had overturned the election of Arnulfo Arias. In many cases, Washington backed unrepresentative rulers long after they had become a liability and then removed or abandoned them too late to establish bona fide democratic credentials with their successors.

It was no accident that those countries with a prior colonial or quasi-colonial relationship with the United States caused her most difficulty as host nations, closely followed by those countries in the Mediterranean with whom she had no previous security relationship. These nations had no deep-rooted democratic traditions of their own, were far from prosperous, and faced little immediate threat to their own security. They were consequently inclined to take advantage of the strategic

[49] *Washington Post* and *New York Times*, 1 July 1981. Cited in W. J. Berry, *US Bases in the Philippines* (Boulder, Co: Westview, 1989).

importance attributed to them by the United States either by pressing for more aid, threatening to curtail the facilities available to the Americans, or pursuing unacceptable domestic policies. By contrast, the countries occupied by the United States at the end of the war tended, in their different ways, to be more accommodating as host nations although there was always an uneasy political relationship with South Korea, a former Japanese colony which had to come to terms with democracy for the first time after 1945. Most accommodating of all was Britain, America's wartime partner who, as her own economic and political power waned, devised a new role for herself as loyal lieutenant to the United States in the post-war global security system.

It would be a mistake to exaggerate the political and other problems faced by the United States in maintaining her global security system in the post-war world or to level undue criticism at the way in which she embarked on an enterprise never attempted before. The policy of containment, which formed the rationale for much of the 'leasehold empire', was eventually justified with the Soviet Union collapsing as a result of it own internal decay rather than direct military conflict. As President Clinton declared in January 1994, the Iron Curtain had rusted from within. The process may have taken longer than anticipated but, in Kissinger's words, 'the ending of the Cold War, sought by American policy through eight Administrations of both parties, was much as George Kennan had foreseen in 1947'.[50] The United States may inadvertently have displayed many of the faults identified with traditional empires, but in policing the world with only limited access to secure bases of her own she was obliged to handle a series of relationships with independent host nations which the empires of old had never contemplated. Although Truman compared the post-war responsibilities of the United States to those of Alexander's Greece or Hadrian's Rome, Eisenhower pinpointed the essential difference which so circumscribed American freedom of action:

We cannot be a modern Rome, guarding the far frontiers with our legions, if for no other reason that they are not politically our frontiers.[51]

Once the force of this basic restriction is acknowledged, the American record in policing the post-war world by stationing troops on the territory of independent sovereign states must be recognized as a considerable success. There were times when the United States, driven by her own imperial pretensions as well as the threat of communism,

---

[50] Kissinger (1994), op. cit. 101.
[51] J. Charmley, *Churchill's Grand Alliance*. (London: Hodder & Stoughton, 1995, 207).

treated the host nations on whom she depended with scant respect. There were other occasions when the strategic imperatives which she faced led her to condone the behaviour of unrepresentative host governments. Nevertheless, the United States took on unprecedented global security responsibilities following the Second World War which, having relatively few overseas possessions of her own, she was obliged to discharge by negotiating the right to station her forces on the territory of other countries. Arrangements of this kind had never been attempted before on this scale and, while they varied from country to country, giving rise to a whole series of social and political tensions, the system described here as the 'leasehold empire' successfully achieved its objectives in circumstances of considerable difficulty. As a result, the United States has emerged with credit and honour from the unique experiment of policing the world, not by imposing garrisons on occupied territory but by agreement with her friends and allies.

SELECT BIBLIOGRAPHY

Official Documents

UNITED STATES

Treaties and International Agreements Series (TIAS). Washington, DC: United States Government Printing Office.

Foreign Relations of the United States (FRUS). Washington, DC, Department of State: United States Government Printing Office.

Annual Reports of the Secretary of Defense to the President and Congress (RSD). Washington, DC: United States Government Printing Office.

Senate Committee on Foreign Relations. (SCFR) *Final Report of the Sub-Committee on US Security Arrangements and Commitments Abroad*. 91st Congress, 1970.

Hearings of the House Committee on Foreign Relations on Diego Garcia. 94th Congress, 1975.

United States Foreign Policy Objectives and Overseas Military Installations. *Report for the Senate Committee on Foreign Relations*. Congressional Research Service (CRS). April, 1979.

Report by the House Committee on the Armed Services. 97th Congress, 1981.

US Military Installations in NATO's Southern Region. *Report for the House Sub-Committee on Europe and the Middle East*. Congressional Research Service. 99th Congress, October 1986.

Discriminate Deterrence. *Report of the Commission on Integrated Long Term Strategy*. January 1988.

Report of the Defense Burden Sharing Panel. House of Representatives. 100th Congress. August 1988.

Keaney, T. and Cohen, E. *Gulf War Air Power–Summary Report*. Washington, DC: United States Government Printing Office, 1993.

Report of the Bottom-Up Review. Washington, DC: United States Government Printing Office, October 1993.

A National Strategy of Engagement and Enlargement. The White House. February 1995.

BRITAIN

UK Treaty Series. Command Papers. London: Her Majesty's Stationery Office.

House of Common Official Reports (H of C). London: Her Majesty's Stationery Office.

Reports and Evidence from the House of Commons Defence and Foreign Affairs Committees. London: Her Majesty's Stationery Office.
Documents on British Foreign Policy. London: Her Majesty's Stationery Office.

General Surveys

Harkavy, R. *Great Power Competition for Overseas Bases* (Oxford: Pergamon, 1982).
Henderson, N. *The Birth of NATO* (London: Weidenfeld & Nicolson, 1982).
Kennedy, P. *The Rise and Fall of the Great Powers* (London: Unwin Hyman, 1988).
Keohane, R., Nye J., and Hoffman, S. (ed.), *After the Cold War* (Cambridge, MA: Harvard University Press, 1993).
Kissinger, H. *Diplomacy* (London: Simon & Schuster, 1995).
Woodliffe, J. *The Peacetime Use of Foreign Military Bases* (Dordrecht: Martinus Nijhoff, 1992).

THE UNITED STATES

Barnet, R. *Allies* (London: Jonathan Cape, 1984).
Blaker, J. *United States Overseas Basing. An Anatomy of the Dilemma* (London: Praeger, 1990).
Cottrell, A. and Moorer, T. *US Overseas Bases: The Problems of Projecting American Military Power Abroad*. Washington Paper No 47. (Beverly Hills, CA: Sage, 1977).
Gaddis, J. L. *The Long Peace* (Oxford: OUP, 1987).
—— *Strategies of Containment* (Oxford: OUP, 1982).
Gerson, J. and Birchard, R. (ed.), *The Sun Never Sets* (Boston, MA: South End Press, 1991).
Lundestad, G. *The United States and the World 1945–1989*. Washington Paper No 95. (Baltimore, MD: Woodrow Wilson Center, 1989).
Lundestad, G. *The American Empire and Other Studies in US Foreign Policy* (Oxford: OUP/Oslo: Norwegian University Press, 1990).
McCormick, T. J. *America's Half Century* (Baltimore, MD: Johns Hopkins University Press, 1995).
McDonald, J. W. and Bendahmane, D. (ed.), *US Bases Overseas* (Boulder, CO: Westview, 1990).
May, E. *The Emergence of America as a Great Power* (New York: Harper & Row, 1961).
Paul, R. *American Military Commitments Abroad* (New York: Rutgers University Press, 1973).
Stearns, M. *Talking to Strangers-Improving American Diplomacy at Home and Abroad* (Princeton, NJ: Princeton University Press, 1996).

Steel, R. *Pax Americana* (New York: Viking, 1967/London: Hamish Hamilton, 1968).

BRITAIN AND HER COLONIES

Baylis, J. *Anglo-American Defence Relations 1939–1984* (London: Macmillan, 1984).
—— *Ambiguity and Deterrence: British Nuclear Strategy 1945–1964* (Oxford: OUP, 1995).
Brown, B. *Strategic Mobility* (London: Chatto & Windus, 1969).
Campbell, D. *The Unsinkable Aircraft Carrier* (London: Paladin, 1986).
Charmley, J. *Churchill's Grand Alliance* (London: Hodder & Stoughton, 1995).
Collier, B. *The Lion and the Eagle* (New York: Putnam's, 1972).
Cross, T. *St Helena* (Newton Abbot, Devon: David & Charles, 1980).
Dimbleby, D. and Reynolds, D. *An Ocean Apart* (London: Hodder & Stoughton, 1988).
Duke, S. *US Defence Bases in the United Kingdom* (London: Macmillan, 1987).
Edis, R. *The Story of Diego Garcia* (London: Bellew, 1993).
Jackson, R. *Strike Force* (London: Robson, 1986).
Jawatkar, K. S. *Diego Garcia in International Diplomacy* (London: Sangam, 1982).
Lamb, R. *The Macmillan Years* (London: John Murray 1995).
Louis, W. R. *Imperialism at Bay* (New York: OUP, 1978).
—— and Bull, H. (ed.), *The Special Relationship* (Oxford: OUP, 1986).
Renwick, R. *Fighting with Allies* (London: Macmillan, 1996).
Reynolds, D. *Britannia Over-ruled* (London: Longman, 1991).
Smith, T. *The Pattern of Imperialism* (Cambridge: CUP, 1981).
Woodward, L. *British Foreign Policy in the Second World War* (London: HMSO, 1970).

EUROPE: GENERAL

Duke, S. *United States Military Forces and Installations in Europe* (Oxford: OUP, 1989).
—— and Krieger, W. (ed.), *US Military Force in Europe: The Early Years 1945–1970* (Boulder, CO: Westview, 1993).
Kaplan, L., Clawson, R., and Luraghi, R. *NATO and the Mediterranean* (Wilmington, DE: Scholarly Resources, 1985).
Sharp, J. M. (ed.), *Europe after an American Withdrawal* (Oxford: OUP, 1990).
Sheehy, E. J. *The US Navy, the Mediterranean and the Cold War 1945–1947* (London: Greenwood, 1992).
Snyder, J. C. *Defending the Fringe: NATO, the Mediterranean and the Persian Gulf* (Boulder, CO: Westview, 1987).

Stuart, D. (ed.), *Politics and Security in the Southern Region of the Atlantic Alliance* (London: Macmillan, 1988).

Europe: Germany

Brookings Institution, *United States Force Structure in NATO. An Alternative* (Washington, DC, 1974).

Haglund, D. and Mager, O. (ed.), *Homeward Bound? Allied Forces in the New Germany* (Boulder, CO: Westview, 1992).

Kirchner, E. and Sperling, J. (ed.), *The Federal Republic of Germany and the United States* (London: Macmillan 1992).

Mako, W. *US Ground Forces and the Defense of Central Europe* (Brookings Institution: Washington, DC: 1983).

May, E. *The Federal Republic of Germany and the United States* (Boulder, CO: Westview, 1984).

Nelson, D. *A History of US Military Forces in Germany* (Boulder, CO: Westview, 1987).

——*Defenders or Intruders?: The Dilemmas of US Forces in Germany* (Boulder, CO: Westview, 1987).

Reed, J. A. *Germany and NATO* (Washington, DC: National Defense University Press: 1987).

Europe: Spain, Greece, and Turkey

Harris, G. *Troubled Alliance: Turkish/American Problems in Historical Perspective 1945–1971* (Washington, DC: ACE–Hoover Policy Studies, 1972).

Rustow, D. A. *Turkey—America's Forgotten Ally* (New York: Council on Foreign Relations, 1987).

Stearns, M. *Entangled Allies: US Policy towards Turkey, Greece and Cyprus* (New York: Council on Foreign Relations, 1992).

Whitaker, A. *Spain and the Defense of the West* (New York: Council on Foreign Relations/Harper/OUP, 1961).

ASIA/PACIFIC: GENERAL

Battistini, L. *The Rise of American Influence in Asia and the Pacific* (Michigan, MI: Michigan State University Press, 1960).

Blum, R. *Drawing the Line: The Origin of the American Containment Policy in East Asia* (New York: Norton, 1982).

Bunge, F. M. and Cooke, M. W. (ed.) *Oceania: A Regional Study* (Washington, DC: The American University, United States Government Printing Office, 1984, 51, 311).

Hess, G. *The United States Emergence as a South East Asian Power* (New York: Columbia University Press, 1987).

Hooper, E. B. *US Naval Power in a Changing World* (London: Praeger, 1988).

Morley, J. (ed.), *Security Interdependence in the Asia Pacific Region* (Lexington, MA: Lexington Books, 1986).
Pringle, R. *American Interests in the Islands of South East Asia* (New York: Columbia University Press, 1980).
Wheeler, G. *Prelude to Pearl Harbor* (Columbia, MO: University of Missouri Press, 1963).

Japan

Ellison, H. (ed.), *Japan and the Pacific Quadrille* (Boulder, CO: Westview, 1987).
Greene, F. *Stresses in US–Japan Security Relations* (Washington, DC: Brookings Institution, 1975).
Iriya, A. and Cohen, W. (ed.), *The United States and Japan in the Post-War World* (Lexington, KY: University Press of Kentucky, 1989).
Langdon, F. C. *Japan's Foreign Policy* (Vancouver: University of British Columbia Press, 1973).
Lee, C. J. and Sato, H. *US Policy towards Japan and Korea* (London: Praeger, 1982).
Mochizuki, M. *et al.*, *Japan and the United States: Troubled Partners in a Changing World* (London: Brassey's, 1991).
Schaller, M. *The American Occupation of Japan* (Oxford: OUP, 1985).
Shiels, F. *America, Okinawa and Japan* (Washington, DC: University Press of America, 1980).

The Philippines

Berry, W. J. *US Bases in the Philippines: The Evolution of the Special Relationship* (Boulder, CO: Westview, 1989).
Brands, H. W. *Bound to Empire* (Oxford: OUP, 1992).
Cottrell, A. and Hanks, R. J. *The Military Utility of US Bases in the Philippines* (Washington, DC: Center for Strategic and International Studies, Georgetown University 1980).
Karnow, S. *In Our Image. America's Empire in the Philippines* (London: Century, 1990).
Taylor, G. E. *The Philippines and the United States: Problems of Partnership* (New York: Praeger, 1964).

South Korea

Bok, L. S. *The Impact of US Forces in Korea* (Washington, DC: National Defense University Press, 1987.
Detrio, R. *Strategic Partners: South Korea and the United States* (NDU, 1989).
Henderson, G. *Korea—The Politics of the Vortex* (Cambridge, MA: Harvard University Press, 1968).

Hinton, H. C. *The US–Korean Security Relationship: Prospects and Challenges for the 1990s* (London: Pergamon/Brassey's , 1988).

Kong, T. Y. and Kim, D. H. (ed.), *The Korean Peninsula in Transition* (London: Macmillan, 1997).

Lewis, D. S. (ed.), *Korea: Enduring Divisions. Keesing Special Reports* (London: Longman, 1988).

LATIN AMERICA

Bonsal, P. *Cuba, Castro and the United States* (Pittsburgh, PA: University of Pittsburgh Press, 1972).

Coniff, M. L. *Panama and the United States: The Forced Alliance* (Athens, GA: University of Georgia Press, 1992).

Griffith, I. L. (ed.), *Strategy and Security in the Caribbean* (London: Praeger, 1991).

LaFeber, W. *The Panama Canal* (Oxford: OUP, 1989).

Meléndez, E. and Meléndez, E. (ed.), *The Colonial Dilemma* (Boston, MA: South End Press, 1993).

Robbins, C. A. *The Cuban Threat* (New York: McGraw Hill, 1983).

Smith, G. *The Last Years of the Monroe Doctrine* (New York: Hill & Wang, 1994).

THE MIDDLE EAST

Long, D. *The United States and Saudi Arabia: Ambivalent Allies* (Boulder, CO: Westview, 1985).

Munro, A. *An Arabian Affair* (London: Barssey's, 1996).

Palmer, M. A. *Guardians of the Gulf: A History of America's Expanding Role in the Persian Gulf 1833–1992* (New York: The Free Press, 1992).

Schubert, F. and Kraus, T. *The Whirlwind War* (Washington, DC: US Army Centre of Military History, 1995).

OTHER PUBLICATIONS

Cardolis, J. *A Friendly Invasion* (Newfoundland: Breakwater, 1990).

Cassesse, A. *Terrorism, Politics and Law: The Achille Lauro Affair* (Princeton, NJ: Princeton University Press, 1989).

Chuter, D. *Humanity's Soldier: France and International Security 1919–2001* (Providence, RI: Berghahn Books, 1996).

Harrison, M. M. *The Reluctant Ally: France and Atlantic Security* (Baltimore, MD: Johns Hopkins University Press, 1981).

Jonsson, A. *Iceland, NATO and the Keflavik Base* (Reykjavik: Icelandic Commission on Security Affairs, 1989).

Memoirs and Biographies

Acheson, D. *Present at the Creation* (New York: Norton, 1969).
Churchill, W. S. *The Sinews of Peace* (London: Cassell, 1949).
—— *Their Finest Hour* (London: Cassell, 1949).
Kissinger, H. *The White House Years* (London: Weidenfeld & Nicolson, 1979).
—— *The Year of Upheaval* (London: Weidenfeld & Nicolson, 1982).
Millis, W. L. (ed.), *The Forrestal Diaries* (London: Cassell, 1952).
Thatcher, M. *The Downing Street Years* (London: HarperCollins, 1995).
Truman, H. S. *Year of Decisions: 1945* (London: Hodder & Stoughton, 1955).
Woodward, S. *One Hundred Days* (London: HarperCollins, 1992).

Articles, etc.

Baylis, B. The American Bases in Britain. *The World Today*, August/September 1986, 115–59.
Converse, E. United States Plans for a Post-War Overseas Basing System, 1942–1948. Unpublished PhD thesis, Princeton University, January 1984.
Goldberg, A. A History of the United States Air Force, 1907–1957. *Air Force Magazine*, August 1957 (Special issue).
Jarvis, R. The Impact of the Korean War. *Journal of Conflict Resolution* December 1980, 563–92.
Krugman, P. The American Economy—Beautiful or Boastful? Foreign Affairs, May/June/1998.
Martínez, R. B. Puerto Rico's Decolonization. *Foreign Affairs*, November/December 1997, 100–15.
Sasae, K. Rethinking US–Japanese Relations. *Adelphi Paper 292*, December 1994.
Zuckerman, M. A. Second American Century. *Foreign Affairs*, May/June 1998, 18–31.

INDEX